GW00702811

THE LIMITS OF

THE LIMITS OF MEANING

Case Studies in the

Anthropology of Christianity

Edited by
Matthew Engelke and Matt Tomlinson

Berghahn Books
New York • Oxford

First published in 2006 by

Berghahn Books
www.berghahnbooks.com
First paperback edition published in 2007

©2006, 2007 Matthew Engelke and Matt Tomlinson

All rights reserved.
Except for the quotation of short passages
for the purposes of criticism and review, no part of this book
may be reproduced in any form or by any means, electronic or
mechanical, including photocopying, recording, or any information
storage and retrieval system now known or to be invented,
without written permission of the publisher.

A version of Danilyn Rutherford's chapter in this volume was published as "Nationalism
and Millenarianism in West Papua" in *Social Movements: An Anthropological Reader*,
June Nash, ed. Copyright 2005. Reprinted by permission of Blackwell Publishing Ltd.

Library of Congress Cataloging-in-Publication Data
The limits of meaning : case studies in the anthropology of Christianity / edited by
Matthew Engelke and Matt Tomlinson
    p. cm.
  Includes bibliographical references and index.
  ISBN 1-84545-170-8 (alk. paper)
  1. Christianity and culture.   2. Ethnology—Religious aspects—Christianity.
  3. Meaning (Philosophy)—Religious aspects—Christianity.   I. Engelke, Matthew.
  II. Tomlinson, Matt, 1970–

BR115.C8L55 2006
306.6'3—dc22   2006042661

British Library Cataloguing in Publication Data
A catalogue record for this book is available from the British Library

Printed in the United States on acid-free paper

ISBN 978-1-84545-170-7 (hbk.) 978-1-84545-507-1 (pbk.)

CONTENTS

Acknowledgements

The papers in this collection (with the exception of the chapters by Ilana Gershon and Andrew Orta) were originally presented in a session entitled, "Christian Ritual and the Limits of Meaning," at the 2002 meetings of the American Anthropological Association in New Orleans. We would like to thank the authors for their contributions to and comments on the larger project. We would also like to thank the other participants in the AAA session who, for various reasons, could not contribute to the volume, but whose thoughts and ideas helped shape it: John Barker, Carol Delaney, Johannes Fabian, Debra McDougal, and Hirokazu Miyazaki. More recently, Michael Scott and Webb Keane offered very helpful advice on draft versions of Chapter One, while Robert Hefner and an anonymous reviewer gave us excellent suggestions on the volume as a whole. Alas, the shortcomings and omissions that remain are our responsibility. At Berghahn Books, we are grateful to Marion Berghahn, Michael Dempsey, and Jaime Taber for shepherding this project through with care and alacrity. And thanks finally to Emilie Hitch for the thankless job of copy editing.

ME & MT
December 2005

1

MEANING, ANTHROPOLOGY, CHRISTIANITY

Matt Tomlinson & Matthew Engelke

The Uses of Meaning

As Stanley Tambiah once said, "the various ways 'meaning' is conceived in anthropology are a deadly source of confusion" (1985: 138). There is certainly no end, however, to the ways in which anthropologists claim to unearth meaning through ethnographic work. There have been disagreements over why Bororo call themselves red macaws, arguments over the subjectivity of Captain Cook, and thick descriptions of Balinese cocks.[1] All of these discussions have focused in one way or another on meaning. Indeed, for an anthropologist to say that an event is "meaningful" might well sound banal. Yet to deny the importance of this claim, we contend, is to surrender one of anthropology's signal contributions to the human sciences. At the same time, it poses questions that should be crucial for anthropologists. If words and things can be meaningful, can they also be not meaningful, or even meaningless? Moreover, is "meaning" always a necessary or even productive analytical category in anthropological work?

The essays in this volume address questions of meaning through studies of Christianity, an area of inquiry that has produced some of the deadly confusion to which Tambiah alluded. Our interest in focusing on Christianity is twofold. First, the fact that Christians often express a concern with meaning provides us with a productive set of ethnographic issues to explore. Second, debates within the anthropology of religion have raised questions about the extent to which a focus on meaning is itself an approach informed by the history of Christian thought (Asad 1993). To focus on Christianity is therefore to address issues that are of central ethnographic and theoretical concern within the anthropology of religion.

The central premise of this book is that anthropologists need to address those cases in their research that challenge "meaning's" fruition to understand when and how it is a relevant, useful term. It is through the limits of meaning, then, that the contributors here seek to discern its analytical and experiential relevance. Rather than taking meaning as a given, the authors reflect on cases in their research where the production of meaningful attitudes is uncertain. In various ways, the cases in this collection address "failure"—sometimes from the point of view of anthropological subjects, sometimes anthropological observers, and sometimes both. The cases include preachers whose sermons fall flat; prophets who are marginal; members of an audience who become bored and fall asleep; congregants who cannot recite the basic tenets of their faith; and born-again Christians who decry their old beliefs as "meaningless." While not a major theme of anthropological work, failure is not a new theme in anthropology, either. The classic invocation of failure is in the critique of functionalism's inability to account for social change through ritual action (Geertz 1973d).[2] In this volume we turn to "failure" to show that just as it has been used to point out the limits of functionalism, so too can it be used to point to the limits of meaning. By analyzing moments of failure, we argue, scholars can approach meaning not as a function or a product to be uncovered, but as a process and potential fraught with uncertainty and contestation.

Religion, Ritual, and the Problem of Meaning

The problem of meaning animates the anthropology of religion. Before beginning the main body of this introduction it will therefore be helpful to outline some of the key debates over the problem of meaning, particularly as they relate to definitions of "religion" and "ritual" informing many of the chapters collected here.

For anthropology, Talcott Parsons and Clifford Geertz have been two of the most important interpreters of Max Weber's interest in the problem of meaning. The problem of meaning concerns the compulsion to create coherent explanations of "bafflement, pain, and moral paradox" (Geertz 1973c: 109). It is the process of interpretation writ large: How can humans tolerate chaos, accept the unexplainable, and endure physical and moral torment, without seeking a reason? For Geertz "it does indeed appear to be a fact that at least some men—in all probability most men—are unable to leave unclarified problems of analysis merely unclarified" (1973c: 100; see also Parsons 1963). In "Religion as a Cultural System," first published in 1966, he suggested that the "quest for lucidity" (1973c: 101) in religion necessitates an analytical focus on meaning; following Suzanne Langer, he forwarded the claim that meaning is "the dominant philosophical concept of our time" (Langer in Geertz 1973c: 89). Geertz criticized anthropologists for neglecting what he considered to be the necessary first step in any investigation of religion: "an analysis of the system of meanings embodied in the symbols which make up the religion proper" (1973c: 125). Indeed, anthropology on the whole is "not an experimental science in search of law but an interpretive one in search of meaning" (Geertz 1973a: 5). Over the past several decades this has become a routine position, particularly within cultural anthropology.

Meaning, however, is not an uncontested "dominant concept." In his critique of Geertz's definition of religion, for example, Talal Asad highlights several problems with the problem. First, Asad argues, religious symbols are not "embodied" with meaning; religion does not have "an autonomous essence" (1993: 28). It follows from this that "there cannot be a universal definition of religion, not only because its constituent elements and relationships are historically specific, but because that definition is itself the historical product of discursive practices" (1993: 29). In Asad's estimation, Geertz's definition of religion as humanity's attempt to generate ultimate symbolic meanings is, in this sense, "a view that has a specific Christian history" (1993: 42). He argues that what makes it Christian is how Geertz "insists on the primacy of meaning without regard to the processes by which meanings are constructed" (1993: 43). Asad traces this perspective to modern Christian hermeneutics, claiming that the attempt to construct a universal definition of religion ought "to be seen in the context of Christian attempts to achieve a coherence in doctrine and practices, rules and regulations" (1993: 29). What is more, Asad wants to highlight the differences between medieval and modern Christianity, the former of which was driven not by these problems of meaning, but discipline. Prior to the Reformation, "coercion was a condition for the realization of truth, and discipline central to its maintenance" (1993: 34).

According to Asad, then, one of Geertz's chief shortcomings is that he does not address questions of power and history. Asad writes that after Geertz many anthropologists of religion have become—like theologians—preoccupied "with establishing as authoritatively as possible the meanings of representations" even as this takes one beyond "indigenous discourses" (1993: 60). Asad's concern with authority is twofold. When it comes to recognizing the role of authority in legitimizing meaning within a given religious discourse, Geertz says too little. When it comes to the authority of the anthropologist to document how "religion is essentially a matter of symbolic meanings linked to ideas of general order" (1993: 42), Geertz says too much. In the wake of the interpretive turn, anthropologists have carried on with "the history of Christian exegesis" (1993: 60). As another critic puts it, anthropologists seem driven by "the will to meaning" (Argyrou 2002), sometimes irrespective of its ethnographic relevance. With such an approach, interpretation can become an end in itself: "Lurking behind our concern for correct interpretation," Vincent Crapanzano warns, "is the fear of a total loss of meaning" (2000: 24).

Not all anthropologists read Geertz's definition as compromised by a Christian history, or as leading into the hermeneut's hall of mirrors. James Faubion still sees Geertz's definition as the most useful, and he recognizes its universalism—which Asad finds so problematic—as "very much . . . strategic" (2003: 73). Indeed, there is a noteworthy disconnect between Geertz-in-theory and Geertz-in-practice. His definition might appear to place the meaning of religion "external to social conditions" (Asad 1993: 32), but his ethnographic work is not, we think, insensitive to context and history (see, e.g., Geertz 1980). Asad himself points out that he is not addressing Geertz's ethnographies. "I stress," he writes, "that this [discussion] is not primarily a critical view of Geertz's ideas on religion—if that had been my aim I would have addressed myself to the entire corpus of his writings on Indonesia and Morocco. My intention . . . is to try to identify some of the historical shifts that have produced our concept of religion as the concept of transhistorical essence" (1993: 29).

A point well taken; we need always to challenge our concepts. But within anthropology, what are concepts without ethnography? Offering a definition of religion is always only a point of departure, shaped and reshaped through ethnographic investigation. Indeed, one of the warrants of the current volume is that the study of such terms as "meaning" and "religion" needs that anthropological grounding. We find it difficult to accept the claim that Geertz is committed to transhistorical essences. As Diana Fuss puts it, when we talk about an "essence" we need to consider "*who* is utilizing it, *how* it is deployed, and *where* its effects are concentrated" (1989: 20). Geertz's essay on religion should be read as a strategic essentialism, not a transhistorical one; it is important to acknowledge that in offering a definition of religion Geertz promises nothing more than a "useful orientation" because "definitions establish nothing" (1973c: 90).

Charles Keyes is not convinced by Asad's claims, either. Keyes questions the charge that the problem of meaning is a Christian (and therefore anthropological) particularity. Citing recent work on religion in Asia (Keyes et al. 1994) and the anthropology of violence (Kleinman et al. 1997), Keyes argues that "problems of meaning continue to impel people in modern societies towards religion" (2002: 243). For Keyes (a scholar of Buddhism) this is not an exclusively Christian concern; nor is it a theoretical anachronism. Keyes finds no evidence for Asad's assertion that religious problems of meaning are not central to modernity "in any but the most vacuous sense" (Asad 1993: 49, n. 33).

We will return to a discussion of Asad's work later in this chapter, and it is also taken up by several of the volume's contributors. But to clarify our focus on the limits of meaning, further examples of religion's disciplinary dimensions might help. In an early essay on ritual and religious language, Maurice Bloch (1989) makes the case against religion being something that is used to make sense of the world. He makes a case, in other words, against Weber, Geertz, and the interpretive genealogy. Bloch does not propose that meaning should play no role in anthropological analysis,[3] but that studies of religious rituals "represent attempts to grasp what, in the end, it is impossible to grasp: what rituals mean to the participants and onlookers. This type of search for meaning, although not pointless, has no end" (Bloch 1986: 11). Moreover, Bloch says there is a disjunction between religious ritual and everyday life, such that we cannot use the former to understand the latter. "It is therefore misguided to argue," he writes, "as so many anthropologists have done, that religion is an explanation, a speculation about such things as man's place in the world" (Bloch 1989: 37; cf. Asad 1993: 33). It is, instead, about authority: Religion is "a special strategy of leadership, the use of form for power" (Bloch 1989: 45).

Asad and Bloch share a concern with Michel Foucault, whose writings on power have inspired a more widespread turn against meaning. "The Foucault move was to insist on looking at cultural forms and practices not in terms of their 'meanings' (which, in this poststructuralist moment, had become a suspect term in any event) but in terms of their 'effects,' both on those to whom they are addressed and on the worlds in which they circulate" (Ortner 1999:138). Marshall Sahlins calls the Foucauldian approach a "postmodern terrorism" in which "the only safe essentialism . . . is that there is no order to culture" (2002: 48). One of his concerns here is with the end of anthropology as a comparative project—a concern we revisit in the second part of this chapter. What we want to highlight for now, based on the strength of evidence in the essays for this volume, is that the concern with discipline or power is not incommensurable with the concern for religion as a "cultural system," in which meaning plays a central role. Both perspectives need to be taken seriously, and in our focus on the limits of meaning we work to show how they are, in fact, parts of the same whole, and not antithetical stances. Just as the limits of meaning can be traced and produced in moments of failure, so too— as Asad, Bloch, and Foucault each suggest—can they be traced and produced through attention to discipline, authority, and power.

Ritual Performance

Like definitions of "religion," definitions of "ritual" have been the subject of much debate within anthropology (Goody 1963; Scott 1994). Given this fact, we will not rehearse them at length. But a few remarks are in order, since many of the contributors here draw their case studies from ritual action. Indeed, because ritual has been one of the most contentious testing grounds for the concept of meaning, it is vital to engage with the limits of meaning in such arenas. At the same time, we think it important to acknowledge that ritual is not the only arena in which the problem of meaning is present or relevant. Some of this volume's contributors (Gershon, Rutherford, Faubion) have accordingly drawn from cases in their research that are not organized primarily around the dynamics of ritual life and ritual action. Taken together, then, the contributions here aim to present a variety of cases in which the limits of meaning emerge.

One of the classic arguments on rituals—although not the final word (see, e.g., Bell 1997; Humphrey and Laidlaw 1994; Keane 1997c)—is that they "make visible, audible, and tangible beliefs, ideas, values and psychological dispositions that cannot directly be perceived" (Turner 1967a: 50). A ritual "makes explicit the social structure" (Leach 1964: 15). As Asad and Bloch have argued, these classic understandings of ritual, like our understandings of religion, are problematic. For Asad in particular they are situated within an anthropological canon that draws implicitly upon arguments about coherence and order in Christian thought. The historian of religion Jonathan Z. Smith has outlined these traditions in some detail, tracing changes in attitudes toward ritual action through the Reformation. In the sixteenth century, Protestant reformers saw ritual as "surface rather than depth" (1987: 100); ritual had little to do with meaning. As Smith goes on to argue, today, "[r]itual is, first and foremost, a mode of paying attention. It is a process for marking interest. It is the recognition of this fundamental characteristic of ritual that most sharply distinguishes our understanding from that of the Reformers, with their all too easy equation of ritual with blind and thoughtless habit" (1987: 103).

The manner in which contemporary anthropological and theological discussions of ritual intersect can indeed be notable. One theologian defines ritual as "a medium or vehicle for communicating or sustaining a particular culture's root metaphor . . . A people's ritual is a code for understanding their interpretation of life" (Worgul in Asad 1993: 78). This is very similar to the foundational arguments of symbolic anthropologists (Ortner 1973; Turner 1967a, 1967b, 1986; cf. Pepper 1942).[4] Such readings of ritual will continue to be challenged by some anthropologists, even as many others will continue to assert ritual's performative and significative potentials in social life. A main emphasis in this volume is indeed on those performative and significative potentials;[5] here, our point is simply to suggest that within debates over problems of meaning, Christian rituals provide us with a fruitful set of problematics to explore, particularly when such rituals explicitly raise questions of meaningfulness and the contested, partial ways in which meanings can emerge in interaction.

In Christian rituals, the perceived efficacy of performance often depends heavily on the manipulation of words. Determining what a phrase means— whether a Biblical passage, glossolalic pronouncement, or prophetic utterance—is often central to Christian ritual practices and their effects. Moreover, Christian emphases on translation of sacred texts (as we outline in the second part of this chapter) have been a notable tool of evangelization, not least in the colonial and postcolonial world (Sanneh 1989). Recent ethnographic investigations of Christianity have highlighted the ways in which Christians often see their religion as "a religion of talk" (Robbins 2001a: 905; see also Coleman 2000; Harding 2000; Placido 2001 for similar observations). Different kinds of Christianity have, of course, come to radically different conclusions about the power of words. For example, Gebusi (Papua New Guinea) Seventh-day Adventists are instructed in a Bible study session that Scripture is "the talk of God himself. You must read the Bible in order to understand. All the words of the Book are hard for you to understand, but you must understand, you must read to understand. . . . You can't be tired of reading the Bible if you want to live forever" (Knauft 2002: 162). In contrast, the Masowe *weChishanu* apostolics of Zimbabwe hold that the Bible, as a printed text, obstructs a "live and direct" connection with God in worship, and therefore should *not* be read, *not* be used—ever—in ritual practice (Engelke 2004; see also chapter 3, this volume). As another example, consider two contrasting understandings of glossolalia: for Pentecostals glossolalia is a manifestation of the Holy Spirit, a sign of blessedness and the vital verbal heart of ritual (Coleman 2000; Wacker 2000); for Roman Catholics, however, doctrine affirms that speaking in "unknown tongues" is a sign of devil-possession. And yet even these different ideologies of language use are not easily categorized by Protestant-versus-Catholic divisions, because some Catholics do speak in tongues (Csordas 2001) and some Protestants—Quakers, for example (Bauman 1974, 1983)—do not see language as a free-flowing stream from heaven. While anthropologists must not rely solely on the words spoken or read in performance to produce their analyses (Bloch 1991), they must not ignore the multiple, consequential ways in which many Christian practices focus first and foremost on language use. Accordingly, throughout this collection there is an emphasis on issues of semantics, pragmatics, and translation.

We want to stress as well that there are important approaches to (and critiques of) meaning that are not taken up here. Within cognitive anthropology, for instance, the problem of meaning is addressed at length by Bradd Shore (1996: 311–342). Shore asks questions about the limits of meaning vis-à-vis "the limits of culture" (1996: 315). He argues that while the semiotic models of culture forwarded by Geertz, Langer, and others have been productive for the analysts' understanding of meaning, they have not always been good at accounting for experiences that people have that cannot, or do not, fit into a framework of cultural knowledge. For Shore, the interface between cognitive anthropology and psychology is a more productive way to understand "meaning" because it can account as well for everyday acts of *meaning-making*. Like Asad, then, Shore raises questions about the dynamism of a semiotic approach. His focus on knowledge and learning, like Asad's on discipline, raises some pertinent issues: "Accounting for how cultural models underwrite meaning construction presupposes that we have a well developed conception of meaning. This is not a simple matter, obviously, and it is especially difficult in anthropology, where a concern with symbols has not been matched by an equal concern with symbol formation and meaning construction as psychocultural processes" (Shore 1996: 337).

Bolstered by the case studies in this collection, and building on our discussions thus far, we will suggest throughout this chapter that semiotic models are not incapable of accounting for symbol formation. Indeed, focusing on the limits of meaning is a productive way to highlight such dynamics. Space prevents us from going into more detail on Shore's argument—or indeed the arguments of other cognitive anthropologists, who have still other critiques to offer (see, e.g., Sperber 1975). The point we want to make in referring to Shore's intervention is that the approaches in this collection are not exhaustive. Our intention is not to be exhaustive, but to suggest that the work here be used in productive dialogue with that of others in relation to a discussion on meaning—and its limits.

The Meaning of Meaning: A Caveat

By the mid 1970s, after two decades of more "scientific" pushes against the regnant Boasian approaches, a number of cultural anthropologists were becoming increasingly optimistic about the place of meaning in anthropological analysis (Basso and Selby 1976; see also Boon 1978). Although it had never been entirely absent from view, it was Geertz's push, starting in the late 1950s, that helped bring meaning to the forefront of anthropological analysis (Ortner

1999: 137).[6] In many ways, the optimism of that earlier generation has been borne out. "Meaning" was not a fad term of the 1970s. It is still central to the discipline, and whether or not it is explicitly recognized as such, the concern with meaning colors a great deal of anthropological writing and analysis. In fact this is part of what we find so interesting about the concept: Meaning is perennially invoked, but also, and too often, taken for granted.

Having sketched some key debates on religion and ritual, we turn now to a caveat on meaning and its definitions, since meaning is the primary problematic of this book. Defining "meaning" is not an easy task. Then again, as Roy Wagner suggests, "The things we can define best are the things least worth defining" (1981: 39). Anthropologists have certainly spilled a great deal of ink trying to define its other key terms, such as "culture." Much less explicit attention has been paid to "meaning." It is, like culture, not an easy word to crystallize, and in general anthropologists have been reluctant to do so.[7] Tambiah's quip over the "deadly confusion" it arouses makes this clear. But even Geertz—the concept's most influential anthropological ambassador—"never formally defines meaning" (Ortner 1999: 137). Neither do Keith Basso and Henry Selby in their landmark 1976 collection, *Meaning in Anthropology*. Were they to have done so, they argued, "a great deal of necessary work would not get done" (1976: 9). Basso and Selby did not want to circumscribe the field. Following this lead, we will not offer a strict definition of "meaning" here. As readers shall see, the contributors to this volume approach the term in a variety of ways. But despite—and because of—its elusive nature, we also feel it will be useful to provide some guideposts for a definition of meaning and its relevance to the study of Christianity.

And so with the backdrop and caveats in place, we now turn to the main body of this chapter. We begin with "Meanings of Meaning," a consideration of some of the most fruitful philosophical and anthropological discussions of meaning, describing how the literature has been used to articulate an anthropological understanding of meaning as a semiotic and sociocultural category emergent in practice. In the next part, "Christian Meanings," we examine ethnographic representations of Christianity to complement the general theoretical overview. In the third part, "The Limits of Meaning," we suggest how the individual chapters of this volume bring together the concerns of the first and second parts. In this final section we outline most clearly how the contributors address the limits of meaning. Throughout all three parts, however, we highlight the ways the essays collected in this volume illuminate the topics under discussion.

Meanings of Meaning

Like sculptors fashioning monuments, scholars of "meaning" have whittled away at vast but variegated surfaces to carve the subject into recognizable forms. In their 1923 classic *The Meaning of Meaning*, C. K. Ogden and I. A. Richards devised a list of sixteen main ways in which scholars have taken something to "mean."[8] Their book has an important role in the history of anthropology.

In their primary focus on denotation—the "direct" meaning of a word or expression—Ogden and Richards addressed what Malinowski recognized as the limitations of "primitive" language; he argued that their approach fit "exceedingly well" the issues raised by his own study of Papuo-Melanesian languages (1946: 298).[9] "Mr Ogden and Mr Richards," Malinowski commented, "have brought out in a most convincing manner the extreme persistence of the old realist fallacy that a word vouches for, or contains, its own meaning" (1946: 336). Malinowski, in other words, was suggesting for anthropology the inadequacy of a denotative theory of language as a theory of meaning.[10]

Well beyond this anthropological intervention, denotation has been a central problematic in the study of meaning and language (Makin 2000). Indeed, whereas Malinowski focused on debates over "primitive thought," his contemporary Ludwig Wittgenstein went somewhat further: Never mind the "primitives," Wittgenstein seemed to say, denotation had misguided the whole of the Western intellectual tradition. For Wittgenstein, previous scholars of meaning had erred in privileging denotation. His chief protagonist in *Philosophical Investigations* (first published in 1953) was Augustine, who, in *The Confessions*, describes the way in which he came to learn the meanings of words as a child:

> When they (my elders) named some object, and accordingly moved towards something, I saw this and I grasped that the thing was called by the sound they uttered when they meant to point it out. Their intention was shewn in their bodily movements, as it were the natural language of all peoples: the expression of the face, the play of the eyes, the movement of other parts of the body, and the tone of voice which expresses our state of mind in seeking, having, rejecting, or avoiding something. Thus as I heard words repeatedly used in their proper places in various sentences, I gradually learnt to understand what objects they signified; and after I had trained my mouth to form these signs, I used them to express my own desires. (Book I, Chapter 8; quoted in Wittgenstein 2001: §1)

Wittgenstein did not deny that Augustine may have learned the meaning of *some* words in such a manner, but as a theory of communication the denotative model is inadequate. Like Malinowski, Wittgenstein called it "primitive"; indeed, Wittgenstein wondered at the "occult process" by which philosophers mystically conjoined words and things (2001: §38). Ostensive definitions are inadequate because they assume that, as in the example of Augustine, "the child could already *think*, only not yet speak" (2001: §32)—that is, that words and things have an essence to be discovered independent of the contexts in which they are referred to or used. To adapt one of Wittgenstein's examples: If an English speaker points to a red apple and says something, there is no way in which a non-English speaker can know what was meant. An apple does not have apple-ness that will make itself known. The person might have said, "that is an apple," or, maybe, "that is red," or, "that is a fruit," or, "an apple a day keeps the doctor away." We cannot learn language simply by pointing at things, because "the meaning of a word is neither an idea in the mind nor an object in reality, no matter whether concrete or abstract" (Hacker 1996: 244; see also Putnam 1996; Quine 1960).

Wittgenstein argued that instead of focusing on denotation we must examine the ways in which meaning is related to function. This is the basis for his well-known argument on meaning-as-use. We want to emphasize here that it provides a useful way to understand how many anthropologists, from Malinowski on, have deployed the concept of meaning in their work.[11] "For a *large* class of cases—though not for all—in which we employ the word 'meaning' it can be defined thus: the meaning of a word is its use in the language" (Wittgenstein 2001: §43). A.C. Grayling summarizes the argument well:

> Meaning does not consist in the denoting relation between words and things or in a picturing relation between propositions and facts; rather, the meaning of an expression is its use in the multiplicity of practices which go to make up language. Moreover, language is not something complete and autonomous which can be investigated independently of other considerations, for language is woven into all human activities and behaviour, and accordingly our many different uses of it are given content and significance by our practical affairs, our work, our dealings with one another and with the world we inhabit—a language, in short, is part of the fabric of an inclusive "form of life." (2001: 79)

Meaning, in this view, is emergent and potentially contestable—"not something complete and autonomous," as Grayling describes language; not a prize to be seized, but a process. This recognition of process has led some anthropologists to question the usefulness of a term like "meaning," just as others have questioned "culture." The main worry seems to be objectification—turning meaning into a thing. "Maybe for the term 'meaning,'" Margaret Trawick proposes, "which is problematic in its thinglikeness, we could substitute 'interpretability,' which indicates the connectedness of a sign with other signs—that is, the fact that the appearance of one sign will make you think of others" (1988: 349). We agree with the intent of Trawick's lexical displacement, but suggest that it is more worthwhile to rethink the term "meaning" critically and fruitfully than to avoid it altogether. There is always the danger of concept-objectification, but in a processual approach careful attention is given to Trawick's concerns, an attention manifest in much of the best literature on meaning.

Ernest Gellner (1998: 145–150) has made the provocative argument that Wittgenstein's later philosophy (developed from the 1930s) was already realized in Malinowski's 1923 supplement to *The Meaning of Meaning*. In the supplement, Malinowski argued that "the meaning of a word must always be gathered, not from passive contemplation of this word, but from an analysis of its functions, with reference to the given culture" (1946: 307). Certainly, anthropologists reading Grayling's account of meaning-as-use might well recognize how key terms in anthropology are related to Wittgenstein's work. What Wittgenstein calls a "form of life," anthropologists call "culture"; his concern with the "rough ground" is the anthropologist's concern with fieldwork and everyday life.[12] The critique of denotation, then, is one obvious starting point in an anthropology volume exploring meaning—not least meaning in Christianity, since Wittgenstein cast Augustine as his chief protagonist.[13] But this critique raises as many questions as it answers. Space prevents us from delving into Ogden and Richards's sixteen categories of meaning, much less the merits of Gellner's overall thesis about the similarities between Wittgenstein's and Malinowski's work. The philosopher H. G. Blocker, however, has provided a useful abridgment of Ogden and Richards's categories, identifying four main types of meaning: (1) structural position, (2) intentionality, (3) symbolism, and (4) "being-as" (1974: 33).[14] Here, we adapt Blocker's scheme for its breadth and flexibility. These four categories touch on a good deal of the literature relevant to anthropological studies of ritual and meaning, and allow us to keep the argument about process, or "meaning-as-use," always in view.

Meaning as Structure

Lévi-Strauss called structuralism "the quest for the invariant, or for the invariant elements among superficial differences" (1978: 8).[15] In many respects, apprehending meaning as a product of structure cuts against the emphases on agency and experience highlighted in this volume, as in our discussions above. But structuralism helped to set the framework for some of the most important discussions of meaning in anthropology.

A key structuralist principle is that meaning arises in relationships: It is the result of combination and selection within a system. Meaningfulness is a product of position, combination, and limitation. Consider language: "Every language makes a selection and from one viewpoint this selection is regressive. Once this selection is made, the unlimited possibilities available on the phonetic plane are irremediably lost. On the other hand, prattling is meaningless, while language allows people to communicate with one another, and so utterance is inversely proportional to significance" (Lévi-Strauss 1969: 94).

Expanding upon Ferdinand de Saussure's linguistic model, Lévi-Strauss used it to engage major subjects such as kinship, exchange, and myth.[16] In each, he hoped "to find an order behind . . . apparent disorder" (1978: 11). Life, for Lévi-Strauss, was too messy. Taken in isolation, the things humans do "are, or seem, arbitrary, meaningless, absurd" (1978: 11). By focusing on structured content, however, one can push past superficial differences to the rules of cultural organization. As he claimed in the final volume to *Mythologiques*, "my analysis of the myths of a handful of American tribes has extracted more meaning from them than is to be found in the platitudes and common places of those philosophers . . . who have commented on mythology during the last 2,500 years" (1981: 639). What Lévi-Strauss claimed to uncover in his analysis of a handful of myths were myth's rules. And for structuralists, "to speak of rules and to speak of meaning is to speak of the same thing" (Lévi-Strauss 1978: 12). In this confident view, different sociocultural products are comparable because humanity shares this tendency to derive meaning from series of oppositions and comparisons in all expressive domains.[17]

Critics of structuralism have long pointed out that it precludes creativity, change, and agency. Geertz is one of Lévi-Strauss's most vigorous critics, claiming his work "annuls history, reduces sentiment to a shadow of the intellect, and replaces the particular minds of particular savages in particular jungles with the savage mind immanent in us all" (Geertz 1973e: 355). Simply put, where Geertz finds meaning in experience, Lévi-Strauss finds meaning in order. Geertz wants to look at people; Lévi-Strauss wants to look at Man.[18]

While there might be an impasse between Geertz and Lévi-Strauss, other anthropologists have developed a reconciliation between structure and agency. Structure is not only a framework for action, but also emergent from action. After Marshall Sahlins, "structure" has come to be seen as the continually revised and negotiated product of historical processes. Sahlins writes of the *structure of the conjuncture*, "a set of historical relationships that at once reproduce the traditional cultural categories and give them new values out of the pragmatic context" (1985: 125; see also Sahlins 1976, 1981). The structure of the conjuncture unites culture and history, but in doing so, it powerfully evokes the creative potential of failures, misunderstandings, uncertainties. It is the recovery of history, and involves the recognition of contingencies (see Biersack 1989: 84–89).

Roman Jakobson also pushed against the ahistoricism of Saussure-inspired semiology. He insisted that "language is an interpersonal (intersubjective) means of communication; that is, it operates between speakers and addressees" (Jakobson 1990:14). With Jakobson, then, emphasis was shifted from *langue* (system) to *parole* (utterance). This move to *parole* was taken up in the 1960s by anthropologists who helped to establish the ethnography of speaking, a subfield premised on the recognition that a "general theory of the interaction of language and social life must encompass the multiple relations between linguistic means and social meaning" (Hymes 1972: 39). As history and context became central anthropological concerns, the ethnography of speaking produced a number of classic studies that dealt with the dynamics of power and meaning in social life.[19]

Where does "meaning" emerge in critical views of structure? "In essence," the Russian literary scholar V. N. Vološinov wrote, "meaning belongs to a word in its position between speakers; that is, meaning is realized only in the process of active, responsive understanding" (1973: 102). Meaning is thus irreducibly social, contextual. Even personal language ("speaking to oneself") is linked in a chain to previous utterances; every utterance exists in dialogue with other ones. Sometimes the "struggle of accents" (as Vološinov put it)[20] builds senses of insider knowledge and exclusive community, as when the Catholic charismatics studied by Csordas (2001) learn to interpret commonplace terms in new ways, or fundamentalists learn to ground their present-day narratives in Biblical typologies (Harding 2000: 55). Sometimes, however, the struggle over meaning creates conflicts without resolution. As Erica Bornstein describes in her paper for this volume, one American NGO worker in Zimbabwe struggled to launch discourse about "success" in a context where "success" was dangerously inflected with the suggestion of witchcraft and understood through the conditions of material impoverishment.

In practice theory, as in the ethnography of speaking, understandings of "meaning" are informed by detailed considerations of power and agency. Bourdieu explicitly linked meaningfulness to the "markets" in which linguistic capital is expended, elaborating the connections between meaning, generic boundaries, and the relations of producers and consumers or receivers in particular fields:[21]

> The objective meaning engendered in linguistic circulation is based, first of all, on the distinctive value which results from the relationship that the speakers establish, consciously or unconsciously, between the linguistic product offered by a socially characterized speaker, and the other products offered simultaneously in a determinate social space. It is also based on the fact that the linguistic product is only completely realized as a message if it is treated as such, that is to say, if it is decoded, and the associated fact that the schemes of interpretation used by those receiving the message in their creative appropriation of the product offered may diverge, to a greater or lesser extent, from those which guided its production. Through these unavoidable effects, the market plays a part in shaping not only the symbolic value but also the meaning of discourse. (Bourdieu 1991: 38)

In other words, meaning is both imposed as a condition and emergent as a process. Meanings are constrained by the markets in which discourse circulates, but the gaps between production and reception, and the "schemes of interpretation" of differently positioned actors, cast meanings in new light and cant them in new directions. The limits of meaning, in Bourdieu's scheme, are both fixed and shifting. They are fixed by the boundaries of decoding, which is to say generic boundaries: Knowing *how* something means is a function of the market in which it circulates. They are shifting, however, due to the interests of actors in different social fields. James Faubion gives us a sense of this dynamic in his contribution to this volume, arguing that sacral actors are "transcendent events" who "bend . . . a given set of rules without breaking them," flitting dangerously at the limits of convention. He coins the term *paranomics* to designate this property. A paranomic actor—such as the Branch Davidian prophet Amo Paul Bishop Roden, with whom Faubion worked in Texas—exists in parallel to the "rules" of religious practice. Ms. Roden is capable of "questioning in practice [the] principles and standards that 'go without saying.'" What Faubion shows is that the limits of meaning, when conceptualized as a set of rules, are neither fixed nor permanent, but can be tangible and effective nonetheless. To speak of rules and to speak of meaning is not necessarily, *pace* Lévi-Strauss, to speak of the same thing.

Meaning as Intention

Another approach to meaning is to understand it as grounded in the intentionality of actions and utterances (Grice 1957; Searle 1983). In fact this is probably the most common English-language colloquial use of the verb *to mean*, as in, "I didn't mean to hurt his feelings." Tambiah, however, has pointed out that intention cannot ground any anthropological definition of ritual meaning, because the more a ritual is entextualized, the less actors' intentions matter: "in conventional ritual like marriage the immediate intentions of the officiating priest or of the bride and groom do not explain the meaning and efficacy of the rite itself (or the unintended meanings)" (Tambiah 1985: 134; cf. Austin 1962).

The view that meaningfulness derives generally from intentions or purposes posits "intentionality" as a universal factor in human action rather than as a culturally specific category. Such an approach cuts against the ethnographic record in many areas, such as divination and spirit possession. For example, Evans-Pritchard (1976: 75–89) described how intention was located in divinatory objects and actions, rather than in his Azande informants. Duranti (1993) has argued that Samoan interlocutors pay little attention to "intention" but pay a great deal of attention to the responsibilities and consequences of speaking. And DuBois (1993) has described how oracles displace the authorship of the signs they read in Yoruba, Azande, and Sisala divination, thus creating "meaning without intention." In all of these cases, displacement of the individual speaking subject (the default subject of Western philosophy) helps to generate significance that emerges not from speakers' motives or (imagined) interior states, but from sociocentric expectations of responsibility.

This dynamic is also evident in the literature on spirit possession, particularly when mediums serve as channels through which spirits communicate (see, e.g., Atkinson 1989; Boddy 1989; Lambek 1993), rather than as actors themselves. As Engelke describes in his chapter for this volume, when prophets in the Masowe Church are filled with the Holy Spirit, their words and actions express divine intentions, not human ones (see also Engelke 2004). In other cases, however, as Fenella Cannell (1999: 88–107) demonstrates in her study of spirit mediums and Catholicism in the Philippines lowlands, a "relationship of intimacy" between medium and spirit develops over time, in which one might come to dominate the other. Michael Lambek makes a similar point from his research on Mayotte, where he suggests that even while mediums on the island are not in control, they can learn to channel spirits with varying degrees of effectiveness; articulate possession is therefore "something to be achieved" (1993: 323). Intention, then, is a product whose importance may be subsumed to other categories in other ideological regimes, or can indeed be defined as "something to be achieved."

Nonetheless, the point that intentionality is fundamental to certain kinds of meaningfulness is a useful one; notions of intention often become central to Christian conceptions of "faith," for example. To speak meaningfully, in some senses, is to speak faithfully, or truthfully, or sincerely. Faith, like sincerity (Keane 1997a, 2002; cf. Miyazaki 2000, 2004), is an individualizing concept resting on notions of interiority, truth versus falsity, and the social obligations of expressing these forms of interiority; faith is perhaps inextricably intertwined with intentionality.[22] Thus, anthropologists investigating Christianity—and especially Christian ritual—must take notions of intentionality into account, particularly when ritual participants themselves struggle to trace and decipher the connections between speakers' inner states and the efficacy of their words. The importance of intention in Christians' senses of meaningfulness and efficacy is seen clearly in Ilana Gershon's account, in this volume, of New Zealand-based Samoans' conversions to new Christian denominations. Gershon argues that in joining new denominations, Samoans often criticize established churches as being enmeshed in "meaningless" rituals of display. Converts, in contrast, have learned to ground morality in private, "continuous" selves that they believe do not depend on others' gazes as the source and audience of moral behavior. "In . . . labeling a more mainline form of Samoan Christian worship meaningless," Gershon writes, "the Samoan converts are discarding the claims to a context-dependent morality in favor of a morality based largely upon a notion of a consistent and self-monitoring person." Such moves toward constructing consistent, internally focused senses of personhood help to position meaning as at least partly determined by models of intentionality.

Meaning and Symbol

Space prevents us from going into detail on the host of anthropologists who have addressed questions of symbolism, but we can perhaps spend time on one approach that addresses Asad's concerns about context and history in Geertz's definition of religion. Since the 1970s a number of anthropologists have focused on how the play of tropes helps to ground meaning in social action in a way that focusing on symbols alone cannot.[23] Metaphor theory, as it has come to be known, grows out of Vico's work on poetic logic, which "considers things in all the forms by which they may be signified" (1947: §400).[24] Poetic logic is based on the embodiment of knowledge through experience—what Leach called "our apprehension of nature" (1970: 16). This apprehension is central to metaphor theory because it grounds poetic logic in social life. Victor Turner defined the ritual symbol as "the smallest unit of ritual which still retains the specific properties of ritual behavior" (1967a: 19). In contrast, James Fernandez argued that ritual symbols were too small—that is, too ungrounded *qua* symbols—to retain any "properties" whatsoever. "Most of the symbols to which our attention is called in symbolic analyses," he wrote, "condense so many and often incompatible meanings as to, in fact, make them difficult to discuss" (1986: 30). By definition, however, tropes exist only through the demarcation of a context. They are figures of speech in which meaning operates on the signifier, not the signified (Sapir 1977: 3), suggesting new meanings. Metaphor makes the unknown meaningful; it is "a predication of a sign-image upon an inchoate subject" (Fernandez 1986: 31). Like all tropes, metaphor is always situated in a system of knowledge and practices. "Tropes and their meanings are dialectical constructs," as Terence Turner (1991: 150) puts it; in other words, they must be understood in relation to a broader social field and the positions of actors within it. And because tropes are creative, because they embody "a new or innovative sequence" (Wagner 1981: 42) of significant associations, they allow us to track articulations of meaning over time.[25]

In metaphor theory, as in most semiotic work, language carries a heavy analogical load. However, it is important for us to note that "meaning and symbol" go beyond the bounds of language (Arno 2003). In this regard, we turn to Charles S. Peirce's theory of signs. Peirce's trichotomy of sign relations (expandable, with refinements, but here we will stick to the basics) has been an increasingly influential model in anthropology, although its emergence in the field can be traced back to a number of anthropologists in the 1970s whose focus was on meaning (Silverstein 1976) and metaphor (Sapir and Crocker 1977; Wagner 1981).[26] In Peirce's trichotomy, *icons* are signs whose relationship to their signatum is based on resemblance; *indexes* are signs related by direct connection, physical or causal; and *symbols* are signs based on convention (although as Emile Benveniste [1971] pointed out, the conventionality is often misrecognized as a necessary relationship).

Peirce's trichotomy helps analysts to see not only the ways that signs work, but also the ways that sign producers and sign consumers interpret the ways that those signs work (see Keane 1997c: 19–20; see also Keane 1997b). For example, religious icons are often held to be sacred by virtue of their iconicity; their sign-status is what sets them apart as holy, or spiritual, or blessed, or cursed.[27] This applies to such religious symbols as the cross, resembling the original crucifix and *thereby* inspiring feelings of devotion; to statues of figures such as the Virgin Mary, which awe viewers by their iconic evocation of transcendent figures; and to words of divinities and prophets, repeated verbatim through the generations so that their original power is not lost. However, anthropologists have recently been turning to indexicality as a relationship particularly worthy of study, partly because of the imputed naturalness people often give to this sign relationship (see, e.g., Keane 1997c, 2002). The naturalness may be conjectural (as in, "I see a footprint in the sand, so someone must have walked on the beach"), and often demonstrably incorrect (as in believing that skin color indicates degree of intelligence), but the deeply felt "fitness" of the relationship makes it particularly worthy of ethnographic study, and compelling within religious arenas. Appeals to indexicality are often claims to power. When divine signs are "natural," they are undeniable, and their enunciation (and perhaps their enunciators) may not be susceptible to challenge.

The image of Jesus, in Christian semiotics, is not only an icon of the sacrificed Son and the future King, but also an eschatological index, the very sign that points to the end of time. But indexical relationships can be unsettled when actors spin the arrow of "direct connection" in different directions. For example, in her chapter for this collection, Danilyn Rutherford describes how in the Koreri movement of Biak (in Papua, Indonesia), Jesus was understood to be Manarmakeri, "an abject hero whose potency resides in his scaly skin." In Koreri's millennial future, Manarmakeri was about to return and usher in "a utopian state of endless plenty." In this example the indexical link between a savior and the millennium was retained, but the identity of the savior was redefined. Such theological sleight is not unique to Biak; Martha Kaplan has described how followers of the Fijian prophet Navosavakadua accepted his claim that Jesus and Jehovah were really the mythic twins Nacirikaumoli and Nakausabaria—and, of course, that "they had returned, like Jesus and Jehovah" (Kaplan 1995: 104). Like Manarmakeri in Biak, the mythical twins take Jesus'/God's place within a host of sign relationships. The process is complicated, however, by the fact that the new signs, like compass needles, swing back magnetically to their previous associations, transforming both prior and future contexts and meanings. Christian practices "always index," Rutherford concludes, but might well threaten the institutional orders from which they arise. Rutherford's chapter suggests how indexicality is productive of, and subject to, the limits of meaning.

Silverstein (1976, 2003) notes how indexes range from highly presuppositional (context-bound) types like deictics, which can only be understood with previous knowledge of the situation (including the discursive context itself) in which they are expressed, to highly creative ones such as honorifics, which can change the contexts in which they are expressed. Such observations are relevant to investigations of meaning when it is considered as a semiotic product emergent in practice. The ability of texts to circulate socially depends largely on their detachability from original contexts, but semiotic relationships can change as texts circulate across contexts, reconfiguring interpretive possibilities. The meaningfulness of ritual action, in turn, often depends on indexical links that may or may not translate well or move stably across cultures, languages, and contexts of performance. Consider Greg Dening's description of the encounter between Spanish friars and Marquesans at the end of the sixteenth century: "The friars acted out the Spaniards' salvation by singing a mass. Under a breadfruit tree they played with symbols of bread and wine. They chanted their Latin phrases; they swung their incense burners; they bobbed about the altar in chasuble and alb. They had all the rubrics and gestures to transport familiar worlds to foreign places, to make beaches seem like churches. The islanders knelt around and mimicked the silence of the believers" (Dening 1980: 10). Making "beaches seem like churches" was easy for the Catholic missionaries. For the friars the ritual was effective because the set of indexical icons marked their action as sacred: bread and wine, Latin, incense, and vestments. The audience, however—unsure of the direction these strange signs pointed in—could only respond iconically, imitating the silence and postures of the rest of the congregation. The boundary of meaningfulness, in this historical example, was drawn relatively neatly between observers and participants. The silence of the Spaniards and the silence of the Marquesans were significantly and qualitatively different.

Meaning as Being

Blocker's fourth category—"being-as" (1974: 33)—is the category of existence and ontology. Meaning here is regarded as an existential condition. To approach the subject anthropologically, we take Blocker's "being-as" to be roughly congruent with the process of *recognition*, which is both interpretation and affirmation:

> people recognize actions and identities in terms of things of which they *already* have some understanding. Objectification depends on an act of comparison in which the new event can be *recognized* as an instance of something that is already known. . . . But . . . what counts as repeatable is at least in part social. . . . It is subject to the playing out of the interaction *between* us and thus begins to take on a more dialectical and potentially power-laden quality than that of a simple embodying of an existing type. . . . In this light, "recognition" as a known type becomes

involved with the social and political dynamics of "recognition" as acknowledgment
or affirmation. (Keane 1997c: 14–15)

Recognition thus depends on semiotic relationships, implicated in social interactions through relationships of iconicity ("the new event can be recognized
as an instance of something that is already known") and indexicality (affirming, for example, that certain texts gain their potential efficacy because of their
causal link to the past).

We can return here explicitly to the problem of meaning as discussed by
Geertz. In attempting to explain intellectual mysteries, suffering, and moral
paradox, people cast themselves in recognizable roles within imagined cos-
mologies. Geertz has argued that everyone does this, not just Christians. But
the questions that emerge from our reading of Asad, as posed above, are:
How do modern Christians draw boundaries of meaningfulness, and how do
emphases on meaning depend on those chaotic "meaningless" spaces beyond
the pale?

Recognition of one's place in a larger religious order, as many of the essays collected here demonstrate, is central to answering these questions. In
her chapter, Gershon notes how Samoan Christian converts often define their
new religious statuses in terms of having moved away from the meaningless
practices of their former congregations. Her work highlights a central paradox of meaninglessness: what is defined as "meaningless" is so understood
by virtue of its position within a meaningful system. A related situation is
described by Andrew Orta in his chapter on the theology of inculturation in
highland Bolivia. Orta describes how the Aymara and resident Catholic missionaries have taken different ideological stances toward the meaningfulness
or meaninglessness of pre-Christian symbols and practices over the course of
the twentieth century. In the "second evangelization" (through the 1980s),
Aymara Catholics were considered not to understand the "true meanings" of
Christian ritual practice. The second evangelization was "about the failure
of meaning, about the limits of colonially derived Catholicism and its shallow roots of faith." From the late 1980s onward, however, the inculturationist
movement has held "that indigenous beliefs and ritual practices reflect and
embody local and culturally particular expressions of what missionaries take
to be universal Christian values." Catholic leaders, then, have turned away
from lamenting "meaningless" worship to positing a universal meaning in all
worship. The situation is fraught, however, as catechists who once attempted
to extirpate certain practices are now called upon to honor them as uniquely
meaningful local Christian phenomena. Both Gershon and Orta show how the
limits of meaning can be tangible and effective when defined by the politics of
recognition, a struggle with political dimensions nevertheless "driven" by the
desire for a meaningful faith.

In this first section, we have surveyed some of the multiple meanings of
meaning, not in an attempt to capture imagined essences but to suggest the
breadth and diversity of analytical approaches to the subjects that emerge out
of concerns with language and semiotics. We want to stress again that these

are not the only viable approaches; they do, however, open up fruitful avenues of inquiry in relation to Christianity because of Christian emphases on language and effective action. Where appropriate, we have tried to illuminate our discussions with ethnographic examples from this volume and the wider literature. We now turn to a more focused consideration of Christianity, to suggest how Christian subjects articulate senses of meaning. The extent to which these senses of meaning resonate with the analytical models is best explored through a reading of this volume's individual chapters. But in the next part of this chapter, we want to offer the outlines of a framework in which the volume as a whole can be situated.

Christian Meanings

Christianity is not a stable, singular object, and the essays in this collection go some way toward further documenting the diversity of its sociohistorical formations. As Orta shows in his chapter, for example, the Catholic Church's approach to inculturation in highland Bolivia has undergone notable shifts within the past generation. Indigenous Aymara rituals—once considered antithetical to Christian faith—are now incorporated as meaningful expressions of local Catholicism. Even within a single "tradition," then, the configuration of Christianity is always unfolding. By bringing together a cross-section of case studies that are sensitive to history and culture, this volume documents the dynamics of Christianity's particularisms.

While the contributors to this collection document specific cases, they are, at the same time, prompting questions of general relevance for studies of Christianity. In this section, therefore, we suggest how they contribute to the emerging interest in "the anthropology of Christianity" (see Cannell 2005, forthcoming; Robbins 2003, 2004, Afterword this volume; Scott 2005b).[28] What is "new" in this interest is not the study of Christianity itself.[29] What is new is a more self-conscious engagement with Christianity as a cultural logic. The main thrust of this recent work is to ask "whether it is possible to say what the properties and dynamics of Christian thought might be" (Cannell forthcoming, p. 5). As its proponents have argued, the importance of Christianity has often functioned in anthropological accounts as something set in opposition to local culture, or as an avenue by which one can advance one's pragmatic or political interests. Such accounts can be fruitful, but they can also eclipse both questions about whether or not Christianity has a cultural logic and, concomitantly, questions about the extent to which people live their lives according to such a logic. In this sense, the anthropology of Christianity is a self-consciously comparative project that seeks to develop "a set of shared questions" (Robbins 2003: 192) that social scientists interested in Christianity might take up, examine, and debate.

The benefits of such a project are made clear by Robbins (2003: 191–194), who suggests how the parallel interest in the anthropology of Islam has, over the past twenty years, produced studies in which ethnographic accounts of

Islamic practice at a local level contribute to an understanding of Islam as a world religion. In other words, what the anthropology of Islam has managed to do is demonstrate how what happens in one corner of the Islamic world is relevant to what might be happening in another, and how fine-grained studies are valuable for what they tell us about not only a local culture but also the ways in which happenings at the local level contribute to the sociohistorical formations of the religion as a whole. At its best, any comparative project manages to sustain a productive tension between what is specific and what is shared. This is precisely what the case studies in this volume seek to do for the question of meaning in, and for, Christianity.

At the outset of this introduction, we highlighted the dual sense in which questions of meaning are relevant to the study of Christianity. On one hand, the focus on meaning is informed by the influence—often unacknowledged—of Christian thought upon the objects of anthropology. The first part of this chapter explored this claim in relation to the arguments of Asad and others, as well as in relation to a particular configuration of the literature on semiotics and language. On the other hand, we remarked, meaning is relevant to the study of Christianity because Christians themselves often focus on it in practice. With the foregoing discussion of the anthropology of Christianity in mind, we turn now to a fuller consideration of this second remark. Drawing upon some key studies of Christianity by colleagues in anthropology and history, and linking these studies to the cases collected here, we highlight the extent to which "ultimate religious meaning" can be considered a "major theme" (Robbins 2003: 196) in contemporary Christian practices.

Meaning, Translation, and Ideologies of Language

When the fundamentalist Rev. Melvin Campbell tells Susan Harding how he accidentally killed his own son, he describes how God defused his pain and bafflement:

> And God didn't speak with a voice that I heard with my ear but he spoke to my heart. He said, "Melvin, you know maybe you don't understand what I've done at this particular time, but, can you accept it?" And I said, "yes sir, I can accept it." And Susan, when I made that statement, and I settled that in my own heart, and I said "Lord, I accept it though I don't understand it," I don't know where to say it came from other than that God gave it to me, but he gave me a peace in my soul. And I have not questioned it since. (Harding 2000: 52)

At first, the Rev. Campbell's words seem to reverse Asad's trajectory of history. It sounds like God is now refusing the creation of meaning, and simply disciplining a man, compelling his acceptance. And yet, note how God's act of discipline involves a *suggestion* of future meaning: Rev. Campbell may not have understood the significance of his son's death, but his bewilderment is only "at this particular time." Presumably, some day in the future, Rev. Campbell will understand the tragedy. Harding suggests that the son's death has already become pragmatically meaningful for Rev. Campbell, because he uses it as his own narrative sacrifice to compel Harding's belief. For the grieving father, the important point is that meaninglessness becomes an impossibility.

This impulse is not necessarily limited to Christianity. For example, one elderly Sumatran Muslim told John Bowen, "If you understand the meaning of the words you recite [in worship] that is fine, but even if you do not know them God understands what you mean, and that is all right" (1993: 289). For this man, as for Rev. Campbell, meaning is an intrinsic condition of religious existence, whether or not it is localized in individual subjects and "their" words.

Christianity does differ from the other Abrahamic religions, however, in its energetic sacralization of new languages. Whereas Islam insists that Arabic is the language of the sacred text and Judaism insists upon Hebrew, Christianity, in contrast, has cast hundreds of new languages as media of sacred performance (Sanneh 1994). Indeed, Schleiermacher distinguished Christianity by its "potentiating linguistic spirit" (1977: 50). The Word of God is meaningful regardless of the language in which it is related. Scripture is always original, always authentic in a way that secular texts cannot be; the Bible is also, as Walter Benjamin put it, "unconditionally translatable" (1968: 82). Christianity is therefore notable because it posits meaning as an achievable, superlinguistic entity.

It is precisely this semantic approach to meaning that Foucault wrote against: "The history which bears and determines us has the form of a war rather than that of a language: relations of power, not relations of meaning. History has no 'meaning,' though this is not to say that it is absurd or incoherent. On the contrary, it is intelligible and should be susceptible of analysis down to the smallest detail—but this in accordance with the intelligibility of struggles, of strategies and tactics" (Foucault 1980: 114). The extent to which intelligibility matters in the history of Christianity is an open question; we need only to recall Asad's criticism of Geertz, remembering not to cast modern emphases on belief, interpretation, and meaning back into an imaginary past. Beverly Kienzle, for example, notes how medieval Catholics sometimes desired that preaching be translated for them, and sometimes shunned it: "Some audiences seemingly preferred a Latin sermon to one in their native tongue . . . . Listeners in Cologne remained attentively while Bernard of Clairvaux preached in Latin but left the site during the German translation of the sermon" (2002: 110). In this volume, Matt Tomlinson describes how nineteenth-century Fijian Methodist converts on Viwa Island protested when they received a revised catechism that was written intelligibly in the Viwan dialect; as one missionary's assistant put it, "some of the critics [do] not like anything they [can] understand." This impulse toward mystification, toward appreciating sacred language *because* it is not intelligible, has not necessarily waned over the centuries. Nor is it exclusive to any single branch of Christianity. But it exists today in a productive tension with an increased emphasis on interpretive agency, an emphasis evident, as Orta shows in his chapter for this volume, in the Catholic mission fields of highland Bolivia. The work of Catholic missionaries among the Aymara is framed by the idea that "all human systems of meaning [are] commensurate expressions of God's Word."[30]

The politics of translation reveal intimate connections between meaning and power. Wresting authority from an institutionalized Church is often justified as a strategy to make Christianity more meaningful, but it is also a method of decentering the political influence of the clergy. It is not the death of discipline by any means, but rather a shift of its locus through arguments over meaning. This can be seen in the earliest encounters of European empire building. At the turn of the eighteenth century, as the Kongolese court of King Pedro IV was struggling with civil unrest, Portuguese slave traders, and Capuchin missionaries, a young noblewoman called Dona Beatriz paid with her life for such a refashioning. Beatriz "rewrote" the *Salve Regina* and *Ave Maria*, claimed Jesus had been born in Africa, and declared herself possessed by Saint Anthony (Thornton 1998; Hastings 1994: 71–129). Beatriz saw her mission as a "purification of Christianity" (Thornton 1998: 109). By rewriting the *Salve Regina* and *Ave Maria*, she was "recovering their original content" (Thornton 1998: 114). What Kongolese Catholics had recited until that point had been, in Dona Beatriz's view, meaningless because of the lack of proper intention in worship. In her new version of the *Salve Regina* (now the *Salve Antoniana*), Beatriz remarked: "*Salve* you say and you do not know why. *Salve* you recite and you do not know why. *Salve* you beat and you do not know why. God wants the intention, it is the intention God takes" (in Thornton 1998: 216). With intention in their hearts, these Christians—the first such significant community in sub-Saharan Africa—did not see themselves needing the empty words and institutions of the Catholic priests.

Meaningfulness is often an intrinsic part of modern Christian language ideologies. Robbins (2001a, 2004) traces the difficulties that becoming Christians posed for the Urapmin of Papua New Guinea. Urapmin, Robbins argues, have had to confront the cultural model of modernity as it is articulated by Protestantism, especially its emphasis on individual truthful speakers. Such a model challenges local listener-focused models of meaning-making, which cast radical doubt on the possibility of knowing a person's inner state. This shift to a modern linguistic ideology depends partly on the placement of an omniscient God, who unquestionably knows subjects' inner states, as the audience for prayer, along with all the people who overhear the prayer. In this scenario, prayer has become an especially frequent ritual practice, gaining particular importance as it casts people in these new roles as individual, truth-oriented speakers and hearers.

Christian language ideologies can entwine meaning and truth as related concepts, and compel their emergence in ritual. Describing the language ideology of a group of Swedish evangelicals, Simon Coleman has written of "the . . . notion that sacred words are signifiers whose meanings are fixed" (1996: 126). This statement echoes Harding's (2000) work on American fundamentalists and Crapanzano's (2000) on textual literalism and the denial of metaphor. Csordas' (2001) work on American Catholic charismatics shows how certain Christian congregations may develop correlated senses of meaning, truth, and efficacy in rituals conducted over a period of years. Members of the Word of God movement pronounce and receive messages from God spoken in the first person. In these prophecies, Csordas argues, Word of God members engage in a dialectic between "motives" and metaphor. Motives are formulaically deployed vocabulary, including such common terms as "world," "word," "people," "power," and "freedom," which believers recontextualize and reinvest with new semantic meaning. Csordas argues that these motives help to generate the prophetic utterances' metaphorical themes; the metaphorical themes, in turn, foster reevaluation of the motives (2001: 202–246). In his examples, unfolding prophecies in the mid 1970s identified Word of God members first as a "bulwark" and then as "an impenetrable hedge" against the growing forces of evil in the world. The importance of the metaphorical shift is its intensification of polysemy; as Csordas explains, the transformation from bulwark to hedge "allows an amplification of meaning" by, for example, resonating with biblical metaphors (e.g., the "good seed" in Matthew 13) and the group's social history (growing from its four founding members). He describes one case where Word of God members took "several years" to interpret one particular metaphorical prophecy satisfactorily, ultimately understanding their new community reorganization as a late achievement of "God's will" (2001: 223). In such ethnographic examples, we see how senses of meaning, truth, and efficacy can become woven together more and more tightly as a congregation develops its ritual practices.

Whatever their stance on the literal or figurative, however God's reasons are read, however God's Word is translated, the Christian subjects discussed in this section all seem to accept the idea that meaning undergirds their actions and expressions.[31] In this brief discussion, we have outlined the ways in which meaning is often a central theme of Christianity. It is also, we contend, a useful heuristic for an anthropology of Christianity. Such a claim is subject to refinement, debate, and rearticulation. But to leave the matter here is unsatisfactory. In the final part of this chapter, we suggest how the contributors to this volume push beyond the functionalism of meaning by testing its limits as both an analytic category and a Christian concern.

Ritual and the Limits of Meaning

If modern Christians emphasize the production of meaning, then with what justification do we attempt to write about meaning's limits? The answer, as we have been suggesting throughout, is simply that an emphasis on meaning entails the potential of its absence, negation, or irrelevance. In the meaning-saturated world of Christianity, where understanding God's message becomes paramount, meanings *as a result* become slippery in performance. Indeed, "in actions meanings are always at risk" (Sahlins 1985: ix). Once people attempt to fix meaning, its limits can be approached, defined, and sometimes superseded, as these chapters illustrate.

The authors of these chapters challenge themselves to find the limits of meaning by asking a number of interrelated questions. How do people define what is "meaningful" in the first place? What does this render not meaningful, or meaningless, and with what political, ontological, or other consequences? And what are the limits of anthropological analysis? When does meaning lose its interpretive salience?

"Meaning" is often an inadequate tool for both anthropologists and their subjects. Faubion shows this in his chapter on the Branch Davidian prophet, Ms. Roden. Living in a tent, drinking water from a stagnant pool, Ms. Roden is today less influential than her counterpart David Koresh—the man killed with his followers at their compound in Waco, Texas, in a standoff with federal marshals in 1993. She is nevertheless assertive in her role as God's messenger. Like many sacral actors, her marginality is a marker of divine sanction; she is both "consecrated" and "accursed." Faubion argues that sacral actions are ritual actions, each "always in need of hermeneutical assessment, of an interpretation of one sort or another." What sacral action accomplishes—like ritual or like anthropological analysis—is a reduction of complexities. This is not always a problem. Ritual action and its analysis are, Faubion shows, "capable of 'working' even when they fail to produce a determinate result." Similarly, in her investigation of Papuan millennial movements, Rutherford considers the internal contradictions of Christian institutions, which are associated in Biak with the "coercive" institutions of the colonial and postcolonial state. For her subjects, Christian texts have secret meanings. They are "evidence of a limited good: a treasure possessed by outsiders, a stubbornly inscrutable truth." Rutherford describes meaning, then, "not as the symbolic content of words, objects, or gestures, but as the lure that fuels efforts to order experience, efforts that can never fully succeed." What Faubion and Rutherford show is that, like the horizon, meaning is always beyond reach. But like the horizon, the point is not necessarily to reach it; sometimes the point is simply to contemplate it.

In contrast to these visions of meaning as unreachable, Bornstein describes an encounter in which interpretations (in this case of "success") were absurdly juxtaposed. When a World Vision official from California told her economically disadvantaged Zimbabwean audience "that it was more graceful to walk with the poor as Jesus did," Bornstein notes that it was a bitter irony. The limits of meaning, in this encounter, were not in hazy or marginal spaces—they were drawn quite sharply between the groups and their regimes of interpretation. Engelke, also writing about Zimbabwe, considers the challenges of boundedness in his discussion of the Masowe Apostolics—"the Christians who don't read the Bible." He points out that while members of the church are not encouraged to emphasize Bible learning, its "absence in church rituals does not correlate to biblical ignorance." Or at least it is not supposed to, although efforts to circulate the Word without the presence of the Book raise questions about the appropriate emphases on Christian knowledge and Christian practice—and whether meaning can be produced from one or the other.

Ritual failure is a topic that emerges in several of the chapters, including Bornstein's account of the World Vision staff meeting and Engelke's story of the Masowe prophet whose attempts to elicit the Ten Commandments from his audience were frustrated. Coleman tells of a Swedish preacher's attempt to provoke his audience into considering what a silence "that is full of God" would be like. Svante Rumar's attempt fails, inspiring mostly tension and embarrassment as he stands still at the end of his sermon, shutting down the "verbal factory" (Coleman 2000: 117) of evangelical Christianity. "It may be," Coleman speculates, "that Rumar was reminding his audience of the value of words precisely by removing them from a part of the service where they were expected to be present in abundance." Rumar's failure is ironic, and also something of a reprimand for scholars who denigrate Christian fundamentalists as part of an uncritical reflex, for, as Coleman shows, "literalism has its own ambiguities and subtleties" (see also Crapanzano 2000; Harding 1991, 2000). Tomlinson also gives an example of failed preaching. He writes that Fijian Methodist sermons, which depend on the explication of Biblical passages and the articulation of their relevance to daily life, are performance sites of explicit meaning-making. As such, he argues, they invoke the possibility that not all preachers can make meanings with equal effectiveness, and that some might fail completely. He describes the case of a Fijian Methodist lay preacher who was unable to produce a sermon—although he stood in the pulpit and had already read the Bible lesson—thus failing within the culturally drawn domain of meaning-making and inspiring both amusement and anger in the congregation.

Gershon and Orta address the intimate connections between meaning and power. It is no accident that many of Gershon's New Zealand-based Samoan converts, rejecting the perceived "meaninglessness" of mainstream Christian worship, meet to worship in a commercial gym. This "subtext of muscular Christianity" helps to set the context in which converts become part of a group that rejects one source of perceived Samoan communal strength: Many evangelical groups prohibit *fa'alavelave* ritual exchanges that are considered by many to be crucial to the vitality of overseas Samoan communities. Gershon argues that converts are not changing religions, but moral economies; however, in doing so, "their own voiced concerns were with meaningful expressions of worship. They spoke often about how worship in more mainline churches felt meaningless—that the services were not adequate vehicles for allowing them to convey and experience their strong connection to God." Orta's chapter shows how indigenous symbolism has gained ascendance in Bolivia through the inculturationist movement. Moreover, "Catholic rituals such as baptism, which, despite their communal aims, sow fragmentation, were depicted graphically as standing outside of the indigenous community (indexing their ongoing failure to transcend their foreign origins)." Present-day rituals explicitly aim at meaningfulness and may reject "foreign" Catholic elements to achieve this aim, but one criterion of such meaningfulness is ritual's ultimate ability to make communities cohere—a difficult task since many of the men charged with leading religious communities in cultural revival were once the agents of abolishing indigenous practices and beliefs.

All of these chapters, then, engage with questions of meaning's limits. The authors all consider how an emphasis on meaning invokes the specter of its absence. They all demonstrate how the "quest for lucidity" in both religious ritual and anthropological analysis is often frustrated, but in doing so suggest that the problem of meaning is not always a problem. Meaning is not a panacea. Nor, to switch metaphors, is it always the rug one must worry about having pulled out from under one's feet. But neither is it something to take for granted, or ignore—or disparage as an analytic tool. To do so is to betray both lived experience and a particular strength of anthropological representation.

These chapters demonstrate how the production of meaning raises the possibility that meaning might not be found. Meaning's absence, opacity, or negation may depend on institutional power and regimes of interpretation; it may be the result of perceived sin and weakness; it may simply be the logical product of boundary-drawing, the "unclarified" space where meaning is unrealized or lost. By collecting these ethnographic accounts of Christianity from diverse settings, we show how Christian practices can be used to inform current anthropological debates about power, authority, agency, and textuality. Tambiah was right: Anthropological conceptions of meaning threaten us with deadly confusion. But the way beyond this confusion, we suggest, is to consider meaning as process and potential. Meaning is a sociocultural product emergent in practice, a consequence of boundary-drawing that is generated in diverse, consequential, and often unpredictable ways.

Notes

1. On red macaws, see Levy-Bruhl (1925), Crocker (1977), and Terence Turner (1991); on Captain Cook, see Sahlins (1985; 1995) and Obeyesekere (1992); on Balinese cocks see Geertz (1973f) and Crapanzano (1986).

2. There are other instances in which anthropologists have focused on "failure" or related themes. These include failure in healing treatments (Lewis 2000); misunderstandings in cross-cultural encounters (Sahlins 1985) and anthropologist-informant exchanges (Fabian 1995); recruitment to social role (Wolf 1990); the uses of ignorance (Gershon 2000); chaos (Scott 2005a) and meaninglessness (Jorgensen 1980); and the uncertainties inherent in ritual action (Dirks 1994; Keane 1997c; Turner 1967b). These various studies do not represent a single line of inquiry and their implications differ, but they can be brought together under the general rubric of what Johannes Fabian, in a different register, calls "recovering the negative" (1991). What these studies suggest, and what we aim to suggest in this volume, are the productive potentialities of failure, misunderstanding, ignorance, chaos, and uncertainty.

3. Other critics of Geertz on this point include Roger Keesing (1987) and Paul Shankman (1984). As Keesing puts it, playing off one of Geertz's Weberian images: "Cultures are webs of mystification as well as signification" (1987: 161). We want to point out, however, that for all of their criticisms none of Geertz's critics discussed here calls for abandoning the concept of "meaning" altogether.

4. Turner, in fact, converted to Catholicism in the late 1950s and was thereafter increasingly influenced by theological perspectives (see Engelke 2002). See also Sahlins (1996) and Cannell (2005, forthcoming) for more general discussions of how Judeo-Christian theologies have played an often unacknowledged role in shaping social theory; Cannell calls Christian theology "anthropology's theoretical repressed" (2005: 341; see also Green 2003).

5. See Kapferer (1983); Tambiah (1985); Turner (1986); Turner and Bruner (1986); and Schechner and Appel (1990) for some of the key formulations of these approaches.

6. Boas' essay "On Alternating Sounds" (1889) showed how phonemes are shaped and rendered recognizable by their combination with other phonemes, and hearers' perceptions of these phonemes are based on previous experience; one hears in a language as well as speaks in

it. His observations on sound (and vision), which helped American cultural anthropology to achieve its degree of relativism, should ultimately unsettle fixed notions of meaning as well (cf. Stocking 1974: 5). A. R. Radcliffe-Brown considered meaning "his central problem" (Stocking 1974: 16). Malinowski, as we discuss presently, wrote explicitly about meaning, first in the supplement to Ogden and Richards' *The Meaning of Meaning* (1923), and later (1935) in the second volume of *Coral Gardens and their Magic*. It might even be said that E. E. Evans-Pritchard's *Nuer Religion* (1956) is a study in meaning: it might well be read as a book-length definition of the Nuer word *kwoth*.

7. Perhaps this reluctance stems from the fact that, unlike "culture," anthropologists cannot claim "meaning" as their contribution to keywords in the humanities and social sciences. There is a long-standing interest in meaning among philosophers, theologians, literary critics, and linguists that does not stem from reading ethnography. Lévi-Strauss is one of the few anthropologists to offer an explicit definition: "'to mean' means the ability of any kind of data to be translated in a different language" (1978: 12). Bruce Kapferer also explicitly characterizes meaning, specifically in regard to a performative theory of ritual: "Meaning arises from a process whereby actors project their own action in relation to themselves and others in such a way as to intend further acts, and it is framed in accordance with typifications or ideational conceptions shared by cultural members as to how typical actors within a culture think or act in typical situations" (1983: 6).

8. These included: denotation; connotation; intention; structural location; consequence; intrinsic properties; and emotional association.

9. Denotation is defined in the *Oxford English Dictionary* as: "A mark by which a thing is made known or indicated; a sign, indication" and "the aggregate of objects of which a word may be predicated; extension" (see also Duranti 1997: 163 for a definition in linguistic anthropology). Michael Silverstein notes that Ogden's and Richards' project to create a standardized "Basic English" was founded, ironically, on an ideological bedrock of denotation's supposed naturalness: adoption of Basic English would lead to "denotational utopia, marked by clear, unambiguous, and easily communicated thoughts. . . . Ogden was formulating and launching a tool toward the end of clarified and rationalized 'pure' denotation, free of messily-encoded emotion and calibrated to 'reality'" (Silverstein 2001: 71, 73).

10. See also Tambiah's discussion of the "denotative fallacy" and the relationship between Malinowski and Ogden and Richards (especially Tambiah 1968: 185–188). Tambiah treats the subject in more depth than we have space to here, but raises some interesting issues around Malinowski's claim—made with "excessive flourish"—that "words had no existence and that texts divorced from context were meaningless" (1968: 185).

11. Some recent examples of anthropologists who acknowledge the influence of Wittgenstein upon their work include Arno (2003), Asad (2003), Das (1998), Geertz (2000), James (2003), and Rosaldo (1999). Kapferer (1983: 5) draws a useful parallel between Turner's performative approach to ritual and Wittgenstein's later philosophy. Indeed, for most anthropologists it is Wittgenstein's later philosophy—in which he takes an antifoundational stance in the development of his ideas on language games, meaning-as-use, grammar, and forms of life—that is particularly compelling.

12. Geertz, for example, cites Wittgenstein's interest in the "rough ground" (language games) as an important parallel to "fieldwork" (Geertz 2000: xii; cf. Wittgenstein 2001: §107).

13. Wittgenstein might well have chosen himself as his chief protagonist; his view of language in the *Tractatus Logico-Philosophicus* was much the same as Augustine's. Moreover, as Henry Chadwick's work suggests, a case can be made that Augustine was not trapped by the denotative fallacy: Augustine expressed his views on meaning in a more subtle way through his essay *De Magistro*: "Words and sounds are significant by convention, but convey meaning only in an ambivalent and limited degree" (Chadwick 1986: 47).

14. Roy Rappaport's scheme is similar to Blocker's, pegging meaning at three levels of social interaction (1999: 70–74). "Low order meaning" is a relation of distinction, i.e. what Saussure identified as paradigmatic difference ("X" means X because it does not mean Y or Z); "middle order meaning" is a relation of similarity, such as metaphor (here, Rappaport includes the problem of meaning's challenge, "What does it all mean?" [1999: 71]); and "high-order

meaning" refers to "identity or unity." See Robbins (2001b) for a reading and partial reformulation of Rappaport's theory. Another effectively simple categorization is Lyons' (1977:
§2.4) distinction of three kinds of linguistic meaning: descriptive, social, and expressive; see
Besnier (1990: 419–420) for a useful criticism.

15. Most of the figures associated with structuralism either never used the term or tried, in various ways, to disassociate themselves from it (or its genesis): Ferdinand de Saussure, Claude
Lévi-Strauss, Roland Barthes, the early Foucault. But in France, where it dominated intellectual circles throughout the 1950s and 60s, apparently even the trainer of the national football
team called for "structural reorganization" in order to improve their win-loss record (Dosse
1997: xix).

16. For Saussure, the linguist/semiologist most often recognized as the "father" of structuralism,
the meaning of any word was a function of its placement in a paradigmatic and syntagmatic
position; he described language as "a self-contained whole and a principle of classification"
(1959: 9). Within all-encompassing *langage* (language), Saussure distinguished between
langue (system) and *parole* (utterance), and designated the former as the proper object of
linguistic study. Saussure argued that language is about form; it is defined by a set of invariant elements, the study of which should conform to a science. As François Dosse sums it up,
"The heart of [Saussure's] demonstration is to establish the arbitrariness of the sign, showing
that language is a system of values established neither by content nor by experience, but by
pure difference. Saussure's interpretation of language firmly places it in abstract terms in order to better remove it from empiricism and from psychologizing" (1997: 44).

17. Lévi-Strauss laments the fact that "a work I know to be packed with meaning"—his own
scholarship—"appears to some as the elaboration of a form without meaning. But this is because the meaning is included, and as it were compressed, within the system" (1981: 693).

18. See Gayle Rubin (1975) for a critique of Lévi-Strauss's work on "Man," incest, and the exchange of women.

19. On the ethnography of speaking, see especially Hymes (1964, 1972) and Bauman and Sherzer (1974). Sociolinguistic studies of inequality took diverse approaches, including investigations of standard and nonstandard language production (Labov 1972); pronominal usage in
social life and literature (Brown and Gilman 1960; Friedrich 1972); and speech communities (Gumperz 1972). Contemporary analyses of race, class, and gender rework and expand
these themes through studies of language ideology (Kroskrity 2000; Schieffelin, Woolard, and
Kroskrity 1998) and entextualization (Bauman and Briggs 1990; Briggs and Bauman 1992;
Duranti and Goodwin 1992; Silverstein and Urban 1996).

20. Vološinov described meaning as interactionally emergent: "It is like an electric spark that occurs
only when two different terminals are hooked together" (1973: 103). In his view, utterances are
meaningful not only in regard to other utterances and contexts of deployment, but also in
regard to producers' "evaluative accents" (1973: 103). These accents, or value judgments, are
an intrinsic part of any utterance, and the resulting "evaluative orientation" is intertwined with
the utterance's meaningfulness: "each element in a living utterance not only has a meaning but
also has a value. . . . A change in meaning is, essentially, always a reevaluation: the transposi-
tion of some particular word from one evaluative context to another" (1973: 105).

21. "Grammar defines meaning only very partially: it is in relation to a market that the complete
determination of the signification of discourse occurs" (Bourdieu 1991: 38). For Bourdieu,
the market is a social context that generates different kinds of *value*. "A field or market may
be seen as a structured space of positions in which the positions and their interrelations are
determined by the distribution of different kinds of resources or 'capital.' . . . Linguistic utterances or expressions are always produced in particular contexts or markets, and the properties
of these markets endow linguistic products with a certain 'value'" (Thompson 1991: 14, 18).

22. Kierkegaard wrote that for Christianity, "Faith is precisely the contradiction between the infi-
nite passion of the individual's inwardness and the objective uncertainty" (1941: 182).

23. See the essays collected in Sapir and Crocker (1977) and Fernandez (1991).

24. Some (Friedrich 1991; T. Turner 1991) prefer the term "polytropy" to "metaphor theory"
because tropes do not, in themselves, have fixed contexts. To borrow and expand an example
from Fernandez (1986: 56), the statement "Frank is a clam" would be understood by most

English-speakers as a metaphor, since Frank (as a human) and the clam (as a bivalve mollusk) are fundamentally "different." However, this statement becomes a metonym if—for some reason—one thinks of Frank and a clam above all as metazoa (bodies composed of more than one cell and displaying differentiation of tissues), and thus as occupying the same conceptual domain. The critiques of metaphor theory advanced by Friedrich and Turner have a precursor in the work of Roy Wagner; see in particular his discussion of controlling contexts (1981: chapter 3).

25. See also Csordas (2001); Lakoff and Johnson (1980); Sapir (1977: 33).

26. Recent work under this rubric includes Keane (1997c; 2002); Lee and Urban (1989); Lemon (2000); Parmentier (1987).

27. Peirce argued that any sign has elements of iconicity, indexicality, and conventional symbolism. The anthropological task is to see which relationships are foregrounded in what contexts, and with what consequences.

28. Both Cannell (forthcoming) and Robbins (2003) have edited collections of papers highlighting an "anthropology of Christianity" approach. A number of other edited collections have, over the past two decades, served as important contributions to the development of such comparative frameworks (Barker 1990; Hefner 1993; Saunders 1988; Stewart and Strathern 1997). Susan Harding's (1991) essay on studying fundamentalists has been credited by both Cannell (2005: 338–339; forthcoming pp. 5–6) and Robbins (2003: 193; 2004: 29) as an important influence on their work. In terms of tracing a genealogy for the anthropology of Christianity, Mary Douglas (1966, 1970) and Edmund Leach (1969; Leach and Aycock 1983) also deserve, in our view, to be singled out because of the comparative frameworks they set for anthropological understandings of Judeo-Christian thought.

29. For example, consider Isaac Schapera's work with the Tswana, which began in 1929. He opened his book *Married Life in an African Tribe* with a set of vignettes that "show rather strikingly the way in which Kgatla culture has been influenced by Western civilization" (1940: 12–13). As Schapera later emphasized in an interview with Adam Kuper, Christianity was the nucleus of this influence and had to be taken seriously in an anthropological study: "[W]hat I saw was a church and people dressed like whites, talking English, and so on. To take them as they were you had to have the church and the rest" (Kuper 2001: 3).

30. The steady increase of Bible translations through the millennia is notable: in 200 c. e., parts of the Bible had been translated into 10 languages; by 1500, the number had reached 60; by 1999, at least one book of the Bible had been translated into 2,233 languages, and 371 languages had complete Bibles (Stine 2001: 108).

31. Even in glossolalia, which involves the apparent denial of explicit meaning or propositional truth in favor of the pure embodiment of divinity, people often translate the sounds streaming from the speaker (Goodman 1969). And yet, even when glossolalia remains untranslated and uninterpreted, it is considered meaningful and true, sometimes precisely because it cannot be understood.

References

Argyrou, Vassos. 2002. *Anthropology and the Will to Meaning*. London: Pluto Press.

Arno, Andrew. 2003. "Aesthetics, Intuition, and Reference in Fijian Ritual Communication: Modularity in and out of Language." *American Anthropologist* 105, no. 4: 807–19.

Asad, Talal. 1993. *Genealogies of Religion: Discipline and Reasons of Power in Christianity and Islam*. Baltimore: The Johns Hopkins University Press.

———. 2003. *Formations of the Secular: Christianity, Islam, Modernity*. Stanford: Stanford University Press.

Atkinson, Jane Monnig. 1989. *The Art and Politics of Wana Shamanship*. Berkeley: University of California Press.

Austin, J. L. 1962. *How to Do Things with Words*. 2nd ed., ed. J. O Urmson and M. Sbisà. Cambridge, MA: Harvard University Press.

Barker, John, ed. 1990. *Christianity in Oceania: Ethnographic Perspectives*. Lanham, MD: University Press of America.

Basso, Keith H., and Henry A. Selby. 1976. "Introduction." In *Meaning in Anthropology*, ed. K. H. Basso and H. A. Selby. Albuquerque: School of American Research, University of New Mexico Press.

Basso, Keith H., and Henry A. Selby, eds. 1976. *Meaning in Anthropology*. Albuquerque: School of American Research, University of New Mexico Press.

Bauman, Richard. 1974. "Speaking in the Light: The Role of the Quaker Minister." In *Explorations in the Ethnography of Speaking*, ed. R. Bauman and J. Sherzer. New York: Cambridge University Press.

———. 1983. *Let Your Words Be Few: Symbolism of Speaking and Silence among Seventeenth-Century Quakers*. Cambridge: Cambridge University Press.

Bauman, Richard, and Charles L. Briggs. 1990. "Poetics and Performance as Critical Perspectives on Language and Social Life." *Annual Review of Anthropology* 19: 59–88.

Bauman, Richard, and Joel Sherzer, eds. 1974. *Explorations in the Ethnography of Speaking*. New York: Cambridge University Press.

Bell, Catherine. 1997. *Ritual Theory, Ritual Practice*. Oxford: Oxford University Press.

Benjamin, Walter. 1968. "The Task of the Translator: An Introduction to the Translation of Baudelaire's *Tableaux Parisiens*." In *Illuminations*. New York: Schocken Books.

Benveniste, Emile. 1971. "The Nature of the Linguistic Sign." In *Problems in General Linguistics*, trans. M. E. Meek. Coral Gables: University of Miami Press.

Besnier, Niko. 1990. "Language and Affect." *Annual Review of Anthropology* 19: 419–51.

Biersack, Aletta. 1989. "Local Knowledge, Local History: Geertz and Beyond." In *The New Cultural History*, ed. L. Hunt. Berkeley: University of California Press.

Bloch, Maurice. 1986. *From Blessing to Violence: History and Ideology in the Circumcision Ritual of the Merina of Madagascar*. Cambridge: Cambridge University Press.

———. 1989 [1974]. "Symbols, Song, Dance and Features of Articulation: Is Religion an Extreme Form of Traditional Authority?" In *Ritual, History and Power: Selected Papers in Anthropology*. London: The Athlone Press.

———. 1991. "Language, Anthropology, and Cognitive Science." *Man* (n.s.) 26, no. 2: 183–98.

Blocker, Gene. 1974. *The Meaning of Meaninglessness*. The Hague: Martinus Nijhoff.

Boas, Franz. 1889. "On Alternating Sounds." *American Anthropologist* 2, no. 1: 47–54.

Boddy, Janice. 1989. *Wombs and Alien Spirits: Women, Men, and the Zar Cult*. Madison: University of Wisconsin Press.

Boon, James A. 1978. "The Shift to Meaning." *American Ethnologist* 5, no. 2: 361–67.

Bourdieu, Pierre. 1991. *Language and Symbolic Power*, ed. J.B. Thompson, trans. G. Raymond and M. Adamson. Cambridge: Harvard University Press.

Bowen, John R. 1993. *Muslims through Discourse*. Princeton: Princeton University Press.

Briggs, Charles L., and Richard Bauman. 1992. "Genre, Intertextuality, and Social Power." *Journal of Linguistic Anthropology* 2, no. 2: 131–72.

Brown, R., and A. Gilman. 1960. "The Pronouns of Power and Solidarity." In *Style in Language*, ed. T. A. Sebeok. Cambridge, MA: MIT Press.

Cannell, Fenella. 1999. *Power and Intimacy in the Christian Philippines*. Cambridge: Cambridge University Press.

———. 2005. "The Christianity of Anthropology." *Journal of the Royal Anthropological Institute* 11, no. 2: 335–56.

———. Forthcoming. "Introduction: The Anthropology of Christianity." In *The Anthropology of Christianity*, ed. F. Cannell. Durham: Duke University Press.

Cannell, Fenella, ed. Forthcoming. *The Anthropology of Christianity*. Durham: Duke University Press.

Chadwick, Henry. 1986. *Augustine*. Oxford: Oxford University Press.

Coleman, Simon. 1996. "Words as Things: Language, Aesthetics and the Objectification of Protestant Evangelicalism." *Journal of Material Culture* 1, no. 1: 107–28.

———. 2000. *The Globalization of Charismatic Christianity: Spreading the Gospel of Prosperity*. Cambridge: Cambridge University Press.

Crapanzano, Vincent. 1986. "Hermes' Dilemma: The Masking of Subversion in Ethnographic Description." In *Writing Culture: The Poetics and Politics of Ethnography*, ed. J. Clifford and G. Marcus. Berkeley: University of California Press.

———. 2000. *Serving the Word: Literalism in America from the Pulpit to the Bench*. New York: The New Press.

Crocker, J. Christopher. 1977. "My Brother the Parrot." In *The Social Use of Metaphor: Essays on the Anthropology of Rhetoric*, ed. J. D. Sapir and J. C. Crocker. Philadelphia: University of Pennsylvania Press.

Csordas, Thomas J. 2001 [1997]. *Language, Charisma, and Creativity: Ritual Life in the Catholic Charismatic Renewal*. New York: Palgrave.

Das, Veena. 1998. "Wittgenstein and Anthropology." *Annual Review of Anthropology* 27: 171–95.

Dening, Greg. 1980. *Islands and Beaches: Discourse on a Silent Land: Marquesas, 1774–1880*. Honolulu: University of Hawaii Press.

Dirks, Nicholas. 1994. "Ritual and Resistance: Subversion as a Social Fact." In *Culture/Power/History: A Reader in Contemporary Social Theory*, ed. N. B. Dirks, G. Eley, and S. B. Ortner. Princeton: Princeton University Press.

Dosse, François. 1997. *History of Structuralism: The Rising Sign, 1945–1966*, trans. D. Glassman. Minneapolis: University of Minnesota Press.

Douglas, Mary. 1966. *Purity and Danger: An Analysis of the Concepts of Pollution and Taboo*. London: Routledge.

———. 1970. *Natural Symbols*. London: Routledge.

Du Bois, John W. 1993. "Meaning without Intention: Lessons from Divination." In *Responsibility and Evidence in Oral Discourse*, ed. J. H. Hill and J. T. Irvine. Cambridge: Cambridge University Press.

Duranti, Alessandro. 1993. "Intentions, Self, and Responsibility: An Essay in Samoan Ethnopragmatics." In *Responsibility and Evidence in Oral Discourse*, ed. J. H. Hill and J. T. Irvine. Cambridge: Cambridge University Press.

———. 1997. *Linguistic Anthropology*. Cambridge: Cambridge University Press.

Duranti, Alessandro, and Charles Goodwin. 1992. *Rethinking Context: Language as an Interactive Phenomenon*. Cambridge: Cambridge University Press.

Engelke, Matthew. 2002. "The Problem of Belief: Evans-Pritchard and Victor Turner on 'the Inner Life.'" *Anthropology Today* 18, no. 6: 3–6.

———. 2004. "Text and Performance in an African Christian Church: The Book, 'Live and Direct.'" *American Ethnologist* 31, no. 1: 76–91.

Evans-Pritchard, E. E. 1956. *Nuer Religion*. Oxford: Clarendon.

———. 1976. *Witchcraft, Oracles and Magic among the Azande*, abridged ed. Oxford: Clarendon.

Fabian, Johannes. 1991. "Text as Terror: Second Thoughts about Charisma." In *Time and the Work of Anthropology: Critical Essays, 1971–1991*. Amsterdam: Harwood Academic Publishers.

————. 1995. "Ethnographic Misunderstanding and the Perils of Context." *American Anthropologist* 97, no. 1: 41–50.

Faubion, James D. 2003. "Religion, Violence, and the Vitalistic Economy." *Anthropological Quarterly* 76, no. 1: 71–85.

Fernandez, James. 1986. *Persuasions and Performances: The Play of Tropes in Culture.* Bloomington: Indiana University Press.

————ed. 1991. *Beyond Metaphor: The Theory of Tropes in Anthropology.* Stanford: Stanford University Press.

Friedrich, Paul. 1972. "Social Context and Semantic Features: The Russian Pronominal Usage." In *Directions in Sociolinguistics: The Ethnography of Communication*, ed. J. J. Gumperz and D. Hymes. New York: Holt, Rinehart and Winston.

————. 1991. "Polytropy." In *Beyond Metaphor: The Theory of Tropes in Anthropology*, ed. J. Fernandez. Stanford: Stanford University Press.

Foucault, Michel. 1980. *Power/Knowledge: Selected Interviews and Other Writings, 1972–1977*, ed. C. Gordon, trans. C. Gordon, L. Marshall, J. Mepham, and K. Soper. New York: Pantheon Books.

Fuss, Diana. 1989. *Essentially Speaking: Feminism, Nature, and Difference.* New York: Routledge.

Geertz, Clifford. 1973a. "Thick Description: Toward an Interpretive Theory of Culture." In *The Interpretation of Cultures: Selected Essays.* New York: BasicBooks.

————. 1973b [1966]. "The Impact of the Concept of Culture on the Concept of Man." In *The Interpretation of Cultures: Selected Essays.* New York: BasicBooks.

————. 1973c [1966]. "Religion as a Cultural System." In *The Interpretation of Cultures: Selected Essays.* New York: BasicBooks.

————. 1973d [1959]. "Ritual and Social Change: A Javanese Example." In *The Interpretation of Cultures: Selected Essays.* New York: BasicBooks.

————. 1973e [1967]. "The Cerebral Savage: On the Work of Claude Lévi-Strauss." In *The Interpretation of Cultures: Selected Essays.* New York: BasicBooks

————. 1973f [1972]. "Deep Play: Notes on the Balinese Cockfight." In *The Interpretation of Cultures: Selected Essays.* New York: BasicBooks.

————. 1980. *Negara: The Theatre State in Nineteenth Century Bali.* Princeton: Princeton University Press.

————. 2000. *Available Light: Anthropological Reflections on Philosophical Topics.* Princeton: Princeton University Press.

Gellner, Ernest. 1998. *Language and Solitude: Wittgenstein, Malinowski, and the Habsburg Dilemma.* New York: Cambridge University Press.

Gershon, Ilana, ed. 2000. "The Symbolic Capital of Ignorance." Special issue of *Social Analysis* 44, no. 2.

Goodman, Felicitas D. 1969. "Phonetic Analysis of Glossolalia in Four Cultural Settings." *Journal for the Scientific Study of Religion* 8, no. 2: 227–39.

Goody, Jack. 1963. "Religion and Ritual: The Definitional Problem." *British Journal of Psychology* 12: 143–64.

Grice, H. P. 1957. "Meaning." *The Philosophical Review* 66, no. 3: 377–88.

Grayling, A. C. 2001. *Wittgenstein: A Very Short Introduction.* Oxford: Oxford University Press.

Green, Maia. 2003. *Priests, Witches and Power: Popular Christianity after Mission in Southern Tanzania.* Cambridge: Cambridge University Press.

Gumperz, John J. 1972. "The Speech Community." In *Language and Social Context*, ed. P. P. Giglioli. Harmondsworth: Penguin Education.

Hacker, P. M. S. 1996. *Wittgenstein's Place in Twentieth-Century Philosophy*. Oxford: Blackwell.

Harding, Susan Friend. 1991. "Representing Fundamentalism: The Problem of the Repugnant Cultural Other." *Social Research* 58, no. 2: 373–93.

———. 2000. *The Book of Jerry Falwell: Fundamentalist Language and Politics*. Princeton: Princeton University Press.

Hastings, Adrian. 1994. *The Church in Africa, 1450–1950*. Oxford: Clarendon.

Hefner, Robert, ed. 1993. *Conversion to Christianity: Historical and Anthropological Perspectives on a Great Transformation*. Berkeley: University of California Press.

Humphrey, Caroline, and James Laidlaw. 1994. *The Archetypal Actions of Ritual: A Theory of Ritual Illustrated by the Jain Rite of Worship*. Oxford: Clarendon.

Hymes, Dell, ed. 1964. *Language in Culture and Society: A Reader in Linguistics and Anthropology*. New York: Harper and Row.

———. 1972. "Models of the Interaction of Language and Everyday Life." In *Directions in Sociolinguistics*, ed. J. Gumperz and D. Hymes. New York: Holt, Rinehart and Winston.

Jakobson, Roman. 1990. *On Language*, ed. L. R. Waugh and M. Monville-Burston. Cambridge: Harvard University Press.

James, Wendy. 2003. *The Ceremonial Animal: A New Portrait of Anthropology*. Oxford: Oxford University Press.

Jorgensen, Dan. 1980. "What's in a Name: The Meaning of Meaninglessness in Telefolmin." *Ethos* 8, no. 4: 349–66.

Kapferer, Bruce. 1983. *A Celebration of Demons: Exorcism and the Aesthetics of Healing in Sri Lanka*. Bloomington: Indiana University Press.

Kaplan, Martha. 1995. *Neither Cargo nor Cult: Ritual Politics and the Colonial Imagination in Fiji*. Durham: Duke University Press.

Keane, Webb. 1997a. "From Fetishism to Sincerity: On Agency, the Speaking Subject, and Their Historicity in the Context of Religious Conversion." *Comparative Studies in Society and History* 39, no. 4: 674–93.

———. 1997b. "Religious Language." *Annual Review of Anthropology* 26: 47–71.

———. 1997c. *Signs of Recognition: Powers and Hazards of Representation in an Indonesian Society*. Berkeley: University of California Press.

———. 2002. "Sincerity, 'Modernity,' and the Protestants." *Cultural Anthropology* 17, no. 1: 65–92.

Keesing, Roger. 1987. "Anthropology as Interpretive Quest." *Current Anthropology* 28, no. 2: 161–76.

Keyes, Charles. 2002. "Weber and Anthropology." *Annual Review of Anthropology* 31: 233–55.

Keyes, Charles, Laurel Kendall, and Henry Hardacre, eds. 1994. *Asian Visions of Authority: Religion and the Modern States of East and Southeast Asia*. Honolulu: University of Hawaii Press.

Kienzle, Beverly Mayne. 2002. "Medieval Sermons and Their Performance." In *Preacher, Sermon and Audience in the Middle Ages*, ed. C. Muessig. Leiden: Brill.

Kierkegaard, Søren. 1941 [1846]. *Concluding Unscientific Postscript to the Philosophical Fragments: A Mimic-Pathetic-Dialectic Composition, An Existential Contribution*, ed. W. Lowrie, trans. D. F. Swenson and W. Lowrie. Princeton: Princeton University Press.

Kleinman, Arthur, Veena Das, and Margaret Lock, eds. 1997. *Social Suffering*. Berkeley: University of California Press.

Knauft, Bruce M. 2002. *Exchanging the Past: A Rainforest World of Before and After.* Chicago: University of Chicago Press.

Kroskrity, Paul V., ed. 2000. *Regimes of Language: Ideologies, Polities, and Identities.* Santa Fe: School of American Research Press.

Kuper, Adam. 2001. "Isaac Schapera—a Conversation (Part I)." *Anthropology Today* 17, no. 6: 3–7.

Labov, William. 1972. *Sociolinguistic Patterns.* Philadelphia: University of Pennsylvania Press.

Lakoff, George, and Mark Johnson. 1980. *Metaphors We Live By.* Chicago: University of Chicago Press.

Lambek, Michael. 1993. *Knowledge and Practice in Mayotte: Local Discourses of Islam, Sorcery, and Spirit Possession.* Toronto: University of Toronto Press.

Leach, Edmund. 1964. *Political Systems of Highland Burma.* LSE Monographs in Social Anthropology. London: Athlone Press.

———. 1969. *Genesis as Myth and Other Essays.* London: Cape.

———. 1970. *Claude Lévi-Strauss.* New York: Viking.

Leach, Edmund, and D. Alan Aycock. 1983. *Structuralist Interpretations of Biblical Myth.* Cambridge: Cambridge University Press.

Lee, Benjamin, and Greg Urban, eds. 1989. *Semiotics, Self, and Society.* Berlin: Mouton de Gruyter.

Lemon, Alaina. 2000. *Between Two Fires: Gypsy Performance and Romani Memory from Pushkin to Postsocialism.* Durham: Duke University Press.

Lévi-Strauss, Claude. 1969. *The Elementary Structures of Kinship*, ed. R. Needham, trans. J. H. Bell, J. R. von Sturmer, and R. Needham. Boston: Beacon Press.

———. 1978. *Myth and Meaning.* London: Routledge and Kegan Paul.

———. 1981. *The Naked Man*, trans. J. and D. Weightman. New York: Harper and Row.

Lévy-Bruhl, Lucien. 1925 [1910]. *How Natives Think*, trans. L. A. Clare. New York: A. A. Knopf.

Lewis, Gilbert. 2000. *A Failure of Treatment.* Oxford: Oxford University Press.

Lyons, John. 1977. *Semantics*, vol. 1. Cambridge: Cambridge University Press.

Makin, Gideon. 2000. *The Metaphysicians of Meaning: Russell and Frege on Sense and Denotation.* New York: Routledge.

Malinowski, Bronislaw. 1935. *Coral Gardens and Their Magic, vol. II: The Language of Magic and Gardening.* New York: American Book Company.

———. 1946 [1923]. "The Problem of Meaning in Primitive Languages." In C. K. Ogden and I. A. Richards, *The Meaning of Meaning: A Study of the Influence of Language upon Thought and of the Science of Symbolism.* New York: Harcourt, Brace.

Miyazaki, Hirokazu. 2000. Faith and Its Fulfillment: Agency, Exchange, and the Fijian Aesthetics of Completion. *American Ethnologist* 27, no. 1: 31–51.

———. 2004. *The Method of Hope: Anthropology, Philosophy, and Fijian Knowledge.* Stanford: Stanford University Press.

Obeyesekere, Gananath. 1992. *The Apotheosis of Captain Cook: European Mythmaking in the Pacific.* Princeton: Princeton University Press.

Ogden, C. K., and I. A. Richards. 1923. *The Meaning of Meaning: A Study of the Influence of Language upon Thought and of the Science of Symbolism.* London: K. Paul, Trench, Trubner and Co.

Ortner, Sherry B. 1973. "On Key Symbols." *American Anthropologist* 75, no. 5: 1338–46.

———. 1999. "Thick Resistance: Death and the Cultural Construction of Agency in Himalayan Mountaineering." In *The Fate of "Culture": Geertz and Beyond*, ed. S.B. Ortner. Berkeley: University of California Press.

Parmentier, Richard. 1987. *The Sacred Remains: Myth, History, and Polity in Belau*. Chicago: University of Chicago Press.

Parsons, Talcott. 1963. "Introduction." In Max Weber's *The Sociology of Religion*. Boston: Beacon Press.

Pepper, Stephen. 1942. *World Hypotheses: A Study in Evidence*. Berkeley: University of California Press.

Placido, Barbara. 2001. "'It's All To Do with Words': An Analysis of Spirit Possession in the Venezuelan Cult of Maria Lionza." *Journal of the Royal Anthropological Institute* (n.s.) 7: 207–24.

Putnam, Hilary. 1996 [1975]. "The Meaning of 'Meaning.'" In *The Twin Earth Chronicles: Twenty Years of Reflection on Hilary Putnam's "The Meaning of 'Meaning,'"* ed. A. Pessin and S. Goldberg. Armonk, NY: M. E. Sharpe.

Quine, Willard Van Orman. 1960. *Word and Object*. Cambridge, MA: The MIT Press.

Rappaport, Roy A. 1999. *Ritual and Religion in the Making of Humanity*. Cambridge: Cambridge University Press.

Robbins, Joel. 2001a. "God Is Nothing But Talk: Modernity, Language, and Prayer in a Papua New Guinea Society." *American Anthropologist* 103, no. 4: 901–12.

———. 2001b. "Ritual Communication and Linguistic Ideology." *Current Anthropology* 42, no. 5: 591–614.

———. 2003. "What is a Christian? Notes toward an Anthropology of Christianity." *Religion* 33, no. 3: 191–99.

———. 2004. *Becoming Sinners: Christianity and Moral Torment in a Papua New Guinea Society*. Berkeley: University of California Press.

Rosaldo, Renato I., Jr. 1999. "A Note on Geertz as a Cultural Essayist." In *The Fate of "Culture": Geertz and Beyond*, ed. S. B. Ortner. Berkeley: University of California Press.

Rubin, Gayle. 1975. "The Traffic in Women." In *Toward an Anthropology of Women*, ed. R. Reiter. New York: Monthly Review Press.

Sahlins, Marshall. 1976. *Culture and Practical Reason*. Chicago: University of Chicago Press.

———. 1981. *Historical Metaphors and Mythical Realities: Structure in the Early History of the Sandwich Islands Kingdom*. Ann Arbor: University of Michigan Press.

———. 1985. *Islands of History*. Chicago: University of Chicago Press

———. 1995. *How "Natives" Think: About Captain Cook, For Example*. Chicago: University of Chicago Press.

———. 1996. "The Sadness of Sweetness: Or, the Native Anthropology of Western Cosmology." *Current Anthropology* 37, no. 3: 395–428.

———. 2002. *Waiting for Foucault, Still*. Chicago: Prickly Paradigm Press.

Sanneh, Lamin. 1989. *Translating the Message: The Missionary Impact on Culture*. Maryknoll, NY: Orbis.

———. 1994. "Translatability in Islam and in Christianity in Africa." In *Religion in Africa: Experience and Expression*, ed. T. Blakeley. Portsmouth: Heinemann.

Sapir, J. David. 1977. "The Anatomy of Metaphor." In *The Social Use of Metaphor: Essays on the Anthropology of Rhetoric*, ed. J. D. Sapir and J. C. Crocker. Philadelphia: University of Pennsylvania Press.

Sapir, J. David, and J. Christopher Crocker, ed. 1977. *The Social Use of Metaphor: Essays on the Anthropology of Rhetoric*. Philadelphia: University of Pennsylvania Press.

Saunders, George R., ed. 1988. *Culture and Christianity: The Dialectics of Transformation*. New York: Greenwood Press.

Saussure, Ferdinand de. 1959. *Course in General Linguistics*, eds. C. Bally and A. Sèchehaye, trans. W. Baskin. New York: Philosophical Library.

Schapera, Isaac. 1940. *Married Life in an African Tribe*. London: Penguin.

Schechner, Richard, and Willa Appel, eds. 1990. *By Means of Performance: Intercultural Studies of Theater and Ritual*. Cambridge: Cambridge University Press.

Schieffelin, Bambi B., Kathryn A. Woolard, and Paul V. Kroskrity, eds. 1998. *Language Ideologies: Practice and Theory*. New York: Oxford University Press.

Schleiermacher, F. D. E. 1977 [1833]. *Hermeneutics: The Handwritten Manuscripts*, ed. H. Kimmerle, trans. J. Duke and J. Forstman. Atlanta: Scholars Press.

Scott, David. 1994. *Formations of Ritual: Colonial and Anthropological Discourses on the Sinhala Yaktovil*. Minneapolis: University of Minnesota Press.

Scott, Michael W. 2005a. "Hybridity, Vacuity, and Blockage: Visions of Chaos from Anthropological Theory, Island Melanesia, and Central Africa." *Comparative Studies in Society and History* 47, no. 1: 190–216.

———. 2005b. "'I was like Abraham': Notes on the Anthropology of Christianity from Solomon Islands." *Ethnos* 70, no. 1: 101–25.

Searle, John R. 1983. *Intentionality: An Essay in the Philosophy of Mind*. Cambridge: Cambridge University Press.

Shankman, Paul. 1984. "The Thick and the Thin: On the Interpretive Theoretical Program of Clifford Geertz." *Current Anthropology* 25, no. 3: 261–80.

Shore, Bradd. 1996. *Culture in Mind: Cognition, Culture, and the Problem of Meaning*. Oxford: Oxford University Press.

Silverstein, Michael. 1976. "Shifters, Verbal Categories, and Cultural Description." In *Meaning in Anthropology*, ed. K. H. Basso and H. Selby. Albuquerque: University of New Mexico Press.

———. 2001. "From the Meaning of Meaning to the Empires of the Mind: Ogden's Orthological English." In *Languages and Publics: The Making of Authority*, eds. S. Gal and K. A. Woolard. Manchester, UK: St. Jerome Publishing.

———. 2003. *Talking Politics: The Substance of Style from Abe to "W."* Chicago: Prickly Paradigm Press.

Silverstein, Michael, and Greg Urban, eds. 1996. *Natural Histories of Discourse*. Chicago: University of Chicago Press.

Smith, Jonathan Z. 1987. *To Take Place: Toward Theory in Ritual*. Chicago: University of Chicago Press.

Sperber, Dan. 1975. *Rethinking Symbolism*. Trans. A. Morton. Cambridge: Cambridge University Press.

Stewart, Pamela J., and Andrew Strathern, eds. 1997. *Millennial Markers*. Townsville: Centre for Pacific Studies, James Cook University of North Queensland.

Stine, P. C. 2001. "Bible Translations, Modern Period." In *Concise Encyclopedia of Language and Religion*, ed. J. F. A. Sawyer and J. M. Y. Simpson. Amsterdam: Elsevier.

Stocking, George W. 1974. "The Basic Assumptions of Boasian Anthropology." In *A Franz Boas Reader: The Shaping of American Anthropology*, ed. G. W. Stocking. Chicago: University of Chicago Press.

Tambiah, Stanley Jeyaraja. 1968. "The Magical Power of Words." *Man* (n.s.) 3, no. 2: 175–208.

———. 1985 [1981]. "A Performative Approach to Ritual." In *Culture, Thought, and Social Action: An Anthropological Perspective*. Cambridge: Harvard University Press.

Thompson, John B. 1991. "Editor's Introduction." In Pierre Bourdieu's *Language and Symbolic Power*, ed. J. B. Thompson, trans. G. Raymond and M. Adamson. Cambridge: Harvard University Press.

Thornton, John K. 1998. *The Kongolese Saint Anthony: Dona Beatriz Kimpa Vita and the Antonian Movement, 1684–1706*. Cambridge: Cambridge University Press.

Trawick, Margaret. 1988. "Ambiguity in the Oral Exegesis of a Sacred Text: *Tirukkōvaiyār* (or, the Guru in the Garden, Being an Account of a Tamil Informant's Responses to Homesteading in Central New York State)." *Cultural Anthropology* 3, no. 3: 316–51.

Turner, Terence. 1991. "'We Are Parrots,' 'Twins Are Birds': Play of Tropes as Operational Structure." In *Beyond Metaphor: The Theory of Tropes in Anthropology*, ed. J. Fernandez. Stanford: Stanford University Press.

Turner, Victor. 1967a. "Ritual Symbolism, Morality, and Social Structure among the Ndembu." In *The Forest of Symbols*. Ithaca: Cornell University Press.

———. 1967b. "*Mukanda*: Rite of Circumcision." In *The Forest of Symbols*. Ithaca: Cornell University Press.

———. 1974. *Dramas, Fields, and Metaphors*. Ithaca: Cornell University Press.

———. 1986. *The Anthropology of Performance*. New York: PAJ Publications.

Turner, Victor, and Edward Bruner, eds. 1986. *The Anthropology of Experience*. Urbana: University of Illinois Press.

Vico, Giambattista. 1946 [1744]. *The New Science of Giambattista Vico*. Trans. T. Bergin and M. Fisch. Ithaca: Cornell Univeristy Press.

Vološinov, V. N. 1973. *Marxism and the Philosophy of Language*. Trans. L. Matejka and I. R. Titunik. New York and London: Seminar.

Wacker, Grant. 2000. *Heaven Below: Early Pentecostals and American Culture*. Cambridge: Harvard University Press.

Wagner, Roy. 1981 [1975]. *The Invention of Culture*. Rev. ed. Chicago: University of Chicago Press.

Wittgenstein, Ludwig. 2001 [1953]. *Philosophical Investigations*. 2nd ed., trans. G. E. M. Anscombe. Oxford: Blackwell Publishers.

Wolf, Margery. 1990. "The Woman Who Didn't Become a Shaman." *American Ethnologist* 17, no. 3: 419–30.

2

WHEN SILENCE ISN'T GOLDEN: CHARISMATIC SPEECH AND THE LIMITS OF LITERALISM

Simon Coleman

The scene is a large hall—part of a warehouse-like building located in an industrial zone on the outskirts of Uppsala, Sweden. The time is 9 p.m. on a September evening, in the late 1980s.[1] Hundreds of people, many of them under thirty, have gathered for the midweek service run by the "Word of Life" Christian ministry (Livets Ord). Of those present, some belong to the group's congregation, which has been in existence for four years and is on its way to attracting a membership of over 2,000;[2] others are studying at its Bible school, which is itself gaining an international reputation in the "Prosperity"- or "Faith"-oriented wing of the charismatic revival.[3] Still others are visitors from rival congregations and a few are even from the press, the former attracted by talk of the fledging ministry being at the center of a national religious revival, the latter by allegations of brainwashing and naïve literalism that have been directed at the group virtually since the day of its inception.

Although the preacher, Svante Rumar, is unaccustomed to leading the service, he is well-known to most of the congregation, since he is Dean of the ministry's Bible school. The theme of his sermon has been songs of praise, and for an hour he has taken the congregation on a breathless sprint through the Bible, cramming in twenty different references to verses in the Old and New Testaments, ranging from the Psalms to the Book of Revelation. Rumar has also asked the congregation a pointed, if rhetorical, question: Have we ever noticed the difference between a stillness that is empty and one that is full of God? Rumar's response is that songs of praise are the best means of achieving the *right kind* of stillness, one where the confusions of the mind (*sinne*) are cleared away, opening up channels of communication to the Lord. He adds that the divine cannot be reached through human understanding (*förstånd*): only through the Spirit can one have fellowship with God.

Rumar's words take on extra significance at the end of the service, when something unusual occurs. Normally, a sermon concludes with altar calls for conversion and healing, during which time the hall is filled with a cacophony of prayer, tongues and music. On this occasion, however, after a period of healing, the noise of the piano dies down. Rumar stands by the lectern, Bible in hand, as if poised to leave. But he doesn't move, and instead stands perfectly still and stares out into the middle distance. Silence falls.

I suspect that I am not the only person to sense the drama of the occasion but also the tension and even embarrassment evident within a congregation that had previously seemed upbeat but relaxed. After a few minutes some people start to file out of the hall, and close to ten o'clock Rumar himself strides out of the service, without a word. After a few more minutes and many more exits there are just thirty to forty people still sitting in silence in their seats.

What had just happened? To this day, I am not quite sure. I also confess that I did not do follow-up interviews with my fellow congregants at the time. However, I would like to suggest a number of ways of interpreting Rumar's act of silence before I show how consideration of this incident brings me to some of the more general themes of this chapter, which concern the ambiguities of meaning relating to literalism in charismatic practices of speaking and reading.

It is initially quite easy to contextualize the service within wider frames of Word of Life patterns of worship. Rumar's verbal statements and illustrative actions were tightly bound together in a manner characteristic of the ministry and of other Prosperity Christians: he noted the power of stillness, and then he *became* stillness—just as at the beginning of the sermon he had stated that his theme would be songs of praise before he did, literally if briefly, break into song. The first part of the service was also familiar, with the singing of praise songs preceding the sermon, thus opening the way for the Word.

At another level Rumar daringly *challenged* the grammar of Word of Life worship, but he did this through a neat logic of opposites. A dauntingly fluent verbosity combined with an exuberant demeanor are strikingly characteristic of the habitus of being a member of the group. Indeed, these signs of commitment are sometimes taken by the Word of Life's many Swedish critics to be manifestations of a form of voluble Americanness imported into the body of the local believer. In such terms, Rumar can be seen to have countered the congregation's expectation of a superfluity of words by deploying an excess of silence and stillness.

So far, then, I have suggested a certain cultural logic for the event, but I have not taken into account an important dimension of what occurred on that September evening: the fact that Rumar's ploy did not appear to "work" in the context of Word of Life worship.[4] How, as an ethnographer, one defines what makes a ritual successful is a problematic issue (see Schieffelin 1995), and in prosperity-oriented charismatic contexts one is unlikely to hear people openly criticize a preacher. Yet, a lot of people did leave the service early—an action explicitly frowned upon in the group—and as far as I know Rumar never repeated the experiment. He had tried something new by presenting an initially puzzling and potentially absurd-seeming ritual *inaction*. In doing so, he had introduced an element of surprise that might have been valued by his fellow charismatics, on the grounds that his risk-taking displayed not only the self-confidence expected of a preacher but also a desire to avoid the routinization of ritual forms. But he had also lost a good part of his audience at the very point at which, according to his own criteria, a "correct" form of stillness should have been developing, and moreover one that would open up the channels of communication to God.

Of course, silence and stillness are hardly strangers to ritual. Bell and Collins (1998) have juxtaposed British Quakerism and Buddhism and argued for the positive, communicative function of silence, since it can imply much more than the mere absence of sound, and can signify messages ranging from political protest to a marked receptivity to the divine. Bauman (1974: 146) shows how the language ideology of early Quakerism stressed that speaking was seen as a faculty of the natural, outward person, and was therefore not perceived to be as valuable as the inward communion with God that could only be achieved through silence: the minister's rhetorical task was therefore to orient people towards introspection.[5]

So, under the right ritual circumstances the suppression of semantic content can imply a kind of meaningful meaninglessness. I am suggesting, however, that Rumar produced the *wrong kind* of "meaninglessness" in his service—one that landed on the unfortunate side of local distinctions between creativity and absurdity. Tomlinson and Engelke note in their introduction to this volume that meaning can be *absent* or *denied*—the two are not the same—and what interests me about the ethnographic scene I have described is that it is unclear whether the preacher remained in control of the dominant interpretation of the ritual act that he himself had initiated: Was the silence that characterized the final part of the service fully intended by him? Or did he expect it to be broken in some way, and if so by whom?

We need to remember that the charismatics I describe are not in principle opposed to the suppression of semantic content from worship. While they take the Bible to be the inspired Word of God, their convictions also prompt them to remain open to other gifts of the Spirit. At the Word of Life and in other parts of the Prosperity-oriented revival,[6] the use of tongues is a powerful and almost ubiquitous technique for the bypassing of conventional—"mind-led"— expressions of meaning, giving voice to divinely derived utterance without demonstrating resemblances to any known human language.[7] So why tongues, but not silence? The answer will be sought in arenas of charismatic life in Sweden that include language use and ideology but also take into account constructions of charismatic subjectivity, authority, and exchange. I shall also be led into still wider considerations, including discussions of not just charismatic, but also *anthropological*, representations of language and meaning.

Signifying nothing?

Meaning and ritual have long been uneasy bedfellows. Robertson-Smith's Victorian emphasis on the primacy of action over meaning was itself a precursor to numerous subsequent emphases on the social *function* of rites. A greater stress on meaning is evident in Turner's (1967: 1) definition of the symbol as "the smallest unit of ritual," though such symbols are presented as vehicles for polarized as well as interconnected cultural meanings. Leach's (1976) presentation of ritual as communicating messages through symbolic language was trenchantly argued, but prompted questions concerning the direction and unanimity of communication (Stringer 1999: 26–27): Who was the final arbiter or decoder of meaning—the anthropologist alone (cf. Lewis 1980)? Turner had raised similar issues in his analysis of symbols in Ndembu ritual, not only by wondering what "the hapless anthropologist" (1967: 35) is to do when faced with conflicting psychoanalytic interpretations, but also by pointedly asking (1967: 26): "Meaning for whom?" In his "performative" approach to ritual, Tambiah (1985) mediated between belief- and action-oriented positions by stressing the mutual constitution of cosmological constructions and rites. More recently, the interpretative wheel has turned back to an explicitly "anti-meaning" position. Humphrey and Laidlaw (1994: 2) argue that ritualization actually severs the link between the intentional meaning of the agent and the identity of the act he or she performs. In this respect, their argument has some parallels with Bloch's (1974) famous assertion that formalized ritual speech restricts propositional meaning (and, in Bloch's argument, consequently bolsters authority).

The wranglings of anthropological theory have had their counterparts in the convolutions of Christian theology. Protestant unease with ritual has classically focused on whether the demands of mediating forms are opposed to the expression of pure meaning, and therefore on the extent to which material, fleshly signs can reveal authentic experience without distortion. I do not wish to delve into these debates, but I do want briefly to highlight one manifestation of conservative Protestant language ideology that is rhetorically highly present at the Word of Life and focuses precisely on the issue of the mediation of meaning: namely, literalism.

Literalist understandings apparently focus on the semantic dimension of language rather than on its pragmatic, context-relating aspects (Crapanzano 2000): the meaning of a text is taken to be ultimately decidable, and traceable to original, authorial intention. While literalism has, for much of the past century, been associated particularly with conservative Protestantism—and thereby politicized positively as a badge of identity, or negatively as a catalyst for scorn—Crapanzano shows that its assumptions are more widespread than might initially be imagined, at least in American society. One could also note its roots in, and resonances with, more general aspects of modern linguistic ideology. Robbins (2001: 901) notes that Western linguistic theory, influenced by such ideology, takes for granted certain assumptions about the relation of intention to meaning, the nature of speaking subjects, and the relative importance of speakers over listeners in processes of semiosis (cf. Stubbs 1983: 45). He adds (2001: 905), intriguingly, that the relationship of Protestantism to modern linguistic ideology has not been widely examined, but that at the heart of such ideology in the West is a tight coupling of intention and meaning, grounded in the postulation of a sincere speaker who has an ability and an inclination to tell the truth (cf. Keane 1997). Further implicit in this ideology are not only the idea that words convey discrete and specific meanings (Stromberg 1993: 7), but also the Western tendency to locate agency or voice in biologically distinct individuals (Keane 1997: 7).[8] Some of the roots of such views on language have been explored in Trilling's lectures on "Sincerity and Authenticity," which assess the romanticist valuation of sincerity—where the "I" is not a persona but stands for the author/speaker (see 1972: 9). Trilling examines the earlier but somewhat parallel Calvinist emphasis on an internalized sincerity that gains authority through the "truth" of personal experience and intensity of conviction of enlightenment (see 1972: 23–24).

One of the most comprehensive ethnographic analyses of Protestant efforts to define the autonomous, "modern" subject has been provided by Keane's work (e.g., 2002) on the twentieth-century Dutch Calvinist missionization of Sumba, in eastern Indonesia. We see how individual agency, interiority, and freedom of the modern, Protestant subject are valorized, and how an important component of this vision of the self is the normative ideal of sincerity in speech: the latter can be seen as a way of characterizing a relationship between words and interior states, of making the inner state transparent. It is associated with that understanding of "religion" that centers on truthful propositions rather than on ritual and/or bodily disciplines (cf. Asad 1993), whilst seeking to locate the responsibility for words in the speaker as a distinct and self-possessed self.

And yet, Keane makes two further points that complicate this picture of linguistic autonomy. First, to the extent that words and things circulate among, and require acceptance by, persons, the very conditions for people's objectification, self-knowledge, and identity necessarily involve other people. Second, the exercise of sincerity is interactive: in being sincere, I am not only producing words that are transparent to my interior states but am producing them for "you"; I am making my inner self available for you in the form of external, publicly available expressions.

We are back to the connections (also raised by the Quaker case) between constructions of personhood and the ritual deployment of language. Prosperity-oriented charismatics, in common with other Protestant nonconformists, downplay what are seen as the dead forms of ritual but do, of course, fill services with words. Such words are not usually described as "sincere" but are deemed to contain "life" and "truth," and ultimately—despite their apparently spontaneous character—either to be sanctioned by, or contained within, holy script. A preacher who relates the words of the Bible to the lives of the congregation is valued. Yet the distinction between truthful proposition and bodily discipline begins to be broken down as we see how charismatic language ideology is translated into specific forms of action relating to words. So we need to ask: What are the practices of *reading, hearing,* and *speaking* that might help to reinforce charismatic faith in a certain view of literalism? What might be the connections between the intentional meanings of speakers and listeners and the identity of the ritualized speech being activated? (After all, the presence of an explicit ideology of literalism does not mean that we can assume a close connection between the intention of the original author of language and that of the current deployer of such language.)[9] And, finally: If Rumar's ploy—or play—with *non*-language did not work, are there other linguistic strategies that are more successful in manipulating the semantics of charismatic faith, producing varieties of "meaningful meaninglessness" that are acceptable to Swedish believers?

Language and Subjectivity

We are now ready to return to the large hall in the Word of Life ministry, and to an examination of local language ideology. Let us start with the words of Ulf Ekman, a former priest in the Swedish Church who founded the Word of Life after studying at Kenneth Hagin's Bible Training Center in Tulsa in the early 1980s. In a chapter entitled "Faith Speaks" in his booklet *Life and Death are on Your Tongue*,[10] Ekman states: "Understanding is limited—it's connected with your soul, your will, your emotions and your intellect, your mental faculties. But in your heart can be found your spirit and that's where you have unbounded resources and assets. That's where you have contact with God himself. It's in your heart that the Word is planted" (1988: 13). Then, a little later: "You must believe and receive the Word. You shouldn't just be, as it says in James's epistle, a hearer of the Word but also a doer of it. To be a doer of the Word, you have not just to hear the Word but also to speak it" (1988: 14).

Note how Ekman starts by mistrusting mere understanding—Rumar did this as well—and links it to the limitation that is said to be inherent within certain aspects of the person (the soul, the emotions, the intellect, and so on). Only one part of the person escapes boundedness, and that is the spirit, the aspect of the inner self that is in contact with God and constitutes a fertile growing ground for the Word. Ekman's implicit distinction between inner and outer selves and concern with mediations between the two is continued in the second passage, where *believing* the Word is juxtaposed with *receiving* it, as if the two were synonymous or at least closely linked. This move from cognition to action and therefore to a form of externalization of language is reinforced in the rest of the quotation, as Ekman shifts us from hearing to doing, and then from doing to speaking (cf. Harding 2000).

As with Quakers, we see how language ideology and concepts of the person are linked, but whereas the ideal Quaker is silent, the ideal charismatic is both hearing *and* speaking, both receiving *and* broadcasting sacred language. Behind this assertion is the theological assumption that charismatics can draw on the power of the Holy Spirit not only to understand sacred text and to receive divine revelation, but also to produce inspired language when preaching, giving testimony, and praying. While the spontaneous deployment of such language should be possible for all believers, preachers are regarded as having been given a particular calling to spread the Word in such a way that it resonates with large numbers of people. Such theology also has practical implications, since it implies that an evidential basis for inspiration—and therefore authority in this religious culture—is provided by the active deployment of such language. We begin to see how the use of words can not only indicate that a person is a believer, but also provide an index of one's ability to express the nature of divine will. Ekman's reasoning is explicitly based in the Bible—hence the reference to James's epistle—but in addition it converts holy writ into a language that is to be bodily appropriated by the believer. In Graham's terms (1987: 7), scripture and other forms of sanctified language are becoming vocal as well as visual facts (cf. Csordas 1997); an ideology of literalism is being articulated where the link between the believing person and the text is created *through* disciplined practices of reading, listening, and speaking. The considerable importance of this point is further demonstrated by the biblical verse that Ekman chooses as the frontispiece for the entire booklet—2 Cor. 4:13: "It is written: 'I believed; therefore I have spoken.'[2] With that same spirit of faith we also believe and therefore speak."

These passages from James's epistle and 2 Corinthians on how to deal with the Word therefore display complex metacommunicative functions (Stubbs 1983: 48). Ekman is not only quoting the Bible and thereby endorsing its sentiment that the believer should have a particular relationship to language; he is also putting the biblical passage into practice in the very act of bringing it to people's attention: admittedly, as author of the booklet, he is not a speaker as such, but he is a writer, a powerful agent in the mediation of language to others. As with Rumar's sermon on stillness, we see how the distance between describing an action and embodying it can be very small indeed. The ideal reader of Ekman's book becomes a link in a chain of language exchange, shifting roles from reader to speaker in further broadcasting a message that becomes multiply authored as it moves from recipient to recipient (bolstering the authority not only of speakers but, albeit sometimes implicitly, of Ekman himself). Indeed, other texts by Prosperity preachers urge the reader to speak rather than merely inwardly register what has been written (see, e.g., Savelle 1982), even when the reader is alone.

Such uses of language can be discerned in many other brands of revivalism, but we should also note some of the specific ways in which they are slotted into Prosperity discourse. In the latter, the healing and material well-being deemed to be the right of the believer (Coleman 2000) are combined with, and indeed dependent upon, a certain type of speaking. "Positive confession" is a statement, made "in faith" (i.e., by a born-again believer), that lays claim to God's provisions and promises. It is grounded in two much-quoted verses that constitute a central biblical trope within Swedish and American Prosperity discourses, Mark 11:23–24 (NIV): "I tell you the truth, if anyone says to this mountain, "Go, throw yourself into the sea," and does not doubt in his heart but believes that what he says will happen, it will be done for him. Therefore I tell you, whatever you ask for in prayer, believe that you have received it, and it will be yours."

Consider this biblical passage in the light of Ekman's earlier ruminations on James's epistle. Belief and reception are again juxtaposed, though in this case what is received results not only from *accepting* the Word but also from *applying* the Word to the world. Metaphor is explicitly denied here—the mountain *can* evidently be made to move—so that a performative dimension of the power of language is being demonstrated. And note again the metacommunicative aspect of the passage, through which linguistic reflexivity is converted into a verbal exchange that ultimately has material consequences.[11] Jesus is addressing an audience and exhorting them to have faith in God, in themselves, and in their externalized language: he urges his listeners to become *speakers* whose words are both indexes of a lack of doubt and vehicles for powerful spiritual agency.

So: a paradigmatic Prosperity view of language displays an ambiguous and at times hostile attitude towards conventional modes of understanding—and, related to this point, emphasizes the limitations associated with certain, non-externalizable aspects of the person. We see also the coupling of belief and expression of charismatic commitment with forms of language-based action, including hearing and speaking. Spoken language is linked to faith but also to performative action in the world, as well as to forms of exchange where listeners of words subsequently become speakers of those words.

These issues are not mere matters of theology. They are deeply implicated in the politics of local charismatic identities in Sweden. Overt membership in the once burgeoning numbers of Prosperity ministries in Sweden, and in particular of the high-profile Word of Life, has over the last twenty years entangled ordinary believers as well as high-profile preachers in macro- and micro-contests of representation in which language has been central. Believers have been surrounded by the words of their many critics—contained in newspaper articles, television shows, sermons, academic reports, and political debates—whom have condemned the group's supposed embrace of pure materialism, rejection of Swedish values of social democracy (such as tolerance and respect for the weak), and adherence to forms of literalism and pastoral authority that have been taken to constitute practices of brainwashing (Coleman 1989).[12] Critics have called, indeed, for the *silencing* of the group, invoking medical and psychiatric as well as theological and political justifications for such action (see Wikström 1988). The speaking charismatic subject has been central to negative depictions of Word of Life members. In interviews I conducted with local, nonaffiliated residents (Coleman 2000: 214–15), I found a frequent rearticulation of an essentializing image of Swedishness—embodied precisely in an acceptance of one's limitations and of the need not to push oneself verbally, socially, or materially ahead of others—in the face of a religious demeanor that seems to encourage the exact opposite.

I also talked to local Pentecostalists, whose church had lost tens of members to the new group. Some of these interviewees interestingly referred to Prosperity behaviors as theatrical, implying a lack of sincerity amongst members of the new group in putting on a positive "show" for the self and others. In terms of relatively more mainstream language ideologies in Sweden, sincerity therefore refers both to an ability to accept limitation and failure, and to a bodily as well as a verbal language in which there appears to be less of a distinction between external and internal aspects of personhood, between expression and thought (cf. Keane 2002).

This last point takes me closer to the issue of the embodiment of local Prosperity identity. We see how ideas about language provide the fundamental ideological underpinnings of a charismatic religious habitus that has become deeply controversial in Sweden. While these ideas are frequently expressed in publications by prominent preachers from Sweden and elsewhere, particularly the US, they are also cultivated in forms of domestic worship that involve deep immersion in linguistic forms. Thus Sune, a 35-year-old man,[13] has described how his desire to reach a higher level of commitment led him to devise a "spiritual gymnastics program," involving him getting up at five in the morning to "stand on the word" (i.e., read the Bible) for an hour, to speak in tongues for the next hour, and then do positive confessions for a further hour, with songs of praise sometimes being mixed into the spiritual cocktail. Sune's experience lies towards one extreme of a continuum of language use amongst believers who spend much of their time away from the ministry, and who may not even officially be members of it, but who can and frequently do surround themselves with its presence by buying its books, videos, and audiocassettes, and accessing its website. The majority of Sune's exercises, though private, are spoken, and he also notes that as a witness to God he has been encouraged to say to himself: "I am a Spirit." Recall that Ekman said that in the heart one can find one's spirit, so that the fundamental identity of the person is to be located in that which constitutes an unbounded growing ground for the Word. Such ground is fertilized not just by having the thought that one is a spirit, however: the words must be *sounded*, so that a description of one's identity is intended performatively to create that identity within the self. Remember also that Keane (see above and 2002) noted that the conditions for self-objectification necessarily involve other people, while the "sincere" person makes the inner self available to others in the form of external, publicly available expressions. Here, we see a variation on this theme: Sune is using a phrase that is broadly biblical in tone but whose origins come more precisely from his teachers at the ministry, and he is repeating it to himself. In Faith terms, words are coming alive through utterance but the "other" to which they are directed is actually part of the self, or more specifically the heart/spirit separated from the fleshly part of the person. What is being said at the level of ideal linguistic practice is tautologous: the spirit is being told that it is spirit, and in the process is becoming reinforced in this identity.

In his analysis of language and charisma, Csordas (1997: 240) draws attention to the "paradoxical situation in which the speaker is at the moment of speaking enmeshed in a voice long preceding itself, in which the speaker stands in the path of the speech that proceeds from him." Part of Csordas's aim is to show how the decentering of intentionality can illustrate the semi-autonomy of language from its speakers (1997: 242–43), as part of the intersubjective constitution of meaning. In the case of Sune, we see how language is deployed not only to empower, but also to objectify the self, with a phrase such as "I am a Spirit" deriving ultimately from God but also more proximately from respected preachers. The irony of the phrase (from a secular viewpoint) is that it dislocates or at least complicates the notion of exactly who the "I" is.

Sune, in common with many other supporters of the ministry, carries out a shorter version of his linguistic exercises before services—thus in effect privately recapitulating his powers as a speaker as well as a listener—and we need to remember that personal linguistic devotions bear a close but also complex relationship to collective speech events. There is admittedly a danger of over-emphasizing the importance of the sermon as a key generator of spoken discourse. As Keane (1997: 5) has noted, many anthropologists are increasingly uneasy with the assumption that formalized ritual holds the key by which an entire culture can be unlocked: certain ritualized activities can be embedded within larger practical arenas of social action, and at the Word of Life we have already seen a little of how contexts of language-use constantly bleed into each other. Yet, it is also important to appreciate Spitulnik's point (2001: 96) that particular kinds of social situations and social institutions can have greater weight than others in establishing the significance of certain sociolinguistic forms. At the Word of Life, sermons are marked not only by their large audiences but also by the fact that they become objects of material diffusion, stored and then sold in numerous mediated forms such as videos, audiocassettes, and magazine articles. Access to the pulpit is also largely restricted to pastors and to the numerous preachers, particularly those from the US, who pass through the group, often to talk at its regular conferences and workshops. Thus while sermons are produced by the few, they are consumed by the many, and gain a social life that extends beyond that of the original event of production.

We need also to take into account the disciplines of *hearing* as well as of speaking that are present at the group. In describing practices of listening to cassette-sermon auditions in Egypt, Hirschkind (2001: 624) refers to how a proper audition requires a particular affective-volitional responsiveness from the listener as a condition for "understanding" sermonic speech. Thus in Egypt to "hear with the heart" is not strictly something cognitive but involves the body in its entirety, as a complex synthesis of disciplined moral reflexes. Indeed (2001: 628), there is a moral physiology acquired through listening exercises that is grounded in Islamic textual traditions, and listening (2001: 635) can itself become a performance, involving a subvocal accompaniment to even an audiocassette. While Hirschkind found (2001: 638) that people did not always agree with each other as to the truth status of some of the accounts commonly found in sermons, all would mimetically represent the narratives in more or less the same way. He notes: "To listen to an Islamic cassette-sermon with the heart means to bring to bear on it those sensory capacities honed within disciplinary contexts that allow one to 'hear' (soulfully, emotionally, physically) what would escape listeners who applied only their 'ears' or *al-'aql* (minds)" (2001: 639).

Egypt and Uppsala present very different religious and cultural contexts, but in both we see embodied metaphors that separate true listeners from others who can only apprehend words through human modes of understanding; and in both cases listening becomes a focused and self-conscious technology of the self. Swedish listeners perceive themselves as "receiving" language by applying so-called "spiritual ears" to what is said, and "spiritual eyes" to the heavily scored and noted Bibles that virtually everybody brings to services. Incidentally, such spiritual perception is seen as non-emotional (unlike the Egyptian case) since emotions disrupt the purity of linguistic reception. In Prosperity terms, what is done by the preacher in such contexts is emphatically *not* to "interpret" the Bible: interpretation is opposed to disciplined speaking and hearing in the sense that it implies ambiguity of meaning in sacred text or inspired preaching—a result of the mind acting as distorting mediator between sacred language and receptive audience.

Yet, from an analytical perspective, such an ideology of embodied literalism provides an incomplete picture of how language and associated meanings are deployed by Swedish charismatics. I want therefore to explore examples of language use that rely upon an *ideology* of literalism but do not necessarily *constitute* literalism as it is conventionally understood—indeed, they implicitly subvert or supersede its implications even as they form fundamental elements of Word of Life disciplines of speaking. Their claim to uphold principles of clarity of meaning, authorship, and agency co-exists not so much with meaninglessness per se as with forms of semantic slippage and ambiguous ownership of words that are actually vital for their continued applicability in charismatic contexts.

Variations on a Theme of Speaking

"Double Talk": Creating Excesses of Meaning

Much charismatic faith in the fixities of language depends upon the illusion of a tight ideological fit between speakers and hearers. However, a necessary feature of language deployment involves addressing others who have not (yet) come under conviction, most obviously through witnessing and therefore deploying conversion narratives (cf. Coleman 2000; Harding 2000; Gershon, this volume). Here I want to focus on a different kind of "public" talk, however, one that is connected to the macropolitics of charismatic speech in Sweden. Ironically, the very outcry against the Word of Life has given Ekman the national platform that he has craved, allowing him to extend his voice beyond the arenas of revivalist discourse and to bring a strongly argued religiopolitical critique of Swedish secularism into the public sphere (cf. Coleman 1991). If the language of Ekman's critics is itself usually secular, we need to realize that Ekman's responses, often relayed through the same media outlets, have a double edge when viewed from the perspective of his supporters. They incorporate a rhetoric of civility appropriate to their broadly based audience but also contain the performative power of a "great man of God." In other words, Ekman is regarded as not merely responding to his critics, but also as "speaking language over them" in a more ritualized sense, even if he is not engaging in a public display of positive confession. Ekman has even incorporated comments on such discursive engagements in sermons given to the congregation, thus reappropriating the significance of his "public language" for charismatic purposes. In sermons I attended during the late 1980s and the 1990s he represented his forays into journalism as involving entry into a secular realm, but certainly not an adoption of the values of that realm. On another occasion in 1987, I listened to Ekman address a large group of uncommitted university students in calm and witty terms. I then asked a believer (who was debating whether to join the Word of Life) how he thought the meeting had gone. To my surprise, he uttered a single word in reply to my question: "War!" In retrospect, I realized that what I had taken to be a civilized exchange of views could also be seen—through Faith eyes—as a battle at an implicit, spiritual level.

A striking, if more trivial, example of the conjoining of esoteric and exoteric dimensions of Prosperity language in the public sphere has been provided by a singer called Carola, very well-known in Sweden and a sometime supporter of the Word of Life. In 1991, Carola won the Eurovision Song Contest, a deeply kitschy but internationally known pop competition, famous for promoting the writing of essentially meaningless "Euro-lyrics" designed to be understood by people from different language communities. But as Carola sang, among other things, of how her "desire awakes when you smile and stretch out your hand" an ostensibly conventional love song could be seen from a Prosperity perspective as a song of praise to God, a potential testimony to the development of a personal relationship with the divine.

At more local levels, in the face of often personally directed hostility, "Word of Lifers" have often chosen not to openly admit adherence to the ministry, and have in work or sometimes even witnessing contexts admitted only to belonging to a "Christian congregation." However, such apparent obfuscation has not prevented subtler attempts to bring sacralized language to life beyond services and Bible school sessions. Tongues may be spoken under one's breath while walking around town, providing a kind of linguistic nimbus in the face of the profane world. Other strategies come closer to the double-edged language of Ekman's civil self or Carola's singing. For instance, a telephone-sales firm was founded by a group of Word of Lifers in the 1980s, not only satisfying the entrepreneurial (middle-class) aspirations commonly expressed in Word of Life discourse but also illustrating the desire to use words to persuade others of the quality of one's "product." Members of this firm talked of how they spoke in tongues in between phone calls to clients, lending apparently secular discourse an added significance known only to the caller.

We see here not only a kind of double agency associated with language projected into the secular sphere, but also the deployment of words that operate at two levels of meaning: "natural" levels—appealing to the mind—coexist with "supernatural" levels—appealing to the activated spirits of a smaller community of interpretation. Such excesses of meaning dwell less in ambiguity per se than in the attempt to create distinct *levels* of significance, appealing to rather different models of personhood.[14] I refer to them as "excess" because, in a sense, they contradict an approach to language whereby unambiguous intention can be related directly to clear meaning. In the instances I have cited, the charismatic speaker is not lacking sincerity so much as assuming that language can bear dual significances and functions. Only spiritual "eyes" and "ears" have the capacity fully to appreciate the fact that the words of a newspaper article or song may be inspired, and may therefore have the potential to create an impact beyond their apparently secular purposes.

"Talk about Talk": The Literal and the Metaliteral

Public, civil speech as I have termed it is not necessarily rooted in the Bible, although it may occasionally refer to the importance of Scripture. Biblical literalism is more explicitly expressed in contexts largely confined to fellow-believers. However, even here referential language can be deflected for charismatic purposes. I look in this section at how literalism is translated into a form of linguistic *practice*, more of a mode of being in and acting on the world than a cognitive focus on the specificities of chapter and verse.

Let me start by noting an irony originally pointed out by Kathleen Boone (1989: 81): she claims that extensive commentary is clearly of great importance in fundamentalist movements that are, nonetheless, deeply wedded to the authority of the text. Such is also the case in Prosperity contexts.[15] Sermons are lengthy perorations ostensibly focused on the Bible, which is brandished by the preacher or placed, ostentatiously open, on the pulpit. The preacher draws on glosses of Bible verses, comparisons of verses, personal anecdotes, and so on, employing a populist and sometimes humorous tone. As I have already implied in looking at Ekman's use of biblical text, Prosperity preachers are very fond of quoting verses that are themselves commentaries on language use, and that in effect provide templates for appropriation not merely as *words* but as actions *in relation to* words. Thus, what I am calling metaliteralism involves preachers deploying scripture to focus reflexively on the iconic value of "the literal" (cf. Stubbs 1983: 47) biblical passages, and then to convert such iconic reading into disciplines of speaking.

I shall give just one extended example of this genre. In the following passage, taken from a sermon delivered in the mid 1990s, the speaker is Jim Kaseman, a frequent visitor to the Word of Life from the US, who on this occasion has been talking to the congregation at various points over a number of days:[16]

> So we talked about Words yesterday and how important it is to watch the Words that we say with our mouth. We talked about spiritual laws but in my life I've found that Mark Four has been a very important chapter to help me understand faith, the importance of God's Word. We're to learn to walk by faith believing that He meant what He said and acting like it. Faith is just simply doing what God's Word says to do!

There then follows a part-quotation, part-summary of verses in Mark Four about the Word being sown, protecting such verbal seed from the devil, and—in classic Prosperity terms—about how putting one kernel of wheat in the ground can produce a hundredfold return:

And I believe that we haven't even begun to see what God's Word can do in our heart. We haven't really seen the fruit yet. But if we could put God's Word into our heart the seed and let it grow unhindered instead of always, you know, stompin' on it and pulling it up every once in a while! But if we'd really take care of that seed then you could begin to see what Jesus meant when he said "All-things-are-possible to him that believeth!" . . . . There is no limit to what you and I can do in Christ if we'll only believe. That precious word is seed and there's no limit to what that word can do in us. We're the only ones that limit that word.

This is talk about talk (cf. Robbins 2001: 904), but it is also talk that denies its sometimes metaphorical status by deploying embodied imagery of *walking* by Faith. Faith consists in "simple" action—*doing* God's Word, watching what one *says* with one's mouth—rather than a focus on interpreting or problematizing the meaning of text. And the second passage invokes an image of limitation that implies the presence of the split charismatic subject: there is no limit in what the Word can do in "us" in our capacities as containers of spiritually open hearts; the active Word is however constrained when "we" as embodiments of mere human agency attempt to get in the way.

It may not seem very clear exactly what Kaseman means when he talks about "letting the Word grow," but his drawing on biblical imagery and focus on practice have the advantage of appearing to avoid cultural specificities and potential differences between American and Swedish understandings of charismatic culture. Such metaliteralism therefore reduces some of the limitations of referentiality (cf. Spitulnik 2001). Furthermore, not only can the trope of Word as seed be invoked anew in multiple contexts, it also indicates the need for a constant self-surveillance in language-use. Our deployment of the Word becomes a reflection of one of two kinds of interiorities: either the limited one of the human self or the sublime one of the self in contact with divinity.[17]

"Transportable Talk" and Circulating Subjectivities

We have seen, then, how charismatic language can contain double meanings in contexts where the "interpretative community" cannot be relied upon, and how it is translated into generic forms of action that can be deployed in multiple situations. In both cases, we see how the semantic function of language is placed in creative tension with the contexts and pragmatics of language use. The final dimension of charismatic speech that I am highlighting here presents a further attempt to transcend context through language by looking at something that has been implicit in much of what I have said so far: language as a means—almost a currency—of verbal exchange, and what such exchanges can tell us about ambiguities of charismatic authorship, personhood, and authority.

Imagining a further dialog between Keane and Spitulnik is again helpful at this point. Keane notes (2002) that we need look no farther than anxieties about plagiarism, quotation, cliché and originality, truth-telling, keeping one's word, mimicry, and finding one's own voice, to find hints of how thoroughly language and in particular heteroglossia (Bakhtin 1981) can trouble the boundaries of the subject. Yet, we also know that many words and phrases are chronically transportable in and across social situations. For instance, Spitulnik focuses on the social circulation of radio discourse in Zambian popular culture, and therefore on "the actual processes of intertextuality, for example, questions about the transportability of speech forms from one context to another and the conditions that enable their decontextualization and recontextualization" (2001: 95). In Spitulnik's analysis, radio becomes a source of phrases and tropes that circulate widely, and that can often be seen as "public words"—standard phrases, slogans, and idiomatic expressions that are remembered, repeated, and quoted. Such words and phrases are likely to retain a degree of semantic open-endedness that allows for ease of recontextualization, but may also function metonymically to index the entire frame or meaning of the earlier speech situation—just as, for instance, the phrase "Make my day" invokes certain associations in Anglo-American contexts.

We need to bring together issues of the transportability of language and the boundaries of the subject when we reconsider Word of Life discursive practices. Firstly, it is clear that what many believers take from sermons, books, and other media are phrases rather than complex narratives. I frequently found that when I asked people after a service to summarize the sermon for me, they would reduce an hour-long talk to a series of familiar verbal tropes. The fact that little new seemed to have been said was not a problem, since what was important was the apparently unmediated invocation of biblical messages, and their translation into easily assimilable form—such as "the power we have in the Word," "the justification we have in Christ," and so on. More generally, the everyday as well as the ritual language of Word of Lifers is peppered with common phrases that are akin to Spitulnik's "public talk," though here the public being invoked is not that of the Swedish public sphere but that of the speech community of fellow charismatics. Thus "God has a plan for my life," "faith conquers all circumstances," "I am a spirit" are all phrases that can be invoked and even repeated, mantra-like, in numerous circumstances: they apparently contain broad reference to the Bible but—in common with metaliteral discourse—are largely unattributable to any single context, and often have the advantage in this self-consciously transnational speech-community of presenting formulas that can seemingly be translated directly from one language into another.

But some forms of language do maintain a more complex relationship with a certain form of context—not necessarily of places/situations so much as of *persons*. Ekman is a central figure here. After some months of doing fieldwork at the Word of Life I noticed two aspects of the local culture of glossolalia that surprised me: first, that tongues, while ubiquitous, were very rarely interpreted into Swedish; second, that the tongues of ordinary believers sometimes echoed that of Ekman to a striking degree, picking up and repeating phrases of his own glossolalia.[18] Thus semantically reduced tongues was not translated, but it was transported from one person to another in a chain of charismatic linkages. Furthermore, a number of believers have spoken of how they have heard Ekman's voice in their head, even when it has been unbidden and in certain cases—of people who have left the group—unwanted. These reports indicate the influence of a powerful speaker, but they also throw into question the authorship of the inspired words that are revoiced inside the person: do such phrases come from God or the preacher? While ultimately deriving from a divine and possibly a textual source, such words are therefore twice-embodied: in both the voice of the preacher and the spirit of the believer, with one penetrating the other. It would be incorrect to assert here that believers simply equate charismatic speech with charismatic authority, or that the adoption by ordinary believers of language spoken by preachers is always done consciously. The reputation of a preacher as a figure of esteem and influence can be built up in many ways: through a biography of spiritual difficulties triumphantly overcome, a reputation for healing, a lifetime of missionizing around the globe, and so on. However, to the extent that a preacher can provide a successful vehicle for language to be passed on in "usable" form to others, he or she can claim particular inspiration in breaking down the potential boundedness of the spirit that is so anathema to Faith adherents. Charismatic renown becomes a product not of the extraordinary powers of the individual, but of social and linguistic processes that illustrate the importance of speech in this religious culture.[19] Occasionally, believers refer to themselves or are labeled by others as having adopted the spiritual character of a great preacher, becoming a "mini-Ekman" and so on. Such labels are of course at least partly ironic, but they also express the power of mimesis in the Swedish ministry.

Practices of hearing and speaking may even encourage ambiguities over the ownership of spirit-filled words. Here, for instance, are some of the opening lines of a sermon preached in 1990 by a now-deceased but formerly popular visitor to the Word of Life from the US, Lester Sumrall:

> We command the blessing of God the Father to be upon you. We command the blessing of God the Son to be upon you. We command the blessing of the Holy Ghost to be upon you. We command you to be blessed. And blessed. And blessed.

Sumrall appears to be commanding God to act on behalf of humans. But he then immediately *enacts* his theme of command, turning the direction of his imperative mood away from God towards his audience:

> Say "I am blessed!" [The crowd responds with "I am blessed" either in English or translated into Swedish.] Say "I am blessed!" [Crowd responds.] Say it again! I am blessed! Hallelujah! Praise God! Tell your neighbor. Say "I am blessed!"

At the very beginning of his sermon, Sumrall is converting his audience temporarily from being listeners to speakers. Exact verbal mimesis of a preacher's words becomes a form of apparent self-empowerment. What is said is not "I shall be blessed" or "I hope to be blessed" but "I am blessed": in narrative terms the act has been completed at the very moment that it has been uttered. Furthermore, the words refer to the self but are spoken to another in a form of self-oriented verbal exchange, catalyzed by the voice of the preacher. While each member of the audience utters the phrase to one partner in faith, it is Sumrall who has used his place on the podium to set off a cacophony of blessings.

Such deployment of language has some parallels with Engelke's description (2004; see also this volume) of Zimbabwean Apostles who prefer to experience faith not in the Bible but via inspired prophets. It also brings us back to Trilling, and his discussion (1972: 61) of Rousseau's worries about how the modern self can understand its own authentic being when subjected to the constant influence, the literal in-flowing, of society—the mental processes of others "which, in the degree that they stimulate or enlarge his consciousness, make it less his own." According to Rousseau (see Trilling 1972: 68), the orator is not susceptible to the corrupting influence of impersonation since, unlike the actor, s/he speaks only in his/her own name. In this regard it is striking that local Pentecostalists also used a theatrical metaphor in criticizing the showy nature of Word of Life worship, but of course for such Christians even the Faith orator is acting out a part, and potentially speaking the words of others.

Whatever the "original" origins of the words that they speak, Ekman and Sumrall appear to encourage the replication of their own discourse in the words of others. As Urban (1996a: 21) points out, any study of such iteration should involve an examination not only of original and copied discourse, but also of the social relationships obtaining between originator and copier. In addition, replication can be compared with response, with the latter providing an alternative and more dialogical form of relationship between discourse instances (1996a: 22). Urban ventures a generalization: "I propose that the tendency to respond rather than replicate correlates with the degree to which the original discourse is viewed as a personal expression of the originator. Replication is more likely to occur where the original represents itself as detached from the originator, for example, as traditional knowledge or as a group rather than an original product" (1996a: 37–38). In the case of Sumrall's call to blessing, the fact that audience members are immediately enjoined to pass the message on to their neighbors implies strongly that the words are designed as currency in forms of verbal exchange. The fact that such exchange takes place so effortlessly is itself an implicitly significant point, since Sumrall is not only a foreign speaker, but is likely to attract an audience from throughout Sweden and beyond. Thus the exchange that he precipitates is an indication in itself of the facility of inspired language to transcend social distance: the "I" of Sumrall's phrase moves from preacher to listener-cum-speaker within an instant.[20]

The private (and, as far as I know, largely unconscious) adoption of Ekman's tongues is perhaps more intriguing. The very lack of semantic content of such phrases involves their appropriation and entextualization away from the context of the service. It is also highly unlikely that any believer who was not very familiar with Ekman's patterns of glossolalia would be in a position to adopt his phrases. Thus the verbal currency deployed here is rather more particular to Ekman as inspired preacher than that deployed by Sumrall, even as it is ultimately attributable to the power and eloquence of the Holy Spirit. In any case, as Urban also argues elsewhere (1996b: 25; cf. the discussion of Spitulnik above), we see how holding constant the physical form of verbal expression can not only expand the social circulation of discourse, but also indicate the relationship it may express between intelligibility and sensibility/palpability. In the ethnographic case Urban describes, that of an Amerindian community in Brazil, it appears that a key to ceremonies is their positive valuation of "experience without conscious scrutiny, of meaning without interpretation through discourse" (1996b: 176ff.). Thus discourse is greater than referential meaning per se, achieving status as an iconic object of sensory experience.

With this last point, we return to the wider debates, mentioned toward the beginning of this chapter, about ritual and the extent to which apparently static forms prevent the expression of pure meaning. Tambiah's attempt to mediate between belief- and action-oriented positions also contains reflections (1985: 132) on the extent to which the formalized qualities of ritual psychically distance the participants from what is being done, and thus endanger the usefulness of intentionality theories of meaning. The point is that rituals as conventionalized behavior are not designed to express the intentions, emotions, and states of minds of individuals in a direct way. According to Tambiah, this characteristic of conventionality poses a problem during periods of religious revivalism, when there is a deliberate attempt to mold new rituals "bursting with meaning" (1985: 165). Such points clearly resonate with the situation of a ministry such as the Word of Life, in which iconic phrases, uttered within or outside services themselves, must not be allowed to become arthritic with use. I shall return to this point in the next section, when I come back to examining Rumar's sermon.

Back to Silence

There is a film by another famous product of Uppsala—Ingmar Bergman—that is called *The Silence* (*Tystnaden*). Produced in 1963, the film sets conflicts between the demands of the spiritual and the physical in a context of spiritual desolation combined with the impossibility of communication. Similar themes are evident in another Bergman film—*Cries and Whispers*—which has been analyzed by Stromberg (1986) in his ethnography of a Swedish church. I mention both of these films not merely because their titles deal with language (or the lack of it), but also because they can be seen as wrestling with issues of sociality in a post-Christian Sweden. In a distant sense, they also refer to the self-stereotype of the country that I mentioned earlier in this piece, as reported to me in interviews: qualities of inward-orientation and acceptance of personal limitations are seen as characteristic of an essentialized national mentality.

It is against such images of silence, stasis and failed communication that Prosperity Christianity in Sweden has railed for the past twenty years. And while it would be too big an interpretative jump to claim that Rumar's act of self-imposed silence on that September evening plugged directly into anxieties over personal mutedness, one can say that he flew in the face of the self-consciously voluble habitus that has been cultivated by the group. In Word of Life terms, the stillness produced by songs of praise is supposed to create the ideal and active listener, who is prepared to use spiritual ears to receive communication from God; Furthermore, the part of the service that normally follows praise songs is the sermon itself, so that such divine communication becomes embodied in the words of the preacher. Yet, Rumar appeared not to understand the implicit grammar of his own service when he moved from speaking to a form of stillness and silence whose ritual resolution could not be found, and where the exchange of language between persons appeared to be blocked. Should any member of the audience speak in tongues or witness in the silence created by Rumar? If so, they might be seen as displacing the preacher's voice with their own. Should they remain silent? If so, they would confirm a position as passive hearers, unable to convert language into speech. Thus the only appropriate response for many of those present was simply to leave the room.

If we ask why Rumar committed such a risky act, I think we can be certain that it was not out of naïveté. Although I cannot prove the point one way or another, I prefer to see his silence as an act of radical purification, even self-inflicted iconoclasm. If, as pointed out by Tambiah and others, convention can sometimes be the enemy of intention, then Rumar can be seen as posing a further uncomfortable question of his audience: Were they themselves becoming too predictable in worship? Were words losing their power to act as vehicles of mutual inspiration? Part of his audience's discomfort may even have come from the realization that spontaneity was no longer permitted in a group that prided itself on bearing the new wave of revivalism in Sweden.[21] It may be, therefore, that Rumar was reminding his audience of the value of words precisely by removing them from a part of the service where they were expected to be present in abundance. Impurity in this charismatic culture is contained in the overtly routine, since it does not reach into the needs and the excitements of the moment, and Rumar may have felt that his listeners—the consumers of his words—were taking his verbal offerings too much for granted. By creating silence rather than speech, Rumar's iconoclasm can be seen as directed more toward the potentially lazy disposition of his listeners than toward the charged language normally expected from him.

A Final Silence

I conclude with another brief image of silence, and one closer to home. As an ethnographer of the Word of Life I have frequently been surprised at the extent to which fellow anthropologists have engaged in their own "muting" practices in relation to a cultural phenomenon that Harding (2000) has ironically called "the repugnant other." Within a day of arriving in Uppsala I found one colleague asking me why I wanted to study those "nuts," and since then I have often encountered a certain amount of incredulity as to why I should wish to spend so much time thinking about such an objectionable area of study. Anthropologists rarely have the power to contribute to political policies that silence others—and one can assume that most of us do not crave such powers—but we can mute others through our representational practices. There are many reasons for anthropological dislike of Prosperity groups (cf. Coleman 2002), but the one I want to mention here is the stereotype many scholars still maintain of the conservative Christian as "simply" literalist. I have tried to show, however, that literalism has its own ambiguities and subtleties—indeed, its own subcultures of interpretation—and there is very little that is simple about it. In using a stereotype of the Christian other as unthinkingly chained to referential views of sacred text we may be in danger ourselves of taking an ideology of literalism rather too literally.

Notes

1. The service took place in 1986. Fieldwork has been carried out on various occasions from 1986 to the present.
2. The Word of Life "Foundation" was started in March 1983, and the congregation was initiated in the same year (Ulf Ekman had been ordained as a priest in the Swedish Church in 1979). The current congregation has around 2,200 members, but the ministry also runs a university, Bible school, secondary and primary schools, a media business, a missionary organization, and numerous offices around the world. It is the premier Prosperity ministry in Scandinavia, while its Bible school has taken students from 80 countries and has some 8,000 alumni. Ekman is a global charismatic figure, formerly resident in Jerusalem. The lives of ordinary believers in Uppsala are still often marked by hostility from family, workmates, or even members of other congregations. Fellow Christians have not unsurprisingly accused the new group of poaching their members, and it is indeed true that, for instance, the local Pentecostalists as well as the Lutheran Church have either lost members or have noticed that some of their members appear to spend much time in the ministry.
3. The nomenclature to describe Prosperity/Faith/Health and Wealth Christianity is much disputed. For an overview of the movement see Coleman (2000). Prosperity Christians belong to a charismatic/neo-Pentecostal trend within contemporary conservative Protestantism that emphasizes both the performative power of words ("positive-confessions") uttered by believers and the right of the Christian to attain physical and material well-being. Followers are found particularly in urban areas in the US, Europe, Africa, Latin America, and some parts of Asia, such as South Korea and Singapore.
4. Compare Tomlinson's description in this volume of a Fijian preacher who does not preach, and Bornstein's American speaker who fails to convey her vision of success to her Zimbabwean audience.
5. See Keane (2002).
6. For discussions of the global spread of the revival, see the special issue on "The Faith Movement" in *Culture and Religion* 3, no. 1(2002).
7. Some parallels with Engelke's chapter (this volume) are evident. We both focus on exchanges between preachers and congregations, and on the (not always corresponding) expectations of both parties. Nonetheless, Word of Life Christians are far more explicitly text-oriented than the Masowe. Whereas personal Bibles are not encouraged by Masowe preachers, they are virtually mandatory for participants in the Swedish services. Both Masowe and Word of Life Christians see knowledge as key to salvation, and in both cases the knowledge obtained is closely associated with the idea of direct, unmediated communication with God. However, the "revelation-knowledge" sought by Swedish Christians is *not* seen as in conflict

with biblical knowledge: the former can only ever complement and reinforce the latter. In another sense Faith ideology does permit the bypassing of referential meanings associated with biblical text. It is sometimes said that sacred words—possibly uttered by a preacher, or read from the Bible—can enter into one's spirit and have beneficial effects even when one does not understand such words with one's conscious mind. A similar effect can be derived from tongues. In such cases conventional meaning is mistrusted on the grounds that it is a form of mediation, a distortion of the performative power of language that should not be compromised by the confusions of fleshly understanding (as opposed to the supernatural capacities of the spirit-part of the self).

8. Cf. Scollon and Scollon's description: "That broad discourse system which we refer to as the Utilitarian Discourse System which has spread as both carrier and producer of the contemporary globalizing and commodity discourse emphasizes certain characteristics such as clarity, brevity, and sincerity in language as if these were simply the natural state of communication" (2001: 59).

9. Irvine (1996: 132) discusses Goffman's (1975) distinctions among several possible realizations of a "speaker," e.g., as Principal, as Animator, and as Figure. She notes that the Principal is the party held committed to the position attested to by the content of an utterance, while the Animator is the party who physically transmits it. The Figure is the character, persona, or entity projected into the audience's imagination by means of the performer's actions.

10. My translation of *Liv och Död är på din Tunga*, Uppsala: Livets Ord.

11. This essay says little about how verbal and material exchanges interrelate, but see Coleman (2000; 2004).

12. Fellow Christians have accused the new group of poaching their members. In common with Gershon (this volume), my essay therefore touches on believers who are not converting from a state of nonbelief, but from a different form of Christianity.

13. Sune's case is discussed in Sjöberg (1988: 44).

14. If in psychoanalysis the conscious acts as a mask for the unconscious, in charismatic ideology the "natural" can obscure "the supernatural" (cf. Trilling 1972: 140–41).

15. Though I am not suggesting here a simple conflation of fundamentalism and charismatic Christianity.

16. I have not addressed issues of translation into and from Swedish. Such questions could focus on the extent to which the performative power of a preacher's language is retained in translation, the extent to which translation apparently indicates the ease with which meaning can be transferred between speakers, and the use of a basic charismatic argot that is common across at least some languages.

17. In a sense, the charismatic sublime is expressed in forms of body language, e.g., the preacher's open-armed stance, often holding the Bible, implying an unmediated "reception" of biblical language; or the more generalized action of "reaching out" into unknown realms with the arms, often accompanied by tongues.

18. With the exception of Ekman's prophetic service each New Year's Eve, when he translates his own tongues for the congregation.

19. Compare the discussions of charisma by Engelke and Faubion, this volume.

20. See Irvine's (1996: 135–36) discussion of how the Bakhtinian notion of multivocality focuses on the forms of discourse that cannot be attributed simply to the act of an individual speaker or author: "The 'double-voiced utterance' is the utterance whose form and significance presuppose a second voice—another party—whose utterances are invoked by the one at hand because they are partly imitated, quoted, or argued against."

21. Rumar's act of ritual risk-taking recalls Faubion's description (this volume) of the effects of "paranomic" actions, in other words "the relativization in practice of the very rules from which they distance themselves." As a religious "virtuoso," Rumar might be expected to challenge rules, but of course in the case I describe he is challenging the implicit model of worship adopted by a congregation that thinks of itself as inherently spontaneous and rule-challenging. Thus, in contesting that ritual model Rumar is simultaneously showing that it exists; he is moving the implicit to the explicit, and ironically illustrating the presence of a ritual model or template in the very process of challenging its existence.

References

Asad, Talal. 1993. *Genealogies of Religion: Discipline and Reasons of Power in Christianity and Islam*. Baltimore: Johns Hopkins University Press.

Bakhtin, M. M. 1981. *The Dialogic Imagination*. Trans. C. Emerson and M. Holquist. Austin: University of Texas Press.

Bauman, Richard. 1974. "Speaking in the Light: The Role of the Quaker Minister." In *Explorations in the Ethnography of Speaking*, ed. R Bauman and J. Sherzer. Cambridge: Cambridge University Press.

———. 2001. "Verbal Art as Performance." In *Linguistic Anthropology: A Reader*, ed. A. Duranti. Malden: Blackwell.

Bell, S., and Collins, P. 1998. "Religious Silence: British Quakerism and British Buddhism Compared." *Quaker Studies* 3, no. 1: 1–26.

Bloch, Maurice. 1974. "Symbols, Song, Dance and Features of Articulation: Is Religion an Extreme Form of Traditional Authority?" *Archives Europeenes de Sociologie* 15, no. 1: 55–81.

Boone, K. C. 1989. *The Bible Tells Them So: The Discourse of Protestant Fundamentalism*. Albany: State University of New York Press.

Coleman, Simon. 1989. "Controversy and the Social Order: Responses to a Religious Group in Sweden." Ph.D. dissertation, University of Cambridge.

———. 1991. "'Faith which Conquers the World': Swedish Fundamentalism and the Globalization of Culture." *Ethnos* 56, no. 1: 6–18.

———. 2000. *The Globalisation of Charismatic Christianity: Spreading the Gospel of Prosperity*. Cambridge: Cambridge University Press.

———ed. 2002. "The Faith Movement: A Global Religious Culture?" Special Issue of *Culture and Religion* 3, no. 1.

———. 2004. "The Charismatic Gift." *Journal of the Royal Anthropological Institute* 10, no. 3: 421–42.

Crapanzano, Vincent. 2000. *Serving the Word: Literalism in America from the Pulpit to the Bench*. New York: New Press.

Csordas, Thomas. 1997. *Language, Charisma, and Creativity: The Ritual Life of a Religious Movement*. Berkeley: University of California Press.

Ekman, Ulf. 1989. *Liv och Död är på din Tunga*. Uppsala: Livets Ord.

Engelke, Matthew. 2004. "Text and Performance in an African Church: The Book, 'Live and Direct.'" *American Ethnologist* 31, no. 1: 76–91.

Feuchtwang, Stephan, and Wang Ming Ming. 2001. *Grassroots Charisma: Four Local Leaders in China*. London: Routledge.

Goffman, Erving. 1975. *Frame Analysis: An Essay on the Organization of Experience*. Harmondsworth: Penguin.

Graham, W. 1987. *Beyond the Written Word: Oral Aspects of Scripture in the History of Religions*. Cambridge: Cambridge University Press.

Harding, Susan. 2000. *The Book of Jerry Falwell: Fundamentalist Language and Politics*. Princeton: Princeton University Press.

Hirschkind, Charles. 2001. "The Ethics of Listening: Cassette-Sermon Audition in Contemporary Egypt." *American Ethnologist* 28, no. 3: 623–49.

Humphrey, Caroline, and James Laidlaw. 1994. *The Archetypal Actions of Ritual: A Theory of Ritual Illustrated by the Jain Rite of Worship*. Oxford: Clarendon.

Irvine, Judith T. 1996. "Shadow Conversations: The Indeterminacy of Participant Roles." In *Natural Histories of Discourse*, ed. M. Silverstein and G. Urban. Chicago: University of Chicago Press.

Keane, Webb. 1997. *Signs of Recognition: Powers and Hazards of Representation in an Indonesian Society.* Berkeley; University of California Press.

———. 2002 "Sincerity, 'Modernity,' and the Protestants." *Cultural Anthropology* 17, no. 1: 65–92.

Leach, Edmund. 1976. *Culture and Communication: The Logic by Which Symbols Are Connected.* Cambridge: Cambridge University Press.

Lewis, Gilbert. 1980. *Day of Shining Red: An Essay on Understanding Ritual.* Cambridge: Cambridge University Press.

Robbins, Joel. 2001. "'God Is Nothing but Talk': Modernity, Language, and Prayer in a Papua New Guinea Society." *American Anthropologist* 103, no. 4: 901–12.

Savelle, J. 1982. *Sharing Jesus Effectively: A Handbook on Successful Soul-Winning.* Tulsa: Harrison House.

Schieffelin, Edward. 1995. "On Failure and Performance." In *The Performance of Healing,* ed. C Laderman and M. Roseman. New York: Routledge.

Scollon, R., and Scollon, S. 2001 [1995]. *Intercultural Communication: A Discourse Approach.* Malden: Blackwell.

Sjöberg, M. 1988. *Trosförkunnelsen och dess Avhoppare.* (RI-rapport 3). Uppsala: Kyrkans Hus.

Spitulnik, Debra. 2001. "The Social Circulation of Media Discourse and the Mediation of Communities." In *Linguistic Anthropology: A Reader,* ed. A. Duranti. Malden: Blackwell.

Stringer, M. D. 1999. *On the Perception of Worship.* Birmingham: Birmingham University Press.

Stromberg, Peter. 1986. *Symbols of Community: The Cultural System of a Swedish Church.* Tucson: University of Arizona Press.

———. 1993. *Language and Self-Transformation: A Study of the Christian Conversion Narrative.* Cambridge: Cambridge University Press.

Stubbs, M. 1983. *Discourse Analysis: The Sociolinguistic Analysis of Natural Language.* Oxford: Blackwell.

Tambiah, Stanley. 1985 [1981]. "A Performative Approach to Ritual." In *Culture, Thought, and Social Action: An Anthropological Perspective.* Cambridge: Harvard University Press.

Trilling, Lionel. 1972. *Sincerity and Authenticity.* Cambridge: Harvard University Press.

Turner, Victor. 1967. *The Forest of Symbols: Aspects of Ndembu Ritual.* Ithaca: Cornell University Press.

Urban, Greg. 1996a. "Entextualization, Replication, and Power." In *Natural Histories of Discourse,* ed. M. Silverstein and G. Urban. Chicago: University of Chicago Press.

1996b. *Metaphysical Community: The Interplay of the Senses and the Intellect.* Austin: University of Texas Press.

Wikström, L. 1988. *RI-Projektet* (RI-rapport 1). Uppsala: Kyrkans Hus.

Worsley, Peter. 1968. *The Trumpet Shall Sound: A Study of "Cargo" Cults in Melanesia.* 2nd ed. New York: Schocken Books.

3

CLARITY AND CHARISMA:
ON THE USES OF AMBIGUITY IN RITUAL LIFE

Matthew Engelke

> One must feel the respect due to a profound lack of understanding for the notion of a potential . . .
> —William Empson, *Seven Types of Ambiguity*

In his work of the problem of meaning, Max Weber focused on how such religious figures as prophets and priests help people make sense of the world. Although Weber said both are committed to metaphysical questions of order, prophets occupy a special place in his discussions. Whereas the priest is a source of stability, "of special knowledge, fixed doctrines, and vocational qualifications" (1963: 29), the prophet is a source of creativity, someone who presents "a unified view of the world derived from a consciously integrated and meaningful attitude toward life" (1963: 59). How this meaningful attitude is structured will vary but "it always denotes . . . an effort to systematize all the manifestations of life" (1963: 59).

Prophets are also the prototypical charismatics (Schnepel 1987: 30). Weber defines the prophet as "a purely individual bearer of charisma" (1963: 46) imbued with a "consciousness of power" (1963: 47). Charisma, in turn, is a term that "will be applied to a certain quality of an individual by virtue of which he is considered extraordinary and treated as endowed with supernatural, superhuman, or at least specifically exceptional powers or qualities. These are such as are not accessible to the ordinary person, but are regarded as of divine origin or as exemplary, and on the basis of them the individual concerned is treated as a 'leader'" (1978: 241). What interests me in Weber's discussion of the charismatic prophet is the extent to which the provision of meaning is connected to a notion of clarity. Implicit in most discussions of the problem of meaning is the argument that religious subjects seek clarity through religious practice (Geertz 1973: 100). This is not to suggest that Weber was naïve (or that Weberian anthropologists are naïve) about the extent to which charismatics rely on obfuscation and ambiguity to maintain their positions of authority. Far from it. But there is, I think, a need to discuss the extent to which Weber's sociology posits a connection between clarity and meaning—a need that can be addressed through ethnographic case studies.

In this chapter, I argue that a focus on charisma can help us understand the extent to which clarity in religious ritual generates a *meaningful attitude*. If charismatics offer a unified view of the world, what role does ambiguity play in the construction of order?

In what follows, I take as granted that clarity is not always the end goal of religious practice.[1] In doing so, I build on a number studies that have challenged the emphasis on the problem of meaning in religious life by stressing religion's disciplinary dimensions (Asad 1993; Bloch 1989; Keesing 1987). Religious practices—like all cultural practices—are "webs of mystification as well as signification" that "empower some [and] subordinate others" (Keesing 1987: 161). But I would also like to suggest that what is unclear to the religious subject is never simply a tool of disciplinary action. Indeed, anthropologists of religion need to problematize the notion of what constitutes clarity and why, in fact, we should expect this as a precondition for the production of meaning (cf. Jorgensen 1980). One way to investigate clarity is by turning to moments in ritual where ambiguity is central to the unfolding of events.[2] Adopting a definition from the literary critic William Empson, I define ambiguity as occurring when an actor discovers ideas in practice, or, does not hold them all in mind at once.[3] This emphasis on potentials rather than products allows us to consider meaning's limits. I will focus here on two examples from the Johane Masowe Church, an apostolic Christian church with congregations found throughout much of Zimbabwe. In each case I focus on an exchange between a "charismatic" prophet and that prophet's congregation. In each, the invocation of charisma leads to ambiguity, not clarity. Focusing on ambiguity in the message of Masowe prophets allows us to consider how meaning and discipline can produce one another in what is left unclear.

The Masowe Apostolics

Before discussing the cases in question, it is necessary to say something about the history of the Masowe Church and examine in particular how its prophets are understood to convey a meaningful attitude toward life. As I show in this section and the next, the medium of the religious message (in this case the spoken word) is often central to the way the clarity of charisma is constituted.

The Johane Masowe *weChishanu* Church, as it is most formally known, was inspired by the teachings of the prophet called Shoniwa/Johane, a young man from the Makoni District in Southern Rhodesia who claimed in 1932 to have been sent by God as an "African John the Baptist." Shoniwa had been working in the colonial capital of Salisbury for a few years before this transformation. As a child he briefly attended the Anglican school at St. Faith's

Mission. He also came into contact with the Catholic and American Methodist missionaries in the area. While working in and around Salisbury, Shoniwa attended the rallies of a popular labor union activist, Charles Mzengeli, and claims to have befriended a Catholic priest. Some time in May 1932, Shoniwa was stricken with painful headaches, and over the next several months was visited by the Holy Spirit in his dreams. It was in these dreams that Shoniwa first learned of his divinely inspired mission, and took on the name "Johane," after John the Baptist. His main task was to rescue Christianity from the brutal and awkward grip of the colonial and mission authorities. Toward this end, he began baptizing Africans, addressing the ill effects of witchcraft that wracked local communities, and encouraging "African initiative" (Sundkler and Steed 2000) in economic and religious life. Today, there are at least three significant churches that lay claim to Johane's legacy, one of which is the Masowe *weChishanu* (hereafter the Masowe apostolics, also known as the Friday apostolics).[4]

There are thousands of African Christian churches in sub-Saharan Africa, most of which were inspired by men and women like Shoniwa/Johane in an effort to "encompass and transform alienating structures of control" (Comaroff 1985: 191).[5] What drew me to the Masowe apostolics in particular is their insistence that they are "the Christians who don't read the Bible." For the first two years of his preaching, Johane expressed deep skepticism over the usefulness of the book, and the *weChishanu* apostolics have followed his sermons on this point down to the present day. This rejection of the text is important for understanding how apostolics produce a meaningful attitude toward life.

Masowe apostolics told me religious faith cannot be expressed through the written word. They say the Bible is an unnecessary and imperfect medium of religious communication and instruction. Above all, this is because it compromises their relationship with God. The book is impersonal; it signifies distance in much the same way a letter signifies distance between its sender and receiver. As a fixed text, the Bible is also problematic because what it contains might be irrelevant or no longer "true." The book, in other words, is a mediation, and the Masowe express concern over how such a compromised channel of communication might affect their faith. As a text, the Bible cannot be usefully employed, and so the Word of God is conveyed through a prophet.

The Bible is also problematic for Masowe apostolics because of its association with colonialism. The Masowe understand Westerners (*varungu*) to be driven by an obsession with the written word as a tool of power. In Africa (Comaroff and Comaroff 1991; Maxwell 2001), as indeed throughout much of the (post)colonial world (Guss 1986; Bhabha 1994), this connection between power and the book has been well documented. In Zimbabwe, it was driven home by missionaries who stressed the connections between literacy and salvation (Ranger 1989; 1999). In the Makoni District, where Shoniwa/Johane grew up, the American Methodists captured this goal in vivid terms, proclaiming that to be Christian "Africa must have books" (*African Advance* cited in Ranger 1989: 126). Of all these books the Bible was preeminent. It became a metonym for texts and a metaphor for colonial might (see Engelke 2003: 300–304). As Walter Mignolo argues, "Christianity secures knowledge in the Book and conveys it through the transmission of signs" (1994: 233).

Yet Mignolo's argument needs a qualification. Christians have not always sought to convey knowledge in the Book—or at least not solely through the Book. This is, I suggest, important for understanding how the Masowe approach the Bible. To their fellow Zimbabweans who question this "rejection" of Scripture, Masowe will respond by saying Jesus and the apostles did not use texts. What Jesus and the apostles stressed was faith, not knowledge. As Paul wrote in his epistle to the Galatians: "[I]f you are led by the Spirit, you are not subject to the law" (5:18). As late as the thirteenth century, even, Thomas Aquinas argued that "it is fitting that Christ did not commit his teaching to writing . . . for the more excellent the teacher, the more excellent his manner of teaching ought to be . . . whereby his doctrine would be imprinted on the hearts of his hearers" (in McLuhan 1969: 122). Saint Francis also criticized the Church for what he saw as "spiritually empty book-learning," a point that has been stressed by Aladura prophets in Nigeria (Probst 1989: 490). Christian cosmology is in no simple way a text-based cosmology. "The experience of Scripture is oral and aural" (Stock 1990: 137–38).

In place of Scripture, Masowe apostolics say religious knowledge must come "live and direct," a phrase borrowed from radio announcers to explain the ways in which the Word of God is revealed through religious language (see Engelke 2004a). In terms of a meaningful faith, then, it is the spoken word that matters.

Charisma and the Problem of Meaning

The Masowe emphasis on the spoken word raises a number of ethnographic and theoretical issues related to the problem of meaning. "It is written, but I say unto you," for example, is the phrase Weber used to sum up the strategy of the charismatic prophet rejecting orthodoxy for innovation (see also Faubion, this volume). Rejecting (or reconfiguring) the role of the text has certainly been key to the history of religious authority within Christianity. As Brian Stock (1990) has discussed, rejection of the Jewish "letter" was a prime motivation of the apostles. Reconfiguring the role of the book was central also to the Protestant Reformation. Martin Luther (Gilmot 1999) and William Tyndale (Bobrick 2001) challenged the Church hierarchy by translating the Bible into the European vernaculars. As Tomlinson and I explain in this volume's introduction, this was a notable moment in the shift from authority to meaning in Christian religious practices. Within colonial contexts, particularly where Christianity and literacy were introduced hand in hand, the problem of the book as a source of meaning and as a tool of discipline was manifested in still other ways. In the Aladura Church in Nigeria, Josiah Oshitelu introduced a new Holy Script in place of the Bible, "claiming the authority of writing for his own ideas" (Probst 1989: 487). In Zimbabwe, as David Maxwell (2001) has shown in work on the

Zimbabwe Assemblies of God, Africa, its founder, Ezekiel Guti, has likewise created his own text, *The Sacred History of ZAOGA*. Weber's work thus evokes a historical dynamic by stressing how the disciplines of charisma signal the social processes of "invention and intervention" (Feuchtwang and Wang 2001: 19) through what people say and do with the text.

And yet, there are a number of problems with Weber's ideal typical charismatic (as there are with any ideal type). As Stephan Feuchtwang and Wang Mingming (2001) point out, charisma is not a term that can be easily translated into non-Western contexts.[6] According to Stock, it is also important to note that Weber "did not speculate at length on how a society's means of communication shapes attitudes toward thinking or behavior" (1990: 113). In other words, Weber did not devote enough attention to how the mediums of charisma he identified help shape a worldview. For these and a host of other reasons, Peter Worsley (1968: 272) rejected the term altogether in his study of Cargo Cults in Melanesia. There are, then, a number of problems with such a "sponge word" (as Worsley calls it) as charisma. Nevertheless, like Feuchtwang and Wang (2001: 19), I do feel it is worth rescuing. In the remainder of this section I would like to discuss how the critique of charisma refines its analytical potential. We can then move on to how ambiguity becomes central to clarifying the apostolic notion of a meaningful attitude toward life.

In their study of charisma in China, Feuchtwang and Wang tell the story of Wumu, an adoptee who found himself in the paradoxical position of being both a marginal son and the family head. In 1901, Wumu founded The Hall of Luminous Good, a spirit-writing hall in the tradition of a practice through which followers heal their own and others' ailments in trance through the production of revelatory texts. Spirit-writing is similar to certain forms of African Islamic possession; it is textual, but the texts are a "representation of speech" (Feuchtwang and Wang 2001: 101). Wumu addressed his personal ills while appealing to a much wider audience, becoming a charismatic figure of some standing. But Wumu, it must be said, was "charismatic not by being possessed but by association with trance and by his organization of a space in which trance can take place" (2001: 111). As founder of the Hall, Wumu coordinated a set of activities and "the possibility of prophetic vision toward which many can contribute" (2001: 112). As a charismatic in the spirit-writing tradition, Wumu's case shows that "charisma is transmission of authority to innovate through a field of intentions" (2001: 116). This attention to revelation through writing reinforces Stock's argument that the means of communication is central to an understanding of how charismatic authority is produced. Charisma in the spirit-writing hall is not a matter of individuals, but collectives—the "performance of authors" creating a "factive, historical but also eternal truth" (Feuchtwang and Wang 2001: 109, 114).

Drawing attention to the social production of charisma has been a strong point in anthropological case studies. Against Weber's claim that charisma is an individual quality, Peter Worsley argues that charisma "needs to be *perceived, invested with meaning, and acted upon* by significant others" (1968:

xi). Charisma is always a relationship. It is not about individuals. More recently, this line of argumentation has been developed by Thomas Csordas in his work on Catholic Pentecostals in the United States. Csordas does not accept Weber's claim that "the charisma of speech is an individual matter" (Weber 1963: 75). Csordas suggests instead that charisma is "not a quality, but a . . . performative [and] intersubjective" (1997: 140) process. It emerges between people, not in them. Charisma, for Csordas, is a form of rhetoric that, like Edward Sapir's notion of culture, is located "in the interactions of specific individuals and the meaning they abstract from those interactions" (1997: 139).

In another critique of Weber, Johannes Fabian points to what he calls "the dark side of charisma" (1991: 61)—something rarely touched upon in sociological analysis. If charisma is a creative social force, it is also a potentially destructive or dangerous one. Fabian is not referring here to the difference between a charismatic Nazi and a charismatic saint, which is another question altogether. Rather, what he suggests is that charismatic pronouncements do not always lead to "invention and intervention," as I termed it earlier. Fabian saw this concern with charismatic arrest in the Jamaa movement in Zaire. Jamaa's founder, Placide Tempels, was ambivalent about the role texts could play in the life of his movement. This approach succeeded somewhat in preventing the formalization of Jamaa ideas. "More than once," Fabian says, "I heard members from the rank and file reject and ridicule intrusions of the mission bureaucracy as the work of *buku na crayon* (notebook and pencil)" (1991: 69). Indeed, the members often "showed their awareness of being caught, even dominated, by their own teachings" (1991: 68–69). Even what a prophet reveals through divine inspiration can become as stifling (or boring or seemingly irrelevant) as anything written in a book. The spoken word, for all of its apparent dynamism, is not immune to routinization. In fact, charisma and routinization are always present in one another: "what has been called charisma is not necessarily even innovatory; it is quite compatible with stability and traditionalism" (Worsley 1968: liii).

These discussions suggest the need to pay attention to the medium of communication of religious authority. In what follows, I present two cases from my fieldwork in which charismatic prophets attempted to articulate a meaningful system of ideas through their sermons. Building on the work discussed here, I hope to show how Weber's implicit emphasis on clarity needs further elaboration. I will highlight what is specific about the dynamics of charisma in Masowe religious life, drawing on both their "live and direct" approach, which I have already touched on briefly, and the concept of *mutemo*, to which I shall presently turn. In each of the cases below the attempt to provide order seems to end in failure, largely due to the inability (or unwillingness) of the congregation to engage in the production of that order by meeting the expectations of the prophet. These are moments in which a "message" does not cohere. However, as I hope to show, such unclear and ambiguous outcomes reinforce some of the fundamental principles of apostolic cosmology. There can be order, then, in the unknown; clarity in what is unclear.

Gilbert and the Apostolics Who "Knew Nothing"

In October 1999, I paid a visit to a Masowe prophet called Madzibaba Gilbert, whose congregation meets in the high-density suburb of Entumbane, Bulawayo.[7] Situated near the rough hills of the Matopos in the country's southwest, Bulawayo is Zimbabwe's second city, and the one-time kraal of Lobengula, the Ndebele king. Today, Bulawayo is still settled primarily by Ndebele speakers, who make up roughly 15 percent of the national population. Since Robert Mugabe came to power in 1980, the Ndebele throughout Matabeleland have suffered at the hands of the state (Alexander et al., 2000).

Gilbert is an outsider (often key to a charismatic's narrative)—a native Shona-speaker from the north. In fact it is only within the past ten years that the Masowe Church has made inroads into Matabeleland. For much of the church's seventy-year history, its strongholds have been in the Shona-speaking areas to the north and east of Harare, Zimbabwe's capital. This is still largely the case, but the recent success of prophets in places like Bulawayo sparked my curiosity about how the church was establishing its presence in new areas.[8]

The Entumbane group had been meeting for about two years when I visited, although its prophet has connections to a more long-standing congregation. Gilbert says he "comes from" the prophet called Sandros. This is an apostolic way of marking a prophetic genealogy. It is also a first step in establishing oneself as a church "leader," charismatic or not. While Johane Masowe is believed to have emerged whole cloth, sent directly by God, every prophet since has undergone a more gradual process of transformation.[9] Usually someone becomes a prophet only after several years in the church, during which time he or she may be given messages through dreams or by singing as part of a special chorus. For apostolics, then, the image of a charismatic leader as someone who might emerge in a flash of divine intervention is tempered by an overriding sense of the process of establishing one's place more gradually. While it would not be accurate to say that certain individuals serve as "apprentices" to a prophet, it is important to stress the idea that prophetic authority derives from a mixture of experience and inspiration. In terms of Weber's ideal types, Masowe prophets might represent something between a prophet and a priest. The most influential prophets—the most charismatic—are those who convey an image of what we might call, following arguments similar to Worsley and Fabian, "stable innovation." (Or, at least, its attempt.) This idea is expressed well in a popular Masowe song:

Nhano, nhano
Kufamba kwakanaka!

Slowly, slowly,
Walk well!

This song suggests religious matters cannot be rushed. It reminds people that church life must be approached with care and at a measured pace.

Gilbert "learned to walk" as a member of Madzibaba Sandros's congregation. At the time of his death in 1996, Sandros was perhaps the most influential
Masowe prophet at work. In the sprawling suburbs of Chitungwiza, just south
of the nation's capital, Sandros had established a congregation that drew in
several thousand people each weekend, many of them looking for Sandros to
restore a sense of order to their lives: through faith healing, through help with
finding a job, or any number of other ways. Gilbert began to have dreams under Sandros, and eventually was filled by the Holy Spirit. And so when Gilbert
moved to Bulawayo in the mid 1990s (for reasons not related to the church),
he took the opportunity to establish a congregation in Entumbane, treating it
as a mission field in need of cultivation.

Like all Masowe, the apostolics in Entumbane meet outdoors, under an
open sky, clad in long white robes. The Entumbane site is, quite literally, on
the edge of the city in a small field. On three sides, the apostolics are surrounded by the ramshackle durawalls characteristic of the African urban landscape. On the fourth the field opens into grassy structures, bounded only by
the train tracks that run north to Victoria Falls and Zambia.

Gilbert is a large, barrel-chested man with a strong voice. His congregation
is made up of about seventy-five men, women, and children. Seventy-five is a
not insignificant number of congregants for only two years of work in an area.
Whether or not we can use such numbers to measure charismatic appeal is not
the point. And no one told me that Gilbert was "charismatic." Yet there was a
clear sense on the part of congregants I spoke to that he provided them with—
to use Weber's words again—a meaningful attitude toward life. The interviews
I conducted with apostolics at Entumbane all followed a similar theme: I
joined this church because I was lost; the prophet explained why I was having troubles; Madzibaba Gilbert showed me what was *really* happening in my
life. These were narratives common in most of the interviews I conducted in
Zimbabwe. They were echoed, as well, in the testimonials of apostolics during
church services. In some congregations, several hours a week might be given
over to apostolics who want to tell the story of how a prophet helped them
"find their way" in life. Apostolics consistently located "the answer" in the
person of the prophet. What the Entumbane congregants said, both publicly
and privately, contributed to Gilbert's authoritative position to provide meaning. It was a position he readily accepted.

However, at the risk of undercutting this sociological analysis, I would say
there was something more about Gilbert. There was something about *him*—
his voice, even the way he just sat on the ground—that made me think of
him as charismatic. What makes this comment interesting, I think, is that not
every Masowe prophet I met did have that *something*, in its spongy or quasi-
material dimensions. Many prophets command nothing like charismatic authority as persons (which is not to say they do not provide "answers" typical
of prophets). Indeed, not every congregation has a leader in Weber's sense.[10]
And in theory, at least, every apostolic will insist that prophets-as-people are
not important, are *never* important; it is always, only, the Holy Spirit that matters. To say that charisma is rhetoric is surely correct, but then some people

are better rhetoricians than others. Inasmuch as Masowe prophets provide answers through what they say, what gives them "clarity" is not expressed through language alone.

On the days I visited Entumbane Gilbert spent most of his time preaching about the history of the church. This is a popular topic in Masowe groups. While newer apostolics can often pick up bits and pieces of the church's past in conversation with those more experienced, occasions on which a prophet or a congregation's "old timers" (as the apostolics call members who have long belonged) speak present the most comprehensive narratives one can expect to receive. For many this is disappointing. There is a strong push from some quarters in the church to make the history more available. Over the past several years, in fact, some Masowe elders (committed to a version of modernity in which texts play a more central role) have argued that the church's history ought to be written down. With the first generation of prophets and elders nearly gone, the sense is that the past needs to be preserved in the written record. One church elder spoke to me about it in terms of protecting a "copyright": people try to use the Masowe "name" without knowing what it means. It needs to be protected in much the same way the Coca-Cola Bottling Company protects their trademark "Coke." By producing a written history (a recipe, if you will), the Church could guarantee its future by marking its past—by staking out a precedent. The more hard-line "traditionalists," however, insist this should never happen. The creation of any religious text (sacred or otherwise) would destroy the "live and direct" emphasis of faith. While even the most "progressive" elders pushing for a written history would never advocate acceptance of the Bible (they make an important distinction between knowledge of history and knowledge of faith), the "traditionalists" are wary of falling down the slippery slope. First a history, then perhaps a book of apostolic songs: eventually, they would be reading the Bible in services, paying no attention whatsoever to the prophet, lost in something akin to Saint Francis's spiritually empty book-learning. Such wrangling only seems to have made occasions on which prophets discuss church history even more appreciated by the rank-and-file. In Entumbane, congregants told me after the services in question that it was particularly valuable for them, since they were relative newcomers—"just children," as many of them put it. I will return to this characterization later.

In one of the sermons I heard, Gilbert traced his work back to Sandros, and Sandros, in turn, to the long line of prophets who came before him. In the course of these lessons, Gilbert stressed a connection between the church's history and the concept of *mutemo*, a Shona word usually translated as "law" that apostolics use also to refer to "knowledge." *Mutemo* is a complicated idea, and we cannot discuss all its dimensions here (but see Engelke 2004b). Suffice it to say that in the absence of a written text, *mutemo* provides a set of guidelines that apostolics should follow in their effort to be good Christians. This includes a number of fairly basic prohibitions, such as abstaining from alcohol and tobacco. It also includes the recognition of basic religious precepts—that Jesus Christ is the Son of God, that He died for their sins, that Friday is the

Sabbath, and so on. More specifically, *mutemo* highlights the apostolic emphasis on a "live and direct" connection to God through the sermons of prophets, as well as prohibitions related to these channels of communication. For example, apostolics are told that bringing a Bible to a church service is a sin because it is disrespectful of the prophet's authority (and therefore the authority of the Holy Spirit). They are told also not to wear shoes, watches, or jewelry at a service, because the wilderness ground (*sowe*) on which they pray is sacred and materials goods will defile it. This is all part of *mutemo*.

Mutemo is similar to what Fabian describes as *mawazo* for the Jamaa movement in Zaire. *Mawazo* means "ideas" in kiSwahili, and refers to "the sum total of [Jamaa] thought, as well as almost any of its particular manifestations" (Fabian 1991: 68). Like Johane Masowe, we may recall that Placide Tempels (the founder of Jamaa) was sceptical of the written word. Both *mutemo* and *mawazo* are, we might say, alternatives to written texts—those mediated, routinized, and stifling objects that characterize (for the African visionary) Western Christianity. Ideally what *mutemo* and *mawazo* provide is what I call a "process of becoming" (Engelke 2004b). Fabian describes *mawazo* as realized through "gradual initiation, so much so that becoming Jamaa and being Jamaa, means and ends, became indistinguishable" (1991: 76). We might say the same for *mutemo*. Constantly aware of the "dark side" of charismatic leadership, Masowe prophets stress the immateriality and potential creativity of *mutemo* through the spoken word. To objectify *mutemo* would be to fall victim to "the terror of the text" (Fabian 1991). As a process of becoming, *mutemo* provides a set of dispositions that apostolics use to make sense of and interpret the world.

When a person expresses the desire to become an apostolic, he or she is taught the meanings of *mutemo* by an elder in the congregation. These teachings are a formal responsibility; elders are chosen by prophets to help them carry out their divinely inspired mission. In addition to providing religious instruction, elders often help prophets prepare the medicinal substances that prophets use in their fight against witchcraft. And if, as often happens during healing sessions, a person possessed by an evil spirit tries to physically attack the prophet, elders will act as bodyguards. In the larger congregations elders also fulfil the more mundane role of coordinating the movements, seating patterns, and comings and goings of the congregation. Since at any given service there will be a number of first-time attendees (most of whom come for healing), part of this involves explaining *mutemo* in its more immediately relevant aspects (such as the need to remove one's shoes before entering the *sowe*).

An elder is usually someone who has been attending the church for a number of years and is familiar with the ins and outs of the faith.[11] In practice, however, Masowe teachings vary in quality from one congregation to the next. Although I never met an apostolic who professed ignorance over the church's policy on alcohol, or an unfamiliarity with the general position on the Bible, there was a significant range in the extent to which apostolics could articulate a knowledge of *mutemo*. By definition *mutemo* cannot be mastered. It is not a book with a beginning and an end. But clearly for some apostolics the process of becoming, of *mutemo* being "incorporated into the believer" (Fabian 1991: 77), is more complete than for others.

This was made evident on my visit to Entumbane during one of Gilbert's sermons on church history. In the course of holding forth, Gilbert began to develop his sermon around the theme of knowledge: "This is the experience of our church; this is our history. You apostolics ought to know these things, just like you know the law [*mutemo*], just like you know our Ten Commandments."

After finishing the sermon Gilbert put his lesson to the test by asking four members of the church to stand up and recite the Ten Commandments. Two men and two women rose to their feet. They were smiling nervous smiles. A buzz rolled over the rest of the congregation. One of the men was near to me. His white robes were perfectly pressed, as apostolic robes often are. He had probably risen before dawn that morning to prepare them. For security he held on to the tip of the belt that gathers the robes at the waist. Very quickly, when it was his turn, he came up with two Commandments: Thou shall not kill; Thou shall not covet thy neighbor's wife. The closest any of the others got was six, and not in any discernable order. Each expressed embarrassment. The congregation tried to remain stone-faced, lest some of them be called on next. Gilbert's disposition was difficult to decipher at first, but it turned decidedly sour by the end of the exercise. He scolded the congregation and exclaimed, "You Apostles don't know anything!"

Later that day, when I met with Gilbert at his home, we sat around his living room watching cartoons on TV and drinking strawberry milk. Gilbert was more ambivalent about the results of his test than I thought he would be, alternately discussing the ways in which it marked the failure and success of his ministry. On the one hand, he was upset that his followers didn't know something as basic as the Ten Commandments. This is *mutemo*—and an important part of it. But Gilbert also remarked that the four apostolics had succeeded in living up to the expectations of apostolic "law"; they had faith in the prophet (and therefore in God) and did not need to abide by a set of rules "written on stone tablets" from "thousands of years ago." Gilbert took a certain pride in the fact that these four men and women had not turned to "book knowledge" in an effort to prove their faith.

Whether or not the apostolics in question could have drawn on such knowledge is another question. Biblical absence in church rituals does not correlate to biblical ignorance. The boundaries between the written and the spoken word are not clearly drawn. Literacy, "book knowledge," and the practice of reading are not one in the same (Boyarin 1993). In fact, most people who become apostolics have previous affiliations with other denominations, many of which emphasize the importance of Bible study. When they join the church, they are not asked to forget, much less renounce, any previous religious education. Even members who have no previous affiliation with Christian churches, or who are illiterate, are not necessarily strangers to biblical narratives. In Zimbabwe, similar to the situation Isabel Hofmeyr (1994) describes in South Africa, Christian imagery has been incorporated into oral narratives and poetry well beyond Christian domains. Indeed, biblical narratives play a central role in the religious imagery of apostolic sermons and rituals. The prophet Pageneck/Nzira, for example—to whom I shall presently turn—made regular allusions to Galatians (see Engelke 2004a). More commonly, river reeds are used in rituals of healing to "protect" apostolics from harm. Whenever I asked why, I would get quizzical looks. The answer was obvious: as an infant, Moses had been protected in the bulrushes from the wrath of Pharaoh. The key point for the Masowe is that these narratives must be enacted or performed in the "live and direct" style, not read. By the end of our afternoon visit, Gilbert was perfectly comfortable with the implications this had in terms of his authority as a prophet. "It is written, but I say unto you" in its Weberian cadences would suit Gilbert just fine.

Another important question to consider here is whether or not the apostolics who were asked to recite the Commandments did, in fact, know more than they let on. Is it possible that one of them—or all of them—could have recited all ten, in order, without missing a beat? Since I spent little time with the Entumbane congregation, I cannot answer this question based on an analysis of this situation. But whether through ignorance, reticence, or—indeed—deference, the image of "knowing nothing" is crucial to an understanding of how apostolics conceive a meaningful faith. The ambiguous results of Gilbert's "test" cannot be reduced to the image of charisma as a tool of authority. In turning to my second example, I hope to explain why.

Pageneck and the Apostolics Who Were Not

In May 1999, several months before my visit to Bulawayo, there was an incident at a congregation called Juranifiri Santa that in hindsight seems related to the incident with the apostolics at Entumbane who "knew nothing."

Juranifiri is situated on the outskirts of Chitungwiza, a community that has grown up over the past several decades just south of Harare's industrial areas. It is now a city in its own right, although most people think of it as an extension of the capital. Chitungwiza is in many ways Harare's Soweto: a space of apartheid. It has always been home to an African labouring underclass—at first migrant workers, but now many families long since settled. While most people maintain close ties to a rural home (musha), the younger generations of Chitungwiza have grown up almost entirely within the city.

The Masowe Church has had a presence in the Chitungwiza area since its beginnings. In the Seke Communal lands that border the city today, a number of prophets (including Johane) established congregations as of the mid 1930s. When the urban areas around Seke began to mushroom in the 1950s and 1960s, the apostolics established a presence there, too. The weChishanu are well known, and while prophets come and go there is a strong continuity of prophetic genealogies in the area.

Juranifiri Santa was established in 1989. Its main prophet during my research was a man called Godfrey Nzira. Like Gilbert, Nzira "comes from" Sandros. In the late 1970s, Nzira's wife, Spiwe, was suffering from stomach pains and began to attend the services that Sandros held near their home. Her husband went with her. They were looking for answers. Why was she suffering from these pains? The doctor could not tell them; the spirit mediums did not know; a Methodist priest dismissed the possibility of spiritual foul play as African superstition. Sandros, finally, explained the misfortune: it was witchcraft, a jealous kinsman. Within a few years, well after she had been cured of her ailments through the work of the Holy Spirit, Spiwe and her husband became apostolics. By 1986, Nzira was having prophetic dreams on a regular basis. It was clear to Sandros and the elders of his congregation that Nzira was on his way to becoming a prophet in his own right. He was learning to walk well. And not only did he have important dreams; what most struck the congregation was Nzira's singing. It is said that when Nzira sang, the evil spirits and witchcraft familiars that plagued members of the congregation would scream out in pain. Singing, indeed, is one of the chief "weapons" prophets use in their fight against witchcraft. Nzira was eventually recognized as a prophet and for a few years worked alongside Sandros (it is not unusual to have two or more prophets in a congregation). The spirit that speaks through Nzira is known as "Pageneck."

In 1989 Sandros and Nzira split because of what was described to me as "the question of leadership." Each saw himself as the main prophet of the congregation and fell victim to what my informants politely called "human nature." Nzira left and took with him only a handful of followers. Pageneck continued to speak through him. For many years his congregation was relatively modest compared to Sandros's. By the time Sandros died in 1996, however, Nzira had come to rival him in popularity. And again, while apostolics stress that there is no "leader" of their church—for they are all subject to God—it is not unusual for members of the five or six most well-known congregations to hint that perhaps their prophet has a more "live and direct" link to the Holy Spirit than anyone else.

By 1999 Nzira was reaching the height of his popularity and power. His congregation topped 1,000 members, and it was not unusual for several thousand more people to attend his healing sessions for the benefit of his singing. Nzira is not a large man but he has a commanding presence. Whereas Gilbert projects himself through his voice, Nzira does so through his eyes. Most of the time he preached in quiet tones punctuated by energetic outbursts and, sometimes, fits of violence. Indeed, Nzira is an intimidating figure; he ran his congregation like a tight ship, taking a much more direct role in day-to-day affairs than do most other prophets. But the apostolics said he can get things done: when you are fighting a war you do not always have time to be gentle.

Nzira's rise as a charismatic prophet follows many standard themes. Endowed with the gift of singing, he stood apart. Challenged by the orthodoxy, he broke away. Down, but not out, eventually he triumphed. Nzira's rise was marked also by the particularities of the "slowly, slowly" apostolic approach. What is more, he first came to the church not on his own behalf, but on that of Spiwe, his wife. Charisma is not an individual matter in at least one other respect, then. Finally, though I was hesitant to reveal my own feelings for Gilbert's charismatic appeal, I must be less so with Nzira. Whatever Gilbert had, Nzira possessed in spades.

One Sunday in the middle of May I arrived at Juranifiri with David Bishau, a Ph.D. student from the University of Zimbabwe specializing in New Testament studies, but interested also in African churches. David had come with me a few times before, so he had a sense of how services were conducted at Juranifiri. We were both struck by what happened that day. I certainly never witnessed anything like it before or after, but despite its uniqueness here it raises a number of important issues about charisma and clarity in ritual.

David and I were late. The service had already started. We took a seat at the back of the crowd of men who had gathered in the middle of the *sowe*. One of the elders was speaking about *mutemo*: "As Masowe we should obey the law." (*Semasowe tinofanirwa kuteedza mutemo.*) Soon, a young girl began a song: "*Tauya Baba kuzopona!*" (Father, we came here to be saved!) The congregation joined in and we saw Nzira stand up. Nzira stopped the singing with a wave of his walking stick, like a conductor, and began to speak in a low voice: "If you are an apostle, don't treat people with disrespect [don't intimidate people]." (*Kana uri mupostori haufaniri kutyisidzira vanhu.*) He was filled with the Holy Spirit and was therefore recognized as Pageneck.

Pageneck, then, went on about the virtues of mercy and kindness. He said apostolics must treat people with kindness. After some minutes the young girl began to sing another song, but the congregation did not pick it up, and she faded out. She tried again and the same thing happened. Pageneck seemed perturbed. Singing is the most direct way in which apostolics can demonstrate their faith, and enact *mutemo*. This was a sign, then, of its absence—that the congregation was not acting as a congregation. "Do we have believers [*vatendi*] here?" Pageneck asked. No one answered. "Do we have believers here?" he said again. Still, no one spoke up. "Okay, okay," he went on, "would all apostles please stand up?" David and I looked around. Everyone was dead quiet. Still, no one stood up. "If we don't have apostles here, if we don't have believers here, then what are you doing? Do you just come here to admire me? To see what I'm going to do next? Okay, go then. You can all go home."

At first the remark did not register. I certainly wondered if I had heard him correctly, and other people appeared confused, too. The congregation sat still. Pageneck started to shout (a rare occurrence): "Now! Leave! Those who've come for healing can get some help now, but the rest of you, you apostles, just go home!" Slowly people got to their feet. A number of the elders rushed off to prepare for the healing session. It was ironic: the only people leaving (with the exception of the elders) were the people in white robes, the people who had distinguished themselves by their commitment to *mutemo*. David and I walked out with an apostle called Madzibaba Chrispine, a young man with whom I had become friendly over the preceding months. We spent the next few hours talking to him about what had just happened.

Chrispine joined the Church in January 1998. He had been coming for about a year before that for help with what he referred to as "problems in school." One year is about the average length of time it takes to become an apostolic. In line with their philosophy of taking things "slowly," elders do not encourage the process to move any faster, and eschew altogether the idea that someone can "convert" on the spot.[12] It is very important from the Masowe point of view that people not rush in to faith—they need to feel the rhythms and cadences of church life. Apostolics always told me that being an apostolic is not easy, and one should give it a lot of thought beforehand. In this respect, then, Chrispine's case was standard. In less than a year and a half in the church, however, Chrispine had become an unusually active member of Nzira's inner circle. He was well known as a particularly devoted member, someone who knew and lived *mutemo*. Just twenty years old when I met him, Chrispine was a promising young artist who hoped to show his work in Harare's galleries. He made a number of paintings for Juranifiri Santa, mostly scenes of apostles praying in their sacred groves. He also did a charcoal portrait of Nzira that hangs in the Nzira family living room.

Chrispine had been meaning to show me his art portfolio, so David and I went back with him to the room he rented in a nearby Chitungwiza neighborhood. We asked him what had happened. Why had no one stood up? Why had no one professed to be an apostolic? To my knowledge there were at least a dozen people there who had been in the church for over a decade. These people are revered members of the apostolic community. Chrispine himself, while relatively new to the Church, had proven his commitment, and in my conversations with him demonstrated an intimate understanding of *mutemo*, often more sophisticated than that of people several years his senior. On the way back to his house he summed it up in matter-of-fact fashion: "Ah, we're just children," he said. Chrispine was not too concerned. "It's like trying to give adult food to little children. We can't take it."

I mentioned above that the apostolics at Entumbane referred to themselves as "children" because they needed to learn about the history of their church. For many of these novices, who were part of a congregation on the outskirts of Masowe influence, this seemed to make sense. There were not many people to whom they could turn to find out about the church, since Gilbert was their best link to its broader movements and traditions. In Chitungwiza, however, the Masowe apostolics have been part of the religious landscape for decades. Within a congregation, certainly, someone like Chrispine, in a place like Juranifiri, cannot be said to "know nothing." What, then, might connect an apostolic "child" in Chitungwiza with one in Entumbane?

For one, this figure of speech is common in much religious discourse. We might expect it to be used on a regular basis, certainly among Christians, who often talk about themselves as the children of God. This logic is also an aspect of Shona religious cosmology, which is expressed through an idiom of kinship. Human beings consult their ancestors about numerous things: the past, for example, or uncertainties in life, or the need for rain. They are children who show respect to elders in their patriline. In each case these images of childhood evoke simultaneous images of meaning and discipline—answers from a higher authority. Both the Entumbane and Juranifiri apostolics were deferring to the authority of the prophet, and in so doing they helped create a framework of religious meaning in the moments of their own "failure" and uncertainty.

There is, however, a key difference in how apostolics and non-apostolics consider themselves "children." This brings us back to the earlier discussion of how meaning is mediated—to the concerns of people like the Masowe who try to live as Christians (see also Robbins 2001a). It has to do with the nature of knowledge, and with how the Masowe understand the ways in which their "live and direct" connection with God allows them to produce a meaningful faith. When a group of apostolics refuse to confirm their faith after being prompted by the Holy Spirit, their refusal is, in one sense, acting on *mutemo*. It becomes a meaningful act because of *mutemo*. As Christians the Masowe recognize that humans and divinity do not speak in the same register; the nature of human knowledge and the nature of divine knowledge are distinct. This is not the case among Shona-speaking peoples more generally. For one thing, the idea of divinity does not translate easily into Shona. The spiritual world and the physical world are parts of the same whole. This is reflected in some of the more awkward formulations of Christian religious concepts. When Catholic and Protestant missionaries began translating Christian ideas into the Shona dialects, the word they used for Heaven was *denga*, which means "sky." The term for hell is *gomba remoto*, "pit of fire." As David Lan points out in his work on spirit mediums in the Dande Valley: "The true relationship between human knowledge and ancestral knowledge is as points on a continuum" (1985: 54). Or, as Marshall Murphree argues in his work on the Budjga, a "patrilineage is both an organic and a spiritual unity" (1969: 41). By refusing to acknowledge their faith when in "live and direct" touch with God, the apostles at Juranifiri meant to suggest their difference from, and deference to, the Holy Spirit. Chrispine's explanation, then, picks up above all on a theme of incommensurability. Here, the apostolics were such young children that it was not a question of needing to be schooled, as it was at Entumbane. Here Chrispine and the others were so "young" they "couldn't take it." They could not answer Pageneck's questions. But this inability—folded into a disciplinary act by Pageneck—was also a capability, a recognition that "live and direct" faith and the precepts of *mutemo* are ontological, not epistemological, concerns.

Conclusion

In anthropological studies of meaning, it is often assumed that clarity is the end goal. At the outset of this paper I discussed this issue in relation to Weber's interest in the problem of meaning. Charismatic prophets are supposed to provide answers, to let people know where they stand in a larger order, to provide a meaningful attitude toward life. Yet such a meaningful attitude will never provide all the "answers," and as the Masowe cases suggest, it is not necessarily supposed to. Indeed, as Dan Jorgensen argues, religious practice is not always about "the promulgation of certainty attended by the suppression of ambiguity and indeterminacy" (1980: 365); neither should the anthropology of religion be.

The historian of religion J. Z. Smith has argued that "ritual precises ambiguities" (1987: 110). This is itself a perfectly ambiguous phrase, and purposefully so. Ritual makes things clear; it also makes them unclear. Ambiguity and clarity are mutually constitutive. Smith's remark can be used to reinforce my arguments here. The case of the four apostolics who "failed" Gilbert's test—who knew nothing—and the case of those who did not confirm their faith—Pageneck's apostolics who were not apostolics—suggest that meaning is not always about clarity. The production of charisma "live and direct," and the ways in which it is understood to be meaningful, are of central concern in each example. And in each ambiguity plays a multifaceted role. For prophets, ambiguity is a useful disciplinary tool. Indeed, for a charismatic prophet to be precise is only to ensure disconfirmation of a message (Worsley 1968: xix). In our conversation, Gilbert suggested he had discovered the meaning of his lesson after the fact. As part of a "live and direct" faith, the failure of his congregation could be interpreted as a success. For Pageneck/Nzira, the failure of the congregation to take up the young girl's song or answer his questions also provided an opportunity to reinforce his discipline in the "live and direct" fashion. Whether this was an intentional outcome I cannot say, but it was significant nonetheless because it fit into the logic of apostolic cosmology.

And yet I hope to have shown through the discussion of *mutemo* that the analysis cannot end here. At both Entumbane and Juranifiri, congregations were supposed to have provided the answers. The prophets had asked the questions. Congregants in the Masowe Church, in addition to contributing to the social relationships of charisma that generate discipline, derive meaning out of moments that reinforce the authority of the prophet, derivations that cut across the constitution of that authority. To paraphrase Empson on ambiguity, meaning is a potential for apostolics. As a potential, as *mutemo*, it is not subject solely to the discipline of the charismatic. It is as much an ontological as an epistemological concern, often highlighted in ritual when the process of becoming runs up against its own limits—as when a religious exchange is left unfinished. For apostolics at both Entumbane and Juranifiri, the unfinished exchange provided the opportunity to reflect on their incorporation of *mutemo*—which is likewise always unfinished. In this way, the mark of discipline (decrying the ignorance of the congregation; accusing apostolics of not being apostolics) can be used in an unpredictable way to generate a meaningful attitude. It is not enough for anthropologists to approach meaning in terms of signification or mystification. In ritual, meaning's limits are defined through their paradoxical interplay, the shading of one into the other.

Acknowledgements

Research for this chapter was supported by the Graduate School of Arts and Sciences at the University of Virginia and a Fulbright-Hays Doctoral Dissertation Research Abroad grant. In addition to the AAA, drafts of this paper were presented to the anthropology seminars at Brunel University and the

University of Aberdeen. My thanks to Stephan Feuchtwang and John Tresch
for their valuable comments, too.

Notes

1. An interesting counter-example to this claim can be found in the work of Eva Keller, whose
    study of Seventh-Day Adventists in Madagascar suggests that clarity is precisely what her
    informants strive for: "what interests and moves church members most about the future is the
    anticipation of finally *seeing* things entirely *clearly*" (2004: 103). While there is not the space
    to develop the parallel here, in many respects Keller's (2004: 101–2) discussion of *mazava*
    (clarity) and my own, below, of *mutemo* (knowledge, law) dovetail in terms of an emphasis on
    processual and gradual realization.
2. See, for example, Victor Turner (1967) and Maurice Bloch (1986) on circumcision rituals.
    One of Bloch's main interests is in "the way rituals are affected by events" (1986: 11). In his
    account of *mukanda*, the boy's circumcision rite among the Ndembu, Turner demonstrates a
    similar concern. Through his discussion of Nyaluhana's desire to perform the rite, against the
    wishes of Machamba and others, Turner shows that "the contemporary state of power rela-
    tions" (1967: 278) plays a direct role in how the rite is both conceived and enacted. Not all
    ritual "specialists" share an understanding of how circumcisions should be carried out. While
    rituals might follow a clear pattern in the abstract, "[i]n social reality circumstances rarely
    go according to plan or norm" (1967: 186). A ritual thus requires a "'certain looseness of fit'
    or discrepancy between its principles of organization" (1967: 271). Turner's focus here is on
    conceiving of society as a process; built into this argument is an understanding that ambiguity
    is central to this process (see also Bloch 1986: 9).
3. Empson's most general definition of ambiguity is "an indecision as to what you mean, an
    intention to mean several things, a probability that one or both of two things has been meant,
    and the fact that a statement has several meanings" (1947: 5–6). Of Empson's seven types of
    ambiguity, that which corresponds most closely to what I will be describing here is the fifth:
    "when the author is discovering his idea in the act of writing, or not holding it all in his mind
    at once" (1947: 155). The central idea I want to highlight here is the process of creating
    meaning in action.
4. Information in this paragraph on the first several years of Johane Masowe's preaching is based
    on oral history interviews collected in Zimbabwe between 1993 and 1999, records in the Na-
    tional Archives of Zimbabwe (esp. files S 138/22, S 1542/P10, and S 1542/M8), Dillon-Malone
    (1978), and Ranger (1999). See also Mukonyora (2000) and Werbner (1985) for important
    discussions of Johane Masowe and his churches.
5. The Masowe apostolics refer to their church as an "African church," which is why I use the
    term here. However, see Fernandez (1978) and Daneel (1987) for important critiques of this
    term in the literature.
6. Feuchtwang and Wang also remind us that charisma is a term with its roots in Christian no-
    tions of grace. This is not a theme I will pursue here: since we are looking at prophets who
    recognize themselves as Christian, a comparative comment would be difficult to make. But
    see Burkhard Schnepel's (1987) essay on Weber for an interesting discussion of how Weber's
    understanding of charisma was informed by his political sensibilities in Wilhelmine Germany
    and family connections to Christianity.
7. "Madzibaba" is a term the *weChishanu* apostolics use to refer to any male in the church;
    madzimai is the term for females. These terms are based on the Shona terms for "father"
    (*baba*) and "mother" (*amai*), although for the apostolics they purposefully cut across genera-
    tional boundaries.
8. About a third of the congregants at Entumbane were native Shona speakers; some had grown
    up in Bulawayo, others had moved there for work or school (one young man I spoke to was a
    student at the local National University of Science and Technology). Most of the native Nde-
    bele speakers I interviewed were fluent in both Ndebele and Shona. Gilbert spoke Ndebele

and would code switch in his sermons. Occasionally he, or other speakers, were accompanied by a translator to translate for those who did not know the language being spoken at a given moment, although there did not seem to be any pattern as to when these translators worked (I was told there *was* no pattern). When Gilbert was filled with the Holy Spirit, he was not accompanied by these translators (but see Engelke 2004a on spiritual interpreters, or *mumiriri wemweya*).

9. Johane emerged "whole cloth," but he still underwent a lengthy process of articulating his message (see Engelke 2005).

10. While there is not space to address the matter here, elders and prophets often strike a fine balance of power in Masowe congregations.

11. This might help explain why Gilbert commanded authority at Entumbane. There were no elders with anything like the experience Gilbert had. However, it is important to note that there is no simple correlation between experience and authority. Most of the congregations in and around Harare had prophets at work for several years, even decades. These men and (some) women stood alongside elders with similar records of involvement, but there was no pattern as to which might command pragmatic authority.

12. See Engelke (2004b) for a more detailed discussion of conversion in the Masowe Church.

References

Asad, Talal. 1993. *Genealogies of Religion: Discipline and Reasons of Power in Christianity and Islam.* Baltimore: The Johns Hopkins University Press.

Bhabha, Homi. 1994. "Signs Taken for Wonders: Questions of Ambivalence and Authority under a Tree outside Delhi." In *The Location of Culture.* New York: Routledge.

Bloch, Maurice. 1986. *From Blessing to Violence: History and Ideology in the Circumcision Ritual of the Merina.* Cambridge: Cambridge University Press.

———. 1989 [1974]. "Symbols, Song, Dance and Features of Articulation: Is Religion an Extreme Form of Traditional Authority?" In *Ritual, History and Power: Selected Papers in Anthropology.* London: The Athlone Press.

Bobrick, Benson. 2001. *Wide as the Waters: The Story of the English Bible and the Revolution It Inspired.* New York: Simon and Schuster.

Boyarin, Jonathan, ed. 1993. *The Ethnography of Reading.* Berkeley: University of California Press.

Comaroff, Jean. 1985. *Body of Power, Spirit of Resistance: The Culture and History of a South African People.* Chicago: University of Chicago Press.

Comaroff, Jean, and John L. Comaroff. 1991. *Of Revelation and Revolution: Christianity, Colonialism, and Consciousness in South Africa,* vol. 1. Chicago: University of Chicago Press.

Csordas, Thomas. 1997. *Language, Charisma, and Creativity: The Ritual Life of a Religious Movement.* Berkeley: University of California Press.

Daneel, Martinus. 1987. *Quest for Belonging.* Gweru: Mambo Press.

Dillon-Malone, Clive. 1978. *The Korsten Basketmakers: A Study of the Masowe Apostles.* Manchester: Manchester University Press.

Empson, William. 1947. *7 Types of Ambiguity.* New York: New Directions.

Engelke, Matthew. 2003. "The Book, the Church, and the 'Incomprehensible Paradox': Christianity in African History." *Journal of Southern African Studies* 29, no. 1: 297–306.

———. 2004a. "Text and Performance in an African Christian Church: The Book, 'Live and Direct.'" *American Ethnologist* 31, no. 1: 76–91.

———. 2004b. "Discontinuity and the Discourse of Conversion." *Journal of Religion in Africa* 34, nos. 1/2: 1–27.

————. 2005. "The Early Days of Johane Masowe: Self-doubt, Uncertainty, and Religious Transformation." *Comparative Studies in Society and History* 47, no. 4: 781–808.

Fabian, Johannes. 1969. "An African Gnosis: For a Reconsideration of an Authoritative Definition." *History of Religions* 9, no. 1: 42–58.

————. 1991. "Text as Terror: Second Thoughts about Charisma." In *Time and the Work of Anthropology: Critical Essays, 1971–1991*. Amsterdam: Harwood.

Fernandez, James. 1978. "African Religious Movements." *Annual Review of Anthropology* 7: 195–234.

Feuchtwang, Stephan, and Wang Mingming. 2001. *Grassroots Charisma: Four Local Leaders in China*. London: Routledge.

Geertz, Clifford. 1973c [1966]. "Religion as a Cultural System." In *The Interpretation of Cultures: Selected Essays*. New York: BasicBooks.

Gilmot, Jean-Francois. 1999. "Protestant Reformations and Reading." In *A History of Reading in the West*, ed. G. Cavallo and R. Chartier. Cambridge: Polity Press.

Guss, David. 1986. "Keeping it Oral: A Yekuana Ethnology." *American Ethnologist* 13, no. 3: 413–29.

Hofmeyr, Isabel. 1994. *"We Spend Our Year as a Tale that is Told:" Oral Historical Narrative in a South African Chiefdom*. Portsmouth, NH: Heinemann.

Horton, Robin. 1971. "African Conversion." *Africa* 41, no. 1: 85–108.

Jorgensen, Dan. 1980. "What's in a Name: The Meaning of Meaninglessness in Telefolmin." *Ethos* 8, no. 4: 349–63.

Keesing, Roger. 1987. "Anthropology as Interpretive Quest." *Current Anthropology* 28, no. 2: 161–76.

Keller, Eva. 2004. "Towards Complete Clarity: Bible-study among Seventh-day Adventists in Madagascar." *Ethnos* 69, no. 1: 89–112.

Lan, David. 1985. *Guns and Rain: Guerrillas and Spirit Mediums in Zimbabwe*. Berkeley: University of California Press.

Maxwell, David. 2001. "'Sacred History, Social History': Traditions and Texts in the Making of a Southern African Transnational Religious Movement." *Comparative Studies in Society and History* 43, no. 3: 502–524.

McLuhan, Marshall. 1969. *The Gutenberg Galaxy: The Making of Typographic Man*. New York: Signet Books.

Mignolo, Walter. 1994. "Signs and their Transmission: The Question of the Book in the New World." In *Writing Without Words: Alternative Literacies in Mesoamerica and the New World*, ed. E. H. Boone and W. Mignolo. Durham: Duke University Press.

Mukonyora, Isabel. 2000. "Marginality and Protest in the Wilderness: The Role of Women in Shaping Masowe Thought Pattern." *Southern African Feminist Review* 4, no. 2: 1–22.

Murphree, Marshall. 1969. *Christianity and the Shona*. London: Athlone Press.

Probst, Peter. 1989. "The Letter and the Spirit: Literacy and Religious Authority in the History of the Aladura Movement in Western Nigeria." *Africa* 59, no. 4: 478–495.

Ranger, Terence. 1989. "Missionaries, Migrants, and the Manyika: The Invention of Ethnicity in Zimbabwe." In *The Creation of Tribalism in Southern Africa*, ed. L. Vail. Berkeley: University of California Press.

————. 1999. "Taking on the Missionary's Task: African Spirituality and the Mission Churches of Manicaland in the 1930s." *Journal of Religion in Africa* 29, no. 2: 175–205.

Robbins, Joel. 2001a. "God Is Nothing But Talk: Modernity, Language, and Prayer in a Papua New Guinea Society." *American Anthropologist* 103, no. 4: 901–12.

————. 2001b. "Ritual Communication and Linguistic Ideology." *Current Anthropology* 42, no. 5: 591–614.

Schnepel, Burkhard. 1987. "Max Weber's Theory of Charisma and its Applicability to Anthropological Research." *Journal of the Anthropological Society of Oxford* 18, no. 1: 26–48.

Smith, Jonathan Z. 1987. *To Take Place: Toward Theory in Ritual.* Chicago: University of Chicago Press.

Stock, Brian. 1990. *Listening for the Text: On the Uses of the Past.* Philadelphia: University of Pennsylvania Press.

Sundkler, Bengt, and Christopher Steed. 2000. *A History of the Church in Africa.* Cambridge: Cambridge University Press.

Turner, Victor. 1967. "*Mukanda*: The Rite of Circumcision." In *The Forest of Symbols.* Ithaca: Cornell University Press.

Weber, Max. 1963. *The Sociology of Religion.* Boston: Beacon.

———. 1978. *Economy and Society*, vol. 1, ed. G. Roth and C. Wittich. Berkeley: University of California Press.

Werbner, Richard. 1985. The Argument of Images: Zion to the Wilderness. In *Theoretical Explorations in African Religion*, ed. W. van Binsbergen and M. Schoffeleers. London: Routledge Kegan Paul.

Worsley, Peter. 1968. *The Trumpet Shall Sound: A Study of "Cargo" Cults in Melanesia.* 2nd ed. New York: Schocken Books.

4

RITUALS WITHOUT FINAL ACTS: PRAYER AND SUCCESS IN WORLD VISION ZIMBABWE'S HUMANITARIAN WORK

Erica Bornstein

Introduction: Ritual Context

It was a special Friday in the Harare office of World Vision Zimbabwe, an international Christian, nongovernmental organization (NGO). The director had convened his staff for the weekly prayer meeting, where on that particular day there was a visiting guest from the United States. This visitor, a member of the international board of directors, had come to the national office of World Vision Zimbabwe to lead a prayer meeting on the subject of success. It was a Bible study and an office politic.

The workers were accustomed to such weekly meetings. The preceding week I had witnessed one with a gospel choir led by one of the staff members. That had been a joyous occasion, an end-of-the week corporate ritual. This week's meeting, however, was more subdued; it was educational and instructive. The board member used the Bible and the metaphor of a ladder to distinguish between spiritual success and the inherent evil of seeking material success. Most of the Zimbabwean staff members attending were comparably wealthy in the context of a Zimbabwe sliding into economic decline, but they too felt pinched. Many had other jobs: the women knitted sweaters and sold and resold what they could. They were certainly not high on the ladder of material success. I was a comparatively wealthy person (and, like the visitor, a Californian), embodying aspirations of NGO staff members who longed to travel. I sat in a similar social space as an institutional board member: foreign, mobile, a woman with resources, from a nation defined by its material success.

During the prayer meeting, a corporate ritual of sorts (which I will elaborate upon at greater length below), the staff members seemed disinterested. The message of placing the spirit above material concerns was met with indifference.

I was alarmed at how the prayer meeting echoed colonial missionary relationships: a foreigner telling native staff that Christianity was a marker of success. But the staff slept in their chairs and slowly filtered out of the meeting. Was this a form of resistance to the visiting board member? No, I was to learn, such an interpretation was held only by me. For the Zimbabwean staff the prayer ritual that had taken place was not filled with corporate conflict. While discussing the event with staff in the subsequent weeks it became apparent that the ritual lacked meaning. This itself became meaningful to me, as an ethnographer on the watch for meanings being made. Where was I to turn to explain such a lack? As much as I tried to interpret it as a matter of misplaced understanding, of political obfuscation, or of disparate registers of understanding, I was mistaken. It was not meaningful, plain and simple. That meaning failed to arrive in this ritual context threatened to make it uninterpretable, which challenged my anticipation of meaning-making in the ethnography of ritual process.

This chapter is a story of my struggle with an ethnographic event, the struggle to make sense of what Victor Turner calls "social drama" (1957) and of anthropological meaning. At first I thought my difficulty was interpretive: I did not know what to make of the event. In retrospect, I see the problem as one of meaning, or rather, its absence. My analysis in this chapter is twofold: To explore an ethnographic absence of meaning and then question why, as an anthropologist searching for meaning, I was alarmed when it ceased to be present. The landscape of meaning's absence appeared on multiple registers. The discourse of Christian development, by both espousing material success and cautioning against its evils, contained the seeds of its own destruction. The backdrop for this meeting was the political context of Zimbabwe after structural adjustment, where a crisis of meaning dominated a rural populace who had lost faith in the state as a provider of social welfare. Finally, my meaning-making task as an ethnographer was challenged by an instance where meaning remained perpetually elusive.

My case focuses on the transnational NGO World Vision in Zimbabwe. At the time of my research in 1996–97, World Vision was involved in rural agricultural development. This included drilling boreholes for clean drinking water, providing education, initiating irrigation schemes, sanitation programs, and micro-enterprise development (Bornstein 2005). Like secular NGOs, World Vision Zimbabwe targeted populations in need and worked with them using the contemporary development paradigms of participatory rural appraisal and needs assessment. Unlike secular NGOs, however, the discourse of development in World Vision was intricately woven with the discourse of Christianity. Simultaneous ambassadors of Christianity and neoliberal economics, Zimbabwean employees of World Vision were lucky to be employed. The economics of the time were such that many employees were not far removed economically from the impoverished rural constituencies that World Vision worked to "develop." In fact, shortly after I returned from Zimbabwe I received a letter from a World Vision employee who had lost his job. Having returned to his rural home, he was writing to source funds for a grinding mill in his own village. Previously part of the staff members who helped others in need, he had—at the moment of losing his employment—become one of those in need. This instability was political, economic, and existential for many Zimbabweans; it formed the backdrop for the programs of economic development World Vision sponsored and for the weekly prayer meeting.

Zimbabwe in the late 1990s was politically and economically precarious. The state, weakened after ten years of structural adjustment, depended upon NGOs like World Vision to provide social services for an increasingly disgruntled populace (Hanlon 2000; Bond 1998). Rising inflation and unemployment exacerbated the effects of structural adjustment, which for most Zimbabweans meant daily economic hardship (Potts 1998). Zimbabweans no longer depended upon the state for social welfare programs. As much as the post-independence history of Zimbabwe was one of promises broken, the rural populace had come to depend on NGOs instead of the state for its social welfare. Many Zimbabweans expressed a sense of hopelessness and a loss of faith in ZANU-PF, the ruling party. One could say that the work of NGOs gained meaning as the primary provider of social welfare. It was in this context that one event—simultaneously a ritual presentation, a staff meeting, and a Bible-study session promoting economic development—came to resemble a drama in the "theater of the absurd."

Development as a Drama in the Theater of the Absurd

There is a danger in comparing the text of a theatrical drama, a map of possibility interpreted in staged form by directors and audiences, and a social event, an ethnographic moment witnessed and interpreted by an anthropologist. Nevertheless, I make the comparison in order to illuminate the elusive nature of ritual, and its challenge to ethnographic assumptions of meaning. The performance of drama as a stage medium is also elusive. It is an ethereal form experienced in the moment. Both ritual and dramatic performance manifest the potential of indeterminacy inherent in social order (Moore 1978), and it is to this indeterminacy that I will turn. The theater of the absurd presents us with the possibility of indeterminacy's dominance, of dramatic moments where meaning fails to arrive. In drawing an analogy between the theater of the absurd and an ethnographic case I do not intend a direct comparison; rather, I offer it as a gesture toward understanding how to conceive, ethnographically, that which eludes meaning.

References to the theater of the absurd usually describe the work of dramatists of the 1950s and 1960s—Albert Camus, Samuel Beckett, Jean Genet, Harold Pinter, Eugene Ionesco—who made the bewildering and deeply troubling assertion that meaning is indecipherable. In theatrical terms, these artists broke dramatic conventions. They shocked viewers with surreal, illogical, and sometimes plotless narratives. Viewers were not shocked into meaning but shocked into the existential possibility that there was no meaning. To interpret the ethnographic event of the NGO prayer meeting as a conflict of meaning or as an act of resistance was at first a tempting alternative. But while these are the more hopeful conclusions I first considered, they are not the conclusions I reached. My comparison of absurdist theater to the development context of post-1990s Zimbabwe is an effort to acknowledge an environment where both human agency and the cosmic assumptions of one's place in the world were thrown into question and remained unresolved. In post-structural adjustment Zimbabwe, the religious ritual of prayer in an NGO meeting came to resemble a play in the theater of the absurd when such questions remained hauntingly unanswered.[1]

The play *Waiting for Godot* (Beckett 1955), for example, is a drama in which nothing happens. It is, perhaps, about indeterminacy itself. There is much room for interpretation in this drama. Meaning is not forthcoming from either the author or the actors. However, the play is not meaningless. It represents a space of logical uncertainty in which indeterminacy dwells. One cannot rely on what is said. Rather, one depends on the total experience of the drama to come away with the anxiety of uncertainty. It is the waiting, as the primary narrative plot, that produces the anxiety of anticipation without end. Here lies my parallel with the economic anxiety of Zimbabwe in the late 1990s. In the prayer meeting with the visiting board member, there was a certain irony in the topic of "success" being conceived in terms of salvation and not materialism. Success was the endpoint, the goal that served as counterpoint to the reality of the apathy, unraveling, and dissipation of the audience. The intent-driven focus of the prayer session on success contrasted with the apathy of the audience that melted away: falling asleep, slowly leaving, and ignoring her address. The visiting board member was cast in a drama of the theater of the absurd in which non sequiturs roamed alongside a lack of meaning.

I ask readers to bear with my ricochet between historical contexts—between an ethnographic moment and the dramatic stage. I do this, again, for the sake of comparative example. The subject of the play *Waiting for Godot* is waiting. The dialogue is nonlinear, timeless yet anticipatory. There is no resolution. At the end of Act I, one of the tramps, Estragon, says "Well shall we go?" Vladimir, the other tramp responds "Yes, let's go." The stage directions note: "(They do not move. Curtain)." Act II begins with the stage direction: "(Next Day. Same Time. Same Place)." At the end of Act II, the characters have switched lines but the lines remain the same. Vladimir asks: "Well? Shall we go?" and Estragon replies "Yes, let's go." The stage directions note: "(They do not move. Curtain)." The end of each act and the end of the play are defined by the closing of the curtain. One could imagine its repetition existing in eternity, of stalemate and stagnation. It is only the dramatic convention of the theater that closes the curtain, forcing an end if not a conclusion. The dialogue of the characters is filled with a tone of futility:

Estragon: I'm tired! (Pause) Let's go.

Vladimir: We can't.

Estragon: Why not?

Vladimir: We're waiting for Godot.

Estragon: Ah! (Pause. Despairing) What'll we do, what'll we do!

> Vladimir: There's nothing we can do.
>
> Estragon: But I can't go on like this.
>
> Vladimir: Would you like a radish?
>
> Estragon: Is that all there is?
>
> Vladimir: There are radishes and turnips. (Beckett 1955: 68)

Vladimir's "Would you like a radish?" does not answer Estragon's question of "What'll we do?" Nor does it respond to the couplet: "There's nothing we can do" and "But I can't go on like this." The response of a "radish" to the existential question is but one instance of the absurdity of this dialogue where non sequiturs are the logic of the narrative.

Absurdist drama highlights human incapacity to grasp the direction of existence. In this theatrical form humans are not in control. There is a seeming lack of human agency. Characters are in a constant frenzy of activity, yet Vladimir and Estragon are not able to *do* anything. They are waiting for a man they have not met. They contemplate suicide as perhaps their only act of agency. Characters are beaten with helpless resignation. Pozzo becomes blind and Lucky becomes dumb by no apparent act except fate. The phrases, "Nothing to be done" and "Nothing to show" are repeated throughout the play as a dramatic refrain. With the backdrop of helplessness, there is the inevitability of fate: "Nothing we can do about it," "It's inevitable," "It's of no importance," and "Nothing happens, nobody comes, nobody goes."[2]

The task of dramas in the theater of the absurd was not to answer philosophical questions but to emphasize the questions themselves.[3] Plays had no story or plot, characters lacked subtlety of motivation, and there was no beginning or end. The plays were not about cause and effect. They explored the contingency and instability of the human being and the impotence of reason. Martin Esslin, one of the first critics to recognize the "absurdist" group, describes this absurdity in an almost musical sense, as "out of harmony with reason or propriety; incongruous, unreasonable, illogical" (1974: 5). Historically, the theater of the absurd emerged amidst the anguish of Europe after the Holocaust, and the post-WWII horror of the nuclear bomb. The 1950s were also the early years of the Cold War, marked by political passivity as well as generalized anger and anxiety, which the theater of the absurd expressed. Absurdist dramas depicted stasis, defeat, and an unshakeable alienation that could not be resolved through intellectualist strategies. It was a theater of rejection, isolation, and futility that directly preceded the politically activist movements of the 1960s, the theatrical experiments of Jerzy Growtowski, the site-specific spectacles of the Bread and Puppet Theater, and the Theatre of Cruelty of Antonin Artaud.[4]

A Dramatic Visitor and Rituals of Prayer and Success

Let us return to my ethnographic case. Against a backdrop of the failing Zimbabwean economy and polity, the daily work worlds of Word Vision employees revolved around discourses of success and the ritual of Christian prayer. At field sites as well as offices, prayer was part of development. In the administrative office in Harare, prayer structured mandatory organizational forums. For example, prayer meetings called "devotions" were held every morning. Prayer functioned in the corporate structure as ritual reinforcement of a World Vision community, linking employees to each other, and the corporate office to the activities of the field. Devotions, sometimes including guest speakers, were a weekly institutional focal point, reflecting and shaping NGO community life. At the beginning of each fiscal year, an Annual Day of Prayer was held in the International Office in California and in each national office, like that in Zimbabwe, where development projects were situated.

Prayer was taken seriously by World Vision as a transnational organization. It was even included in the NGO's corporate origin myth. I was repeatedly told how the founder, Bob Pierce, started World Vision through prayer. A monthly "Prayer Guide" was printed by the International Office, listing a different country to be prayed for each day, and details of what should be prayed for. In addition to daily devotions, Fridays consisted of devotions that broke into departmentally clustered staff meetings. In each office, prayer formed an integral aspect of corporate order, one in which an inspirational atmosphere could be maintained, and problems and concerns could be aired.[5] In Zimbabwe, the assistant to the national director described prayer as an important part of faith in the organization, something that brought people together and transcended the workaday world of duties and responsibilities. It created a community in which employees were concerned about each other and depended on prayer. He explained: "We are always praying for each other. Praying even for major decisions, praying for water to be found, or for resources to be found and things like that."

As much as the act of prayer ritually integrated the development work of World Vision, the discourse of success formed its axis. Success in World Vision was measured in terms of acceptance of Christianity and of material improvement. This dual measure was applied to development projects and staff performance alike. For example, staff members were evaluated annually on their "commitment to Christ" as well as their performance in the economic duties of administering funds and managing projects. Rural projects were also evaluated in terms of their "improvement"—evangelistically according to the acceptance of Christianity, and economically in terms of boreholes drilled, irrigation schemes initiated, and micro-enterprise programs commenced. This dual nature of success in World Vision produced a critical contradiction: while World Vision strove to make the economic success of individuals morally acceptable in the face of widespread suspicion of such practices (primarily because of witchcraft), it advocated the "Christian" behavior of benevolence and selflessness. While promoting the materialism of micro-enterprise strategies, which carried with it the temptations of greed and avarice, Christianity was presented as an antidote to this potential evil. In an attempt to create an ethnographically coherent structure of meaning, one could say that Christian development contained the seeds of its own destruction. Analytically, it can be interpreted as either a contradiction or a lack of meaning: a tension within the organization that inspired employees to continually reposition their own orientation to institutional theory and practice. It was a space where meaning had the potential to be continually remade. However, in the instance with which I began, and to which I shall now turn in more detail, contradictory pulls of meaning created a site where meaning failed to attain its unity and thus ceased to exist.

I present this ritual context to situate the prayer meeting as part of a larger picture. It is only one case, after all, but it is a case of something significant within World Vision. It was an ethnographic moment where things seemed to come together for me in the field, where I felt, analytically, that I was on to something really important. Once again, prayer was a structure within World Vision where institutional meanings were made. Through institutional pedagogy, these meanings were enforced. However, I was not prepared for the absurd, the space of meaning's absence that emerged surrounding the topic of success during a prayer meeting. In this event, an example of ritual process, the potential for corporate meaning and solidarity was met with silence, apathy, and desertion.

During staff devotions at World Vision Zimbabwe in Harare on that particular Friday there was a guest speaker. She was an older woman, American, blond, and a member of World Vision's international board of directors who had come to lead the weekly devotions on the topic of success. Her reason for coming to Zimbabwe from southern California was to lead what one World Vision staff member called the weekly "hour of power," an hour of prayer, as part of a worldwide tour called "Scripture Search" that explored, as she described it, the "practical life of the scriptures and what we are doing about that as an organization." Devotions that Friday were more akin to a corporate seminar than a prayer session, although there was plenty of praying. The meeting was an extended weekly prayer meeting. It lasted three and a half hours, and I perceived it to encapsulate the essence of World Vision's transnational, corporate Christian strategy. To me, it was ethnographically meaningful.

The room was filled with rows of chairs, as in a theater. At the front of the room stood a table with an overhead projector, and some posters and dioramas of World Vision's projects were displayed at the periphery of the room. On the wall hung a map marking World Vision's sixty four community project sites in Zimbabwe. A senior staff member gave an introduction and asked us, the audience, to pray and dance to show that we were "happy." The field officers and NGO staff suddenly became the subjects of World Vision's development. No longer facilitators, they were being evaluated by the director and the board member in the same manner that these employees had been accustomed to evaluating the rural beneficiaries of aid: through their performance. We sang and prayed with Shona songs. Rounds and choruses, one woman started, others followed, clapping in syncopated rhythms. The assistant director of World Vision Zimbabwe talked about the "activities and what we become in the process of what we do," and told the group that we were "setting aside the day to look at us becoming people that God can use in spirit." He explained that later in the afternoon there would be a review of World Vision Zimbabwe's activities by the director of Field Ministries (the staff member in the Harare office who oversaw all the development projects in Zimbabwe). The director of Field Ministries made her presentation on the work of World Vision in Zimbabwe. It was long and detailed, and geared for the ears of the visiting board member. Most of the Zimbabwean staff looked bored; some were falling asleep. It was their world, their life, being told back to them. At the end of the presentation, the board member remarked on how thorough the presentation had been. A promotional videotape of World Vision's projects in Zimbabwe was then shown. The staff members, residents of Zimbabwe, were very familiar with this tape. Thus far, my depiction may sound familiar: a corporate ritual—secular or religious—enacted for the benefit of the visiting board member.

After being formally introduced by the national director, the board member addressed World Vision Zimbabwe about the Christianity of World Vision: "The core phrase is: we follow Jesus Christ. We follow Jesus, and we find ourselves taken into this particular work. We want to focus on following Jesus. I will begin with a metaphor, an image, to define success in life. But first I want you to break into small groups." She directed us into small groups and told us to define success. Staff members came and went; no one seemed particularly interested in the topic of the day. We came back together as a group and listened to the board member define success as moving from a "lower to a higher level, and success as following Jesus." She contrasted success in the material world with success in following Jesus. She drew a picture of a ladder with a felt marking pen on a large pad of paper, and explained:

> With a ladder you go from lower to higher level, the ladder is a powerful metaphor in the culture of the world as a way of thinking about defining the success of human beings. Climbing the ladder of success, moving from lower to higher areas like status. Success is achieving higher and higher status, reputation, what people think, having more and more people think more of us. Power is personal success, achieving more power.

The seminar, to me, seemed terribly familiar, terribly American. The board member continued:

> People are born to different places on the ladder. The poor sometimes can't get on the ladder. The ladder of success involves status, reputation, power, and rewards. People measure how well they are doing in terms of a ladder, in comparison with other people. We tend to think: if I am not moving up, climbing, if I am staying where I am, I am not succeeding. It feeds competition and creates discouragement. This is the way the world uses as a way of thinking. It can lead to discouragement and despair.

She directed us to look at the Scriptures, leading a group Bible study on success. Her next concern was the account of the temptations faced by Jesus. She began to talk about World Vision. "We are those who have been called—we have heard the Good News. We are called in ministry with the poor, the captive . . . between the two experiences, there is the temptation account." Her preaching blurred distinctions between biblical verse that described Jesus' directives, and the work of World Vision; they became one and the same. World Vision field officers followed in the footsteps of Jesus. They were contemporary Jesuses. In practice, I thought, working for World Vision, for Zimbabweans, was more a matter of having an excellent job than a spiritual quest.

At the time, I was struck by the gulf of meaning between the World Vision board member who came from the United States with a vision of what motivated people, and the economic realities that propelled people to survive in Zimbabwe. Staff members of World Vision in Zimbabwe were poor in the global context, and they were also trying to help themselves out of their own poverty, materially. An NGO job was a good job. It meant someone was doing well in Zimbabwe. Yet this board member was saying it was a temptation to try and succeed materially, that it was more graceful to walk with the poor as Jesus did. The irony seemed a bitter one. By helping others less fortunate than themselves, poorer than themselves, they defined themselves through comparison—they stood on a higher rung on her ladder of success.

We broke into our small Bible study groups again to analyze specific Bible passages for "temptations," and came back together to discuss our biblical reflections.[6] After each small group told the larger group what it had found, the board member advocated bringing the love of God to the world as World Vision's mission. She described three temptations that Jesus, and World Vision staff, faced while helping the poor:

> The devil also quotes scripture. It is not enough to quote the Bible; you must understand what the Bible means. The challenge is the confusion of means and ends. Jesus has a mission, which is to be the Savior, to be God's messiah, and to bring the love of God to the world. It is the same as World Vision's mission. The challenge is the Kingdom, and Jesus' call to be the King is the end. Temptation is about how should the rule of God be established? And what is the way, the relationship between the methods used and the results sought. Must we adopt the world's methods to achieve God's purpose?

The first temptation, she explained, was to be self-absorbed and to meet one's own needs. She described how the temptation, for Jesus, was to meet his own needs first rather than being concerned for others to whom he was called. She explained as a correlative a World Vision "Core Value," which was: "We value people." In the work of World Vision, this temptation was manifested as a focus on the material instead of the spiritual dimension of success:

> Temptation asks, which people do we value? Jesus is tempted to value himself and not to discipline himself for those he is to serve—to center on himself and meet his own needs. Jesus responds: It is written, one does not live by bread alone. Bread is necessary, Jesus is hungry. The physical needs of people are important. Jesus says: I must meet both the spiritual and physical needs of the people. It is God's will. God's disclosure is the revelation of his love. This is as important as the physical for human beings. Jesus is being tempted to focus only on the physical. The world considers success more to succeed on the physical side; it doesn't care about the spiritual side. Jesus declares his ministry is to meet the needs of the poor, and to preach the good news of the gospel.

The second temptation, she said, was to impress, to be spectacular and flashy instead of being a humble servant. She said,

> People are wanting only what Jesus could give them—to be part of spectacular suc-
> cess. In World Vision we want to succeed and fulfill the will of God, and there
> are right ways and wrong ways to achieve success. A wrong way is with outward
> spectacular [*sic*]. A right way is through quiet servitude, small acts of compassion,
> unimpressive ministry, walking beside people, touching the leper to bring healing,
> speaking to the sick with kindness. Jesus didn't do the spectacular thing. He did the
> quiet servant thing.

At this point I wondered to myself, rather cynically, whether the African audience wanted to be quiet servants. The word servant connects two things:
serving others, and being economically subservient. In this presentation, the
contemporary missionary meaning of servitude harmonically converged with
its colonial interpretation. It sounded like preaching subservience, to people
who knew its meaning far more than she did, in the form of corporate ritual.
She continued:

> Jesus did not want to use the world's methods to achieve the word of God. He did
> not go for reputation; he did not climb the ladder. He came down and became a
> servant. The way of Jesus is the opposite of the way of the world. It is not the way of
> climbing. When he was tempted by the way that would give him a reputation. God
> has not promised spectacles, miraculous deliverance from putting yourself in a place
> of foolishness (as in jumping from the top of the temple). You must not test God,
> but must submit. Faith that says 'I don't need to do the small things' is arrogance.

The third temptation in her recounting was being offered worldly things.
Again, the analogy between the work of World Vision and the work of Jesus
was direct. Jesus was offered all the kingdoms in the world and all their splen-
dor. She explained it in terms of power:

> In communities, sometimes it is tempting to rely on power—the one who has the
> gold rules instead of the golden rule. Using power, domination, or force to achieve
> what God wants to do can be emotional, coercive, asserting dignities and privi-
> leges. To worship the ways of the world is to worship the false God, at the wrong
> altars. The path of power is the path of destruction and domination. Jesus chose
> not to be born in Rome, in the emperor's palace, but in Bethlehem, in poverty. We
> follow the one who walks with people, who refused the way of power and might.
> Instead, he chose the way of listening, of love, of learning, of obedience. Jesus
> learned obedience from the things he suffered. I have been on the board of World
> Vision for 17 years. I know that money and resources will not fix all the problems
> of the world. The problems must be fixed through the heart with the love of God,
> person to person . . .

We took a ten-minute break and then returned for a summary discussion on
Jesus and biblical approaches to success. The board member spoke of following "the way of love, of Jesus, the way of the cross, of sacrifice, servanthood"
instead of the "values and methods of the world, society, culture outside of the
faith." She urged the workers to remember that the mission of World Vision

was sharing the love of Jesus Christ "with those who need to know it through the disciplines of prayer, knowing and reading the scriptures, studying the scriptures, and the way of worship." She continued:

> Prayer, scripture, and worship are the spiritual under girding of our sense of identity. This is what we mean when we talk in the mission statement about following Jesus. It isn't just the work we do with the poor, but the way we do the work, and the motivation and strength we find. We believe what we believe, and we walk in the way of Christ.

Once again, she read the "Core Values" that constituted World Vision's institutional mission. The national director then asked her to talk a bit about World Vision's structure and work in other countries, which she did. World Vision Zimbabwe staff members were then encouraged to ask questions.

I wondered what the Zimbabweans thought of this woman from southern California, and whether or not they felt these devotions were corporate indoctrination. I asked around after the meeting, but I seemed to be the only person who was interested. To the rest of the staff, it was simply irrelevant, another weekly prayer meeting with an invited guest. After the break, many of them did not return. The room was only half as full as it had been in the morning. As the meeting closed, the assistant director thanked the board member and said, "I feel I have become Christian for the first time after having the [biblical] passage explained to us. Now I know what it means to be Christian for the first time. We need this kind of teaching, to measure our Christianity on world standards. It is a very special day for us, to develop us from where you have left us." I turned to the communications director sitting next to me to see her reaction to this statement, and noticed that she was asleep. The assistant director asked the audience to give songs of praise and a closing prayer. This time, we sang in English: "He will lift you up. Humble yourself before the Lord. And He will lift you up." The national director stopped our singing. It was not lively enough. He told us to start over again, to be more cheerful. So we, the audience, started again.

When Rituals Become Social Dramas Without Final Acts

If this case resembles a drama in the theater of the absurd, what does that add to our ethnographic understanding of ritual? The use of a theatrical paradigm is not new in anthropology or in the study of ritual. Victor Turner has used the framework of social drama to analyze a particularly reflective social form through which meaning is made (Turner 1957). If daily living is theater, then social drama is metatheater in which actors dramatize what they are doing to an audience. Perhaps my use of existentialist playwrights as an analogy to World Vision Zimbabwe's social dramas is a stretch. But I make it in order to challenge an ethnographic assumption about the search for meaning, which emerges from Geertz's semiotic concept of culture and the interpretive process through which the ethnographer searches for meaning and constructs it while writing ethnography (Geertz 1973).[7]

Victor Turner's analysis of social drama is based on his work among the Ndembu of Northwest Zambia. In his essay "The Anthropology of Performance," he quotes dramatist Richard Schechner describing his work: "Victor Turner analyzes 'social dramas' using theatrical terminology to describe disharmonic or crisis situations. These situations—arguments, combats, rites of passage—are inherently dramatic because participants not only do things, they try *to show others what they are doing or have done*. Actions take on a 'performed-for-an-audience' aspect" (in Turner 1986: 74). Crisis arises because any change in status involves the readjustment of a social scheme, which is effected ceremonially through theater. Social dramas are "units of aharmonic or disharmonic social process, arising in conflict situations" that have four phases of public action: (1) the breach of regular norm-governed social relations; (2) a crisis, during which the breach tends to widen; (3) redressive action ranging from personal advice and informal mediation or arbitration to formal juridical and legal machinery and the performance of public ritual; and (4) the final phase, which consists either of the reintegration of the disturbed social group, or of the social recognition and legitimation of the irreparable schism between contesting parties (1986: 74–75).

Building on Turner's processual approach, Sally Falk Moore's work on reglementary processes (1978) explores the tension between law as rules, man-made intentional action, and efforts to circumvent this action. Thus law is both an intentionally constructed framework of social order and, at the same time, the manipulation of the system. Moore's work offers an interesting counterpart to Turner's work on ritual. Specifically, her focus is on the inherent uncertainty and indeterminacy in order and law making (and for the sake of this argument, I will bring it back to ritual as does Turner's later work on social drama [see Turner 1974]). Although Turner does factor in "anti-structure" in his model of ritual action and its role in maintaining social order, it is not quite the same as Moore's idea of indeterminacy. For Moore, as much as law attempts to organize and control behavior through the use of explicit rules, the study of rules also involves occasions when rules are not communicated or invoked. While Moore is in agreement with Turner that making symbolic order is an active process, she focuses on how orders are vulnerable to being unmade, remade, and transformed. The processual analysis that Moore proposes emerges from Turner's analysis of ritual, analyzing social situations over time to explore continuity and change. Yet in contrast to Turner's model of redress after a breach, and the restoration of social order, for Moore order never completely takes over. Rules and customs exist but always in the presence of indeterminacy and ambiguity. The whole matter of reglementary action contains a paradox: every action includes elements of the regular (order) and elements of the indeterminate. Both are "used" by individuals (Moore 1978: 40). Rituals are part of a process of regularization, and for Moore they "constitute the explicit cultural framework through which the attempt is made to fix social life, to keep it from slipping into the sea of indeterminacy" (1978: 41). Yet, there are instances when rituals fail and where meaning is indeterminate.[8] In my ethnographic case of the prayer meeting and in absurdist drama, meaning is elusive. Although ethnographers may search for the possibility of narrative resolution, dramatists in the theater of the absurd offer a representational alternative that may be troubling for anthropologists. Social life that remains logically indeterminate and unstable challenges anthropological assumptions of human agency in ritual process.

In Turner's later work on social drama he made a direct connection to stage theater (1974). Although Turner has been critiqued for this move, his work is worth revisiting for its lasting contribution to debates surrounding agency. Some anthropologists of ritual consider it to be a form of agency and praxis (see Firth 1974; Devisch 1993; De Boeck and Devisch 1994). Their critiques of Turner argue that he was too cognitivist (Devisch 1993), found too much of a focus on order and on conflict resolution (De Boeck and Devisch 1994), did not, in his model, allow for the agency of individuals (Firth 1974), and, did not sufficiently elaborate upon the moral aspects of redress and its fulfillment (Jules-Rosette 1998). Devisch takes Turner to task for conceiving a model of ritual process with a Western, linear temporality. But in my ethnographic case his model happens to be applicable, since the speaker from California represented Western temporality in her corporate-structured presentation on success. Firth has critiqued Turner's use of drama as a descriptive and analytical device (1974). He argues that to consider it a paradigm for understanding conflict resolution and the "disharmonic aspects of social life" is to rely upon an element of fatality. Action is taken not out of choice, but as "a kind of preordained mental pressure upon individuals by codes of their society which they hold to be axiomatic." Firth finds fault with Turner's use of social drama to interpret social life, and asks, "Who is to recognize the dramatic, representational or symbolic quality of what is happening . . . ? The people themselves or the anthropologist?" (1974: 966). He finds the actor to be a dangerous model because it stresses the performance of a role rather than individual initiative. Using social drama as a model with lead performers may "undervalue" the roles of all others concerned to the degree that they become spectators rather than participants. In this way, the drama concept polarizes the "interests" and "actions" of ordinary folk. Finally, Firth argues there is a danger of using such a stylized aesthetic concept as an interpretive model. The anthropologist risks becoming the dramatist who shapes, distorts, and contrives the data!

The prayer meeting, however, actually did take place in a dramatic context; it was theatrical and it was staged. There was an actor, the visiting board member, and an audience, the World Vision Zimbabwe staff. The group prayer study was a staged event, a literal drama, as well as a social drama in Turner's ritual use of the term with all of its allusions to social order. The visiting board member may very well have been trying to maintain corporate order in the transnational NGO. Perhaps it was a form of social engineering, a demonstration of reglementary structure. The directive was to remind staff members how to act in relation to success: to pay attention to spiritual instead of material gain. Yet while the ethnographic context may lend itself to bringing back Turner and his critics, the conclusion is not one of conflict resolution and redress. Moreover, the conflict did not lie between actor and spectators. Instead it existed, if at all, between actors and the backdrop of the wider economic context that produced a sense of fatalism in the audience (precisely what Firth argues against). If there was a breach in the meeting when the staff left and slept there was no redress, no sanction, only apathy.

Here Moore's contribution of indeterminacy as part of social process may assist us in understanding the ritual of the institutional prayer meeting. That this meeting echoed the larger structure (as in Turner) of weekly prayer meetings in all of World Vision was important. Ritual was a means of maintaining order and hence a corporate objective. If, as my informants told me, the weekly prayer meetings were places where problems could be discussed and grievances aired, in some ways it did resemble Turner's model of social drama among the Ndembu. However, the actors (the sleeping and waning audience included) were not necessarily in a generative process of worldmaking (cf. De Boeck and Devisch 1994). The silence, helplessness, and apathy that the audience exhibited, spoke to cosmic dissonance instead of harmony. This instance of theatrical narrative in the dialogue about prayer and success lends itself to analogy with the theater of the absurd, where meaning is not clear or does not exist. Instead of social drama as a ritual space where individuals make their worlds, the social drama of the Zimbabwean prayer meeting was one where actors did not have agency. To leave the meeting or to sleep was not an act of resistance to authority. Praxis simply did not exist.

How does an overture to order become an absurdist drama without a final act? In my case of the prayer meeting in World Vision's Harare office, there seemed to be the potential to reaffirm the solidarity of membership. Structurally, the prayer meeting fit into Turner's ritual structure. Staff members gathered together weekly, often with a guest speaker. At some point the staff was broken into smaller groups for Bible study. This liminal phase had the potential for breach or crisis, giving staff members an opportune moment to leave. There was some risk of desertion, or even greater, of conflict between Zimbabwean staff and management and/or between national and international staff. Thus there were plenty of possible fissures where the indeterminacy of ritual process might break through. After the work groups, the entire group came together. This structure was part of World Vision's larger structure of weekly prayer. Prayer meetings in the Harare office frequently devolved into staff meetings, sites to resolve crisis or for crises to be brought up, aired, and worked through. Ideally, the corporate goal was harmony and order.

However, in my case there was no resolution. The crisis was itself the backdrop for the ritual of performance. The performance dramatized an irresolvable existential predicament. Hence my ethnographic case deviates from Turner's analysis of ritual and performance to consider the possibility of failure, of there being no resolution. Here is where the theater of the absurd once again becomes relevant. As in dramas in the theater of the absurd, irresolvable existential anguish may become the preamble for political action. One could interpret the later violence of 2000 in Zimbabwe as such action emerging from the anguish. But the acknowledgment of the absurd and irresolution is not political itself, even if it does represent nascent politics and change. My case is an instance where the structure of the Zimbabwean economy was in such disarray that a non-action, or an absence of meaning, came to the front of the stage and spoke through its silence. As actors in this social drama, NGO employees not only percieved the stage they performed on in a different social register from that of the visiting board member that came to direct them in a weekly prayer reflection on the topic of success, they lived the struggles she preached about. As such embodied participants in the drama, their response to her presentation was a performance of absurdist proportions: exhaustion, boredom, apathy, and anomie.

Conclusion: Ethnography and the Elusion of Meaning

Meaning's absence, as I have been discussing it here, is not the same as meaninglessness. In Beckett's play *Waiting for Godot*, the anticipated arrival of Mr. Godot does not occur. This is not the same as a play with no end. Such an anticipatory drama offers the possibility of hope (Bloch 1986; Miyazaki 2004). The work of Jacques Derrida (1976) has alerted us to the interpretive possibility of meaning's substitution, and of the potential for meaning to have perpetual arrival. But what if meaning fails to arrive?

There is no space for the absence of meaning in ethnography. Such events are ignored, put aside, or not written about. Ethnographically, they vanish and fade; they disappear from our analysis. The prayer meeting on success was not meaningful for Zimbabwean employees of World Vision. Meaningful statements depend on discursive formations—fields of use in which a statement must be placed to acquire its meaning (Foucault 1973). That the discourses of success were different for the Zimbabwean staff of World Vision and for the visiting board member is one explanation for the lack of meaning. One could argue that the American board member introduced a rhetoric that did not have the same discursive bearings in Zimbabwe as it did in the United States. This would be a simple conclusion. One could also interpret the event as an example of resistance to authority, or of contextual incongruity. But although the visiting board member spoke from a position of power and privilege, the workers' response was one of paralysis, not quiet resistance. The event was more than an instance of internal colonialism, of an attempt by a board member visiting from the West to discipline and educate the native Zimbabwean staff of a transnational NGO. In discussions with staff after the prayer meeting, I was struck by the extent to which the meeting was a non-event. They did not consider it important. One might interpret the event ethnographically as a radical misunderstanding. For example, one might argue that the visiting board member was insensitive to the fact that many Zimbabweans lived and struggled with poverty in their personal lives as well as in their jobs.[9] In contrast to this analysis, what if the concurrent perspectives of the board member and the Zimbabwean staff canceled each other out in the noise of radical incoherent coexistence? Without an analysis of power and resistance, one soon faces the possibility that a crisis of meaning has reached proportions of the absurd.

For me as an ethnographer, the absence of meaning of the event was shocking, and its indeterminancy was ethnographically destabilizing. This is what has led me to the conclusion I prefer to draw. As in the post-WWII context that inspired the existential crises of playwrights in the theater of the absurd, poststructural adjustment Zimbabwe was overtaken by the loss of meaning. It was a political and economic crisis in which the ground of expectation was removed. Zimbabweans had lost faith in the government and the promises of independence that guaranteed the education, health, and social welfare of newly liberated citizens.[10]

How does one discuss the absence—the non-presence—of meaning ethnographically? Perhaps this is a contradiction in terms. In my attempts to analyze the board member's visit, the lack of meaning was multidimensional. Meaning failed to emerge between the board member and her audience, as well as in my ethnographic understanding. Hence the multiple dimensions of absurdity as well. Prayer, as a ritual, created cohesion in the organization. This is what I heard and what I saw. However, when I attended this particular prayer meeting it was empty, vacuous of meaning. Of course, one might argue that people sleep in churches, prayer meetings, and corporate seminars all over the world. One could interpret this practice as passive resistance. But then, one again must assume there is meaning. There is no space for meaninglessness in ethnography. Written out, it does not appear. In my account of the board member's visit, language no longer mattered, and the absence of meaning became meaningful itself. I too found myself, ethnographically, making meaning of meaning's absence.

The search for meaning is bound to assumptions of agency in ritual process. To deny fate as an analytical possibility, in favor of human agency, is to reinforce the humanist and secularist assumptions upon which the discipline of anthropology is founded. To look at rituals from this perspective is to eliminate the possibility of the illogical. For something to be illogical or uninterpretable, ethnographically, is for it to be absurd. To interpret ritual as agency or worldmaking (De Boeck and Devisch 1994; Devisch 1993) as a productive process is to eliminate the possibility of ritual manifesting the absurd, the meaningless, and the helplessness of humans in the face of larger forces—whether political, economic, or divine. Rituals are only absurd when, having assumed that meaning is being made by and through them, we find that meaning is elusive. When we, as ethnographers, embrace the possibility of indeterminancy in ritual, we also acknowledge the realm of the sacred: that which cannot be spoken. To see a ritual as a social drama in the theater of the absurd no longer denies the sacred. No longer bound by logical impossibility, by the un-translatability of the sacred by the secular, ritual remains powerful even when it eludes ethnographic interpretation.

Acknowledgements

Support for the research and writing of this project was generously provided by the Pew Charitable Trusts (via OMSC) and Charlotte W. Newcombe Foundation. A fellowship at the Society for the Humanities at Cornell University 2003–04 provided a wonderful opportunity to rethink this material. Many thanks to World Vision staff in Zimbabwe for their patience with my presence.

Notes

1. Although the 1950s playwrights of the theater of the absurd were not religious, Esslin (1974) has argued that they sought to question the possibility of meaning in a world where religion no longer provided answers to questions of one's place in the universe.

2. Raymond Williams (1966) has written eloquently of the intimacy that emerges in the desolation of *Waiting for Godot* as the marker of a tragic rhythm. The travelers, Pozzo and Lucky—representing the "world of effort and action"—change places as master and slave between the two acts. These two characters represent relationships, of power and exploitation, which can easily be reversed, and eventually they consume themselves, becoming the blind leading the dumb. The two tramps, Vladimir and Estragon, on the other hand, do not change. They represent the "world of resignation and waiting," the way of compassion in degradation. "The possibility of human recognition, and of love, within a total condition still meaningless" (Williams 1966: 155). It is love in a stalemate, and the human condition is absolute. Yet the tramps stay together "with nothing to go for and nothing but disappointment to wait for, yet staying together, an old and deep tragic rhythm is recovered" (Williams 1966: 155).

3. Smallwood (1966) links this to existentialist philosophy.

4. Gaensbauer notes that the theater of the absurd, as a movement, was not completely apolitical: "For Sartre and Camus, recognition of the absurd was not an end in itself, but a springboard to a unique concept of freedom and from there to political engagement" (1991: xviii).

5. On ritual and social order see Turner (1969).

6. We discussed the Gospels of Matthew 4:1–11; Mark 1:12–13; and Luke 4:1–13, and focused our Bible study on Luke 4:1–13:

   Jesus, full of the Holy Spirit, returned from the Jordan and was led by the Spirit in the wilderness, where for forty days he was tempted by the devil. He ate nothing at all during those days, and when they were over, he was famished. The devil said to him, "If you are the Son of God, command this stone to become a loaf of bread." Jesus answered him, "It is written, 'One does not live by bread alone.'" Then the devil led him up and showed him in an instant all the kingdoms of the world. And the devil said to him, "To you I will give their glory and all this authority; for it has been given over to me, and I give it to anyone I please. If you, then, will worship me, it will all be yours." Jesus answered him, "It is written, 'Worship the Lord your God, and serve only him.'" Then the devil took him to Jerusalem, and placed him on the pinnacle of the temple, saying to him, "If you are the Son of God, throw yourself down from here, for it is written, 'He will command his angels concerning you, to protect you,' and 'On their hands they will bear you up, so that you will not dash your foot against a stone.'" Jesus answered him, "It is said, 'Do not put the Lord your god to the test.'" When the devil had finished every test, he departed from him until an opportune time. (*New Oxford Annotated Bible* 2001: 102–103 [NT])

7. I set out to conduct my fieldwork with Geertz's use of Weber in mind: that "man is an animal suspended in webs of significance he himself has spun" (Geertz 1973: 5). Culture is these webs, and the analysis of culture is the interpretive search for meaning. If, as Geertz has written, "doing ethnography is like trying to read (in the sense of 'construct a reading of') a manuscript—foreign, faded, full of ellipses, incoherencies, suspicions, emendations, and tendentious commentaries, but written not in conventialized graphs of sound but in transient examples of shaped behavior" (1973: 9), then the "text" of Christian development was like a play in the theater of the absurd.

8. Geertz raised this question several decades ago in his critique of functionalism and call for distinguishing between culture and social systems (see 1973 [1959]), as is discussed by Tomlinson and Engelke in chapter one of this volume. I ask the question here in a broader sense, with a more explicit focus on meaning and its limits vis-à-vis a comparative exercise with the theater of the absurd. Jules-Rosette (1998) also discusses the possibility that redress may not occur, although she still analyzes such situations in terms of conflict and the possibility of its eventual resolution.

9. I would like to thank Carol Delaney for her comments on an earlier presentation of this paper (at the AAA meetings in New Orleans), which helped clarify this aspect of my argument.
10. Compare this example with the expectations of modernity and the ethnography of decline in Zambia (Ferguson 1999).

References

Beckett, Samuel. 1955. *Waiting for Godot: A Tragicomedy in Two Acts*, trans. S. Beckett. London: Faber and Faber London.

Bloch, Ernst. 1986. *The Principle of Hope*, vol. 1. Trans. N. Plaice, S. Plaice, and P. Knight. Cambridge: MIT Press.

Bond, Patrick. 1998. *Uneven Zimbabwe: A Study of Finance, Development, and Underdevelopment*. Trenton: Africa World Press.

Bornstein, Erica. 2005. *The Spirit of Development: Protestant NGOs, Morality, and Economics in Zimbabwe*. Stanford: Stanford University Press.

De Boeck, Filip, and Rene Devisch. 1994. "Ndembu, Luuanda and Yaka Divination Compared: From Representation and Social Engineering to Embodiment and Worldmaking." *Journal of Religion in Africa* 24, no. 2: 98–133.

Derrida, Jacques. 1976. *Of Grammatology*. Trans. G. C. Spivak. Baltimore: The Johns Hopkins University Press.

Devisch, Rene. 1993. *Weaving the Threads of Life: The Khita Gyn-Eco-Logical Healing Cult Among the Yaka*. Chicago: University of Chicago Press.

Esslin, Martin. 1974. *The Theatre of the Absurd*. Rev. ed. London: Eyre Methuen.

Ferguson, James. 1999. *Expectations of Modernity: Myths and Meanings of Urban Life on the Zambian Copperbelt*. Berkeley: University of California Press.

Firth, Raymond. 1974. "Society and Its Symbols." *Times Literary Supplement*, September 13.

Foucault, Michel. 1973. *The Order of Things: An Archaeology of the Human Sciences*. New York: Vintage Books.

Gaensbauer, Deborah B. 1991. *The French Theater of the Absurd*. Boston: Twayne Publishers.

Geertz, Clifford. 1973. "Thick Description: Toward an Interpretive Theory of Culture." In *The Interpretation of Cultures: Selected Essays*. New York: BasicBooks.

Hanlon, Joseph. 2000. "An 'Ambitious and Extensive Political Agenda': The Role of NGOs and the AID Industry." In *Global Institutions and Local Empowerment: Competing Theoretical Perspectives*, ed. K. Stiles. New York: St. Martins Press.

Jules-Rosette, Bennetta. 1998. "Prophetic Performances: Apostolic Prophecy as Social Drama." *The Drama Review* 32: 140–59.

Miyazaki, Hirokazu. 2004. *The Method of Hope: Anthropology, Philosophy, and Fijian Knowledge*. Stanford: Stanford University Press.

Moore, Sally Falk. 1978. "Uncertainties in Situations, Indeterminacies in Culture." In *Law as Process: An Anthropological Approach*. London: Routledge and Kegan Paul.

The New Oxford Annotated Bible (New Revised Standard Version with the Apocrypha). 2001. Oxford: Oxford University Press.

Potts, Deborah. 1998. "'Basics Are Now a Luxury': Perceptions of Structural Adjustment's Impact on Rural and Urban Areas in Zimbabwe." *Environment and Urbanization* 10, no. 1: 55–75.

Smallwood, Clyde G. 1966. *Elements of the Existentialist Philosophy in the Theatre of the Absurd*. Dubuque: Wm. C. Brown Book Company.

Turner, Victor. 1957. *Schism and Continuity in an African Society: A Study of Ndembu Village Life*. Manchester: Manchester University Press.

1969. *The Ritual Process: Structure and Anti-Structure*. Ithaca: Cornell University Press.

1974. *Dramas, Fields, and Metaphors: Symbolic Action in Human Society*. Ithaca: Cornell University Press.

1986. *The Anthropology of Performance*. New York: PAJ Publications.

Williams, Raymond. 1966. "Tragic Deadlock and Stalemate: Chekhov, Pirandello, Ionesco, Beckett." In *Modern Tragedy*. Stanford: Stanford University Press.

5

NATIONALISM AND MILLENARIANISM IN WEST PAPUA: INSTITUTIONAL POWER, INTERPRETIVE PRACTICE, AND THE PURSUIT OF CHRISTIAN TRUTH

Danilyn Rutherford

What is the relationship between people's experience of Christian institutions and the meanings they attribute to Christian texts? Anthropologists have offered a straightforward answer to this question. Christian missions, schools, and churches promote particular interpretations of scripture and ritual in an effort to produce particular kinds of believers (see Asad 1993; Rafael 1993 [1988]; Comaroff and Comaroff 1991, 1997; Cannell 1999; Schrauwers 2000; Aragon 2000; cf. Bowen 1993, Foucault 1979). Christian institutions achieve this "disciplinary" outcome because they are dense sites of power, "the effect of a network of motivated practices" ranging from brute force to spiritual and material sanctions and incentives, from ecclesiastical law to routinized habits of self-cultivation and control (Asad 1993: 35).[1] Yet this straightforward answer does not offer us a way of accounting for the mixture of Christian images and references deployed by the people of Papua—from the Indonesian province formerly known as Irian Jaya—in fighting for their independence. Throughout the predominantly Christian province, pro-independence groups have resorted to texts, practices, and technologies associated with Christianity and the colonial and postcolonial state. To understand the conditions that have made it possible for Papuan separatists to read the Bible for signs of God's support for their struggle, we need to understand the history of Christian organizations in the province. But we also need to understand how such institutions can come to feature in people's lives and imaginations as something other than a disciplinary force. On the offshore island of Biak, the part of Papua that I know best, some prophets once accused foreign evangelists of tearing a page from the Bible—the one that accounted for the wealth and potency wielded by outsiders (see Kamma 1972: 161). When it comes to the linkage between institutions and interpretations, our own approaches may be missing a page.

Take Talal Asad's (1993) critique of the approach to ritual and religion promoted by Geertz (1973) and others who have read social practices for their symbolic meaning. Asad foregrounds what Geertz takes for granted: the institutions through which a ritual's purposes, and what counts as religion, are defined. Asad offers evidence of a transition in the West from the monastic use of prayer and other practices as disciplinary techniques, toward a more modern sensibility that searched for the meaning behind public acts. Asad shows how the medieval church set the boundaries of proper worship through "authorizing discourses," which at the same time represented the clergy's measures as "instruments of God" (1993: 35). But he neglects to explain how institutional power might become the object of alternative interpretations: ones that undermine, rather than uphold, the official monopoly on the "truth." Roy Rappaport's (1999) account of the universal problems addressed by ritual misses the point from the other direction. Rappaport distinguishes between the "highest order meanings" embedded in a religion's "Ultimate Sacred Postulates," and the concrete politics involved in the enforcement of the "lower order" rules. Institutions may derive legitimacy from conceptions of the sacred, but the vector only runs one way. The historical contingencies of social life seemingly exist on a different plane from the species-level threats to social order that religion supposedly evolved to address. Edmund Leach (1983) comes closer to bridging this gap by showing how particular institutional arrangements relate to particular understandings of power and mediation. Leach's argument turns on an analysis of the Arian heresy, which held that Jesus Christ was the human receptacle of the divine, and the threat that this interpretation posed to early ecclesiastical authorities. Still, in sharply contrasting the church to the heretical millennial movement, Leach fails to account for how the trappings of orthodoxy can come to serve heterodox ends. What is missing from these approaches can be stated plainly: people's treatment of the Christian message is surely related to the specific ways in which they have negotiated the traffic in people, practices, goods, and, often, violence, opened by organizations acting in the name of God.

In this chapter, I explore this under-examined aspect of the link between institutional power and interpretive practice in the context of two episodes in western New Guinea's checkered history: a millennial movement known as Koreri that occurred on Biak from 1939 to 1943, and the campaign for West Papuan independence that has followed the fall of Indonesian President Suharto's authoritarian New Order regime in 1998. In approaching these episodes, I take meaning not as the symbolic content of words, objects, or gestures, but as the lure that fuels efforts to order experience, efforts that can never fully succeed. The conventional threats to coherence described by Geertz (1973) certainly figure in my analysis: death, suffering, and injustice loom large in West Papua. But I intend to focus on dilemmas inherent to the institutions that disseminate Christian texts and rituals and attempt to control their meaning and use. I use the term *institutions* to refer to what Max Weber called "compulsory organizations" (1978: 52). For Weber, these included the church, which exercised "psychic coercion," and the state, which claimed a monopoly on the legitimate use of force. Like Weber, I view the actions undertaken by these organizations as fueled by a combination of abstract ideals and concrete motivations and constraints, including the collective interest of functionaries in a "secure existence" and the resources at their disposal for pursuing this end (1946: 199). But unlike Weber, I do not hold the "ideological" and the "functional" purposes of an organization in stark opposition. "Ideas such as 'state,' 'church,' 'community,' 'party,' or 'enterprise'" only exist to the degree that they are evoked in social practice (Weber 1946: 199). Purposes, including "functional" ones, are never simply given; these values and the subjects who pursue them are discursively produced.[2] As such, institutions are subject to what Keane (1997) calls the "risks of representation": organizations depend for their authority—and their social reality—on instances of social interaction involving words, things, and forms of behavior that are always open to multiple uses, that can always be seen from multiple points of view. In the course of a Christian ritual, one such point of view might fix upon the officially sanctioned symbolism of an utterance, gesture, or object. Another perspective might foreground the ties between these phenomena and broader contexts and enabling conditions: the Sunday school or seminary where the participants learned these verses and movements, the money that paid for this bread and wine. A further perspective, which comes into focus in the cases I consider here, would highlight the links between the Christian institutions that introduced these texts and practices and other "coercive" organizations, including the colonial and postcolonial state. However official doctrine treats these ties—with some Protestant forms of Christianity doing their best to obscure the believer's dependence on established social forms—Christian genres of practice always *index*, that is, derive from and potentially point to, broader institutional orders (see Bauman 1983; Collins 1996; Mertz 1996; Shoaps 2002). Potentially a threat, but also a resource for believers, this aspect of Christian ritual elicits interpretation, figuring in local struggles for authority derived from the divine.

These struggles are local because, as I hope to make clear in this chapter, historically particular understandings of the nature and powers of coercive organizations shape people's participation in Christian rituals and their interpretation of Christian texts.[3] One effect of such participation might be something akin to what Benedict Anderson (1991: 55–58) describes as the consciousness born of the "bureaucratic pilgrimage." Through their participation in a translocal institution, colonial officials develop a sense of "connectedness" and "interchangeability" with one another as they traverse the same administrative space. In the context of Christian institutions, which are almost always translocal and often transnational, a parallel instance might entail a situation in which participants, in imagining their global peers as equivalent "brothers and sisters in Christ," experience a sort of "practical transcendence" that calls to mind the divine transcendence of an otherworldly God. But other possibilities exist. Participating in a ritual can appear as a means of demonstrating one's privileged access to wealth and potency from beyond the reach of local worlds. The coexistence of these alternatives presents a dilemma to institutions whose pretensions to universality require them to extend personnel and resources across political boundaries. By virtue of an institution's role in the pursuit of status within a particular social context, Christian texts can appear as evidence of a limited good: a treasure possessed by outsiders, a stubbornly inscrutable truth, whose revelation unleashes extraordinary power.

Ever since European missionaries set foot in western New Guinea, the region's inhabitants have attempted to seize the potency of Christian institutions by laying claim to the truth behind official doctrine (see Kamma 1972; Giay and Godschalk 1993; Giay 1986, 1995a, 1995b; Timmer 2002; Rutherford 2000, 2003). In this chapter, my discussion of this dynamic begins with an analysis of Koreri, the millennial movement on Biak, and its relationship to the islands' history of conversion and colonization. I then turn to my current research on the resurgence of Papuan nationalism in the province. In both cases, a particular orientation to officially sanctioned institutions may well have created a space for the pursuit of decidedly unsanctioned ends. In the conclusion, I explore the wider implications of these findings. But first, let us consider a case in which, for reasons related to the dynamics of a local society shaped by a particular experience of colonial expansion, the link between the power of Christian institutions and the secret meaning of Christian texts comes particularly vividly into view.

Koreri and the Power of the Foreign

In my previous writings, I have set the long tradition of Biak millenarianism, which dates back to the earliest days of colonial contact in New Guinea, in the context of the practices through which the people of these islands have pursued value, authority, and prestige (see Rutherford 2003). In arenas ranging from marriage to the performance of sung poetry, Biaks have reproduced an image of the so-called Land of the Foreigners as a source of excessive wealth, pleasurable surprises, and inscrutable texts. Under the New Order, this aspect of Biak social life had a corrosive effect on the identities imposed on the islanders by the regime. The islanders suppressed the referential meaning of official rhetoric by deploying it as evidence of a speaker's proximity to distant sources of wealth and power. This fetishization of the foreign, I have suggested, is the product of this region's history on the frontiers of powerful polities, beginning with the Moluccan sultanate of Tidore, where Biaks delivered tribute in return for trade goods and titles. This dynamic found its limits in the millennial movement, Koreri. Drawing on a myth that made a Biak ancestor, Manarmakeri, into the source of foreign potency, Koreri occurred at moments when Biaks were drawn to adopt the perspective of powerful outsiders on their society. Signaling a collapse in distances and differences, this recognition sparked expectations of Manarmakeri's imminent return. Whereas today's pastors present their sermons as glosses originating in an encounter with a sublimely alien original, Koreri prophets claimed to have discerned the Bible's secret significance: it was a rendering of Biak myth. Jesus Christ was really Manarmakeri, whose name means "The Itchy Old Man," an abject hero whose potency resides in his scaly skin. This revelation heralded Manarmakeri's return and the opening of Koreri, a utopian state of endless plenty, which literally means "We Change Our Skin." Koreri prophets thus drew upon and superceded the strategies of leaders who used translation as a means not of overcoming, but rather of positing difference, that is, of creating the very "foreignness" that was the source of their prestige (see Rutherford 2000, 2003: chapter 4).[4] But there is another way to look at Koreri, one that locates the movement in the context of the region's colonial institutions, which took a particular form.

The Netherlands Indies government laid claim to the western half of New Guinea in the early nineteenth century. The first missionaries to work in the region were two German cabinet makers, Carl W. Ottow and J. G. Geissler, who settled in Doreh Bay, on the Bird's Head Peninsula, in 1855.[5] They were the protégés of O. G. Heldring, the famous Dutch Pietist reformer, and Johannes Gossner, a defrocked German priest. Sharing a strong distrust of official institutions, Gossner and Heldring hit upon the idea of sending unpaid "Christian Workmen" to the colonies to spread the Gospel as they plied their trade. The local Papuans had little use for cabinets, but they did want trade goods, which the missionaries supplied in return for food and forest products, which they collected for a trader based in Tidore's sister polity, Ternate, seat of the residency that included western New Guinea. When the Utrecht Mission Society took over the field, its leaders pushed for the elimination of this practice. But the brothers in New Guinea found that they needed trade to attract the Papuans' attention. Very few Papuans converted to Christianity during the first fifty years of the mission; those who did were manumitted slaves. But coastal natives did take an interest in the mission post. Biak seafarers came to Sunday services, where they received tobacco and trade goods, along with snatches of sermons, which they repeated verbatim in their home communities or even sold for rice.

Needless to say, this tendency to turn Christian words into "booty" exasperated the missionaries. Even worse, would-be converts declared that Jesus belonged to the "Company," that is, the colonial state. That Papuans associated Jesus with the colonial government should come as little surprise, given the conditions in which the missionaries operated. Elsewhere I have described how the Dutch pursued a "policy of display" in western New Guinea during the nineteenth century (Rutherford 2003). Rather than investing in settlements in this vast and seemingly unprofitable land, officials traveled along the coasts erecting escutcheons and confirming the appointment of local chiefs. They also relied on the missionaries to create the impression of Dutch authority. Ottow and Geissler earned a small stipend from the government for rescuing shipwreck victims from competing colonial powers. Occasionally, the resident launched punitive expeditions, often to placate the missionaries, who kept the government informed of the Papuans' "evil" acts. The remarkable security enjoyed by the Protestants in this "unpacified" land attests in part to the value attributed to the commodities they traded, in part to their association with a violent colonial state.

By the end of the nineteenth century, the missionaries had become convinced that their efforts would never bear fruit until the government applied a firmer hand in New Guinea. Protestant pressure in the Netherlands contributed to the Dutch Parliament's decision to fund the expansion of the colonial bureaucracy into New Guinea. At the turn of the century, new victories for the mission accompanied the establishment of permanent government posts. North coastal communities suddenly took an interest in converting, and the demand for evangelists soon exceeded the supply. Having battled prophets in the past, the missionaries worried that the "great awakening" might signal another round of Koreri. But as the Dutch lieutenant who "pacified" Biak in 1915 observed, Christianity's appeal lay in the access the mission offered to evangelists fluent in Malay, the Indies lingua franca and language of administration, which later became Indonesian (see Feuilletau de Bruyn 1916: 244; see also Rutherford 2005). Faced with a head tax, forced labor, and the prosecution of Papuan "criminals," Biaks no doubt felt the need for advocates who could speak on their behalf. At the same time, conversion gave Biaks access to Christian narrations, which they incorporated into Biak myth as a means of interpreting their changing experience of colonial power.

The Biak communities that requested evangelists got more than they bargained for. The first native teacher to visit Biak was a manumitted slave who had attended a native seminary in Java with a handful of other Papuan "foster children." But Papuan evangelists soon found themselves outnumbered by native Christians from Ambon and Sangir, whom the mission imported in large numbers to staff their government-subsidized schools. Natives from other parts of the Indies also monopolized the lower ranks of the colonial bureaucracy. The officials and teachers worked hard to suppress local practices, including "heathen" feasts and song and dance genres, which the missionaries associated with warfare, licentiousness, and other heathen "sins." By the 1920s, despite the missionaries' efforts to impose a division between the affairs of church and state, the two remained interchangeable in the local imagination. On Biak, people used the same word, *pandita* (Malay, "pastor"), to refer to colonial officials and mission teachers (see Hartweg 1926). Both were also known as *amberi*, a Biak term meaning "foreigner" drawn from the adjective *amber*, used in such expressions as the Land of the Foreigners, *Sup Amber*.

At the same time, the intensified experience of colonial rule and mission guidance gave rise to new opportunities for the pursuit of status in Biak. One Papuan nationalist told me how his father, an evangelist trained in the 1930s, had managed to marry his mother, the daughter of a titled village chief.[6] Such a woman could only marry the son of a man with a similar Tidoran title unless the suitor was a teacher, whose association with the mission and government gave him equivalent rank. The remarkably high literacy rates observed for Biak in the 1930s and 1940s indicate the attraction of these new ties (see de Bruyn 1948). Even coolies, stevedores, and mission carpenters enjoyed a certain cache. Biak workers spent some of their wages buying the imported cloth and porcelain that circulated as bridewealth, along with silver bracelets made from colonial coins (see Rutherford 2001a). Commodities and money, often regarded as instruments for dissolving distinctions, became evidence of encounters in distant lands.

The World War II outbreak of the millennial Koreri movement must be set in this context, in which institutions that Biaks confronted appeared as sources of both violence and value. I have argued elsewhere that the mission contributed to the movement by reviving *wor*, a forbidden song and dance genre, for use in church (see Rutherford 2003: chapter 6). This surprising act of recognition occurred at a time when the colonial landscape was quickly changing. Although Koreri is sometimes called a "cargo cult," the movement had much in common with uprisings that occurred throughout the territory that later became Indonesia (see Lanternari 1963; Worsley 1968; see also Kahin 1985). The Japanese occupation of the Netherlands Indies led to the destruction of the colonial administration. On Biak, as elsewhere, local people responded by attacking the elite natives through whom the Dutch had ruled.

The first stage of the movement, which began in 1939, was led by a former plantation coolie named Angganeta Menufandu.[7] Angganeta was deathly ill when Manarmakeri appeared to her in a vision and explained his plans for her and "Papua," as he called her homeland. Angganeta miraculously recovered and soon was healing others, who gathered around her on a nearby island. She called for people to perform *wor*, the formerly banned genre, and drink palm wine, which was still forbidden. The faithful had to trade their imported clothing for loincloths and follow food taboos derived from the myth of Manarmakeri, who soon would return to his chosen land.

The encampment grew quickly, and soon thousands had gathered to drink and sing and dance to *wor* songs. While these practices reflected a certain "nativism," a closer look complicates the picture. For reasons I explore elsewhere, *wor*, which had attracted so much "foreign" attention, served as a privileged method for providing evidence of encounters with new and startling things.[8] Angganeta spent the nights crouched in what her followers called a "radio room," where she received transmissions that she turned into songs, which her followers repeated. Carried along by the music, some participants went into a trance and spoke English, Dutch, and Japanese, channeling the voices of outsiders and the dead. At a later stage, those who spoke in tongues earned the right to serve as the representatives of Angganeta and her successors: they were the *bin dame* (Biak/Malay: "women of peace") deputized to spread the movement and punish (perhaps "pacify") those who opposed it. Like Angganeta, their authority derived from their power to embody alterity. Their incomprehensible words made present absent worlds.

As the uprising progressed, its leaders increasingly laid claim to the authority of "foreign" institutions, as the *bin dame* example suggests. Angganeta, now known as the "Queen," held court in her hut, where Tidoran etiquette prevailed. After the Japanese arrested and executed Angganeta, some Biak warriors recently released from colonial jails wrote by-laws for the movement, supposedly inspired by rumors that the Japanese had promised to recognize existing nationalist organizations. Among other things, the by-laws designated an upside-down Dutch tricolor as the new Papuan flag. In addition to establishing an "army," one of the warriors founded a "city" where people from different communities followed a strict schedule of activities. Word spread that this warrior owed his power to a tiny Bible.[9] Another leader built a replica of an airplane, around which his followers drilled, danced, and prayed.

Along with this recourse to objects, texts, and practices associated with the colonial church and state—and their Japanese and Indonesian opponents— went a radical reversal of colonial hierarchies. When Koreri came, the prophets proclaimed, all the *amberi* would be Papuans, and all the Papuans would be *amberi*. An Ambonese teacher later described to the mission how a huge band of believers had confronted him (see Picanussa n.d.). After beating him up, they forced the teacher to listen to a statement, which began with an announcement: "Our movement is called the New Religion and the New Government." The statement went on:

*Our Manseren has returned from Holland, so the Dutch people are now poor and the Papuan people are going to become rich. Queen Wilhelmina is now wearing a loincloth and we Papuans are going to be wearing fine clothing. We also have a clothing factory. The Dutch people now have to work in the garden planting cassava, sweet potato, taro and so forth, and we Papuans are going to be eating the food Dutch people usually eat.

*You *amberi* from Ambon, Java, Menado, etc. who still remember and follow only the Dutch Government, now we are going to imprison all of you just like the Japanese have imprisoned the Dutch. Now we want to chase away all the Dutch people and other *amberi* from our land because they have oppressed us too much. Now we want to be free and stand on our own.

*We want to become our own government [Dutch, *Bestuur*], our own local head of government [Dutch, *HPB*, acronym for Hoofd Plaatselijk Bestuur] our own teachers [Malay, *Goeroe*] and preachers [Malay, *Pendeta*].

*The Dutch people and you *amberies*, you have deceived us Papuans. You have hidden many secrets from us.

On the face of it, this effort to clarify the Bible's secret meaning seems at odds with Angganeta's radio transmissions and her followers' outpourings of "foreign" words. Where the crowd questioning the elder focused on the significance of foreign discourse, the singers and dancers highlighted its material qualities: its startling effects, its strange sounds. Yet if we view interpretation as itself a social act, then the paradox disappears. Both sets of practices demonstrated Angganeta and her successors' privileged access to Manarmakeri and proved that the Biak ancestor soon would return. In this way, these prophets compelled their followers to see themselves from a new perspective. The missionaries who served in New Guinea envisioned their Papuan converts as submitting to a similar force. For these Pietists, as for Kierkegaard, Christianity's significance lay in its implications for "existing individuals" and their "eternal happiness," not in the abstract, communicable logic of a doctrine.[10] Suddenly subjected to the gaze of an invisible, inscrutable Other, the new Christians were supposed to forgo worldly ties for spiritual treasures stored up in an other-worldly realm (see Derrida 1995; Kierkegaard [1943] 1985). The myth of Manarmakeri, I have argued elsewhere, thematizes this transformation (see Rutherford 2003: chapter 5). It describes startling moments of recognition and the "leap of faith" required to sacrifice old obligations on behalf of the new. But the Biak narrative results in a productive sort of failure: Manarmakeri leaves New Guinea after Biaks reject his offer of prosperity and eternal life because these changes would eliminate the conditions underlying Biaks' pursuit of prestige. Through Koreri, Biaks acknowledged a force that they had obscured by making the church and state into sites to raid. Refracted through a myth that deified the most degraded of characters, Biaks caught a glimpse of themselves as these institutions' official ideologies defined them: as ignorant and sinful, yet subject to salvation. But this acknowledgement could only occur at a millennial moment, spelling the end of the (colonial) world.

Koreri thus offered an account of biblical "truth" that laid bare an imperative embedded in the prewar mission and colonial government. The movement marked the limits of an approach to these institutions that made their "foreignness" into a source of value and prestige. Not surprisingly, Koreri left a lasting mark, not only within Biak society, but on the organizations established in its aftermath. With the Indonesian revolution raging in distant Java and Sumatra, postwar officials banned all "paraphernalia" associated with the movement and once again prohibited the performance of *wor* (see Galis 1946). These measures contributed to the success of Dutch efforts to retain western New Guinea as a separate colony after the Netherlands transferred sovereignty over the rest of the Indies to Indonesia in 1949. Indonesia disputed the Netherlands' claim that the "Melanesian" Papuans should eventually form a separate nation-state. A new understanding of Koreri soon emerged among Dutch officials, who cited the movement as evidence that the Papuans had an innate aversion to Indonesians—but not to Dutch colonial rule.[11]

In August 1962, when the Netherlands submitted to US pressure and agreed to a settlement that entailed western New Guinea's transfer first to the United Nations, then to Indonesian control, this new reading of Koreri came to the foreground. As part of the arrangement, Indonesia was to hold a consultation in which the Papuans would be given a chance to choose between independence and integration into the Republic. It quickly became clear that the Indonesian authorities were not going to risk the so-called "Act of Free Choice" yielding anything but one result (see Saltford 2000). Some of the Papuan nationalist leaders from Biak who emerged during this period of violence and repression presented Koreri as part of an age-old tradition of Papuan resistance (see, e.g., Sharp with Kaisiëpo 1994). But this vision of Koreri was not universally shared among Biak leaders, as I learned in a conversation with Seth Rumkorem, a Biak who long served as commander of an armed wing of the Free Papua Organization (Organisasi Papua Merdeka, or OPM).[12] Koreri was a "false religion" (Indonesian, *agama palsu*) that could only lead to death—as, indeed it had on a massive scale, when the Japanese military finally wiped out the movement. Rumkorem had spent much of his time in the forest fighting similar "false religions," movements led by people loosely affiliated with the guerillas who suddenly became convinced that they themselves had become the embodiment of a divinely liberating force.[13] Rumkorem had little patience for such nonsense—or for fellow exiles who have talked of reviving Koreri as part of the official culture of Papuan nationalism. Rumkorem's opposition to Koreri is not surprising given his personal background; his father was one of the Biak teachers that the crowds attacked.

Clearly, when Papuan nationalists tap the power of the province's Christian institutions, they are doing so in a fashion different from that of their millennial predecessors and competitors. But rather than following Rumkorem in distinguishing "true" and "false" religions, we need to pay heed to the range of interpretive strategies that can coexist within a particular social field. The fact that both the Koreri prophets of 1939–42 and Seth Rumkorem have mobilized the term *religion* (Indonesian/Malay, *agama*) indicates that they all, in some fashion, have sought to tap this official category as a source of legitimacy (cf. Timmer 2002; Giay 1986; 1995a; 1995b; Giay and Godschalk 1993). Today's elite Papuan nationalists have faith that someday Jesus will free the Papuans. But unlike the prophets, few have dared to declare how and when this will occur.

Something like the millennial "truth" of Koreri may well provide the horizon toward which contemporary nationalist performances gesture. In the second half of this chapter, I explore this possibility by examining the more recent history of Christian institutions in western New Guinea. I focus on the Gereja Kristen Injili, or GKI, heir to the Protestant mission whose authority Koreri leaders sought to supersede.

Papuan Nationalism and the Power of Prayer

In a 1973 study of the GKI, Ukur and Cooley (1977: 27–29) point out that the Koreri uprising of 1939–42 is in part to be thanked for the speed with which the native church gained autonomy during the 1950s. The Koreri movement traumatized the Protestant missionaries by showing them how quickly the local schools and congregations they had created could crumble. Before World War II, the missionaries failed to delegate any of their responsibility for performing Christian sacraments. When the Japanese military rounded up the European missionaries and sent them to distant camps, no one was on hand to baptize infants and serve communion or, even more importantly, to determine who would be allowed access to these rites. The Protestant mission's response to Koreri's call for a reversal of colonial hierarchies was to attenuate prior relations of inequality. As a result, growing numbers of Papuans did become "*amber*," albeit without a radical transformation of the colonial conditions under which they lived.[14]

These changes entailed the expansion of opportunities for participation in Protestant institutions on all levels.[15] In 1918, the Utrecht Mission Society

funded a school to train Papuan evangelists and teachers at the mission head-
quarters at Doreh Bay. In 1925, the mission moved the school to Miei, at the
base of the Bird's Head, where it remained in operation until the 1950s under
the guidance of Isak Semuel Kijne, a missionary from the Nederlandse Hervormde Kerk, which took over the New Guinea field after World War II. When
Jan P. K. van Eechoud, the first Resident of Netherlands New Guinea after the
war, began the task of cultivating a small corps of Papuan colonial officers,
he recruited the school's best students (Derix 1987: 133–156). Eventually, the
school for teachers faced competition from the new educational opportunities offered by the colonial government and the Catholic Church.[16] But Protestant institutions still provided a privileged avenue to social advancement.
The Protestant mission began ordaining Papuan ministers in 1952, beginning
with a handful of experienced teachers and evangelists, then turning to graduates from a school of theology founded in 1954 (see Ukur and Cooley 1977:
29–30). Although Ambonese and Sangirese church workers remained prevalent, Papuan pastors began to appear in greater numbers.[17] Among these early
pastors was a Biak named William Rumainum who became the first chairman
of the GKI.[18]

At the same time, on a local level, the church created new possibilities for
involvement. Before the war, mission evangelists and teachers exercised a great
deal of control over the Papuan congregations. The congregations in turn were
divided into resorts, each overseen by a European missionary who answered
to the chairman of the mission convention, the most senior Dutch pastor on
hand. In 1956, when the GKI gained autonomy, this form of governance gave
way to a Presbyterian system, in which a board of elders and male and female
deacons governed a congregation (Ukur and Cooley 1973: 45–46, 53–72).
Elders shouldered a range of responsibilities, from visiting the ill to leading
Sunday services to enforcing policies laid down at higher levels of church organization. Local congregations elected their elders, who chose representatives
to make up the parish governing body, which in turn sent representatives to
the synod council, which met once every three years.[19]

Yet even if the mission satisfied, however partially, desires associated with
Koreri, the missionaries who implemented these measures did so in the hope
that the new order would undermine some of the presuppositions on which
the movement rested. Even as the church's Dutch advisors introduced new
avenues to authority for Papuan villagers, they sought to deny that authority was primarily at stake. A booklet written by the mission anthropologist,
F. C. Kamma, author of a seminal study on Koreri, reflects this contradiction.
"Eldership is a form of service," as Kamma (n.d.: 3) puts it at the beginning of
the text, which contains frequent references to the Bible. "To serve means: to
help, to provide everything that people need. Thus although eldership must
also be called: a **position** or even often a **rank**, its meaning is **not** to command people, to seek or demand to be served, but rather just the contrary"
(Kamma n.d.: 3). Despite the fact that a congregation selected its own elders,
these servants should always remember that their true source of authority lay
elsewhere. "Elders are appointed by Jesus Christ through the intercession of

the Congregation. Because of this, the choice is prayed for, so that Christ will use the Congregation to designate His servants. In this way, elders become the instruments of Christ. Christ governs the Evangelical Christian Church (GKI) by way of these office holders" (Kamma n.d.: 6).

A similar publication for deacons makes much of the example provided by Christ, who served his disciples food—and even washed their feet—behavior that the booklet insists was utterly degrading at the time (see Teutscher n.d.: 1). In Biak, and perhaps elsewhere, this effort to control the meaning of Christian "service" may well have had ironic effects. The very effort to limit the church officers' authority may well have provided a means of enhancing it, through proximity to Jesus, the ultimate "foreign" power. A similar possibility lies in the booklet's advice on conducting home visits, which are presented as occasions to comfort the suffering and reprimand sinners. The elder should bring along a list of suitable Bible verses to read to the household, rather than speaking in his own words (see Kamma n.d.: 52–55). As I have noted, such a displacement was key to the strategies of New Order-era Biak leaders, who sought to be recognized as purveyors of "foreign" words. Perhaps in response to this possibility, Kamma insists that the elder should neither present himself as a "spiritual policeman" (Malay, *polisi rohani*) nor as a "Christian magician" (Malay, *tukang hobatan kristen*), who in a heathen (Malay, *kafir*) fashion presents himself as holding the monopoly on a community's religious resources; rather, every father should lead his family in prayer (Kamma n.d.: 49–50). Again, this advice opens the way to its own subversion. The very move that would have the institution's authority penetrate ever more deeply allowed for the dispersal of spiritual skills.[20] The "democratization" of Protestant rituals also carried with it the danger that entrepreneurs could emerge outside the institutional boundaries of the church.[21]

A further set of productive contradictions comes into focus if one considers the ways in which Christian institutions responded to a changing political context during the postwar period of Dutch, then Indonesian rule. During the same year that the GKI was founded, the Nederlandse Hervormde Kerk issued a Call to Reflection on the New Guinea question (Generale Synode der Nederlandse Hervormde Kerk 1956; see also Henderson 1973: 84–85). The statement urged Dutch Protestants to carefully scrutinize the motivations behind the Dutch decision to retain western New Guinea, which, rather than serving a greater good—the Papuans' right to self-determination—could be read as an effort to preserve Dutch national pride. But aside from the higher purposes that a negotiated settlement with Indonesia would serve, the Call appealed to more practical imperatives. The implications of the dispute for the Dutch church's operations in Indonesia were potentially devastating. For Dutch missionaries working in New Guinea and their Papuan flock, the event revealed the risks that went along with the benefits of belonging to an organization that could channel resources from afar.[22]

In the aftermath of western New Guinea's transfer to Indonesia, the GKI's close relationship with the Indonesian Council of Churches (Indonesian, *Dewan Gereja Indonesia*), which was a legacy of the episode, helped the church survive in tumultuous times (see Ukur and Cooley 1977: 210, 295). Many Papuans in the colonial administration lost their jobs in the 1960s, when scores of Indonesian officials flocked to the new province of West Irian.[23] In contrast, the departure of Dutch missionaries vacated positions in the GKI hierarchy that were filled by the "Irianese," as the Papuans were now called. These Irianese pastors presided over a growing, increasingly multiethnic flock, thanks to the Council of Churches' policy of encouraging Christian migrants to join the GKI instead of founding branches of their home churches in the new province.[24] Similar pressures on the Catholic Church did not yield the same windfall for the indigenous faithful. European priests, many of whom became Indonesian citizens, were more willing to weather the change in administration than European pastors. Given the strict standards imposed for ordination, there were very few Papuan priests qualified to staff the dioceses, so the Europeans who did leave ceded their posts to Javanese and Eastern Indonesian colleagues (Hadisumarta 2001). Under Indonesian rule, the relatively stronger European presence in the Catholic Church—and its relatively more formalized links to the outside world—provided Catholic leaders with more leeway to criticize the government. But both the GKI and the Catholic Church moved within a space of possibility that depended on their playing the role of mediator between the government and the population, rather than acting as the champion of either. Both institutions pursued this role not simply in the name of "peace," but because their institutional survival was at stake.

Official Indonesian state ideology played a key role in setting the rules of the game. In an effort to stem the growth of pro-Indonesian sentiment, Dutch propagandists had warned the Papuans that if Indonesia gained control of western New Guinea, the Indonesian government would force its inhabitants to convert to Islam, Indonesia's majority religion (see Ukur and Cooley 1977: 285). In fact, a generalized "belief in God," rather than Islam per se, was and remains the first pillar of Indonesia's official state ideology, Pancasila, which was introduced by Indonesia's first president, Sukarno, and revised by Suharto, the general who replaced him in 1966 after an aborted "communist" coup and military-led massacres that cost close to a million Indonesians their lives (see Kipp 1996: 107–8). Several months before the coup, an Indonesian brigadier general explained to religious leaders from West Irian that "to pray for God's help and blessings for the good of mankind and the prosperity of the State is the essence of the Indonesian personality in everything they [*sic*] do."[25] Under Suharto's so-called "New Order" regime, "belief in God" was more than a description of the Indonesian national character—it was prescribed. All Indonesian citizens had to list an approved world religion on their identity cards, or risk being labeled communists. The central government's promotion of *agama*, that Indonesian term for institutionalized religion, served the regime's purposes (see Kipp 1996). Religious-based identities tempered the grip of those associated with ethnicity, or residence suppressed allegiances based on class.

As a result, in Irian Jaya, as western New Guinea was once again renamed in 1973, Christianity provided a safe refuge for indigenous leaders and provided a passage into national networks through which New Order patronage freely flowed. Many members of the Papuan elite now participating in the movement have ties to Christian institutions: they include church officials, the rectors of schools of theology, graduates from Christian universities, and staff-members from church-backed NGOs (see Rutherford 2001b: 195–200; see also Mote and Rutherford 2001). Since colonial times, Indonesian Christians have claimed more than their share of positions in the national elite by virtue of the opportunities for social mobility and alliance building offered by participation in church-based institutions.[26] Under the New Order, these pathways led in just one direction: to the center, where the regime used its control over export earnings, foreign investment, and military power to harness religiously based *aliran* or "currents." Indonesians came to view the center as holding a monopoly on the sources of their life chances and status as legitimate social actors (see Pemberton 1994; Siegel 1997, 1998). But Irianese participation in the Catholic and Protestant "currents" seems not to have resulted in this level of subjugation. The churches in Irian Jaya operated in a different political environment from that found in other parts of Indonesia. Elsewhere, the lingering threat was "communism"; in Irian Jaya, it was the specter of Papuan separatism that haunted the Indonesian nation-state.

The GKI came to occupy a particularly fraught position between the administrative and military apparatus and an often rebellious indigenous population. Intelligence officers attended church services during the 1960s to monitor the messages issued from the pulpit.[27] The authorities expelled some foreign pastors, including a German Lutheran who reportedly gave a sermon in which he touched on the question of whether West Irian might in fact be God's chosen land. The government soon found uses for indigenous pastors, who risked being imprisoned, tortured, or worse if they misspoke. Early on during the Indonesian period, the church distributed letters to local congregations, reminding the members of their duties "as Christians and citizens of the Indonesian Republic" (see Ukur and Cooley 1977: 295). On the eve of the Act of Free Choice, the GKI played an active role in promoting the Indonesian position. Many pastors served on the consultative councils that took part in the heavily manipulated event. One of the speakers at the GKI's Fifth Synod Convention called on the delegates to rise above any "personal disappointment" and place their trust in Jesus. After all, "Jesus already endured a choice that was free: to be crucified at Golgotha. Christ is the implementer of the *Act of Free Choice*: for the salvation of people with faith" (Ukur and Cooley 1977: 295; italicized words are in English.)[28]

In a similar spirit, the GKI participated in military operations in which church officials distributed leaflets urging those who had joined the Operasi Papua Merdeka (Free West Papua Movement; OPM) to return to their communities and families (Ukur and Cooley 1977: 289–90). But on occasion, the church's authority was directed against the Indonesian military as well, as when one pastor saved some four hundred captured "rebels" from execution by begging for forgiveness, then kneeling to pray in front of the commanders and their troops (Ukur and Cooley 1977: 290).[29] In addition to Protestant rituals, the GKI itself sometimes appeared to be up for grabs. This point was brought home to me when Seth Rumkorem, the OPM leader mentioned above, turned from "false religions" to speak of his own view of the place of faith in the struggle.[30] In the forest, he told me, the guerillas always held Sunday services, divided according to denomination.[31] In the mid 1970s, Rumkorem went so far as to send a letter to the chairman of the GKI, urging him to send an official delegation to confer with the armed separatists. The pastors and the guerillas would pray together, and if God indicated that the Papuan nationalist cause was just, then the GKI would agree to support the struggle openly; if not, the OPM would give up the fight.[32] New Order ideologies and imperatives clearly could not fully define Christian institutions in the eyes of the province's inhabitants; the churches' power still remained, in some sense, at large.

Perhaps for this reason, the post-Suharto period in Papua has yet to see the religious violence that has plagued other parts of Indonesia. Elsewhere, the sudden collapse of the institutional networks that connected local communities and the national center has given rise to intense anxieties about identity. A key theme in nationalist literature is the fear that one could be a traitor to the nation without knowing it (Siegel 1997). Under the New Order, one was either recognized as a proper Indonesian, or one stood with the forces of disorder and death. These anxieties arguably account for the ferocity of conflicts in places like Ambon and Poso, where, under conditions of democratization, being Muslim or Christian entails membership in potentially threatened political "currents" (see Sidel 2003; van Klinken 2001). But in Papua, the possibility of seeing something unexpected in oneself is not unwelcome: Papuanness is what has suddenly come (back) to light.

This moment of recognition has not resulted in the suppression or replacement of existing institutions. Instead of founding a new religion, the current movement's leaders have recontextualized the old, turning the churches and practices associated with them into a source of legitimacy for a new national order. FORERI, the Forum for the Reconciliation of the People of Irian Jaya, was founded at the instigation of the churches to open a dialogue between provincial leaders and the central government following a series of flag raisings that ended with the death of demonstrators in July 1998. In February 1999, a team of one hundred representatives met with then President Habibie, whom they startled by announcing that the province's population wanted to secede. Reportedly, the delegates' main activity in Jakarta was prayer, including at a service led by a famous Indonesian evangelist (Mote and Rutherford 2001: 126). Upon their return to the province, the delegates "socialized"—that is, broadcasted and explained—their message by urging their constituents to pray for the nonviolent movement's success. Theys Eluay, a charismatic Sentani chief who participated in the Act of Free Choice, assumed the role of "Great Leader" at a birthday celebration in November 1999, which no doubt included prayers to his good health. The period of relative openness that followed culminated in June 2000 in the Second Papuan National Congress in Jayapura, which was attended by thousands of participants from throughout the province and beyond (see van den Broek and Szalay 2001: 89–90; King

2002).[33] Prayer was in abundance at this event, with representatives of each of the provinces' religions and denominations opening each day's session by leading a brief devotion. The secretary of the Presidium, the executive branch confirmed during the Papuan congress, is a Papuan Muslim who, I have been told, prays for West Papua's liberation along with everyone else.[34]

I have heard rumors of strange occurrences associated with the contemporary Papuan nationalist movement. A group of Papuans near Wasior, where an attack on a military-controlled logging concern led to harsh reprisals and many civilian deaths, supposedly found the "original" Bible in a cave.[35] But the movement's institutionally sanctioned invocations of Christianity are worth scrutiny as well. Those who organized the Congress seemingly followed the lead of Indonesian ideology in deploying a generalized notion of religion as one of the "pillars" established to represent the new nation's bases of support (see King 2002: 101) But at the same time, like the Koreri prophets, they gave new meaning to Christian practices and texts. As one consultant told me, "All the people pray for independence, the Presidium, everyone. They also hope and depend on God. They always pray for this. They have the hope, the faith, that someday it will arrive. Faith that what they are struggling for is right, and because it is right, God is on their side."[36] Speaking in English and Indonesian, he concluded by calling this faith a "force within the heart of every Papuan" that "military weapons" would never "kill." Papuan nationalist prayer evokes the checkered history of Christian institutions in the province. But in doing so, like Koreri's millennial rituals, it gestures towards the moment when God's true intentions will be revealed.

Conclusion: The Politics of Transcendence

In this chapter, I have dwelt upon the conditions that have enabled Papuan leaders to turn Christian texts and rituals toward their own ends. These conditions include the materiality of institutions—their dependence on concrete acts and objects—and their embeddedness in wider social and political fields. In paying heed to these aspects of institutions in a context that has brought them to the fore, I have sought to illuminate how institutional power can be appropriated. But my materials at the same time shed light on some of the ways in which institutional power is produced. The traffic in authority between official institutions and unofficial practices runs in both directions, as Steve Caton (2006) suggests. By turning Christian prayer into a separatist weapon, today's Papuan nationalists have reinforced the churches' authority, even as they have run foul of these organizations' officially neutral stance. In the same fashion, Indonesian leaders have created a resource for Papuan separatists through their own deployment of Christian practices and texts. Even the practices of Koreri prophets, who radically rejected the mission's legitimacy, had a constitutive effect on the province's religious institutions. As I have suggested, coercive organizations owe their authority—and their very existence—to such concrete practices and evocations. Institution, after all, is a word with two meanings:

an instituted order and the instituting processes through which such an order, however provisionally, comes into force (see Weber 2001).

The interpretive practices described in this chapter have played a critical role in shaping Papua's religious institutions as sites of contestation. Human rights workers who have visited OPM groups still at large in the province report that their commanders now spend much more time preaching than planning attacks.[37] Against these guerillas-turned-pastors, the Indonesian authorities are currently deploying their own version of Christian truth. A crackdown against separatists has been underway in Indonesia, where a massive military campaign has been waged in another restive province, Aceh. On Biak in 2003, Papuan separatists were given three months to turn in their weapons and insignia, or else face the full force of the law.[38] The Indonesian police "socialized" the call for surrender by way of the island's Protestant congregations. The letter inaugurating the operation ended with three Bible verses: Matthew 5:9, Hebrews 12:14, and Psalms 34:15.[39]

With the US-led "war on terror" reshaping global realities, the future looks grim for the current generation of Papuan nationalists. This is not to say that, when it comes to the true meaning of the Bible, the Indonesian authorities are sure to have the final word. I hope I have made one thing clear in this paper. Institutional power both shapes and is subject to interpretive practices. This is why, some fifty years after Koreri, the forces capable of making West Papua a reality still go by the name of the Lord.

Notes

1. Asad (1993) shows how the medieval church set the boundaries of proper worship through "authorizing discourses" that at the same time represented the clergy's measures as "instruments of God" (1993: 35). Compare Rappaport (1999) and Leach (1983).
2. See Caton (2006) on how institutions and the traditions they promulgate depend for their authority on what Vološinov called "behavioral ideology": their tacit invocation in practices that are always "dialogic" to the degree that they consist of a range of contending "voicings," that is, socially locatable points of view. I discuss this point at the end of this chapter. On the ways in which processes of surveillance both call into being and vex bureaucratic subjects in the context of colonial state formation, see Rutherford (2003).
3. Much as linguistic ideologies present a partial image of the "multi-functional nature of linguistic communication," ideologies of institutionality present a partial view of the social, technological, and material preconditions and effects of actions undertaken in the name of church and state. See Woolard and Schieffelin (1994); Kroskrity (2000); see also Silverstein (1976).
4. This orientation to translation would be at odds with that classically associated with the Protestant vision of the Word as a bearer of a universally transmissible meaning. See Rutherford (2003: 250, n. 16; 2005).
5. The following account draws on Rutherford (forthcoming) and Rutherford (2003: chapter 6).
6. Interview, Seth Rumkorem, Wageningen, 14 October 2002.
7. The following account is drawn from Kamma (1972) and Rutherford (2003: chapter 6).
8. See Rutherford (1996, 2003: chapter 3). *Wor* composers invent songs instantly and automatically after they experience something startling or striking. Their lyrics take the form of almost identical couplets. The second couplet fills in words that are omitted in the first: place names, personal names, and nouns that specify the meaning and origin of the song.

9. The man's relatives reported that he had received it in a colonial prison from Indonesia's first president, Sukarno, who was then a famous nationalist.

10. See Rutherford (forthcoming). Kierkegaard insists upon the paradox embedded in Christianity's proposition that "the individual's eternal happiness is decided in time through a relation to something historical that furthermore is historical in such a way that its composition includes that which according to its nature cannot become historical and consequently must become that by virtue of the absurd." See Kierkegaard ([1846] 1992: 385). By contrast, the Biak response to Christianity outlined here and in Rutherford (2003: chapter 5) does not presume the sheer division between the temporal and the eternal on which this paradox turns. Koreri and the narratives associated with it in large part account for how Biak's God has remained a divinity whose power is "of this world."

11. de Bruyn (1948: 22) refers to Koreri as an expression of "self-conscious Papuan nationalism." See also van Baal (1989, vol. 2: 167).

12. Interview, Wageningen, 14 October 2002.

13. Rumkorem is a member of the Calvinist *Gereformeerde Kerk* in the Netherlands, where he lives in exile. He recounted his troubles with a group of Catholic villagers who staged a crucifixion, promising that the victim would rise in three days, at which time Papua would be free. He told me of other villagers who tried to recruit the guerillas to submit to a scheme in which they would lay down their arms, pray, and sound a trumpet outside the provincial capital, Jayapura, which, like Jericho, would fall. Rumkorem was sometimes inclined to trace these disturbances, if not to Satan, then to the Indonesian special forces, who sought to discredit the OPM internationally by portraying it as a cult.

14. Biaks first used the term, *amber*, to refer to themselves in the early 1960s, I was told; at first it was a joke. Zachi Sawor remembered the names of the two Biak students who started the habit, jokingly calling out, "Hey amberie!" Interview, Wageningen, October 11, 2002. But this practice, of calling elite members of one's group by the name used for non-Papuan Indonesians and other foreigners, may be prevalent elsewhere in the province (see, e.g., Giay 1995a).

15. See Ukur and Cooley (1977); Kamma (1977).

16. The Catholic Church established a mission in the south at Merauke in 1905, then expanded into the mostly Protestant north in the late 1930s, when territorial restrictions on evangelization were lifted (see Mewengkang 2001; Hadisumarta 2001). Members of several different religious orders proselytized in New Guinea, including the Jesuits, the Augustinians, and the Franciscans. The province is now divided into four dioceses, with bishops based in Jayapura, Sorong, Merauke, and Agats.

17. Scores of Christians from Ambon, in particular, flooded into Netherlands New Guinea after the Indonesian Republic crushed a separatist rebellion in the southern Moluccas.

18. Rumainum was the descendant of a Papuan evangelist of Petrus Kafiar's generation, also trained in Depok.

19. Henderson (1973: 90) notes that the Protestant church was the first institution in the colony to entrust the average Papuan "with the promotion of his [sic] own interests via a democratic system."

20. The long-term effects of these policies were evident on Biak in the early 1990s, when lay people regularly mounted the pulpit to deliver sermons and everyone, myself included, was expected to be able to lead a prayer (see Rutherford 2003: 125–126).

21. There is evidence of the lasting effects of these policies. The early 1990s saw the emergence of vaguely millennial "prayer groups" on Biak, which attracted the suspicion of church officials and the military (Rutherford 2003: 129). My initial research suggests that lay participation is equally important in the functioning of Catholic institutions in the province, despite the very different model of mediation and authority Roman Catholicism is generally understood to promote (see Hadisumarta 2001).

22. Although Catholic leaders in Java supposedly engaged in a similar lobbying effort, their initiative was much less open. Interview with Nicolaas Jouwe, Leiden, 17 October 2002.

23. West Irian was a relatively attractive posting for Indonesian officials, given the economic crisis then underway in the rest of the Republic.

24. In September 2003, a former GKI officer explained this policy. He had never seen official documents telling how this deal had been struck, although he was sure they existed somewhere.

25. Sutjipto (1965: 10). Sutjipto gave this address during an "Orientation Week on the Aims and Means of the Indonesian Revolution."

26. Some analysts have gone so far as to argue that the rise of reformist Islam in the 1990s represented an attempt on the part of elite Muslims to compete with elite Christians on the same terrain (see Sidel 2003; see also Schrauwers 2000: 14). An example is the founding of ICMI (Ikatan Cendiakawan Muslim Indonesia, Indonesian Muslim Intellectuals Network) in the early 1990s. This initiative was originally supported by Suharto, who used the group to offset rival factions within political and military circles. ICMI's chair was B. J. Habibie, Suharto's vice president and longtime protege, who assumed office after his mentor resigned.

27. Some Papuans left the GKI as a result of these incidents, joining the growing ranks of Papuan evangelicals or converting to Catholicism. Interview with Nicolas Jouwe, Leiden, 17 October 2002.

28. Tjakraatmadja also warned the delegates not to let anyone "turn the *Act of Free Choice* into a determination of the future made on the basis of personal disappointment uninformed by just consideration, revenge, tribal or ethnic hatred."

29. For GKI members, this story would recall the tale of Ottow and Geissler's arrival in New Guinea, which has the Germans dropping to their knees to thank the Lord and ask for his help (see Kamma 1976).

30. Interview, Wageningen, 14 October 2002.

31. Whether they were Catholic, Protestant, Seventh-Day Adventists, or Pentecostals, all the freedom fighters worshipped God in their own (institutionally) sanctioned ways.

32. If God was not behind them, why should they risk their lives? Seth pointed out. This proposal calls to mind one of the demands made by today's Papuan leaders. In official statements, they have called on members of the Indonesian central government to sit down with them to consult, not God, but the historical record, with the understanding that if history shows that the Papuans are really Indonesians, the separatists will give up their struggle (see Mote and Rutherford 2001: 128).

33. The event's emotional climax was the raising of the Morning Star flag and the singing of the national anthem, "Hai Papua Tanahku." Introduced in 1961 by the New Guinea Council, a colonial advisory body set up in a last-ditch effort to accelerate the territory's progress towards self-rule, the flag features a design supposedly inspired by the Christian triad of virtues, faith, hope, and love, with the single star representing hope. For its part, the national anthem, a song composed by Kijne during the 1930s, begins with a pledge of loyalty and ends with a prayer. Interview Nicolaas Jouwe, Leiden, 17 October 2002.

34. Interview, Washington, D.C., 3 October 2002.

35. Interview, Seth Rumkorem, Wageningen, 14 October 2002.

36. Interview, Washington, D.C., 3 October 2002. A non-Papuan pastor who advocates on behalf of the Papuan cause described trying to convince the Papuans that it would take more than prayer to win their liberation. God had already granted them their rights; now they had to struggle to realize them. Interview, Jakarta, 6 June 2003.

37. Papua's premier human rights organization, ELSHAM, has led a campaign to transform Papua into a zone of peace. As part of this campaign, human rights workers have visited some of the OPM commanders still at large in the province's dense forests. To their surprise, these commanders responded enthusiastically to the human rights workers' call to lay down their weapons. Many no longer behave as military commanders, but rather as the leaders of religious communities whose main function is to pray for Papua's salvation. Personal communication, John Rumbiak.

38. In fact, Koru Konsup, the aging OPM fighter who recently resurfaced to found a pro-independence community in West Biak, has no weapons. The community's main activities are marching and prayer.

39. See "Semua Warga Biak yang Terlibat Separatis OPM Diancam Menyerah Sebelum Batas waktu yang Ditetapkan Berakhir," *Elsham News Report*, 28 July 2003. The verses are, "Blessed are the peacemakers, for they shall be called sons of God," "Strive for peace with all men, and for the

holiness without which no one will see the Lord," and "The eyes of the Lord are toward the righteous, and his ears toward their cry."

References

Althusser, Louis. 1971. "Ideology and Ideological State Apparatuses (Notes towards an Investigation)." In *Lenin and Philosophy*. London: New Left Books.

Anderson, Benedict. 1991. *Imagined Communities: Reflections on the Origin and Spread of Nationalism*. Rev. ed. London: Verso.

Anonymous. n.d. Raport tentang Koreri. Unpublished manuscript. Files of F.C. Kamma, Hendrik Kraemer Institute, Oegstgeest, the Netherlands.

Aragon, Lorraine V. 2000. *Fields of the Lord: Animism, Christian Minorities, and State Development in Indonesia*. Honolulu: University of Hawaii Press.

Asad, Talal. 1993. *Genealogies of Religion: Discipline and Reasons of Power in Christianity and Islam*. Baltimore: Johns Hopkins Press.

Ballard, Chris. 1997. "Irian Jaya." *The Contemporary Pacific* 9, no. 2: 468–74.

———. 2002. "The Signature of Terror: Violence, Memory, and Landscape at Freeport." In *Inscribed Landscapes: Marking and Making Place*, eds. B. David and M. Wilson. Honolulu: University of Hawai'i Press.

Bauman, Richard. 1983. *Let Your Words Be Few: Symbolism of Speaking and Silence among Seventeenth Century Quakers*. Cambridge: Cambridge University Press.

Bowen, John R. 1993. *Muslims through Discourse*. Princeton: Princeton University Press.

de Bruyn, Jan Victor. 1948. *Jaarverslagen 1947 en 1948 van Onderafdeling Biak*. Nummer Toegang 10–25, Stuk 188. Nienhuis Collectie van de Department van Bevolkingszaken Hollandia Rapportenarchief. The Hague: Algemeene Rijksarchief.

Cannell, Fenella. 1999. *Power and Intimacy in the Christian Philippines*. Cambridge: Cambridge University Press.

Caton, Steven C. 2006. "What is an 'Authorizing Discourse'?" In *Powers of the Secular: Talal Asad and His Interlocutors*, eds. D. Scott and C. Hirschkind. Stanford: Stanford University Press.

Collins, James. 1996. "Socialization to Text: Structure and Contradiction in Schooled Literacy." In *Natural Histories of Discourse*, eds. M. Silverstein and G. Urban. Chicago: University of Chicago Press.

Comaroff, Jean, and John L. Comaroff. 1991. *Of Revelation and Revolution: Christianity, Colonialism, and Consciousness in South Africa*, vol. 1. Chicago: University of Chicago Press.

Derix, Jan. 1987. *Bapa Papoea; Jan P.K. van Eechoud, Een Biografie*. Venlo: Van Spijk.

Derrida, Jacques. 1995. *The Gift of Death*. Trans. D. Wills. Chicago and London: University of Chicago Press.

Feuilletau de Bruyn, W. K. H. 1916. *Militaire Memorie der Schouten-eilanden*. 31 August 1916, Nummer Toegang 10–25, Stuk 183. Nienhuis Collectie van de Department van Bevolkszaken Hollandia Rapportenarchief. The Hague:Algemeene Rijksarchief.

———. 1920. *Schouten en Padaido-eilanden*. Mededeelingen Encyclopaedisch Bureau 21. Batavia: Javaasche Boekhandel.

Foucault, Michel. 1979 [1975]. *Discipline and Punish: The Birth of the Prison*. Trans. A. Sheridan. London: Penguin Books.

Galis, K. W. 1946. *Dagboek over April 1946*. Nummer Toegang 10–25, Stuk 179. Nienhuis Collectie van de Department van Bevolkingszaken Hollandia Rapportenarchief. The Hague: Algemeene Rijksarchief.

Geertz, Clifford. 1973. "Religion as a Cultural System." In *The Interpretation of Cultures: Selected Essays*. New York: Basic Books.

Generale Synode der Nederlandse Hervormde Kerk. 1956. *Oproep van de Generale Synode der Nederlandse Hervormde Kerk tot bezinning op de verantwoordelijkheid van het Nederlandse volk inzake de vraagstukken rondom Nieuw-Guinea*. No. 825.35/3690. June 27, 1956. The Hague.

Giay, Benny. 1986. *Kargoisme di Irian Jaya*. Sentani, Irian Jaya, Indonesia: Region Press.

———. 1995a. *Zakheus Pakage and His Communities: Indigenous Religious Discourse, Socio-political Resistance, and Ethnohistory of the Me of Irian Jaya*. Amersterdam: Amsterdam University Press.

———. 1995b. "The Conversion of Weakebo: A Big Man of the Me." *Journal of Pacific History* 34, no. 2: 181–90.

Giay, Benny and Jan A. Godschalk. 1993. "Cargoism in Irian Jaya Today." *Oceania* 63: 330–44.

Giay, Benny, and Yafet Kambai. 2003. *Yosepha Alomang: Pergulatan Seorang Perempuan Papua Melawan Penindasan*. Jayapura: Elsham Papua.

Hadisumarta, Mgr. F.X., O. Carm. 2001. "Keuskupan Manokwari-Sorong Gerak dan Perkembangannya." In Dr. F. Hasto Rosariyanto, SJ, *Bercermin pada Wajah-Wajah Keuskupan Gereja Katolik Indonesia*. Yogyakarta, Indonesia: Kanisius.

Haga, A. 1884. *Nederlandsch Nieuw-Guinea en de Papoesche eilanden: Historische bijdrage*. 2 vols. Batavia: Bruining's-Gravenhage: Nijhoff.

Hartweg, F. W. 1926. Letter to the Board of September 23. UZV K31, D12. Oegstgeest, the Netherlands: Archives of the Hendrik Kraemer Institute.

Henderson, William. 1973. *West New Guinea: The Dispute and Its Settlement*. Seton Hall: Seton Hall University Press.

Kahin, Audrey R., ed. 1985. *Regional Dynamics of the Indonesian Revolution: Unity from Diversity*. Honolulu: University of Hawaii Press.

Kamma, F. C. n.d. *Pembangunan Djemaat: Tentang Kepenatuaan*. Hollandia: Panitia Pembangunan Djemaat.

———. 1972. *Koreri: Messianic Movements in the Biak-Numfor Culture Area*. The Hague: Martinus Nijhoff.

———. 1976. *Dit Wonderlijk Werk*, vol. 1. Oegstgeest: Raad voor de Zending der Nederlandse Hervormde Kerk.

———. 1977. *Dit Wonderlijk Werk*, vol. 2. Oegstgeest: Raad voor de Zending der Nederlandse Hervormde Kerk.

Keane, Webb. 1997. *Signs of Recognition: Powers and Hazards of Representation in an Indonesian Society*. Berkeley: University of California Press.

Kierkegaard, Søren. 1985 [1843]. *Fear and Trembling*. Trans. A. Hannay. London: Penguin Books.

———. 1992 [1846]. "Concluding Unscientific Postscript" to *Philosophical Fragments*, trans. H. V. Honig and E. H. Honig. Princeton: Princeton University Press.

King, Peter. 2002. "Morning Star Rising? *Indonesia Raya* and the New Papuan Nationalism." *Indonesia* 73, no. 1: 89–127.

Kipp, Rita Smith. 1996. *Dissociated Identities: Ethnicity, Religion, and Class in an Indonesian Society*. Ann Arbor: University of Michigan Press.

Kroskrity, Paul V. 2000. "Regimenting Languages: Language Ideological Perspectives." In *Regimes of Language: Ideologies, Polities, Identities*, ed. P. V. Kroskrity. Santa Fe: School of American Research Press.

Lanternari, Vittorio. 1963. *The Religions of the Oppressed: A Study of Modern Messianic Cults*. London: MacGibbon and Kee.

Leach, Edmund. 1983. "Melchisedech and the Emperor: Icons of Subversion and Orthodoxy." In *Structuralist Interpretation of Biblical Myth*, ed. E. Leach and D. A. Aycock. Cambridge: Cambridge University Press.

Lee, Benjamin. 1997. *Talking Heads: Language, Metalanguage and the Semiotics of Subjectivity*. Durham: Duke University Press.

Liklikwakoe, P. n.d. "Tentang agama Koreri (Manseren)." Unpublished manuscript. Files of F. C. Kamma, Hendrik Kraemer Institute, Oegstgeest, the Netherlands.

Mertz, Elizabeth. 1996. "Recontextualization as Socialization: Text and Pragmatics in the Law School Classroom." In *Natural Histories of Discourse*, ed. M. Silverstein and G. Urban. Chicago: University of Chicago Press.

Mewengkang, Jus F., MSC. 2001. "Arah Dasar Keuskupan Agung Merauke." In Dr. F. Hasto Rosariyanto, SJ, *Bercermin pada Wajah-Wajah Keuskupan Gereja Katolik Indonesia*. Yogyakarta, Indonesia: Kanisius.

Mooiy, D. n.d. "Perhambatan Koreri." Unpublished manuscript. Files of F. C. Kamma, Hendrik Kraemer Institute, Oegstgeest, the Netherlands.

Mote, Octovianus, and Danilyn Rutherford. 2001. "From Irian Jaya to Papua: The Limits of Primordialism in Indonesia's Troubled East." *Indonesia* 72, no. 1: 115–40.

Munn, Nancy. 1986. *The Fame of Gawa: A Symbolic Study of Value Transformation in a Massim (Papua New Guinea) Society*. Cambridge: Cambridge University Press.

Pemberton, John. 1994. *On the Subject of Java*. Itasca: Cornell University Press.

Picanussa, J. n.d. "Soetoe Ibarat dari Hikajat Manseren Manarmaker (Manseren Konori)." Unpublished manscript. Files of F. C. Kamma, Hendrik Kraemer Institute, Oegstgeest, the Netherlands.

Rafael, Vincente L. 1988. *Contracting Colonialism: Translation and Christian Conversion in Tagalog Society under Early Spanish Rule*. Ithaca: Cornell University Press.

Rappaport, Roy A. 1999. *Ritual and Religion in the Making of Humanity*. Cambridge: Cambridge University Press.

Rutherford, Danilyn. 1996. "Of Birds and Gifts: Revising Tradition on an Indonesian Frontier." *Cultural Anthropology* 11, no. 4: 577–616.

———. 2000. "The White Edge of the Margin: Textuality and Authority in Biak, Irian Jaya, Indonesia." *American Ethnologist* 27, no. 2: 312–39.

———. 2001a. "Intimacy and Alienation: Money and the Foreign in Biak." *Public Culture* 13, no. 2: 299–324.

———. 2001b. "Waiting for the End in Biak: Violence, Order, and a Flag Raising." In *Violence and the State in Indonesia*, ed. B. Anderson. Ithaca: Cornell Southeast Asia Program Publications.

———. 2003. *Raiding the Land of the Foreigners: The Limits of the Nation on an Indonesian Frontier*. Princeton: Princeton University Press.

———. 2005. "Frontiers of the Lingua Franca: Ideologies of the Linguistic Contact Zone in Dutch New Guinea." *Ethnos* 70, no. 3: 387–412.

———. forthcoming. "The Bible Meets the Idol: Writing and Conversion in Biak." In *The Anthropology of Christianity*, ed. F. Cannell. Durham: Duke University Press.

Saltford, John. 2000. "United Nations Involvement with the Act of Self-Determination in West Irian (Indonesian West New Guinea) 1968–1969." *Indonesia* 69, no. 1: 71–92.

Schrauwers, Albert. 2000. *Colonial "Reformation" in the Highlands of Central Sulawesi, Indonesia, 1892–1995*. Toronto: University of Toronto Press.

Sharp, Nonie, with Markus Wonggor Kaisiëpo. 1994. *The Morning Star in Papua Barat*. North Carlton: Arena.

Shoaps, Robin A. 2002. "'Pray Earnestly': The Textual Construction of Personal Involvement in Pentecostal Prayer and Song." *Linguistic Anthropology* 12, no. 1: 34–71.

Sidel, John T. 2003. "Other Schools, Other Pilgrimages, Other Dreams: The Making and Unmaking of Jihad in Southeast Asia." In *Southeast Asia over Three Generations: Essays Presented to Benedict R. O'G. Anderson*, ed. J. T. Siegel and A. R. Kahin. Ithaca: Cornell Southeast Asia Program Press.

Siegel, James T. 1997. *Fetish, Recognition, Revolution*. Princeton: Princeton University Press.

———. 1998. *A New Criminal Type in Jakarta: Counter-revolution Today*. Durham: Duke University Press.

———. 2000. "Suharto, Witches." *Indonesia* 71, no. 1: 27–78.

Silverstein, Michael, and Greg Urban, eds. 1996. *Natural Histories of Discourse*. Chicago: University of Chicago Press.

Smeele, Rogier. 1988. "De Expansie van het Nederlandse Gezag en de Intensivering van de Bestuursbemoeienis op Nederlands Nieuw-Guinea 1898–1942." Doctoral Thesis, Institute of History, Utrecht University.

Sutjipto S.H., Brigadir Djendral TNI. 1965. "Irian Barat: Agama dan Revolusi Indonesia." Address given by the Sekretaris Koordinator Urusan Irian Barat/Sekretaris Umum Musjawarah Pembantu Pemimpin Revolusi/Ketua Gabungan V Komando Operasi Tertinggi at "Pekan Pengenalan Tudjuan dan Upaja Revolusi Indonesia" bagi Rochaniawan dan Rochaniawati Daerah Propinsi Irian Barat, sponsored by the Sekretariat Koordinator Urusan Irian Barat in Jakarta, 2–10 June 1965. Jakarta: Projek Penerbitan Sekretariat Koordinator Urusan Irian Barat.

Teutscher, H. J. 1961. "Pembangunan Djemaat: Katechismus Ketjil tentang Kesjamasan." Unpublished ms.

Timmer, Jaap. 2000. "Living with Intricate Futures: Order and Confusion in Imyan Worlds, Irian Jaya, Indonesia." Doctoral thesis, Centre for Pacific and Asian Studies, University of Nijmegen, the Netherlands.

Ukur, Dr. F., and Dr. F. L. Cooley. 1977. *Benih Yang Tumbuh VIII: Suatu Survey Mengenai Gereja Kristen Irian Jaya*. Jakarta: Lembaga Penelitian dan Studi Dewan Gerja-gereja di Indonesia/Ende, Flores, Indonesia: Percetakan Arnoldus.

van Baal, Jan. 1989. *Ontglipt Verleden*, 2 vols. Franeker: van Wijnen.

van den Broek, Theo, and Alexandra Szalay. 2001. "Raising the Morning Star." *Journal of Pacific History* 36, no. 1: 77–91.

van Goor, J., ed. 1986. Imperialisme in de Marge: De Afronding van Nederlands-Indie. Utrecht: HES.

van Hasselt, F. J. F. n.d. *Petrus Kafiar: Een Bladzijde uit de Nieuw-Guinea Zending*. Utrecht: Utrechtsche Zendings-Vereeniging.

van Klinken, Gerry. 2001. "The Maluku Wars: Bringing Society Back." In *Indonesia* 71, no. 1: 1–26.

Weber, Max. 1946. *From Max Weber: Essays in Sociology*, ed. H. H. Gerth and C. W. Mills. New York: Oxford University Press.

———. 1978. *Economy and Society*, ed. G. Roth and C. Wittich. Berkeley: University of California Press.

Weber, Samuel. 2001. *Institution and Interpretation*. Stanford: Stanford University Press.

Woolard, Kathryn A., and Bambi B. Schieffelin. 1994. "Language Ideology." *Annual Review of Anthropology* 23: 55–82.

Worsley, Peter. 1968. *The Trumpet Shall Sound: A Study of "Cargo" Cults in Melanesia*. 2nd ed. New York: Schocken Books.

6

THE LIMITS OF MEANING IN FIJIAN METHODIST SERMONS

Matt Tomlinson

In this chapter, I examine Fijian Methodist sermons as meaning-making performances, and argue that by emphasizing the generation of meaning, preachers also create a chaotic space of potential meaninglessness that is realized in failed performances. This argument is inspired partly by Talal Asad's well-known criticism of Clifford Geertz's definition of religion—that it derives from "a view that has a specific Christian history" (1993: 42; cf. Keyes 2002; see also chapter one of this volume). Asad's charge—that Geertz "insists on the primacy of meaning without regard to the processes by which meanings are constructed" (1993: 43)—is perhaps overstated, but it can lead scholars in a promising direction. In this direction lie explorations of "meaning" as potentially (but not necessarily) emergent from ritual interactions, and analyses of the ways that meaning, authority, and effectiveness are correlated in certain ritual performances. In undertaking these explorations, new questions emerge. For example, if Christianity generates strong interest in meaningfulness, then how do its rituals accomplish this? How do ritual participants ground their claims regarding what is meaningful and what is not, and what are the effects of perceived ritual failure in this regard?

I begin this chapter by considering the topic of textual circulation and meaningfulness. I discuss the ways that unintelligible texts circulate socially, and the ways that Fijian Methodism has grappled with questions of explicit meaningfulness, particularly in Bible and catechism translations. In the second section, I examine some of the ways that boundaries between meaningfulness and meaninglessness are drawn in Fijian Methodist ritual contexts, drawing on data from my fieldwork in the Tavuki church circuit, Kadavu Island.[1] I focus on sermons, a genre of ritual speech performance in which explicating Biblical texts is a central goal. In emphasizing the creation of meaning, however, sermons also define spaces of potential meaninglessness—spaces that are filled when meaning-making performances fail, as I show in the third section. Finally, I ask how anthropologists should approach meaningfulness and meaninglessness, given the discipline's own impulses toward meaning-making in ethnography.

Translation, Circulation, and Meaning

A momentous historical shift is seen in the work of religious scholars such as Martin Luther, John Wyclif, William Tyndale, Miles Coverdale, and Erasmus. By attempting to make the Bible available in the vernacular to as wide an audience as possible, these scholars necessarily shifted attention to, and responsibility for, the meanings that can emerge from Biblical texts. Emphasizing accurate translation raises questions of interpretation, and thus questions of meaning.

The vigor of modern Bible translation is remarkable in light of early scholars' difficulties (which were not just intellectual; Tyndale was executed for his translations). Henry Knighton's well-known complaint from the fourteenth century shows the depth of feeling that certain scholars had about putting meaning-making into the hands of the masses:

> This master John Wyclif translated the gospel, which Christ had entrusted to clerks and to the doctors of this church so that they might minister it conveniently to the laity and to meaner people according to the needs of the time and the requirement of the listeners in their hunger of mind; he translated it from Latin into the English, not the angelic, idiom . . . so that by this means that which was formerly familiar to learned clerks and to those of good understanding has become common and open to the laity, and even to those women who know how to read. As a result the pearls of the gospel are scattered and spread before swine, and that which had been precious to religious and to lay persons has become a matter of sport to ordinary people of both. (In Hudson 1986: 87)

For Knighton, English was "not . . . angelic," and casting the Bible into English was spiritually ruinous. Holy language was correlated with holy meaning, so translation inevitably debased the gospel's meaningfulness, turning eternal truth into a "matter of sport" that would amuse the "swine."

The early translators felt differently, and their notions of meaning that transcends particular languages became a firmly established aspect of Protestant language ideologies. William Tyndale's "determination to put nothing in the way of being understood" (Daniell 1994: 113) was the same impulse later felt by Methodism's founder, John Wesley, who insisted on "plain language" in preaching (Rack 1989: 344). Wesley was so intent on communicating particular meanings that he told this story about himself: "[A]s a young man he preached a learned sermon which left the congregation open-mouthed; tried again and left their mouths half-open. He then read the sermon to an intelligent servant, and every time Betty cried 'Stop,' he wrote in a single word, until it reached a form that the congregation could understand" (Rack 1989: 344). Wesley's efforts reflect Christianity's historical shift from the pole of discipline to the pole of meaning. This shift is what Asad calls "the transformation of rites from discipline to symbol, from practicing distinctive virtues (passions) to representing by means of practices" (1993: 79). That is, earlier emphases on discipline and coercion had become replaced by emphases on interpretation and belief. Such new emphases were grounded partly in gospel verses such as Matthew 24:14, "And this gospel of the kingdom shall be preached in all the world for a witness unto all nations . . . ."

The men who translated the Bible into Fijian, however, pulled strange rabbits out of their philological hats. The linguist Paul Geraghty describes the language of the Fijian Bible as a creation of the missionaries, not simply a bastardization of the standard tongue: "The language this small band of well-intentioned amateur language-planners . . . forged was far from native; it even verged on the pidgin in some respects, yet the Bible was written in it, and, wholly or partially, most Fijian literature since" (Geraghty 1989: 385). The Fijian Bible's awkward phrasings and archaisms reflect the missionary translators' lack of fluency and dependence on eastern dialects (Cammack 1962: 11). Drawing a connection between eastern Fijians' reputation as "papaw [papaya] eaters" and eastern dialect in the Bible, one of Floyd Cammack's informants complained that the language of Methodism "smells of papaw" (1962: 14). Geraghty (1989: 393) argues that "those who know even a little English prefer to read the English translation of the Bible because it is so much clearer than the Fijian"; i.e., clarity is just as important as prestige in choosing to read English rather than Fijian versions of the text.

Because of the Fijian Bible's semantic awkwardness, Fijian hermeneutics is not based in textual literalism, the linguistic ideology analyzed by anthropologists such as Vincent Crapanzano (2000) in which interpreters imagine a simple correlation between words and semantic meanings transcending context (see also Coleman, this volume). In other words, Fijian Methodists do not scour the Bible for "pure" meanings; ritual performances such as sermons are not held to strict criteria of accurate textual replication. Biblical mispronunciations and misquotations are a standard feature of Fijian Methodist religious life because the written text deviates so far from idiomatic language. Indeed, a ministerial entrance examination for a Fijian Methodist theological college misquoted the Bible (see Tomlinson 2002b: 295 n. 63). Clarity is not always the goal of religious action, however, in Fijian Methodism or any other arena (see Engelke, this volume; see also Tomlinson 2004). The religious historian Andrew Thornley relates an amusing tale of how an idiomatic version of the Fijian Methodist catechism was rejected by one community because it was understood *too easily*:

> When the catechism was delivered towards the end of 1843, it aroused a lively debate on Viwa [Island]. There were objections from those who knew the old catechism. Noa [a Fijian man who assisted the missionary Rev. John Hunt] came to Hunt's defence and contended with the critics. He reminded them that the new catechism was using the Viwa language as it had been before missionaries came and that the old catechism was the 'language of the [Christian] people since the introduction of Christianity' [that is, it was not really the local language, but was

the way Europeans spoke Fijian and the way Fijians imitated Europeans speaking Fijian]. Noa told Hunt that some of the critics did not like anything they could understand! He gave as an example his student colleague: 'If Ezekiel prays and says 'vaka funumalia vakayapayapa' [this sounds mockingly nonsensical] etc. they like him much but they do not like to hear the truths of the gospel so as to understand them.' Hunt finally declared that the catechism was to be read and understood, not criticized. (Thornley 2000: 232)

Thornley's example is vividly ironic. The catechism, a text whose sole function is to provide answers to questions of doctrine, was more popular with some Viwans when its semantic meaningfulness was minimized; people were more impressed with its evocative meaninglessness. Because religious practice often demands that ritual participants "suspend or alter certain aspects of everyday ways of speaking" (Keane 1997a: 49), obscure, foreign, archaic, and mystical language is often considered ritually powerful. Thornley's tale shows that reverence for holy texts does not necessarily create a desire to decode all of those texts' meanings.

The Standard Fijian language, an outgrowth of the Fijian Bible translation efforts, is now spread through national newspapers, radio, and education. It has also become the language of worship in Fijian Methodism, particularly for prayer. During my research in Kadavu (described below), people generally prayed in Standard Fijian. Many preachers gave their sermons in Standard Fijian, too, although some ventured to preach in the Kadavuan dialect. The linguist Robert Dixon, who carried out research in Taveuni, tells a revealing story in this regard. Invited to say a prayer in the Methodist church, he prayed aloud in the local dialect, Boumā, undoubtedly supposing that his efforts would be appreciated. Instead, he tells us, "I received a reprimand—God, the Christian priests had said, only likes to be addressed in [Standard Fijian]" (Dixon 1997: 105).

Firm knowledge is a prerequisite to becoming a Fijian Methodist authority, someone who is licensed to speak in official church contexts. People who want to become ministers must pass a difficult test to gain entrance to the Davuilevu Theological College for training; the test covers a range of topics including history, theology, pastoral studies, and the English language. Moreover, as I will describe below, Rev. Isikeli Serewai (Kadavu's superintendent Methodist minister from 1995 to 1999) emphasized to preachers that they needed to know thoroughly the Biblical passages on which they planned to preach. However, textual knowledge was not the only criterion for gaining a position of authority in the Methodist Church. For example, when one young man who wanted to attend Davuilevu told me about all the gardening work that students had to do there—hours and hours each day—I said to him, "But this is time you're supposed to study." He replied that Fijians' "theology" was that a person needs to know the *qele*—the soil—and that if someone got in the pulpit to preach but did not do garden work, people would think that the preacher did not know anything. A Methodist preacher's effectiveness in preaching, then, comes not just from reading the Bible and having strong textual knowledge, but also from working the earth.[2]

I have presented these brief historical and ethnographic examples to suggest some of the ways that meaning, textual circulation, and institutional authority are correlated in Fijian Methodist contexts. Although meaning is a cultural product that emerges interactively and partially, in ritual performances such as Methodist sermons authorized speakers (i.e., preachers) may attempt to fix and control meanings. These attempts are not always successful; indeed, they can be disastrous failures. Scholars of ritual have argued that ritual performances are often considered efficacious through invoking the specter of failure—and, paradoxically, by occasionally being unsuccessful (Dirks 1994; Keane 1991, 1995, 1997b; Luhrmann 1989; Shelton 1976). Below, I will describe one remarkable failure in the Tavuki Methodist church, an example that illustrates the ways in which attention to meaning potentially generates meaninglessness.

Sermons and Meaning-Making

Sermons are given by qualified lay preachers, or by church officers such as ministers and catechists. [3] In the Tavuki circuit, the superintendent minister assigns preachers to different churches on different Sundays; there are two main Sunday services, one in the late morning and one in the mid afternoon. In roving about the landscape, preachers help to stitch together a larger community with both their tongues and their feet. This system is ultimately derived from British Wesleyan Methodism's original evangelical system of field preaching that developed into a network of local circuits (see Tomkins 2003: 115–18).[4]

Each sermon is based on a passage from the Bible. Preachers usually choose their own verses to expound upon, but some consult the Fiji Methodist Church's calendar for its daily recommended Bible passage as a default choice for preaching. Preachers often relate Bible verses to contemporary Fijian concerns, explaining the practical relevance of holy text for people's daily lives. Such relevance is usually grounded in moral criticism. As Miyazaki has observed, for Fijian Methodists "a sermon often introduces a critical picture of village life as a *problem*" (2000a: 37). The "problem," as depicted by Fijian Methodists, is usually a lack of attention to "traditional" Fijian standards of conduct.

For example, on Christmas Day in Tavuki, 1998, Ratu Josaia Veibataki preached on Galatians 4:1–11, verses that describe humans as sons of God and contain a condensed summary of the New Testament: "But when the fulness of the time was come, God sent forth his Son, made of a woman, made under the law, To redeem them that were under the law" (verses 4–5). Veibataki, a lay preacher who was then also Nagonedau village's steward (*tuirara*),[5] explained the passage by comparing redemption to purchasing something in a store; this metaphor resonates with other Bible verses such as 1 Corinthians 6:20 and 1 Corinthians 7:23. Infusing the metaphor with a moral lesson, Veibataki brought the Galatians verses into conjunction with Fijian social expectations of compliance, and people's experiences of shopping in the capital city:[6]

Dana ina gauna nidavu	See the present age
ina visitoa lelevu dra tu mai Suva	in the big stores in Suva
dua na ere nodra	it's something, their
segata me lutu sobu[,] nodra	lowering their prices, the
viqajitakina jiko na visitoa lelevu	stores' competition
na lutu sobu ni nodra ivoli.	the reduction of their prices.
Me rawa ni voli varawarawa	To make buying easy
me kora laivi	to finish off
na	the
na iyaya makawa	old stock
me rawa ni kau tale mai iso na iyaya vou.	to be able to bring in some new stock.
Nona sucu mai na Turaga o Jisu Karisito	Our Lord Jesus Christ's birth
i via mai voli iko jiko vata kei au ina siga nidavu.	is to buy you and me today.
Via mai volia na bula	He wants to buy life
jiko kari vata kei na bula jiko ka.	there and life here [i.e., your life and my life].
Ka dodonu ke vei keda	And it's proper for us
me da kua ni vasaudredretakina	[not to make our lives cost too much.
na bula i jiko vei keda.	

Veibataki was urging his audience to be easy to "buy," not to be difficult. Such a code of cooperation—and submission to authority ("it's proper for us" not to be stubborn or recalcitrant)—is an exemplary Fijian value. Nonchiefly people, who are the large majority of the population, are ideally *talai rawarawa*, "easily sent"; i.e., people who do as they are told and do not act on their individual desires. Fijians, commoners and chiefs alike, generally accept the assertions of texts such as Romans 13 and 1 Peter 2, that temporal rulers gain their authority from God. By drawing on the verses from Galatians and comparing his listeners to goods on a shelf in a store, Veibataki was introducing a vivid, memorable metaphor and reinforcing a common Fijian social ethic. In short, he attempted to make Galatians 11:4–5 meaningful to Tavuki villagers in a practical and evocative way.

Meaning is a cultural product that emerges interactively and partially; thus, audience members necessarily share in meaning-making endeavors. Yet during Fijian Methodist church services, audiences are almost always silent. Responses are mostly limited to an occasional "*vinaka*" (good) in support of the preaching; in addition, children who sit up front are sometimes asked simple questions by preachers to convey a main point, and sometimes preachers tell obvious, innocuous jokes that earn laughter. Most of the time, however, the audience sits passively.[7] Considering the audience's expected lack of responsiveness, the rare joke that earns hearty laughter may be especially effective in making a point. In these cases, the intertextual dynamic is the same as in Bible citation: a text is used to lend authority to an assertion of general significance.

For example, here is a tale about "ice-blocks" (popsicles) that a preacher, Rev. Seru Tokalau, told in the Tavuki church on 15 June 2003. The story, which earned exuberant laughter, explains that God is all-good and evil is inherent to humanity.

Nanuma na
dua na kai Jaina, bula dede mai Levuka.

Kilai taucoko, au qai ka lailai mai sa kilai
  tu ni kai Jaina oqo, na yacana o Lal

sitoa ni gunu ni ice-block, gunu vinaka
  duadua.
Au qai tubu cake mai, sa ka lailai jiko
au se rogoca tu na sitoa oqo

ice-block, ko via gunu ice-block, sitoa
  ga nei Lal, kai Jaina . . .
Dua na siga sa lai voli ice-block mai e
  dua na kenaturaga
leqa jiko na drakana
a, vosota
qai veve jiko na gusuna.
Ni kilai tu na vica sagavulu na yabaki
ice-block vinaka duadua.
Sa lai voli ice-block na kenaturaga oqo
baleta ni veve jiko na gusuna.
Volia ga na ice-block
tovolea
sa complain vei kai Jaina
"Na cava sa ca kina, ice-block, sa dua na
  ice-block gunu ca."
Ka kaya kai Jaina:
"Sa sega ni ca na ice-block, sa ca ga na
  gusumu."
[Laughter]
Vei keda i Nacolase

ka kece vinaka e vakarautaka na Kalou
sega ni dua na ka e ca.
Na ca ga
sa jiko e lomada . . .

[I] remember
a Chinese man who's lived for a long
  time at Levuka.
Everyone knows him, I knew when I
  was just a kid that this Chinese
  man, named Lal[8]
[has an] ice-block store—the best-
  tasting drink.
I was growing up, I was a kid
I would hear about this ice-block
  store, if you want
to drink ice-block, [go to] Lal's store,
  the Chinese man . . .
One day, an old man goes to buy an
  ice-block
his mouth was messed up
oh, sorry
his mouth was crooked.
It's been known for how many decades
[this is] the best ice-block.
This old man goes to buy an ice-block
because his mouth is crooked.
He buys the ice-block
tastes it
complains to the Chinese man
"What's wrong with the ice-block, this
  ice-block tastes bad."
And the Chinese man says:
"The ice-block isn't bad, your mouth
  is bad."
[Laughter]
For us in Nacolase [Tavuki's dominant
  clan]
God provides all good things
nothing is bad.
Evil
is inside us . . .

The claims that God is all-good and that humans are responsible for evil are accepted by the Tavukian congregation, so the preacher was not using humor to smooth over a difficult subject. He was simply entertaining his listeners, but doing so to make a fundamental claim about the location of evil in the world. By proposing a parallel between the old man's crooked mouth and everybody's crooked hearts or intentions, Rev. Tokalau was attempting to make a meaningful claim about moral cosmology.

Preachers are not given commentary at the time of performance, so if feedback emerges it comes later, usually at casual kava-drinking sessions.[9] I should note, however, that I did not generally hear people comment on sermons after the fact; when drinking kava in Kadavu, people are more likely to comment on other village events such as current news, activities of visitors, results of rugby games, movements of boats and ships around the island, and the like.

Not all sermons are judged to be equally good, however. During his term of service on Kadavu, Rev. Serewai was both critic and guide for local preachers. Like John Wesley, Rev. Serewai had specific "ideals for preaching" and instructed his preachers on how to deliver effective sermons (Rack 1989: 344–45; see also Tomkins 2003: 118). In July 1996, after hearing what he apparently thought was a bad sermon, the minister held a meeting with the local lay preachers. As he later explained it to me, the congregation is "very wise," and conversant with Bible stories. He said that if a preacher announces he will be speaking on Luke 15, people already know that this chapter has the tale of the prodigal son, as well as two other parables, the lost sheep and the lost coin. Rev. Serewai emphasized that preachers need to "be well prepared" and to speak surely. To symbolize sure, confident preaching, he rattled off a string of plosive syllables—"pu pu pu pu pu," similar to the sound of a machine gun. He said that preachers ought to prepare by reading their chosen Biblical text repeatedly, thinking about it, praying, and even fasting. Similarly, in January 1999, he gave the villagers of Baidamudamu some preaching tips; the setting for this lesson was a friendly kava-drinking session. The minister told the Baidamudamu preachers that they really had to know the passage they were expounding upon, and he quoted Ephesians chapter 6, verses 10 through 14, which speak of putting on "the full armor of God." One has to suit up properly—i.e., be fully prepared intellectually and spiritually—to explain the word of God to a congregation.[10]

Not only did Rev. Serewai give advice; on at least one occasion, he lent his sermon notes to another preacher. In May 1999, Ratu Josaia Veibataki preached a sermon on Stephen being the first martyr. Surprised at how familiar it sounded, I eventually realized that it was the same sermon on which Rev. Serewai had consulted me for translation advice. The minister had been reading the Scottish theologian William Barclay's reference works, and I discussed translations with him as he prepared his sermon notes. So the sermon had a complicated history, from William Barclay to Rev. Serewai, with some help from me, and then on to Veibataki in a flow of translations. When I asked Rev. Serewai if he helped other preachers with sermon notes, he said no, he had helped only Ratu Jo. But discourse often slips the bonds of authorship. Once, catechist Tomasi Laveasiga preached a sermon based partly on feedback he had gotten from Baidamudamu villagers on a sermon that Rev. Serewai had preached there. As these various preachers moved about the landscape, so did their texts.[11]

The example below is a rare case of a sermon being commented upon publicly—but it was a doubly complicated context, because this was a sermon itself, in which the preacher told about a kava-drinking session from the night before in which he had asked people about the assertions in another preacher's sermon. In this pastiche of texts, the preacher, Sevanaia Takotavuki, jumped from example to example as he danced around the central point, which is that if one commits one's life to Jesus, he or she will ensure eventual eternal rest in heaven:

Jiko ina bogi au vataroga jiko vei kedra na turaga	Last night I was asking the chiefs—
viqaravi jiko ina vuku ni	[we] were serving the

vuvale mai Vale
taroga jiko
"Kemutou bau marautakina jiko na mate?

"Mu marautakina jiko vavinaka na mate?"
Lako mai na kena isau
dui vakasama
totoka na kena isau.
Au sa qai tarogi . . . au mai, "Io.
"Au sa marautakina jiko na mate."
"Baleta?"
Baleta na vanua kacei
na vanua tawa mudu.
Da rogoca na ivunau nei
nei
Tuikilakila
Talatala Tuikilakila.
Tukuna ke
tukuna o kia
vua na turaga bale sa mate
"He's going home."
Kena ibalebale, sega ni noda vanua
sega ni rawa ni o na vakacegu jiko ina
    vuravura ka.
O iko sa via muri Jisu.
Noda vanua
noda vale
waraki keda jiko mai lomalagi. . . .
Sa tukuni vei kedra, kena gauna ka

tukuni vei kemi ina somiyaqona jiko kacei

kena gauna ka, mo cakacakatakina
kevani ko marautakina jiko
na yaco na gauna o na mate.
Baleta na yava?
Mo rawata na vanua kacei.
Cakacakatakina
kena irairai au tukuna jiko ka. . . .
Tukuna o Jisu, "Oi au na sala.
"Oi au ga na salevu ki na vanua kacei."
Mino tale i dua.
Muria jiko na gone turaga o Jisu Karisito.
Sa kacivi nomu bula.
Sa yaco na vanua ko kacivi ke, toso jiko.

Baleta na yava? Ta cake ki na vanua kacei.
Vani ga na ivunau ni Talatala Tuikilakila
"We are going home."
Vanua sa vakatabaki dua ga
vei kedra ga na vakabauta
kedra ga na liga savasava
kedra ga
muri Jisu jiko
ina bula ka.

family at Vale House[12]
[I] asked,
"Are you happy about death? [i.e., do
    you welcome it?]
"Are you quite happy about death?"
Answers came
different thoughts
they were good answers.
Then I asked . . . myself, "Yes.
"I am happy about death."
"Why?" [they asked].
Because that place
is eternal.
We heard the sermon of
of
Tuikilakila
Reverend Tuikilakila.
⌈He said
about the high chief who died [recently]
"He's going home."
This means, it's not our place
it's impossible for you to rest in this
    world.
You want to follow Jesus.
Our place
our house
awaits us in heaven. . . .
[I] told them, this time [i.e., the
    eternity of heaven]
[I] told us at the kava-drinking
    session there
you should work for this time
if you are happy about
the arrival of the time that you will die.
Why?
So you can get to that place.
Work for it
that's what I said. . . .
Jesus said, "I am the way
"Only I am the path to that place." [13]
There is no other.
Follow the Lord Jesus Christ.
He's calling your life.
[When] that place comes that you are
    called to, go.
Why? Look up to that place.
It's like in Rev. Tuikilakila's sermon:
"We are going home."
This place is only for
those who believe
those with clean hands
only those
following Jesus
in this life.

The preacher, who was the village catechist (*vakatawa*) at the time he delivered this sermon in July 2003, was not only expressing the central practical imperative of Protestant Christianity, to commit one's life to Jesus, but he was also evidently making claims about his own authority.[14] Note how he describes himself questioning people in a chiefly house, and then revealing the truth to them, at the Vale kava-drinking session. He attempts to build his own authority by presenting his words along with those of a famous Fijian preacher who had recently been in Tavuki, Rev. Tuikilakila Waqairatu (quoted in English, n.b.), and also the words of Jesus. Even as he obviously seeks some personal glory in this sermon, however, Takotavuki is fundamentally concerned with making a meaningful statement. In fact, his statement concerns one of the sources of Weber's problem of meaning, namely, death and how to suffer properly.

In these three examples, preachers are displaying their "competence" by relating texts to contexts (Briggs 1988); but more than simply flourishing their rhetorical talents, they are staking claims to meaningful exposition. This exposition depends on style as well as substance. Sermons' style highlights their distinctiveness and reinforces the sense that words spoken from the pulpit have particular gravity. Fijian Methodists often imitate Western-style evangelical preaching through dramatic intonation, raising their voices to a crescendo of volume, then dropping down to a restrained tone, like waves crashing on a shore. Some preachers, less subtle, shout most of the time. In 1921, the missionary Rev. Wallace Deane wrote wryly, "All have volubility in preaching" (1921: 114). Sermons are stylistically distinct from other forms of Fijian public discourse, being one of the rare occasions when a man can yell for a sustained period. Notably, preachers' intonational pattern is generally the opposite of chiefly speakers' intonational pattern, which is "relatively slow, almost halting in some cases. . . . The pitch register is even and low" (Arno 1990: 254). The implicit rule seems to be that when chiefs speak, you must make yourself listen to them; they do not need to persuade you to listen (Arno 1990: 254).[15] When chiefs speak during Methodist Church services, they maintain (or import) their quiet, chiefly style of speaking. Buell Quain commented, "Wesleyan services, which permit men of low status . . . to speak presumptuously from the dais in the church, amuse most chiefs" (1948: 410).

Susan Harding's description of American fundamentalist sermons applies well to Tavukian Methodism: "Sermons occur in the context of clear ritual format, of a collective, sanctifying scenario in which the mode of interpretation is enacted" (2000: 36). By virtue of their distinctive style of performance and their placement near the end of the service, sermons are positioned to be eminently meaningful religious action in Fijian society. In other words, sermons are vehicles for meaning-making effected by their style and structural position as well as their content. With preachers orating dramatically, yelling and then murmuring, sermons stand apart from ordinary speech events; by their placement near the end of the service, completing the collective ritual of Christian gathering, their significance is emphasized. Sermons are not just another item in the syntagmatic presentation of Fijian Methodist services; they are the main clause at the end of the sentence.

Metasemantics

In Fijian Methodist preaching, meaningfulness is often claimed in a specific, formulaic way. A phrase uttered by some preachers, and other orators, as will be described below, is *kena ibalebale*, which translates literally as "its meaning [is]" and can usually be glossed as "that means" or "what it means is," or simply "meaning" (as a verb).[16] In other words, *kena ibalebale* is a metasemantic phrase, explicitly making a claim to meaningfulness. Speakers use this formula as a pivot between what-needs-to-be-explained and its explanation. For example, they might use *kena ibalebale* as a bridge between Biblical passages and the ways they should be understood in Tavukian terms.

A good example of such an explicit metasemantic declaration comes from Ratu Josaia Veibataki's sermon given at Namuana village in October 1998. He preached:

Sa sega ni noda na vanua oqo.	⌈This land is not ours.
Kena ibalebale beka kacei	**That means**
keda da i sa mai	we are
keda da i sa vani tu beka ga	we are like
keda da i sa wili tu talega	we are counted as
kedra na vulagi dra mai tu ena noda vanua.	the foreigners who are in our land [i.e., Indo-Fijians].
Dra mai lisi tu beka ga.	They lease [the land].
Kena ibalebale	**That means**
na nomu bula jiko ina vuravura ka	your living in this world
ko i na mini bula tawa mudu jiko ke	you will not live forever
jiko na gauna	there is a time
ko na lesu vua.	you will return to Him.

Here, Veibataki forged a complicated chain of meaning. First, drawing on the Book of Exodus' story of the Jewish exile, he made the claim that "This land," Fiji, "is not ours." He drew a comparison that his Kadavuan listeners would find threatening: Fijians are just like immigrant Indo-Fijians—that is, in danger of not really belonging in Fiji. This was a strong political claim to derive from the Book of Exodus, echoing themes of a rightful homeland and raising the specter of its loss. After this pronouncement, Veibataki inflected the statement "this land is not ours" with a different significance, turning to ultimate metaphysical issues: "you will not live forever," he told the congregation, "there is a time you will return to Him"—that is, you will die and go to the afterworld. In this short passage from his sermon, Veibataki articulated his political and religious statements by using the metasemantic pivot of *kena ibalebale*.

Because *kena ibalebale* is a claim to meaningfulness based on the speaker's understanding, its public utterance is a claim to authority. Accordingly, not all speakers use it in the same ways, and it is not heard in all performance genres (see Tomlinson 2002b). For example, only once have I noted hearing *kena ibalebale* used in a prayer, which is not surprising because prayers

are either supplications or praises, offering little opportunity for the explication of meaning per se. On the other hand, formal interviews seem to elicit
many uses of *kena ibalebale*, which makes sense because of their pedagogical
nature. My point, however, is that when *kena ibalebale* is used it usually positions the speaker authoritatively: "There is a whole dimension of authorized language," Bourdieu (1991: 76) wrote, "its rhetoric, syntax, vocabulary
and even pronunciation, which exists purely to underline the authority of
its author and the trust he demands." *Kena ibalebale* is an example of such
authorized language, and its prominence in sermons calls attention to links
between meaning and power.

As meaning-making rituals, sermons are *kena ibalebale* writ large. The syn-
ecdoche of "its meaning [is]" stands for what preachers attempt to accomplish
in the pulpit. In other words, sermons are ritual attempts to generate explicit
meaningfulness. Sermons (or, rather, preachers) explain things. They relate
Bible verses to social concerns, present models of ideal vs. actual society, and
after describing what proper Christianity is, exhort people to live up to it.
Preachers' claims (such as, in the above examples: one should make oneself
easy to "buy" with the blood of redemption; humans are responsible for evil;
people should not be afraid of death, for it leads to eternal rest in heaven)
become resonantly meaningful when preachers cite Bible verses, draw parallels with present-day Fijian life, and tell personal stories, spinning the "webs
of significance" that Geertz (1973a: 5) famously wrote about. However, audience members may judge the meaningfulness of sermons in ways that are
different from what the preacher intended.

When meaning-making becomes an explicit endeavor, one begins to see
the shadowy outlines of meaning's limits. As Hirokazu Miyazaki has shown,
Fijian ritual actions involve moments at which the *limits* of agency and
politics are emphasized (Miyazaki 2000a, 2000b). Here, I attempt to build
on his work and show how Fijian Methodist sermons suggest the limits of
meaning. In other words, rituals that focus on the articulation or achievement of meaning can also suggest meaning's boundaries and, perhaps, violate those boundaries.

The Limits of Meaning

On Sunday, 28 February 1999, approximately ninety people attended the late
morning service in Tavuki village's Methodist church. For most of the service,
everything went normally: the service leader prayed, a money collection was
taken, and everyone sang hymns. Jona (this is a pseudonym), a middle-aged
man, read a lesson from Daniel chapter six.

Then it came time for the sermon to be preached. Jona stood in the pulpit
. . . And then, nothing happened.

Or, rather, Jona refused to deliver a sermon. He mumbled a few short
words, and asked for the final hymn to be sung. He had spoken in a low,
quiet voice, but not in an authoritative chiefly way. Apparently, Jona did not

want to be heard. Sitting toward the back of the church, I had no idea what he had said.

That afternoon, I watched the fallout from the non-sermon. Rev. Serewai told me how, after he had given the final prayer which closed the service, he told Jona that his sermon had been too short—this was a mocking understatement—and Jona bowed his head in shame. Rev. Serewai joked that the failed preacher's name was not "Jona," it was "Daniel," presumably referring to the fact that all Jona had done was to read the lesson from Daniel chapter six. One of my best friends laughed at the hapless preacher but also said he should not be allowed to preach again. Indeed, Jona would not reappear in the pulpit for five months, and then only as an assistant helping to lead the service, not as a preacher.

The story of Jona's non-sermon suggests how the obligation to make meanings in Fijian Methodism can actually have the reverse effect, and call attention to the inability to make meanings—or, if forced to speak, to the fact of doing so meaninglessly, as Jona did. He mumbled and then ended the service by calling for the final hymn. Because Fijian Methodist sermons are performance sites for making meanings explicit, failure to deliver a sermon is a marked failure to create meaning. Jona was supposed to preach on a passage from Daniel chapter six, and so he got up to speak, stood in the pulpit, and delivered utterances. But, in this context, they did not make any sense. Or, rather, the sense that they made was nonsense; thus the mixed reactions of humor and anger.

By critically emphasizing preachers' need to be well prepared, Rev. Serewai had raised the possibility to preachers that they might *not* be adequate to the task of explaining the Bible from the pulpit. As he had told them, they should put on "the full armor of God" to explain God's word to the congregation, and they should be able to preach confidently—"pu pu pu pu pu," as he put it, sounding like a machine gun. Jona, though, was unable to fire any meanings at the congregation. Other preachers who did not feel ready to preach had the good sense to bow out gracefully in advance, asking the catechist to take their places. Reasons people gave for missing their assigned preaching dates included adherence to traditional obligations and drinking too much kava the night before.[17] Jona, however, was simply unable to preach, even though he stood in the pulpit. The moment for ritual pronunciation of meaning had arrived, but he failed conspicuously at the task.

Bourdieu described rituals as "the limiting case of situations of *imposition* in which, through the exercise of a technical competence which may be very imperfect, a social competence is exercised—namely, that of the legitimate speaker, authorized to speak and to speak with authority" (1991: 41). But when technical competence fails completely, legitimate authority vanishes. Just as not all speakers have equal rights to explain all subjects, not all preachers can make claims to meaningfulness with equal effectiveness. Rituals of meaning-making necessarily create the possibility of a vague and chaotic realm in which meanings might be present but cannot be made, or might be absent and have attention to be called to such absence.

Ethnographic Meanings

If Fijian Methodist preachers are called upon to generate meaningfulness ritually, then what about the anthropologist who sets out to produce an ethnography? Michael Silverstein describes culture as, "with the exception of a small part of language, but a congeries of iconic-indexical systems of meaningfulness of behavior" (1976: 54). That is, culture emerges from semiotic relationships construable as meaning(ful); the limits of meaning are thus a necessary subject of ethnography. Seen in this light, the ethnographic project seems a bit like the Fijian Methodist preacher's project, recontextualizing texts and practices in order to make greater realities intelligible. The desire to make meanings explicit is not only, perhaps, a modern Christian desire; it is also an ethnographic desire.

Some texts, however, refuse to sit comfortably on the page. In his ethnography *Kapingamarangi*, Kenneth Emory retells a local story about a rat. When the rat saw a fish that was in trouble from fishermen, he put on a kilt made from *Scaevola* (fan flower) leaves, then danced and chanted: "The Scaevola leaves at your ear will not float." In a footnote, Emory tells us: "When I asked for the meaning of the chant given by the rat, they said they did not know because it was composed by the rat" (1965: 351). In other words, the people of Kapingamarangi knew the chant, but could not explain the unintelligible phrase "The . . . leaves at your ear will not float." The rat's chant was unintelligible discourse, but it was circulated publicly. People could not understand it, but they could—and did—speak it.

Is it meaningless? Most scholars would say no. The meaning of the rat's chant might not be apprehensible to a reader, but its significance emerges from the contexts of authorship and performance—it is a text embedded in another text (the story itself), and in the embedding, the telling, and the hearing, some kinds of meaning surely emerge, whether phrased as "rats are inscrutable," "rats are magical," or something similar. Yet as ethnographers increasingly describe culture as heteroglossic (and write in experimental prose styles to reflect this state), meaning may increasingly seem partial, flexible, and unbounded. What was Emory supposed to do when people in Kapingamarangi told him that they did not know the meaning of the rat's chant? He might have responded as Jean Comaroff did when she was confronted by the letter H. She describes how, since the letter H appears in all the visions of one South African Zionist bishop, his congregation's ritual vestments display this letter. However, she tells us, "He seemed unclear as to its significance . . . it is not the subject of discussion in the church—and suggested that it might stand for both the English 'holy' and Afrikaans 'heilig'" (Comaroff 1985: 205). Later in her chapter, Comaroff speculates, "H . . . suggests perhaps a double cross, but it is also emblematic of the power of literacy itself" (1985: 226). A Geertzian compulsion to create meanings is at work here, for the ethnographer if not for her subjects.

It is not just isolated symbols and decontextualized texts that threaten to push past the limits of meaning, however. In trying to apprehend culture, anthropologists create an *a priori* category of meaningfulness that they then attempt to achieve. For example, when Gregory Bateson told Jane Fajans that the Baining were "unstudiable" because they did not have "any formulable culture," she took this as a challenge and not a warning. After all, as Geertz had pointed out: "Men without culture . . . would be unworkable monstrosities" (1973b: 49). What did Bateson mean by the adjective "formulable," though? For Fajans, it was a claim about meaningfulness: "My own insight into the underlying order of meaning which informs Baining social relations came when I realized that the Baining themselves felt their social life to be constituted of very few types of repetitive activities. Far from being amorphous, deficient in meaning or lacking in form, social interaction to them appeared rather strictly ordered, its constituent activities charged with meaning and value. . . . Baining social interaction is saturated with meaning . . ." (Fajans 1997: 6). Faced with a society that takes very little interest in interpreting its actions, Fajans gamely carries on the ethnographic project, figuring out what the real "underlying order of meaning" must be. But such an attempt, I suggest, is hobbled by the certainty that "meaning" exists on its own in structures, sites, and institutions.

One proponent of the "new ethnography" of 1980s and 1990s anthropology criticized the anthropological "desire for decontaminated 'meaning,' the need to require that visual and verbal constructs yield meaning down to their last detail" (Stewart 1996: 26). I agree with her criticism, and suggest that ethnographers begin by asking if and how meaningfulness emerges in ritual action. Once meaningfulness is seen as a cultural project, meaninglessness necessarily becomes a possibility. In his non-sermon, Jona showed the limits of meaning in Fijian Methodist sermons by violating the boundaries of meaningfulness when he failed at his assigned task of making meaningfulness explicit. Christian sermons—and scholarly ethnographies—approach the limits of meaning in their determination to attain fixity.

Notes

1. Tavuki is the chiefly village of Kadavu Island. Nearly all of Kadavu's total population of approximately 9,800 are indigenous Fijians, and over 93 percent are members of the Methodist Church (Government of Fiji 1995). Tavuki village's own population is approximately 125, and includes the paramount chief Tui Tavuki; the leading government-appointed chief for the island, the Roko Tui Kadavu; and superintendent Methodist ministers who are appointed to the island for five-year terms. On church statistics, see n. 4 below.
2. For a satirical comment on this kind of education in Oceania, see Hau'ofa 1994: 57. For an analysis of the sacralization of soil in Fiji, see Tomlinson 2002a.
3. Andrew Arno (2003) argues that ritual meanings can circulate vigorously through time and space without being expressed in language: "Nonlanguage meaning sunken into the self forgetfulness of action is a powerful referential resource in ritual and, in association with coherent patterns of social activity and sentiment in everyday life, it can demonstrate an endurance over time that parallels that of language" (Arno 2003: 816). In this regard, all the taken-for-granted aspects of attending Methodist services in Fiji—that people will come, that they will have bathed and oiled, that they will have dressed in formal clothes and sit in pews appropriate to their positions in the social hierarchy, etc.—are integral parts of the ritual's effect for

participants, although they are not often commented upon. However, in this chapter I am focusing on the explicit, verbal articulation of claims to meaningfulness, which is the primary task of the preacher standing in the pulpit.

4. In April 2002, the Tavuki catechist recorded a total of 171 congregants in Tavuki and neighboring Nagonedau village, with a total of 19 preachers. The superintendent minister's statistics for 2003 listed 14 preachers in Tavuki and Nagonedau, and a total of 110 preachers for the entire circuit of Tavuki, comprising ten villages, the town of Vunisea, the high school at Richmond (Rijimodi), and the settlement of Busa.

5. The steward's role is to represent the Church to the chiefs and vice versa. See Tomlinson 2002b.

6. In this chapter, lines of transcription are broken at speakers' pauses.

7. Bruce Knauft (2002) suggests that active engagement with "modern" institutions, including Christianity, can require learning how to be passive. He coins the term "recessive agency" for this phenomenon, and suggests that such engagements can both foster "modern" desires and effectively thwart them.

8. "Lal" is an Indian name, but the original Chinese name is presumably close in pronunciation.

9. Kava is a beverage made from the dried and pounded roots and stems of a pepper plant, *Piper methysticum*. It is drunk for hours every night by almost all adult men in Tavuki; women drink a fair amount too, but not with the everyday regularity and volume of the men. Kava-drinking is valued not only as an index of "traditional" village life, but also for its practical function of bringing people together into groups for storytelling, gossip, discussion, debate, etc.

10. This sense of subordinate preachers' getting meanings wrong has a long history in Fiji. In the 1840s, the great Methodist missionary John Hunt complained about teachers who could not explain the Bible adequately: "Among the teachers of Viwa Circuit, he found their theology deficient and their explanation of the biblical text nonsensical. 'The result of their [Fijian teachers'] preaching,' said Hunt, 'is to make the people sour not affectionate'" (Thornley 2000: 245).

11. Compare Besnier (1995, especially chapters 6 and 7), who describes how Tuvaluan Congregationalists share preaching notes from their "sermon notebooks" according to "traditional" patterns of the exchange of intellectual property (1995: 135).

12. By "serving the family at Vale House," he means he was drinking kava in observance of the recent death of a man who lived in that house. "Vale" is a pseudonym.

13. This is Takotavuki's homespun adaptation of John 14:6, "I am the way, the truth, and the life: no man cometh unto the Father, but by me."

14. For a resonant example of a Fijian speaker posing Christian questions and positioning himself authoritatively, see Miyazaki's description of a Bible study session (Miyazaki 2000a: 34–35).

15. Arno's descriptions from Lau (eastern Fiji) are accurate for Kadavu as well.

16. *Ibalebale* ("meaning") comes from the verb *bale(ta)*, which Dixon translates as "caused by, mean" (1988: 358).

17. As an example of traditional obligations preventing someone from preaching, I knew one man who had been assigned to preach at Solodamu village, but felt he could not go there because he still owed Solodamuans particular gifts for a funeral he had been unable to attend.

References

Arno, Andrew. 1990. "Disentangling Indirectly: The Joking Debate in Fijian Social Control." In *Disentangling: Conflict Discourse in Pacific Societies*, ed. K. A. Watson-Gegeo and G. M. White. Stanford: Stanford University Press.

———. 2003. "Aesthetics, Intuition, and Reference in Fijian Ritual Communication: Modularity in and out of Language." *American Anthropologist* 105, no. 4: 807–19.

Asad, Talal. 1993. *Genealogies of Religion: Discipline and Reasons of Power in Christianity and Islam*. Baltimore: The Johns Hopkins University Press.

Besnier, Niko. 1995. *Literacy, Emotion, and Authority: Reading and Writing on a Polynesian Atoll*. Cambridge: Cambridge University Press.

Bourdieu, Pierre. 1991. *Language and Symbolic Power*. Ed. J. B. Thompson, trans. G. Raymond and M. Adamson. Cambridge: Harvard University Press.

Briggs, Charles. 1988. *Competence in Performance: The Creativity of Tradition in Mexicano Verbal Art*. Philadelphia: University of Pennsylvania Press.

Cammack, Floyd McKee. 1962. "Bauan Grammar." Ph.D. diss., Cornell University.

Capell, A. 1991. *A New Fijian Dictionary*. 3rd ed. Suva, Fiji: Government Printer.

Comaroff, Jean. 1985. *Body of Power, Spirit of Resistance: The Culture and History of a South African People*. Chicago: University of Chicago Press.

Crapanzano, Vincent. 2000. *Serving the Word: Literalism in America from the Pulpit to the Bench*. New York: The New Press.

Daniell, David. 1994. *William Tyndale: A Biography*. New Haven: Yale University Press.

Deane, W. 1921. *Fijian Society: Or, The Sociology and Psychology of the Fijians*. London: Macmillan.

Dirks, Nicholas B. 1994. "Ritual and Resistance: Subversion as a Social Fact." In *Culture/Power/History: A Reader in Contemporary Social Theory*, ed. N. B. Dirks, G. Eley, and S. B. Ortner. Princeton: Princeton University Press.

Dixon, R. M. W. 1988. *A Grammar of Boumaa Fijian*. Chicago: University of Chicago Press.

———. 1997. *The Rise and Fall of Languages*. Cambridge: Cambridge University Press.

Emory, Kenneth P. 1965. *Kapingamarangi: Social and Religious Life of a Polynesian Atoll*. Honolulu: Bernice P. Bishop Museum.

Fajans, Jane. 1997. *They Make Themselves: Work and Play among the Baining of Papua New Guinea*. Chicago: University of Chicago Press.

Fiji, Government of. 1995. "Provincial Profile Report, 1994–1995: Kadavu." [Photocopy in author's possession.]

Geertz, Clifford. 1973a. "Thick Description: Toward an Interpretive Theory of Culture." In *The Interpretation of Cultures: Selected Essays*. New York: BasicBooks.

———. 1973b [1966]. "The Impact of the Concept of Culture on the Concept of Man." In *The Interpretation of Cultures: Selected Essays*. New York: BasicBooks.

Geraghty, Paul A. 1989. "Language Reform: History and Future of Fijian." In *Language Reform: History and Future*, vol. IV. Ed. I. Fodor and C. Hagège. Hamburg: Helmut Buske Verlag.

Harding, Susan Friend. 2000. *The Book of Jerry Falwell: Fundamentalist Language and Politics*. Princeton: Princeton University Press.

Hau'ofa, Epeli. 1994. *Tales of the Tikongs*. Honolulu: University of Hawaii Press.

Hudson, Anne. 1986. "Wyclif and the English Language." In *Wyclif in His Times*, ed. A. Kenny. Oxford: Clarendon Press.

Keane, Webb. 1991. "Delegated Voice: Ritual Speech, Risk, and the Making of Marriage Alliances in Anakalang." *American Ethnologist* 18, no. 2: 311–30.

———. 1995. "The Spoken House: Text, Act, and Object in Eastern Indonesia." *American Ethnologist* 22, no. 1: 102–24.

———. 1997a. "Religious Language." *Annual Review of Anthropology* 26: 47–71.

———. 1997b. *Signs of Recognition: Powers and Hazards of Representation in an Indonesian Society*. Berkeley: University of California Press.

Keyes, Charles. 2002. "Weber and Anthropology." *Annual Review of Anthropology* 31: 233–55.

Knauft, Bruce M. 2002. *Exchanging the Past: A Rainforest World of Before and After*. Chicago: University of Chicago Press.

Luhrmann, T. M. 1989. _Persuasions of the Witch's Craft: Ritual Magic in Contemporary England_. Cambridge: Harvard University Press.

Miyazaki, Hirokazu. 2000a. "Faith and Its Fulfillment: Agency, Exchange, and the Fijian Aesthetics of Completion." _American Ethnologist_ 27, no. 1: 31–51.

———. 2000b. "The Limits of Politics." _People and Culture in Oceania_ 16: 109–22.

Quain, Buell. 1948. _Fjian Village_. Chicago: University of Chicago Press.

Rack, Henry D. 1989. _Reasonable Enthusiast: John Wesley and the Rise of Methodism_. Philadelphia: Trinity Press International.

Shelton, Austin J. 1976. "Controlling Capricious Gods." In _Language in Religious Practice_, ed. W. J. Samarin. Rowley: Newbury House.

Silverstein, Michael. 1976. "Shifters, Linguistic Categories, and Cultural Description." In _Meaning in Anthropology_, ed. K. H. Basso and H. A. Selby. Albuquerque: School of American Research, University of New Mexico Press.

Stewart, Kathleen. 1996. _A Space on the Side of the Road: Cultural Poetics in an "Other" America_. Princeton: Princeton University Press.

Thornley, Andrew. 2000. _The Inheritance of Hope: John Hunt, Apostle of Fiji_. Suva, Fiji: Institute of Pacific Studies, University of the South Pacific.

Tomkins, Stephen. 2003. _John Wesley: A Biography_. Grand Rapids: William B. Eerdmans.

Tomlinson, Matt. 2002a. "Sacred Soil in Kadavu, Fiji." _Oceania_ 72, no. 4: 237–57.

———. 2002b. "Voice & Earth: Making Religious Meaning and Power in Christian Fiji." Ph.D. diss., University of Pennsylvania.

———. 2004. "Ritual, Risk, and Danger: Chain Prayers in Fiji." _American Anthropologist_ 106, no. 1: 6–16.

7

Converting Meanings and the Meanings of Conversion in Samoan Moral Economies

Ilana Gershon

Samoans are no innocents to the experience of conversion. Samoans have both been converted and converted others to Christianity since 1830. That year John Williams of the London Missionary Society began formal conversions after he landed felicitously (guided by a Tongan follower) in the harbor of Malietoa, the next titular head of Samoa. He brought Christianity to his host, and through Malietoa to Samoans in general. Samoans then became missionaries themselves, traveling under the aegis of the London Missionary Society or the Methodist church to Tuvalu, Rotuma, Niue, many parts of the Solomon Islands, Papua New Guinea, and other parts of the Pacific (Lange 1997: 19). In the last fifty years, this penchant for conversion has become involuted. Samoans continue to convert others and each other, but the conversion is now frequently from one form of Christianity to another. In the process, Samoans must distinguish between different relationships one can have to Christianity, and to moral orders in general, to justify their conversions. Conversion encourages Samoans to evaluate what kinds of Christianity and what kinds of worship are right—that is, it provokes comparisons that are also critiques. In this chapter, I will discuss how contemporary conversion requires that Samoans attribute meaning and meaninglessness anew to various forms of Christian worship, generating reflexive explanations of their personal transformations. I focus on Samoan migrants in New Zealand who join evangelical churches, rejecting Catholicism or more established Protestantism.

The types of conversion I am discussing here—shifting from one form of Christianity to another—is not a rejection of one set of moral guidelines for another. While my interlocutors would tell me occasionally that people who worship in more established Samoan churches (such as Catholic or Congregational) are not truly Christian, this critique seemed based on their assessment of mainline Christian practices and the authenticity of others' beliefs, not a doctrinal difference. What intrigues me in particular about these conversions is that my interlocutors were not rejecting the content of a former Christianity. Many in fact were willing to attend a more mainline church in the morning, and worshipped in evangelical churches in the afternoon.[1] I argue that they were rejecting the reflexive stance taken to a moral order by members of a Samoan church congregation involved in ritual exchanges, and instead adopting a different stance, one they considered more valid. This transition is based on the ways in which ritual exchanges and capitalism structure certain reflexive stances as moral. People are literally moving between different moral economies, not religions.

When my interlocutors discussed their decisions to change churches with me, they did not talk about moving between moral economies. While the content of their preoccupations has led me to this analysis, their own voiced concerns were with meaningful expressions of worship. They spoke often about how worship in more mainline churches felt meaningless—that the services were not adequate vehicles for allowing them to convey and experience their strong connection to God. In this chapter, I am arguing that my interlocutors' attributions of meaning and meaninglessness to particular forms of worship are the tangible ways in which they experience their connections to moral orders. Moral orders that allow them to structure their practices in ways they find compelling are experienced as meaningful; moral orders that do not are experienced as meaningless. So where I would speak of one's stance toward a moral order, my interlocutors would speak of meaning.

I am departing from other recent scholarship on new religious conversions in the Pacific. The focus in literature on conversion in the Pacific has been primarily on initial conversions to Christianity, not how people choose to move from church to church (Firth 1976; Barker 1990; Ballard 2000; see also Hefner 1993). Even when looking at conversion between Christian denominations, other analysts have emphasized the ways in which Polynesians retain the pre-contact spiritual beliefs up until they convert to a new form of Christianity by joining a Mormon or an evangelical church (Ramstad 2000, Ernst 1994). These scholars view conversions as transformations of worldviews, in accordance with Bennetta Jules-Rosette (1975), who describes conversion as "a powerful clash resulting from the shift of one realm of thought and action to another . . . ." This is not the perspective I take here. In this article, I am taking seriously the fact that the people I interviewed had been Christian prior to their conversion experience. They were not switching moral orders; rather, they were changing the ways in which they related to the moral orders in which they participated. I am departing from other scholarly perspectives by focusing on the Christianities my interlocutors left behind, instead of uncovering the lingering vestiges of non-Christian spiritual beliefs.[2] In this sense, in response to Joel Robbins' (2003) call to look at the ways in which Pentecostal religions can be socially constructed to offer discontinuities, I am noting that both continuity and discontinuity must be examined with a critical gaze. Robbins points out that Pentecostal believers often view their faith in terms of discontinuities, which is at odds with scholars' focus on continuities in traditions. He calls for analyses that examine how people imagine and use ruptures as well as perceived continuities.

I am arguing that when my interlocutors converted, they were responding to the ways in which the moral is created in the various moral economies in which they engage. My interlocutors were leaving behind not only churches, but also ways of presenting themselves as moral beings through complex economic exchanges. When they entered new congregations, they learned new ways to be reflexively linked to moral economies. At the same time, my interlocutors would attribute meaninglessness to the ways that their former church economies are still experienced by others as moral. These shifts in meaning and morality were often also shifts in reflexivity—people were learning to carve out different personhoods through these conversions as well. What was at stake in conversion for my interlocutors was not the type of doctrine they believed but the type of moral self they fashioned. Thus the meaninglessness that my interlocutors found in mainline Samoan churches had little to do with texts, and everything to do with how best to practice Christianity, which included how best to demonstrate their faith.

The Accidental Fieldworker

I did my research for this paper accidentally, in the pursuit of other questions. During my fieldwork in New Zealand, I was interested in how differences in Samoan families are made into cultural differences, so I was interviewing couples in mixed marriages. I used what is formally called a snowball sample—asking people at the end of the interview if they knew of anyone else I should interview. This technique generated its own dynamic in my fieldwork, providing entry to a community of people, all of whom knew each other. For a period of three or four months I interviewed a number of couples who attended evangelical Christian churches. After several of these interviews, I learned that a good way of eliciting complex life stories was asking how they had received the Lord into their life. This question would trigger a narrative, well-rehearsed and illuminating. I would learn about respondents' conversions, about how their lives had profoundly changed in response to a powerful spiritual insight. I was always clear that I did not share their faith. I am Jewish, which was a curiosity for them, but also made me into a possible convert. While this is not necessarily what was at stake in every, or even many, of these interviews, it was an undercurrent (largely because in the evangelical Christian imaginary, testimony about receiving Christ into one's life is often given in an enunciative space of nonbelievers [see Crapanzano 1994: 871; Harding 2000: 39]). But I was a single-minded interviewer, who cared only about the nuances of families. I did not appreciate what people were trying to tell me about how relating to Christian precepts from an evangelical perspective had changed them. In this paper, I am responding to the conversion element in the stories that I collected and to the people I spoke with, albeit in hindsight.

Most of the couples I interviewed attended a born-again church that met every Sunday in a benefactor's commercial gym. Meeting in a gym, surrounded by mirrors and stuffed nylon mats, created a subtext of muscular Christianity. People dressed casually, sometimes in T-shirts and jeans, in contrast to the more formal attire that Samoans would wear to other churches. This church was a culturally mixed congregation, although its founding families—who were still its most active members—were Samoans or married to Samoans.[3] While I was in Auckland, this fact sporadically elicited criticism that the church was too Samoan. Those running the church were often connected through family ties—the pastor, for instance, was an Australian whose mother-in-law was a very influential Samoan and a prominent figure in several of the conversion stories I collected. Her children and relatives were also active church members. There were many young families, as well as a cadre of single people, many of whom were evaluating each other as potential spouses. Of the Samoans who attended, many were New Zealand-raised Samoan. The church also met late in the afternoon, thus allowing people to attend other churches. While the church itself was based in West Auckland and drew most of its congregation from surrounding neighborhoods, some people would travel from Central Auckland or even make the hour long trip from South Auckland to worship there. Several of the members I interviewed were part of an emerging Samoan socioeconomic group, working for job training and in other government-sponsored programs for assisting the unemployed. Three Samoan members of the All-Blacks, New Zealand's national rugby team, attended while I was doing research. It was a congregation full of people learning how to negotiate their surrounding systems successfully, and teaching others how to do so as well.

While many of the interviews I collected were with members of this church, the body of conversion narratives in my fieldwork was by no means limited to this particular church. The people I spoke with were, however, limited by age. With a few exceptions, interlocutors were under fifty; for the most part the people I interviewed were in their mid twenties to late thirties. As I will explain, this was the age range most likely to be impacted strongly by family- and church-related financial demands, and least likely to be gaining obvious benefits from participating in family and church exchanges.

Rational Choice or Revelation?

The narratives I was collecting operated for me at two levels, and it is the contradictions between these levels that I hope to reconcile through the course of this chapter. People offered me heartfelt and strongly emotional stories of experiences that I kept re-reading through a sociological lens. They would tell me stories about how they had experienced a strong physical connection to Christ at the moment of becoming born-again, stories such as this one:

> The following year I actually once again went with my cousin and his wife who were
> in the same kind of movement to their church, and had the same kind of service,

like clapping and chanting and singing and dancing and speaking in tongues. And I was just standing there and, and I thought. And I didn't know what to say, what I said was I think I prayed two things like—Please God, or Please Jesus. And suddenly this power that just came, it was just over my head and all the way down. It was like a bucket of water, it was just very cleansing. My whole being was like transforming into things, it was really dynamic.

It is possible to read this as an account of anxieties over group membership, or rituals of initiation. But that focus does not address the other elements of my interlocutor's experience, the sense of cleansing and transformation in her encounter with the spiritual. Other anthropologists have discussed this particular dilemma, most notably Edith Turner (1992) in her revision of Victor Turner's (1968) account of healing among the Ndembu. Edith Turner argues that perhaps there are forces to be accounted for in healing ceremonies that transcend functionalist arguments of newly created social harmonies. Others have written about instances in which their analytical frameworks were not only at odds with their informants' beliefs, but insulting to them (see Brettell 1996). I experienced the same tensions time and time again as my interlocutors and I discussed their reasons for becoming evangelical Christians. The sociological explanations I suggested were not welcome to the people I spoke with in New Zealand, who often gently told me that the motivations I attributed were not people's actual motivations at all.

So, to what motivations did I persistently insist on attributing to people's conversions? I fear that my explanations never revolved around revelation or faith, my first mistake. The explanations I used to offer my interlocutors in the field, when discussing these conversions between Christianities, all presumed that people were acting as makers of rational choices. Moreover, I was suggesting that it was economically advantageous for people not to attend churches that my interlocutors would describe as more traditionally Samoan, such as E.F.K.S. (originally London Missionary) or the Catholic Church. People who attend evangelical churches typically contribute less money, less often, than those who belong to E.F.K.S., Catholic, or Congregational churches. My interlocutors would politely but firmly reject these explanations, and would occasionally discuss instead the fundamentally meaningless worship they perceived to be present in these churches. My explanation, although salient from a distanced perspective, was too limited to explain the transformations that conversion enables—the new allocations of meaning and meaninglessness in how people experience their relationship to a Samoan moral order.

Knowing Pride When You See It

My first encounter with Samoans who attended non-mainline churches occurred during one of my first mixed marriage interviews in Auckland. The respondent was a New Zealand-raised woman who had grown up in the Seventh-day Adventist (SDA) church. Her mother was present, so the conversation included a generational perspective. We chatted about the role cultural differences had played in the daughter's relationship with her Tongan partner. The daughter, Lotu, explained to me that she had not learned to speak Samoan growing up, which constantly surprised her partner Pita. When Pita first found out she did not speak Samoan, he assumed that she was a snob, that she was rejecting her Samoan heritage. Lotu had had to explain to him that this was not the case; she simply hadn't been raised speaking the language. Nor did she observe many Samoan cultural conventions, such as the *feagaiga*—a covenant between brother and sister that generates behavioral taboos and responsibilities. This became quite a significant issue when she moved in with her partner's family, who did practice the feagaiga, albeit a Tongan version. Lotu told me animatedly how she had suffered as the daughter-in-law in a Tongan family—how her husband's sisters had complete authority to take any of her daughter's clothes, and so on. Later, when Lotu's mother Sara drove me home, she turned to me and asked me what one word I thought would sum up the whole interview. I had only recently taken my doctoral qualifying exams—one-word answers did not leap easily to mind. I muttered something about the dynamics of kinship, and she glanced at me, tolerant but bemused. "No," she said, when I finally stopped floundering in academic phrases, "power—it is all about power." Sara was right: the entire time her daughter had been telling me about the ways in which her Tongan in-laws invoked tradition to control her behavior. From that moment on, whenever Sara summed up a situation for me, I always listened very carefully.

During the months that I went to this SDA church, Sara would occasionally ask me what I was discovering. And then, each time, she would ask me if I had come to the conclusion that Samoans are a very proud people. Pride, for Sara, was as weighty a word as power. I started to listen quite carefully to discern what work "pride" was doing for Samoans—aside from contributing the slogan "Samoan Pride" to T-shirts festooned with muscle-bound tattooed Samoan men. As I listened more carefully, I began to notice that pride, along with its ever present conceptual partner shame, was one of a small number of motivations people consistently attributed to each other. And pride was one of the few motivations (among the small set of constant options such as respect, love, desire for power, desire for companionship, selfishness, and so on) that Samoans used to explain other people's commitments to family or communities when they were expressed through *fa'alavelave*s (ritual exchanges). Pride was the word people used to explain others' emotional motivation for performing the moral in a Samoan moral economy.

The Moral in Samoan Moral Economy

When Sara asked me whether I had noticed the extent to which pride motivated Samoans, she was asking me about people's commitments to a Samoan moral economy—commitments about which many of my interlocutors had very mixed feelings. She was in fact rejecting the reflexive position one must take in order to see that the fa'alavelaves occurring in church contexts are part of a Samoan moral economy. Here I am discussing moral economy in a way that might be unfamiliar to my readers. Scholars often use the term moral economy to refer to the moral assumptions that underlie economic practices (Thompson 1971 and 1991; Scott 1976). Frequently these moral assumptions are not visible or clearly articulated until people are confronted with the possibilities of alternative economic practices that violate their moral principles.[4] I am suggesting that in order to act on the precepts of a moral economy, one must assume a particular reflexive stance defined in situ by the moral economy. From the perspective of someone rejecting the assumptions of a Samoan moral economy, the reflexive stance rejected is discussed as a prideful mindset.

So just what are fa'alavelaves, that they should be moral? These ritual exchanges—at weddings, funerals, church dedications—are the primary medium through which Samoan migrants present their family as a unit to others in their local Samoan community. As I have discussed elsewhere (Gershon 2000), back in Samoa fa'alavelaves are not the only arena for expressing one's complex connections to different families and communities, but are simply the most public arena. After migration, however, these exchanges become the dominant form through which people's relationships, and particularly the strength of the relationships, are made known. When Samoans would describe to me why they personally make these gifts, they would invariably cast their sacrifice in terms of a strong sense of obligation and affection for their family. When describing other people, they might discuss pride, as Sara did. But their own reasons were invariably couched in the language of moral sentiments. To be part of a family engaged in the project of being a Samoan family is to be committed to making the family's strength and status visible by contributing money, food, and fine mats to one's church and to fa'alavelave. The family reveals its capacity in these moments and expresses both pride in and *alofa* (respectful love) for the family. So there are strong moral valences attached to contributing to fa'alavelave—when one contributes to the church, one is revealing love for God and family in one fell swoop. And through this public ritual, one is also affirming the family's position vis-à-vis other families in the community. This particular combination of alofa and pride was frequently described to me as a potent motivating force.

Moral Exchange, Meaningful Economy

In this section, I will sketch the effects of migration on the Samoan ritual exchanges that take place in churches. By looking at how church exchanges allow people to make their moral fiber visible, I will outline the ways in which a contextual morality is fashioned within migrant Samoan communities. Churches enable Samoans to display unities at two different levels—both as a congregation and as members of families that constitute a congregation. Here I am pointing to a distinction between levels of scale constituted by exchange.

When operating as a congregation, people's attentions tend to be occupied by supporting their minister, building new churches, paying off church mortgages through monthly contributions, and contributing to other churches. At stake in these exchanges is Samoans' ability to demonstrate what their congregation can accomplish together. Samoans' financial obligations are not limited to their own church's building.[5] Congregations also engage often in historically complex exchanges with other local churches. Ministers visit other congregations constantly and must be treated with proper respect, which includes gifts of food, money, and fine mats. In addition, when other churches consecrate their new buildings, costly financial obligations are often borne by participants in those celebrations. For example, while I was doing fieldwork in Auckland in 1997, the E.F.K.S Otara church rebuilt its church buildings. The all-day celebration included contributions, from churches all over Auckland, that ranged from NZ $10,000 to NZ $75,000 per congregation.

I have been describing the pressure to contribute to the support of one's church's reputation among larger Samoan communities. Belonging to a church also means responding to one's own congregation as an imagined judging gaze. Families compete in numerous ways within a congregation to demonstrate their relative strength as well, most visibly toward the end of every Sunday church service, when a deacon reads the lists of who contributed and the amount. People do not always contribute as a family or a household. In one of the churches I attended, women contributed one week, men the next. Yet the names for the most part reference households' resources, not individuals.' This Sunday donation is the most predictable contribution one has to make: meanwhile, belonging to a church also involves contributing at fellow congregants' weddings, funerals, birthdays, and so on in a competitive context that can quickly escalate.

My interlocutors were mainly of an age or status where they might contribute to their families' exchanges but did not often make the decisions about how much to give as a family. In my interviews, people would mention that they frequently did not know who was getting married, who had died, or how they were related. They would receive phone calls from their parents or sometimes an uncle or aunt, asking for money for an upcoming fa'alavelave. Sometimes news of a fa'alavelave would be introduced at a family meeting, or would be the reason for a family meeting in the first place. Sometimes my informants had not been present for the actual ritual exchanges, and hardly any of them had ever represented the family in the exchanges. My interlocutors were not the generation who knew the long histories of exchanges between relatives and between families—they were perhaps ten or twenty years too young. Older family members elicited resources for fa'alavelaves, and monitored their family's varied commitments. They were the ones actively engaged in producing family unity and interconnections through exchange, not my interlocutors. This lack of knowledge often contributed to the distance and disengagement people felt from the exchanges.

The fa'alavelave is not the only way people show family or community unity when engaged in the project of being Samoan, but it becomes a far more central medium after migration. Migration has ensured the church's new role as the site for determining a family's relative status. Prior to migration, competition occurred in several different arenas, and was framed largely in terms of how hierarchies were variously transformed historically within villages. After migration, people did not recreate village hierarchies by living in the same neighborhood or even using villages as a basis for association until the late 1990s. Church congregations began to be the primary site for determining relative worth within the local New Zealand Samoan communities. When money was sent back to Samoa, the contributions were merged into a display of family strength in the village. These resources were sustaining a nostalgic unity, not the one that family members tried to make visible in their daily lives. In contrast, during fa'alavelaves held in local New Zealand churches there would be a public display of the connections created through their contributions—that is, their contributions would be publicly and ritually acknowledged in ways that were rendered invisible for overseas remittances. In short, for Samoans overseas, mainline Samoan churches have become the primary site through which people can enact being moral Samoans through fa'alavelaves.

When people are engaged in the project of being Samoan in a foreign country, they are straddling two contradictory perspectives. From the perspective of Samoan capitalism, involvement with fa'alavelaves can seem overwhelming—one has to contribute substantial amounts of money at an unpredictable rate. This conflicts with a guiding principle of the capitalist perspective—that people use plans and budgets to manage themselves and their resources. Funerals or sudden weddings can occur at any time, so people cannot easily anticipate how much they will need to contribute from week to week or month to month.[6] But from the perspective of Samoan ritual exchange, it is difficult not to exchange. The reasons for contributing are emotionally charged. Not giving is a sign of not wanting to support one's family, of not wanting to be part of the complex emotional connections of familial affection made visible through exchange.

Samoans reading this may think I am blaming *fa'asamoa* (the Samoan way) for particular financial conundrums that Samoan migrants experience. This is not the case. In other work (Gershon 2000), I have pointed out that the problems arise because people are operating within two exchange systems, Samoan capitalism and Samoan ritual exchanges. It would be easy to blame Samoan ritual exchanges for placing Samoans in particular traps. But this would disguise the pragmatic ways in which capitalism in New Zealand discourages people from supporting their family through familiar Samoan avenues. It is not fa'alavelaves per se that are the problem, it is negotiating two contradictory (moral) economies at the same time.

Converting Out of Context

Converting to being a born-again Christian (or a less mainline Christian) reformulates one's relationship to each of these two perspectives. When Samoans convert from one form of Christianity to another, they are most often leaving a church that is more involved with Samoan ritual exchanges and entering a church with strong injunctions against these ritual exchanges. This was particularly true of the first wave of reformist Christianities to be adopted by Samoans, such as Seventh-day Adventism or Mormonism. To belong to the Seventh-day Adventist church is to refuse to worship on Sunday; to avoid pork, dancing, tattooing; and most importantly, to refuse to exchange fine mats. Born-again Christians observe similar injunctures against engaging in Samoan ritual exchange, although dancing and eating pork are not taboo. Importantly, most of the churches do not tithe publicly—the church service does not approach a conclusion by having a deacon call out the amounts specific people have donated. Several of my interlocutors stressed how important it was to them that they attended a church with anonymous collections. One evangelical minister offered the following comparison:

> I found out in the islands, I observed it myself as a young man, on a Sunday every month they used to take up the love offering for the *faifeau* [church minister]. The way it is conducted in the church is just like money changers in the temple that Jesus threw out. Now the secretary would go up to the front of the church, the old faifeau sitting there half-asleep, fat stomach [laughs] and I am not being critical because I could have been caught up in it only the Lord has changed my life and my whole outlook. And then the secretary says, "right, today is the love offering for the faifeau. I would like you to give generously for God's servant." And so the family gets up and goes up—one hundred dollars. And then the next family goes up. And they announce it. The family of John Groendahl have now contributed 100 dollars for the love offering for the minister. And the next family goes up and they say now Ilana's family has now contributed 200 dollars to the minister. And the next thing this guy John sends up the kid and he whispers, "my dad said to add another 150 to the offering" it is now that the Groendahl family will increase their offering to . . . it's like an auction. And in our church here we have offerings, we call it a free will offering. We have bags and nobody knows what the next person puts in. And we emphasize to the folk that what you put in, some people are able to put in more than others, those who can not afford it, don't you feel obligated. You are just as much a part of this church.

In this minister's account of Samoan giving, he mentions conversion, pointing out that this form of giving would have been meaningful for him still if the Lord had not intervened and changed his whole outlook. Notice also that it is not giving to the church that is the problem for my interlocutor, it is the public, and thus the competitive, nature of the giving in mainline Samoan churches. My interlocutor was very aware that public giving encouraged church members to give more than they had anticipated giving. From his perspective, mainline Samoan churches were arenas of evaluation and competition expressed through supposedly more' traditional Samoan ritual exchanges. The less traditional Christian churches create new venues through which Samoans can demonstrate their moral character, venues that do not require public displays of giving. This minister and my other interlocutors were pointing to the fact that these churches do not compel Samoans to negotiate both Samoan capitalism and Samoan ritual exchange. Instead, the churches encourage their congregants to restructure their relationships to Samoan ritual exchanges.

I interviewed a Mormon couple who were quite explicit about the costs families incurred by contributing to fa'alavelave, and the escapes the new Christian churches could provide. In the following conversation, a mixed couple discuss ritual exchanges as "culture," providing what I mentioned earlier as a common focus on pride as the principal motivation:

> **Thomas:** I work in South Auckland and I see it everyday. I see how Polynesian families are just struggling to cope with the social ills of that area.
>
> **Sina:** And it doesn't help when the culture, when their culture, when some families' culture is the main focus of their life. I am not kidding, I have seen it. And it is so sad. Because their children get neglected—so much pride and they just give, give, give and the children suffer.
>
> **Thomas:** There should be an even balance of everything as far as I am concerned. But some families, the main priority is their culture, their church perhaps. We believe that there should be a fair balance of everything.
>
> **Sina:** We support my culture. If my family needs help, like if one of my brothers gets married, or someone goes on a mission, or a relative dies, we give what we can afford. But my parents don't. Before they used to, eh? But they don't put pressure on us. Now they don't. They are really adapting to the church culture.

Culture becomes a slippery term in this conversation, moving from referencing what it means to be Samoan to what it means to be Mormon. Mormonism has provided this couple with a perspective that encourages focusing their resources on their nuclear family rather than their extended family (see Gordon 1990 for discussion of this process among Mormon Tongan families). In addition, Mormonism has changed their relationship to the Samoan wife's parents, who recently converted.

Because of this restructuring, it is quite compelling from a Euro-American analyst's perspective to read this conversion as a movement toward becoming a rational choice actor. Samoans are doing what is economically feasible. Caught in a system in which they must spread their financial resources too thin, they turn to newer forms of Christianity to be able to continue engaging in producing community with Samoan valences, but without the financial costs of producing a community structured along Samoan exchange principles. From a perspective formed by capitalist impulses, it is a compelling reason to switch forms of worship is to reduce the contributions that more mainline Samoan churches seem to demand.

But I suggest that the change people are experiencing is a different one—they are not becoming rational choice actors as much as they are becoming different kinds of moralists. They are choosing to move away from a faith that is exhibited to a faith that is emoted. People address this shift in their comparisons of mainline and evangelical churches. Most frequently, my interlocutors would compare the styles of worship, pointing out that in mainline churches people sit formally and quietly, whereas in evangelical churches the worship is exuberant, replete with energetic singing and movement (see Tiatia 1996: 160–65 for a comparison of styles of worship). The difference between these styles of worship can be described as a distinction between being and achieving. In more mainline churches, people are worshipful without revealing the effort that goes into producing faith. In evangelical churches people reveal the effort; they make visible the labor that goes into making a worshipful self.

In sum, what people are rejecting is a morality based upon public displays of family strength and public evaluations. My interlocutors had rejected the importance of others' gazes as the fount of moral behavior. Having rejected this morality, they begin experiencing it as meaningless. Bradd Shore (1982) has argued that others' gazes are a crucial moral restraint for Samoans, as a consequence of the Samoan concept of personhood. He argues that for Samoans morality is sociocentric, and human nature is supposed to be instinctual and socially destructive. As he writes: "Perhaps most significantly, village law and authority are understood to protect people from themselves—from passions and desires that, uncontained by culture and customary authority, would lead to moral and social chaos" (Shore 1982: 118). In this account, it is the cultural context, not an internally cohesive intentionality, that determines how Samoans will behave. Shore argues that the Samoans believe that motivation is only partially linked to the actor's internal qualities or decisions. "Samoans commonly talk about actions and feelings as if the body were a decentralized agglomeration of discrete parts, each imbued with its own will" (1982: 173). The social context determines which part of the conglomerate Samoan self will be made explicit. One of the consequences is that people in public might appear to behave in ways that dramatically contradict their private behavior.

A corollary to this ethnographic claim is that Samoans hold licit selves to be public, and illicit selves private. Shore describes this as the Samoan link between knowledge and responsibility. He argues that for Samoans, a misdeed is not a misdeed until the person is publicly held responsible: "private or purely personal knowledge of one's own actions is not sufficient grounds for responsibility for them. Knowledge of one's actions must be public to some extent for one to be responsible" (1982: 175). An action is neither good nor bad until it has been judged so by others. Meaning from a Samoan perspective—or in Shore's case, morality—must be co-produced (see also Duranti 1994). There is no such thing as a private morality—morality exists only when one is judged by others.

Evangelical Christianity offers Samoans an appealing alternative to this form of morality—a church in which the main focus is the labor of self-making. One of my interlocutors gave a direct and pithy summary of this transformation, saying: "We kind of had to reevaluate who we were. But I think Christianity does that to you, it forces you to reevaluate, renew your mind. It causes you to stop, think, look, and renew your mind." These evangelical churches differ from mainline churches in one aspect that has become crucial for my interlocutors: instead of a context in which one should not make visible the labor that goes into making oneself moral, they provide a context in which this labor is glorified. In mainline churches, people are criticized for not obeying the contextual cues, for not fulfilling their roles properly. In evangelical churches, they are commended for precisely the behavior that drew condemnation in their previous churches—the *effort* to be good.

Born-again Samoan Christians describe their conversion experiences time and again as a move away from a morality based on context, although they use differing terminology, preferring to depict the conversion as away from a meaningless form of worship toward a more meaningful form. They told me that people went to Samoan mainline churches to gossip and compete with everyone else, not to worship. As other authors in this volume have illustrated (see Bornstein; Tomlinson), fashioning meaninglessness is also refashioning context. Upon labeling a more mainline form of Samoan Christian worship meaningless, a Samoan convert discards claims to a context-dependent morality in favor of a morality based largely upon the notion of a consistent and self-monitoring person. The moral meaninglessness that they discover or learn to recognize in a particular form of worship is a meaninglessness emergent from the ways in which Samoans conceive of themselves as reflexive and reflexively moral within a particular context. In a more mainline Samoan church, the onus is on the production of morality through the demonstration of familial strength and piety or proper behavior. The focus is entirely on the external presentation, a match between contextual demands and appearance. In the born-again churches, the creation of meaning occurs in a different way, through one's reflexive management of oneself as a moral being.[7]

At stake is not the content of the moral beliefs, but rather the moral stance itself. When Samoans convert from one form of Christianity to another, they do not learn that new behaviors have become immoral. Rather, they learn a new reflexive stance toward being Christian. The strength of their commitment is no longer shown through exchange, but through monitoring the self. One interviewee explained the problems with Samoan churches as a critique of a contextual moral self:

> **European New Zealander Wife:** That's what he likes. He doesn't want to go to a Samoan church.
>
> **Samoan Husband:** There is a different way that I understand and the way that they understand what it is all about. How to take the Word into yourself, that's what's different. How to put it? In the way I take it, in a European way, it's really deep in me and also it's really serious. In the Christian way of fellowship or worshipping God it is doing a lot to feed the Holy Spirit in people or in myself. And in Samoa—I haven't been to a Samoan church in a long time. They are only going to church on Sunday for two or three hours to listen to the minister, and that's it. Oh, and Sunday school for the kids. No program to feed the Holy Spirit, no support. That's why they only have the Spirit in themselves on Sunday. And then they walk out and the next day they go back the same way they are.

My interlocutor criticizes the lack of context through which people can demonstrate their Christian faith—according to him (though not in my experience), in Samoan churches people must be visibly moral only on Sundays. For this Samoan man, the conversion was a movement toward understanding how to be moral in a new way, conferring a form of meaninglessness on previous ways of finding moral certainty.

Peter Stromberg discusses the ways in which conversion can serve to create a coherent self, resolving people's previous emotional contradictions. He writes: "The conversion narrative, like the ritual, induces a sort of 'solidarity,' in this case a solidarity of motives. The conversion narrative enables the believer to forge a sense of coherence by using the ideological language to embrace intentions that, as the analysis has shown, persist in spite of being denied. It is this sense of coherence that signals, both to the believer and to the observer, a transformed identity" (1990: 54).

Stromberg specifically describes how identities that were previously experienced as meaningless become meaningful through the conversion (1990: 53). I am arguing for a cultural specificity to Samoans' conversion experiences. By shifting morality from its social construction to an internal management of emotions, and demonstration through emotions, Samoans are moving from having morality defined through contextual selves to having morality defined through continuous selves.

The sermons at the churches I frequented were often narratives framed in terms of acquiring tools by which to manage oneself. The stories captured my Samoan interlocutors' imagination—even those who went to more mainline churches on a regular basis often found this particular aspect of evangelical Christianity especially appealing. I went with two Samoan men, who went regularly on Sundays to their family's mainline churches, to hear a visiting Korean evangelical minister who was attracting large crowds. The visiting preacher was popular enough to fill a large church hall and a huge tent behind it. We watched on a large screen as the minister told the audience an inspirational story about a woman who came to him one day seeking advice. She told him that she prayed constantly, but God was not answering her prayers. The preacher asked her what she was praying for, and she replied that she wanted a husband. The preacher wondered if she prayed with any specificity, and the woman replied that she did not. So the preacher told her that if she wanted something, she should pray in detail. She should develop a list of the characteristics she wanted—a thoughtful man, a teacher, a good Christian, and so on. Then, with a list of ten attributes she wanted in a husband, she should pray for precisely that person, and God would provide. She followed his advice, and the next time he visited that town, she was married to a man who fit her wish list exactly. This, of several similar stories the minister told, turned out to occupy my two Samoan interlocutors for the ride home. The driver turned enthusiastically to his friend as we were heading across a long bridge into the city: "this is what you need to do. You want a wife, you should come up with a list of exactly what you want and start praying for that." What evangelical churches offered were clear and concrete guidelines for how to develop a self that could be regulated and managed. The churches were offering templates for how to be a reflexive self, guidelines for how to think of oneself as an emotional, and often powerfully emotional, person with needs, all of which could still be constructed in a moral valence.

What I have been arguing is that in a Samoan context, morality is more often linked to social contexts and created by others' gazes than derived from internal impulses or consistent selves. But Samoan morality based on social context hinges on two elements that are increasingly missing in a Samoan

Auckland: cultural knowledge about the cues and guidelines that others' gazes provide, and appropriate performative contexts. My interlocutors often told me that one of the ways in which they experienced the results of migration was precisely these disruptions in being culturally knowledgeable and in being in appropriate performative contexts.[8] When Samoans convert to evangelical churches, some of these pressures are removed. They are no longer concerned with being good Samoan Christians, as much as they are with practicing how to be good Christians (see Taule'ale'ausumai 1990; cf. Engelke, this volume). Visible effort is irrelevant from a mainline Samoan Christian perspective but valued as meaningful from an evangelical perspective. As a consequence, others' gazes cease to be as relevant as guides to morality; instead my interlocutors wanted to be moral by fashioning and experiencing a faith-filled self.

In this chapter, I have argued that the transition implied in conversion from one form of Christianity to another is not a movement between Christian principles, but a movement between moral economies. Moral economies are not only guidelines for how best to exchange, they also entail the proper stances for being moral and for revealing one's morality. While I have analyzed the stances as reflexive connections to moral orders, my interlocutors discussed conversion in terms of meaning, of moving from meaningless forms of worship to meaningful ones. In short, because my interlocutors found the moral compasses offered in more mainline Samoan churches increasingly difficult to follow, they turned to a Christianity that required a different reflexive stance to a moral order. In these cases, conversion was not about the content of one's faith but about the way of being faithful—not about principles but about personhood.

Notes

1. Cluny and La'avasa Macpherson (2001) have written about Samoans who move between churches over a lifetime, leaving the more mainline churches in their late teens and twenties, and returning once they have children. They argue that their construction of their own ethnicity is central to this cycle. They also point out, apropos of this chapter, that their decisions to return to more traditional Samoan churches are often based on their desire to provide their children with appropriate Samoan contexts.
2. See Barker (2001) for a direct critique of this tendency in Ernst (1994).
3. This strong Samoan contingent might be unusual for congregations Samoans choose to join. Both Macpherson and Macpherson and Melani Anae (1998) found in their research that the converts they spoke to preferred to attend evangelical churches with less of a Samoan influence.
4. See E. P. Thompson (1971) for an account of how food riots in the sixteenth to eighteenth centuries were peasants' responses to violations of their moral expectations of farmers and millers' economic practices.
5. I am focusing here on exchanges in New Zealand, but I want to point out that family members must often send money to Samoa to help their family there contribute to various church obligations.
6. Families often pool money in a reserve for fa'alavelave to which every family member contributes a small sum weekly or biweekly. This creates a cushion in case of unexpected fa'alavelave.

7. It is no accident that several of the people I interviewed were also engaged in teaching other people how to transform themselves into consistent and manageable selves for the job market by running job training programs.
8. New Zealand-raised youth often become icons of the ways in which migration has produced these tensions. It is not surprising that many converts to evangelical churches are New Zealand-raised Samoans.

References

Anae, Melani. 1998. *"Fofoa I Voa Ese*: The Identity Journeys of New Zealand-born Samoans." Ph.D. diss., University of Auckland.

Ballard, Chris. 2000. "The Fire Next Time: The Conversion of the Huli Apocalypse." *Ethnohistory* 47, no. 1: 205–25.

Barker, John, ed. 1990. *Christianity in Oceania: Ethnographic Perspectives.* Lanham, MD: University Press of America.

Barker, John. 2001. "Recent Changes in Pacific Island Christianity / Les mutations récentes du christianisme en Océanie." *The New Pacific Review / La Nouvelle Revue du Pacifique* 1, no. 1: 116–27, 108–17.

Brettell, Caroline B., ed. 1996. *When They Read What We Write: The Politics of Ethnography.* Westport, CT: Greenwood Publishing Company.

Crapanzano, Vincent. 1994. "Kevin: On the Transfer of Emotions." *American Anthropologist* 96, no. 4: 866–85.

Duranti, Alessandro. 1994. *From Grammar to Politics: Linguistic Anthropology in a Western Samoan Village.* Berkeley: University of California Press.

Ernst, Manfred. 1994. *Winds of Change: Rapidly Growing Religious Groups in the Pacific Islands.* Suva, Fiji: Pacific Conference of Churches.

Firth, Raymond. 1976. "Conversion from Paganism to Christianity." *Royal Anthropological Institute News* 14: 3–7.

Gershon, Ilana. 2000. "How To Know When Not To Know: Strategic Ignorance When Eliciting for Samoan Migrant Exchanges." *Social Analysis* 44, no. 2: 84–105.

Gordon, Tamar. 1990. "Inventing the Mormon Tongan Family." In *Christianity in Oceania: Ethnographic Perspectives,* ed. J. Barker. Lanham, MD: University Press of America.

Harding, Susan Friend. 2000. *The Book of Jerry Falwell: Fundamentalist Language and Politics.* Princeton: Princeton University Press.

Hefner, Robert, ed. 1993. *Conversion to Christianity: Historical and Anthropological Perspectives on a Great Transformation.* Berkeley: University of California Press.

Janes, Craig. 1990. *Migration, Social Change and Health: A Samoan Community in California.* Stanford: Stanford University Press.

Jules-Rosette, Bennetta. 1975. "The Conversion Experience: The Apostles of John Maranke." *Journal of Religion in Africa* 7, no. 2: 132–64.

Lange, Raeburn. 1997. *The Origins of the Christian Ministry in the Cook Islands and Samoa.* Christchurch: Macmillan Brown Centre for Pacific Studies.

Macpherson, Cluny, and La'avasa Macpherson. 2001. "Evangelical Religion among Pacific Island Migrants: New Faiths or Brief Diversions?" *Journal of Ritual Studies* 15, no. 2: 27–37.

Ramstad, Mette. 2000. "Conversion in the Pacific: Eastern Polynesian Latter-Day Saints' Conversion Accounts and Their Development of an LDS Identity." Ph.D. diss., University of Bergen.

Robbins, Joel. 2003. "On the Paradoxes of Global Pentecostalism and the Perils of Continuity Thinking." *Religion* 33, no. 3: 221–31.

Scott, James. 1976. *The Moral Economy of the Peasant*. New Haven: Yale University Press.

Shore, Bradd. 1982. *Sala'ilua: A Samoan Mystery*. New York: Columbia University Press.

Stromberg, Peter G. 1990. "Ideological Language in the Transformation of Identity." *American Anthropologist* 92, no. 1: 42–56.

Taule'ale'ausumai, Feiloaiga. 1990. *The Word Made Flesh*. Wellington: Presbyterian Church of New Zealand.

Tiatia, Jemaima. 1996. *Caught Between Cultures: A New Zealand-Born Pacific Island Perspective*. Auckland: Christian Research Association.

Thompson, E. P. 1971. "The Moral Economy of the English Crowd in the Eighteenth Century." *Past and Present* 50: 76–136.

———. 1991. *Customs in Common*. New York: The New Press.

Turner, Edith. 1992. *Experiencing Ritual: A New Interpretation of African Healing*. Philadelphia: University of Pennsylvania Press.

Turner, Victor. 1968. *The Drums of Affliction*. Ithaca: Cornell University Press.

8

DUSTY SIGNS AND ROOTS OF FAITH: THE LIMITS OF CHRISTIAN MEANING IN HIGHLAND BOLIVIA

Andrew Orta

Introduction

"We don't yet know what people really understand by the customs that they do. *They* don't know." So suggested William, a Catholic missionary from the United States, who has been active since the 1960s in indigenous parishes of the Bolivian highlands. Father William was referring to what he saw as a "mixture" of Christian and indigenous practices found in rural and peri-urban communities in the Bolivian *altiplano* (highlands). He explained: in contrast with Catholicism in the United States, which, as an immigrant offshoot of European Catholic traditions, benefited from those "roots of faith" sunk "deep" in the European past, the roots of Latin American Catholicism were shallow and immature. The result, he told me, was a "patina" of Catholicism, a "cultural Catholicism" without meaning (cf. Gershon, this volume).

The status of Christian meaning in Latin America has been a vexatious issue for Catholic missionaries to the region. From the earliest idolatry scandals through the contemporary period, metaphors of patinas of Christianity, superficial evangelization, and indigenous meaning in Christian clothing abound. Confounded by the devil, by the intransigence of the Indians, or by the imperfections of the missionaries themselves, Christian meaning seems endlessly to be stretched past its limit in Latin America.

The anthropology of the region has reflected similar preoccupations. As anthropologist Tristan Platt has suggested, "Andean studies have long emphasized a distinction between new Christian forms and an underlying concrete logic of pre-Columbian origin, suggesting that pagan mythic thought, accompanied by many practical concepts and ideas, has been able to survive unobtrusively till today, beneath the deceptive appearances of a dominantly European public aesthetic" (1987: 141). Reporting events from a rural parish in Bolivia, Platt describes an "eccentric ex-priest" who related to him with a "wild look in his eye": "These Indians don't believe in God at all. They're not *really* Christians. It's the Sun they worship—the Sun! the Sun!" (1987: 140).

In this chapter I draw upon ethnographic research with Catholic missionaries and the indigenous Andeans they seek to serve to examine the limits of Christian meaning in the Andes. In doing so, however, I hope to avoid an assertion of meaninglessness or the failure of meaning in indigenous Christian practices. Nor do I mean to claim, with Platt's priest, that the missionaries and their flocks are at cross purposes, that the natives resist and redirect Christianity by hiding—literally or figuratively—pagan idols under Christian altars. Rather, what I propose to think about here is a limited sense of "meaning" in approaches to Christianity in places like the Andes, including the limitations of what may well be *Christian* approaches to meaning in such missionizing circumstances. I wish to stress two features of these Christian missionary approaches.

As others have noted, these circumstances are marked by processes of translation, which align systems of meanings and seek to read and evaluate one in the terms of another (e.g., Rafael 1988). In his discussion of colonial Spanish Catholicism in the Philippines, Rafael stresses the asymmetric relationship among Latin, Castilian, and Tagalog, with Latin taken by the missionaries as the medium for the transparent expression of God's meaning, Castilian as a vernacular that could be grammatically ordered to approximate Latin, and Tagalog as subject to a similar process of grammatical "reduction" as a condition of the possibility of successful evangelical translation. The point to stress is that translation here is not, as it could be, an explicitly reciprocal process. In her work on intercultural education among the Nasa of Colombia, Joanne Rappaport (2005: 95) describes a process of "back translation" of terms—from Spanish to Nasa and back to Spanish—in ways that explicitly mark the different conceptual spaces enabled by the engaged linguistic systems. The universal, outside grounding of Christian meaning necessarily drives a different sort of translation project. As the case that I present below makes clear (cf. Orta 1998, 2004), even when its aims are explicitly intercultural and localizing, Christian missionization is framed always by a transcendent point of reference and by an anticipated transparency that might align all human systems of meaning as commensurate expressions of God's Word.

This approach to meaning, moreover, is a process of "fixing" in the double sense detailed by Diane Nelson (1999): reforming meaning, and stabilizing it. This is the second feature I wish to stress. That is, missionary goals of reforming indigenous practices turn on efforts to understand them. Such understandings, grounded in the comparative bias inherent in "religion" as a category that is taken for granted, tend to reduce a nimbus of meaning to more focal, systematic, and thus comparable content. Such fixing, moreover, often blurs pragmatic as well as semantic content. Writing about Christian evangelical strategies in Indonesia, Webb Keane (1996) describes missionary efforts to reform indigenous ritual practices by reducing them to their pragmatic social functions (communal feasts of thanksgiving, for instance) and replacing them with "functionally equivalent" rites that are seen as serving the same purposes without the pagan details that made the indigenous practice objectionable. What I gloss here as a Christian (missionary) approach to meaning has to do with these "fixing" aims and the one-to-one correspondences they entail. It has to do with an exegetical aesthetic of legibility and an institutional accounting of meaning from a vantage at some remove from the situated unfolding of Christian practice (cf. Scott 1998; Orta 2002a).

Sensuous Catechisms and Local Marginalia

Students of colonial missionization in Latin America will rightly point out that this characterization overlooks a robust repertoire of missionary strategies and lumps together a diverse—and sometimes quite divided—set of pastoral positions. Platt (1987), for example, discusses the colonial evangelical strategy of instituting calendrical feasts and indigenous religious brotherhoods honoring Catholic saints. This, he notes, constituted a "sensuous catechism," weaving Catholicism across the landscape, across the calendar, across the indigenous life cycle, and across the sociopolitical processes that reproduce local indigenous society in ways that are not (and for some of the early evangelizers arguably were not) premised on a one-to-one correspondence of practice and meaning. It was enough to enact these practices regularly (religiously) and reverently (cf. Asad 1993). Indeed, colonial evangelizers, witnessing some of the last public rites of the Inca Empire in the high lakeside sanctuary of Copacabana, openly admired the reverence and respect evident in the worshipers and commented that believers back home in Spain could learn a thing or two from these idolatrous Indians (Ramos Gavilan 1621).

Platt's point of departure is the mid twentieth century tendency to dismiss the impact of colonial evangelization as superficial. In reply, he posits the colonial amalgamation of Andean ritual sensibilities with official Christian practices as institutionalized in Andean life through the sensuous catechism of early modern Catholic evangelization. Platt focuses on Corpus Christi celebrations in indigenous highlands parishes. Combining his field observations with parish records of Corpus Christi festivities in the seventeenth century, he argues further that these highland enactments of Corpus Christi are performances of an indigenous Catholic theology.

Specifically, after noting a number of reductions and modifications in these ritual celebrations as he observed them in the 1970s, Platt identifies a set of contemporary practices that were also described in the official parish accounts from the eighteenth century. He characterizes these—"Mass," "Procession," "vispera" [vigil]—as the "elements of the orthodox *text*" evident in the colonial account (1987: 157). Pushing the metaphor further, he presents the more markedly indigenous practices as "the ritual *marginalia* on the liturgical nucleus"—indigenous emendations of the official Catholic ritual text, generating, from the margins, practical and meaningful coherence (1987: 157). Where other analysts have posited an unresolved tension—a "theological problem for [Andean] thought"—between Christian messages of divinity and indigenous concepts of cosmic power and fertility, or suggested the watershed replacement of the latter by the former, Platt takes his indigenously annotated ritual text as evidence of a "specifically Andean reading of Christianity" (1987: 173). Platt argues that Andean Christians thus ritually enact a theological "critique of Manichaeist dualism" (1987: 174) that transcends an opposition missionaries have cast between Christian and Andean beliefs.

There is much to admire in Platt's discussion. His historical refutation of facile claims of an ineffectual evangelization is correct, and his juxtaposition of contemporary ethnography and colonial records is provocative and effective. Yet he shares with the contemporary commentators he hopes to engage a narrow one-to-one view of meaning. This shortcoming is compounded by his analytic reduction of ritual to text, reflecting the historical transformations of marginalia, but tending always to a stable composite form. It also bears noting that Platt's metaphoric recourse to textual totality is a function of the scale of his analysis. Driven in part by the available historical data (parish-level records) and the vantages they offer, Platt is focused on regional social systems and the large-scale ritual networks that reproduce them. In his reading, this is the principal interface between indigenous and Catholic meaning; it is here that the sensuous catechism had its system-generating effect.

I take this example as a parable illustrating both the sort of "legibility" that is a concern of Christian approaches to meaning in such contexts, and the risks of reinforcing it through an anthropological analysis pitched at a comparable level of scale. The Andean Christian theology Platt evokes is the ideological engine for the production and reproduction of regional sociopolitical structure in post-Conquest circumstances. The life of Christian practice and the negotiation of what are genealogically distinct but inextricably entangled cultural forms however, take place across multiple social scales. It is an irony that mission studies often overlook the methodological opportunity afforded by the case of missionization to cut across multiple scales (Orta 2002a). It ought to be asked as well to what extent ethnographic discussions of Christian ritual hold themselves accountable to exegetical vantages of doctrinal systems at the cost of an engagement with the more situated experiential dimensions of meaning in and through which ritual necessarily unfolds.

In the remainder of this chapter I present data from my own research with Catholic missionaries and Aymara in highlands communities to further examine these limitations and opportunities. The missionary case at hand involves a pastoral ideology known as "inculturation," premised upon the revitalization of indigenous practices understood as local expressions of Christian meaning. In the following section I introduce a communal Andean ritual called *ayuno* that is promoted by inculturationist missionaries and that also embodies the syncretic "theological problem" mentioned by Platt. I then review the history, ideology, and pastoral practices of inculturation, before returning to a more detailed discussion of the ritual. On the one hand I aim to illustrate the process of "fixing," and to unsettle such ambitions through a closer examination of the ritual. At the same time, in addition to asserting the irreducibility of ritual practice to such schema of meaning I want, like Platt, to give Christian evangelization its due. To this end, over the course of the discussion, I am tracking the force of Christian missionization across multiple scales of inclusion in the Andes. The limits of (Christian) meaning are not the absence of (Christian) meaning and my argument, ultimately, is that rituals such as the ayuno "mean" in ways shaped and constrained by encompassing contexts of missionization. Yet, the upshot is not an alternative local theology. Rather than fix such ritual as an indigenous reply in kind to a missionary message, the task as I see it is to set the always irreducible phenomena of ritual meaning making within complex circumstances that include the institutions and ideologies of missionary Catholicism.

Of Feasts and Fasts: The Ayuno of Santa Barbara

In December 1991, on the Catholic feast day of Santa Barbara, I attended a ritual in a highlands Aymara community (*ayllu*) of the region of Jesús de Machaqa, Bolivia. It was an ayuno (fast)—a community-level event marking the completion of the year of service provided by community authorities, an honor and an obligation long taken as a foundation of indigenous community in the Andes. Through a collective fast and an intercommunity rite of "pardon" (during which community members, on their knees and weeping, embraced one another expressing reciprocal forgiveness for their trespasses of the past year), the community prepared the way for the entrance of new local authorities in January. The event also coincided with the early weeks of the growing season, and an offering to earth and sky was performed to help secure an abundant harvest.

Community members assembled early in the morning at the local Catholic chapel at the base of a small foothill overlooking the community. Over the course of the rite they ascended to the top of the hill, where a *yatiri* (ritual specialist), holding aloft a flat stone with smoldering embers, instructed the outgoing authorities to kneel. He placed an offering of flowers, fronds, and incense upon the embers to burn. Pouring a cup of wine, he arced the red liquid high in the air toward the noontime sun. As the smoke drifted into the sky, the rest of the community, on their knees, circled around the authorities and yatiri, pausing to recite the Our Father and read aloud the Christian liturgy of the Stations of the Cross, the Via Crucis.

This excerpt—an enacted page from an indigenous theological text?—might be taken as an illustration of Platt's priest's point. The spatial arrangement of the ayuno appears to disclose a fragmented, syncretic history of partial assimilation, localized resistance, and clandestine survivals by which a marked Andean core endures within the perimeter of imposed Christian form. There is reason to be wary of such readings. Also notable about this ayuno performance is that the event had been all but abandoned in recent years. In part, this was a product of sometimes violent interreligious tensions in the region in the 1960s and 1970s, when a growing number of Protestant converts and an emerging movement of neo-orthodox Catholics publicly denounced what they saw as idolatrous and fraudulent traditional beliefs and practices. Intersecting with these developments has been a more general decline affecting a number of traditional practices: like the ayuno, fiesta celebrations in the region were suspended or reduced, and a host of regalia marking ayllu authorities was abandoned. Indeed, the very site of the ayuno celebration bears the mark of apparent cultural decadence: stone cairns that once sequenced the space up the side of the foothill behind the chapel in accordance with the stations of the cross have been destroyed (or allowed to tumble down), and a hilltop shrine (*calvario/apacheta*)—a common spatial complement to rural chapels—is similarly in ruins. The crumbling calvario walls were the site of the yatiri's offering and the focal center of the circular Via Crucis.

The locally enacted "recovery" of the ayuno, and of the meanings of this enactment for the participants, requires more than the bird's-eye vantage of evangelical battlefields and textual metaphors of culture. It requires ethnographic attention to the rite itself and to the history out of which it emerged—a history in which such bird's-eye vantages and textual metaphors themselves have some force and must be reckoned with analytically. The enactment of the rite and the trajectories of the various participants all disclose the embeddedness of meaning across multiple levels of phenomena, multiple scales of action/ meaning. Missionization institutionalizes this multiscalar phenomenon. It is particularly good to think with in this regard, and it is exceptionally ironic that such a process, which enacts a veritable cascade of meaning across levels, so often itself turns on a much thinner sense of meaning.

The Second Evangelization

The recovery of the ayuno reflects the missionary strategy of inculturation. Premised on the revitalization and celebration of indigenous cultural practices—seen by missionaries as local expressions of universal Christian meanings—inculturation emerged as a significant pastoral ideology in Bolivia in the late 1980s. It followed on the heels of "liberation theology," and its ascendance reflects a broader turn at the fin de siècle toward culture and ethnicity and away from class as politically salient and globally transposable categories of identity (Orta 1998, 2004).

Inculturation might also be seen as the latest in a series of explicitly modern efforts to wrestle with the concerns of Platt's priest. While the sensuous catechism of the colonial evangelization is crucial to understanding the necessity of Catholicism in places like Machaqa, equally significant for recent generations of Andeans has been the impact of what some in the Church refer to as the second evangelization: an institutional reengagement with Latin America dating roughly from the end of the Second World War. For a variety of reasons—concerns to check the influence of Protestantism, comparable fears about communism and secularism, an uneasiness within the Church regarding its position in the "modern" world, a desire that the Church remain a player in the postwar geopolitical order in which its historical relationship to the newly identified third world gave it unique standing—the postwar moment was the start of a new missionary era, heralded most clearly in Pius XII's 1957 encyclical *Fidie Donum*. In Bolivia, new missionary orders such as the Oblates and Maryknoll joined the growing ranks of Jesuits and other orders already in the region. Secular priests from a number of dioceses in the U.S. also arrived in Bolivia. Between 1956 and 1968 the number of regular and secular priests in Bolivia increased from 495 to 899.

The phrase "second evangelization" itself—familiar to Latin American Catholics for more than a generation—bears some scrutiny. In places like Bolivia, it implies a second missionary bite at a so far unevangelized indigenous apple and so dismisses the efficacy of the colonial sensuous catechism. It is patently about the failure of meaning, about the limits of colonially derived Catholicism and its shallow roots of faith. In his tellingly titled book, *The Aymara Indians: Evangelized or Only Baptized?*, Jacques Monast, one of the early Canadian Oblates to work on the altiplano, observed:

> Christianity provided the Indians above all a new vocabulary to express in Catholic terms their traditional beliefs. . . . The subjects of the Incas, overwhelmed by the fervor of the conquistadors and the Spanish preachers, accepted the religion of the invaders without resistance. They did not understand. Defeated, they retreated into a disconcerting religious muteness. In truth, no one today knows their true religious sentiments. They know with precision when and how to organize their worship and their religious fiestas; at the desired moment, they send for the priest. And if he is not initiated in their religious customs, they explain in detail what they expect from him in the given circumstances (1972: 18–19).

Father William agrees:

> what was happening was ritual celebration with almost no instruction and what the hope was . . . [was to have] much more preparation of at least a nuclear group of people who began to pull their villagers together around the idea that more than just the ritual is involved in these sacramental celebrations and fiestas, whether it is a personal celebration of first communion or baptism or a marriage or a communal celebration of the village feast, that the people have to know why they're doing it at some minimal level.

Missionaries of the second evangelization found themselves necessary strangers, often uncomprehending participants in apparently Catholic practices. Priests arriving in Latin America were immediately pressed into ritual service. Many of the missionaries of the period whom I consulted in my research recounted and complained of this in ways that echo Monast's observations (Orta 2002a). But the problem they identified at that time was not their own incomprehension but that of the Aymara. The task was not understanding their meaning to the Aymara or that of Catholicism in the Aymara context, but systematically revaluing that meaning through formal instruction. The challenge, as William recounted, was "[t]o go to where nobody was, to reach out to people who had this patina of Catholicism from Spain and this cultural Catholicism and to say 'we have to give them instruction,' that we can't go on with the repetition of the customs, traditional fiesta celebrations, etc., that we have to find a way to catechize, to instruct and to give people reasons for faith."

The history of Catholic missionization in Bolivia over the second half of the twentieth century reveals a two-pronged approach to the problem. On the one hand there was a push for instruction—catechisms, Bible classes, the *cursillo* movement. As part of this effort, missionaries began the systematic training of indigenous catechists, local-level agents of missionization who, along with the weekly worship groups ("faith groups") they formed around themselves, were to be a constant evangelical presence in their rural communities. It was these catechists who would "go to where nobody was," or rather, since they were already there, the new evangelization would be spatially diffused through the recruitment of catechists who would come periodically to pastoral centers to receive instruction and carry it back to their faith groups and communities.

The catechists and the weekly services they offered were to be a vehicle for establishing a routinized sense of Christian community, beyond the infrequent celebrations of calendrical and life-cycle rituals that tended to occupy much of a priest's contact with his dispersed flocks. As William explained: "[M]issioners of the 50s and 60s came to the point where they said, 'We just can't keep up these rounds of fiestas. [They just] have absolutely no relationship to anything else.' So they almost said to the villages, 'We won't come anymore to do the fiestas unless you name a catechist, who becomes your delegate responsible for the continuation of the Church community here.'" The sense that periodic priestly visits merely punctuate with Catholic ritual an otherwise non-Christian Aymara life offers a temporal analogue to other notions of an incomplete evangelization. The catechists' ongoing presence, further multiplied by a community of followers in the faith group, was to serve as a permanent enactment of Christian identity in dispersed communities. The catechists were the prototypes of a newly conceived Aymara-Christian.

The second prong of this approach, hinted at by William, was a systematic institutional rejection of what were seen as the ritual trappings of a superficial, meaningless Christianity. "Sacramentalismo" was (and is) the scornful label missionaries used to designate this defective Catholicism. Overwhelmed by the liturgical demands placed upon them by their "unevangelized" flock, many pastoral workers refused to celebrate fiesta masses, retreating from a repertoire of expected actions that had meanings beyond their comprehension or control. In some cases, the catechists served as gatekeepers to the sacraments: regular faith group attendance or other preparation certified by the catechists was required before priests would agree to celebrate a fiesta mass for the annual sponsors or to baptize a child. In other instances, priests sought to strip Catholic ritual practices of all sacramental and performative excesses—particularly those linked to the veneration of local images of Catholic saints, and forms of dancing and drinking and feasting linked to saint's day festivals.

Dubbed "neo-Catholicism" by some, these reformist concerns dominated Catholic missionization during the 1960s and 70s. Denouncing the drunkenness, dancing, the excessive costs incurred by festival sponsors, and the worship of man-made statues, Catholic missionaries and catechists sounded very much like their evangelical Protestant rivals. Aymara I interviewed in the 1990s would list *catequistas* as kind of religion, part of series that included a range of Protestant churches, and distinct from the unmarked "Catholic" (cf. Buechler and Buechler 1978: 93). Neo-Catholic missionaries and the local catechists they trained were not only concerned with the imperfections of inherited colonial Catholicism; what they saw as pagan or idolatrous indigenous practices also drew their attention. Indigenous ritual specialists (yatiris), local place deities, and a host of rituals were denounced as part of this modern extirpation campaign. The ayuno I witnessed in 1991 reenacted a community practice that had been abandoned some years before in the face of these pressures.

The Theology of Inculturation

I have addressed the postwar history of neo-Catholicism in the Andes in more detail elsewhere (Orta 1995, 2004). In broad strokes, its landmarks include the convergence of neo-Catholicism and theologies of liberation in the wake of the Second Vatican Council and meetings of the Latin American Bishops Conference. Though it reverses many of the conservative political aims that gave rise to the second evangelization, liberation theology, which emphasizes exegesis of biblical texts in the light of contemporary social reality and mistrusts both more conventionally conceived ritual and what it condemns as a colonial derived alienating piety, reflects a similarly modernizing/rationalizing approach to Christian meaning. For a variety of reasons—ranging from successful repression of radical priests by the Bolivian state, to the suppression of key missionaries by the Vatican, to what I suspect was a strong dissonance between the reformist extirpative bent of neo-Catholicism and liberation theology on the one hand, and the integration of Catholic ritual in rural Andean life on the other—a number of these pastoral initiatives collapsed in the early 1980s.

Emerging in their wake was a new pastoral paradigm: the theology of inculturation. The guiding premise of inculturation is that indigenous beliefs and ritual practices reflect and embody local and culturally particular expressions of what missionaries take to be universal Christian values. Where colonial missionaries strived to convince Andeans to abandon their indigenous ways and thereby to become Christian, inculturationists insist that Andeans were Christian all along. Where missionaries of the second evangelization sought to complete an evangelization that had not successfully penetrated indigenous society or souls, having instead been co-opted to do the work of indigenous meaning, inculturationists seek to dismantle the colonial legacy and to revitalize what they see as indigenous religion.

In practice, this shift in pastoral ideology has entailed a double objectifying and codifying move. The first involves the construction of an Aymara identity. This is not, of course, the exclusive purview of missionaries: Aymara have been codified as a group in a variety of ways and in many contexts may think of themselves as component members of an extensive ethnic group (Orta 2002b). However, in other contexts communal or regional affiliations predominate. As missionaries in the field strive to identify local practices as representative of a more inclusively constructed Aymaraness, they often encounter friction between the salience of local, community-level frames of ritual action and the more general Aymaraness to which they aim to reduce it (Orta 1998). Second, the theology of inculturation involves the alignment of Aymara identity with a grid of Christian meaning taken to be universal. Indeed, it is through this alignment that it effects the construction of Aymaraness in theological terms.

Some vignettes from missionary courses may serve to illustrate this process. These are drawn from my observations of a regional pastoral training center serving catechists from a number of altiplano parishes. I then turn to look in more detail at an event from a parish-level course for catechists. This was the course in which catechists were first exhorted to undertake community-level performances of the ayuno.

In November 1991 I observed a course for catechists led by Quintin, an Aymara pastoral worker of long standing who had been at the forefront of the turn to inculturation. The theme was "Exodus." Building upon the implicit parallel between the "people of Israel" and the "Aymara people," the course was focused on the implications of Jesus' teaching for Israel—and by analogy for the Aymara. Quintin's message condensed much of the inculturationist perspective, stressing historical ethnic continuity: Jesus' "project" is the fulfillment of the Hebrew (Aymara) cultural past, not its overturning.

Quintin depicted these points through a diagram of a tree representing Israel. The roots of the tree corresponded to the "past," while the trunk was described as the "history" of the people. Together, the roots and trunk are the Old Testament, yet the tree is incomplete, Quintin noted, without beautiful branches. As a result of the carelessness of the people of Israel, weeds grew around the tree and some of the branches became twisted. Jesus' "project" as detailed in the New Testament, Quintin explained, is to "complete" the tree. Jesus, he continued, did not come to reject the ways of the past, but rather to fulfill them. This fulfillment involves a two-fold process of enabling the healthy branches to grow, by cutting away the deformed bad branches. "So," stressed Quintin, "Jesus' purpose is to construct this same tree, not to make another tree."

There is an implicit criticism of previous Catholic missionaries here. "For a long time," Quintin told the catechists, "they have told us, 'this [part of your culture] has to be removed, this is bad, this is not written in the Bible, the word 'ayllu' is not there, it has to be removed. 'Pachamama' (the earth/place deity) must be removed, waxt'a (offerings to place deities) [also].' Our ancestors didn't know God, so we have to get rid of that. And music, 'since they are not the horns of the Apocalypse, you must get rid of the tarkas [vertical duct flutes].'" Amid much laughter, Quintin made his points, erasing branches of the tree for each word denied Aymara culture by Christian evangelization.

The tree that once represented the biblical history of Christian revelation now stands for Aymara history: the roots and trunk index an Aymara past; the severely pruned branches the engagement of Aymara culture with Christianity. Having parodied missionary priests, Quintin now assumed the voice of Jesus and, paraphrasing Matthew 5:17, told the catechists: "I did not come to cut the laws that you had since the Incas . . . Rather I came to fulfill the laws that you had since your *achachilas* [ancestors]. You have beautiful laws for living in community. . . . You have beautiful laws for creating solidarity." As with the Jews, noted Quintin, there are many bad customs in Aymara communities that must be removed. But he exhorted the catechists to see the Bible not as a "new project," but rather as a vehicle for fulfilling what he identified as the "historical project of the Aymara people."

Revelation through inculturation is thus cast as the end of cultural history. The Aymara are to realize their own New Testament as the contemporary unfolding of Aymara history is harnessed to the narrative poetics of Christian revelation and salvation. As an Aymara priest commented: "The Holy Scripture is the fruit of a people's history. To create an Andean theology, we have to take account of our history." Yet the Aymara are also said by missionaries to "no longer know their historical memory." This rupture with the past is indexed sociologically (in the decline of community solidarity; in the Westernized ways of the younger generation) as well as physically (in the declining use of traditional medicinal practices; in the increased dependence on imported foodstuffs—noodles, rice, sugar—said to be less nutritious than the native diet of potatoes and highland grains). Inculturation, as well as the conversion it predicates, entails a recommitment to historical continuity. It organizes a range of metacultural discourses around a posited Aymaraness anchored by a newly remembered history.

"You are the grandchildren of the yatiris. What are their grandchildren like?" At a course offered a few of months after his discussion of Exodus, Quintin began with this challenge to the assembled catechists. He instructed everyone to leave the classroom where we had gathered, and assembled us outside around a small stone altar covered with a *thari* cloth and set with coca, cigarettes, and alcohol. Quintin asked one of the older catechists to prepare a *ch'alla*—a libation of the sort performed in the context of a range of traditional ritual practices. The catechist prepared a shot glass of alcohol in which he placed three coca leaves; he aspersed the altar with the alcohol and then invited another female catechist to perform a ch'alla with the wine. The older male catechists spoke to me, addressing me as "Padre." I told him he was mistaken—I was not a priest; furthermore, I was married. This did not put an end to the matter, for he insisted that I was simply a priest who had married a nun. This became a familiar line of (teasing?) banter over the course of my research. It was performed here quite publicly before an amused audience of catechists and Quintin. When he learned that my wife and I did not have children—a public index of adulthood—he spent some time telling me how young and immature I was and how little I knew about life. He then informed me (and his audience) that he could read coca (a capacity usually limited to yatiris—the archrivals of catechists, by the lights of earlier pastoral ideologies), and began an impromptu coca reading workshop as a number of catechists asked his opinion about the significance of variously shaped leaves. "I can read coca better than I can read the Bible," he boasted, adding that each was the "Word of God." Quintin then led the catechists in prayer around the altar and distributed cigarettes (also important to the practices of yatiris), which we all smoked. We returned to the classroom to begin the course.

These autoethnographic performances are for immediate consumption by the catechists. Quintin adeptly elicits a ch'alla from an older catechist framed by his call to the catechists to assess their relationship to their yatiri/ancestors. In addition to authorizing what for some of the catechists were scandalous practices, the ch'alla enacts a quasifamilial relationship of descent linking generations of catechist, and so reinforces the meta-Aymara community of catechists, while underscoring implicit doctrinal messages about the evangelical promise of remembered Aymara culture. Indeed, it is revealing that this catechist segued to his authoritative performance of a metonymic culture trait in the wake of making me stand for a foreign priest and publicly scorning my utter ignorance of life.

This appeal to elder catechetical authority is risky business, given the tendency for older catechists to be among those most strident in their opposition to the new postures of inculturation. In this light, Quintin's orchestrated ch'alla is also an autoethnography of penance, calling catechists to align themselves anew with their own cultural past. As Quintin remarked to the catechists in the course of his discussion of Exodus and the extirpative position of many Catholic missionaries: "I remember as a young catechist telling the *awkis* [elders] to stop with their customs, that the culture was ruining them. I don't know who I was then."

Inculturation as an Ideology of Conversion

At the same time, Quintin's discussion makes clear that inculturation is an ideology of conversion. Notwithstanding the value placed on the organic unfolding of cultural traditions, not all the branches on the tree can remain. Local cultures are to be judged in the light of "Christian values," and the resulting pastoral pruning is referred to as "purifying" cultural practices. As I once heard a missionary from Brazil put it (to the catechists themselves): the task of the missionaries is not to judge Aymara culture, but rather to prepare the Aymara themselves to undertake the task of judgment. "All that which facilitates life, living in community," she explained, "this should be conserved and dynamized. I cannot do this [selecting] for you. The inculturation of the Gospel is for you to do. We give you the criteria."

Practices that are seen as fostering community solidarity are held to be consonant with Christian values, often contrasted with practices that cause division or "fear." Father Hernando frequently cited the Gospel of Matthew (7:16–20)—"you shall know the tree by its fruits"—as a reference point for catechists in assessing their culture:

I say to you what I have always said: "when the fruit of something is fear, you ought to think, 'this must not be good.' God does not want the people to go in fear." . . . If people go to Mass out of fear, because it is forced on them, although it is Mass and the Mass is the greatest thing Christians have, it will not be good. If the people after a *wilancha* [llama sacrifice] are afraid, then that wilancha is badly done, it is not good. You should know that anything that causes fear in people is not of God. You must go thinking, what fruits these things produce. All that is good comes from God. This is the way you must analyze. It is not whether you can do or not do [a particular ritual act]. Each one of you must answer for yourself, in your heart, honestly, "I do this out of fear," or "because I do this I am in peace, I am happy, I am with love." There are many [Aymara rituals] so we must read them with the eyes of Jesus from the Bible.

Dusty Signs

Hernando's comments came as part of the parish-level course for catechists that I observed in December of 1990. For Hernando, this course represented an effort to revitalize his work with catechists; he described it to me as a self-conscious effort to introduce the inculturationist theme of "culture" to the catechists. This was discomforting to a number of the catechists present, some of whom directly reflected the cultural conservatism of old-line neo-Catholicism and so found themselves encouraged to embrace practices they had once had a hand in extirpating. The course was marked by nervous laughter and silence in places (cf. Bornstein; Coleman; Engelke; and Tomlinson, this volume); the discomfort was palpable to me despite my then limited experiences with such courses. I turn here to discuss that course in more detail.

The three-day course began under the leadership of Manuel, a young Aymara seminarian assisting Hernando. Working at a chalkboard, Manuel drew a chart listing two categories of "ministries": those that are "ours" and those that are "foreign." He illustrated this with a sketch map showing Latin America and Europe, with arrows depicting the movement of things from Europe to Latin America. He also glossed this movement with references to "Columbus" and "conquest." "Evangelization" and "baptism" were quickly listed under the heading "foreign." The goal of these foreign ministries, Manual suggested, is "to create community." He illustrated the need for this by drawing a pie diagram of a contemporary Aymara community, which he depicted as fraught with divisions between Catholics and Protestants, members of different political parties, and so forth. Slyly implicating the catechists in this state of affairs, he noted that baptism creates other kinds of divisions, because it excludes people who have not received the proper catechetical preparation.

As to "our" ministries, waxt'as, wilanchas, fiestas and ayunos were listed as local practices unknown in Europe. Fiestas and ayunos, of course, are not unproblematically autochthonous; their categorization as "our" (viz. indigenous) stemmed in part from their oppositional relation to recent generations of official Catholic doctrine. At this point we were already on a complex composite terrain of locality, autochthony, ethnicity, and the popular, generated and referenced in contemporary interactions. From the point of view of the catechists as well, the list was a potentially scandalous one. The mention of "wilancha" (blood sacrifice of a llama, sometimes overseen by a yatiri) elicited a fair amount of nervous laughter, prompting Manuel to erase the term. Comparing the lists, Manuel asked "which are more communitarian?" The answer is "our ministries." Catholic rituals such as baptism, which sow fragmentation despite their communal aims, were depicted graphically as standing outside of the indigenous community (indexing their ongoing failure to transcend foreign origins).

The task as Manuel posed it is a kind of a double unification. On the one hand the contemporary fragmentation of the Aymara community is to be overcome. Manuel used a variety of Aymara terms that connote a productive merging of parts characteristic of ayllu structures: *mayachasiña* (becoming one), *sawthapiña* (weaving). But at the same time, this unification of the community entails the authentic placement of foreign ministries at the center (*taypi*) of the community. As representatives of foreign ministries, the catechists were thus challenged to position themselves at the centers of their communities. In this effort, Manuel told them, the catechists are singularly capable (and culpable). "We have been following other footsteps along another path," noted Manuel. "We have gone wrong." But, catechists know the correct path, the path of Aymara ministries "from when we were young." Unintentionally underscoring the entanglements entailed in this movement towards a more perfect Aymara-Christian future through their memory of their lived Aymara past, Manuel added, "So the Padre is going to guide us in how we will weave this together."

Hernando remained at the back of the classroom as a number of catechists spoke about what they saw to be a general state of cultural decline in their communities. For the most part, their nostalgia focused on a contemporary breakdown of respect and proper sociability—as more and more young Aymara migrated to the city; as the current generation of *mallkus* (ayllu authorities) seemed less capable of leading the community than those of past decades—rather than on the decline of waxt'as and fiestas. Still, Manuel seemed to have hit his mark.

At this point, Hernando intervened to sketch out his goals for this course, which were to see "how we can achieve a faith that is communitarian. These types of celebrations—ayunos or fiestas—are very communitarian. Everyone participates. In contrast, baptism, marriage, in reality this is only for me . . . we have to do something."

Hernando then turned to elicit a ritual calendar—"an Aymara liturgical year"—to represent the sequence of communal ("our") rites practiced in the region. Here the course turned into an extensive ethnographic interview. Under each month of the year, he listed the rituals celebrated in the home ayllus of the catechists.

As a range of Andeanist work makes clear, the notion of community as a unit of analysis in the Andes is neither unproblematic nor transparent (Abercrombie 1998; Molinie Fioravante 1986; Platt 1987). Yet this inculturationist ethnography preselects a particular level and locus of ritual activity—the community—as a principal site of authenticity, holding foreign rites such as baptism accountable to the same sociological level. Hernando's liturgical list does not address what priests might judge to be more fragmentary Aymara practices, such as household-level rituals, or indigenous analogues to baptism such as first hair-cuttings (*ratucha*). Similarly, this fabricated Aymara liturgical year codifies a set of practices as communal—thus making this community-constituting function the most salient dimension of the rite—when in fact such practices are differentially salient for different actors depending upon their positions in their own life cycles, in the genealogical contexts of their families, and with respect to the complex sequence of community service obligations out of which Aymara locality is ceaselessly constituted (Orta 2004).

More significantly, this missionary ethnography homogenized a diverse range of practices across the region, establishing a prototypical liturgical calendar as well as a prototypical community/ayllu. Hernando went on in this ethnographic encounter to focus on the ayuno, eliciting detailed descriptions of the rite from various catechists. In some cases these were narrations of extant practices. In others there was a whiff of salvage ethnography made more troubling as the very catechists responsible for the decline of such events memorialized their passing. Hernando, who has a subtle and deep knowledge of his parish, was well aware of these variations across communities, and it is not my purpose to criticize him. My point is that the pastoral position shaped by inculturation trades upon a homogenized conception of Aymara locality as a serial component of an overarching Aymaraness. One function of the course was to extract a generalized template of the practices being discussed. This generation of a normative, prototypical version of the ritual is key, for the ayuno was being promoted as a principal ritual to be revitalized: a privileged forum for the catechists and faith group members to achieve the aims of inculturation.

Part of the inculturationist message involves a privileging of "ritual." Hernando, for instance, often exhorted his catechists to communicate with their faithful using "signs" rather than "words." By "signs" he meant the repertoires of gestures and objects that compose rituals; yatiris were held up here as role models. As examples of the excessive use of words, missionaries pointed to the interminable speeches of self-important schoolteachers during national holiday celebrations at rural schools. This was an indirect criticism of many of the catechists themselves, who, inspired by the text-based liturgical reforms introduced as part of earlier waves of the "second evangelization," were infamous for speaking to their congregations for hours.

But if earlier missionary cohorts sought to fix Catholic practices by emphasizing (educational) words, inculturationists' enthusiasm for ritual signs did not signal a return to a sensuous catechism, but rather sought a different medium through which to continue this missionary interest in legibility. In fact, they sought to recuperate signs precisely for their legibility in at least two regards. The first had to do with what they took to be the communicative efficacy of signs, which they saw as bypassing interpretation (and hence misinterpretation) by speaking more directly to the "heart" of the interpretant (cf. Orta 2000). The second concerns signs as an enduring archive of meaning. In his comments to the catechists, Hernando voiced this as a parable: "When one is walking down a road, although he begins very clean, by the end it may be that he is full of dust and his clothing all disheveled. That is to say there are signs that, sometimes if we don't look at them a little, they may be losing their meaning. So it is important to look at them." Although they appear idolatrous to us now, Hernando was suggesting, Aymara signs such as those used in the ayuno retain a reserve of (commensurably Christian) meaning through time, which can be recovered in spite of the dust of conquest and faulty missionization.

As I suggested at the beginning of this chapter, however, this approach to meaning is a limited one. At the limits of this sense of meaning can be found opportunities for a richer evocation of the significance of such rituals. For more than enacting systemic (if dusty) theological content, rituals like the ayuno constitute local social worlds and reference the complex contexts of their constitution. Further, in cases like the one at hand, the contexts of the production of Aymara locality include Catholic missionization and its long legacy of systematizing intent. A final section of this chapter, returning to the ayuno as enacted, is intended to bring both the irreducibility of ritual and the particular contextual force of missionization into shared focus.

The Ayuno

The ayuno performance described earlier reflects the gradual assimilation by catechists of the premises of inculturation, and the increasing exposure of Aymara in the region to a range of other discourses of cultural revalorization. I return here to that performance as a prescribed enactment of a local cultural practice that exceeds the legible meanings intended by the missionaries. In this regard I want to consider the ayuno in two analytic dimensions: first, as a capillary performance of a newly officialized practice; second, as an example of a cultural practice by which situated agents produce locality. Far from a stable local frame anchoring the ritual performance of indigenous theology, such ritual practices produce and transform localities in ways that both engage and escape the official glosses of missionary Christianity. In this regard, they enact a form of meaning that is always irreducible to the commensurability, legibility, and fixity of Christian meaning.

To review, the ayuno is an intracommunal event correlated with the beginning of the planting season and with the completion of the tenure of annually rotating community authorities. Once celebrated under the direction of yatiris, the ayuno had effectively been extirpated in the mid 1970s by Bonifacio, the more senior of the two catechists serving the community and, significantly, a son of one of the most powerful yatiris in the region.

By the early 1990s, the region was reeling from a series of disasters ranging from the impact of neoliberal economic structural adjustments, to floods, droughts, and, in the 1990–91 growing season, devastating frosts. More than a few people muttered that this was a consequence of forgetting the ways of the ancestors. This fear of further punishment motivating some to revive the ayuno practice was the opposite of what missionaries intended, but it clearly reinforced in unanticipated ways a discourse of "recuperating and revalorizing culture," which was seeping in from many sides. Another factor shaping the recuperation of the ayuno was the fact that one of the authorities (mallkus) serving that year was a Protestant. This is more remarkable than may be apparent. Among the duties of a mallku are regular use of alcohol and coca—activities prohibited by most Protestant churches and until recently by catechists and faith group members. In the current case, the man complied with his obligations to the community, explaining that for the current year he would drink and chew coca, and then return to the life of temperance. His ecumenism further enabled the self-conscious performance of the ayuno.

The morning of the ayuno began with intense interactions between the mallkus and Alejandro, the other catechist from the community, with whom the authorities had arranged to celebrate the ritual. I arrived early with Alejandro at the chapel, where the principal community authorities, along with a handful of faith group members, were already waiting. Standing together on the raised chancel of the adobe chapel, the authorities and Alejandro conferred. They were looking to Alejandro for an explanation of the ritual, to get a sense of what an ayuno involved.

Other community members arrived, including a group of yatiris invited by the mallkus. The mallkus exited the chapel to the churchyard, leaving Alejandro and the faith group inside. Three spatial groupings were taking shape at this point: Alejandro and the faith group inside the chapel; a larger group including ayllu authorities and yatiris in the churchyard gathered around a low stone table (*misaqala*) that serve as the socioritual focal point of the enclosure; and a third group outside the churchyard, looking in. Among these detached spectators was Bonifacio, the other catechist from the community, who had been responsible for the extirpation of the ayuno.

As the event began to cohere, the principal mallku addressed those in the churchyard. (Alejandro and the faith group members emerged from the chapel to watch, but remained apart.) The mallku praised the community for celebrating the ayuno, stressing repeatedly that the ayuno be undertaken "voluntarily." His stress on voluntary participation reflects a sort of interreligious détente reached in the region, turning on the assertion that no one should be compelled to participate in any ritual. This acknowledges the refusal by Protestants and neo-Catholics to participate in some practices, and so ratifies a certain weakening of tradition. It also suggests a specific vision of personhood as the discrete rational basis for legitimate ritual participation. Finally, it indexes the contentious multifaceted social frame within which the ayuno performance and consequent production of locality is achieved.

The lead yatiri (Bonifacio's father, Cornelio) began the preparation of a complex offering composed principally of flowers and ground copal (incense). The flowers were presented by lesser authorities (*p'iqis*) representing different sections of the community. The yatiris bundled these together. The chunks of copal were similarly offered and then ground into a fine powder. This was done in a bowl resting upon the misaqala, using a rock as a pestle. Cornelio then invited each member of the community to spoon the copal into a bowl. As they did, people muttered prayers for a good year to come and invoked place names of significance to their household. The offering thus embodies a merging of the community into a single homogenous totality composed of people differentially aligned with various microlocalities (households) within the ayllu. But note that the ayllu (of interest both to the missionaries and to the various participants in the ayuno) is neither unproblematically already there nor a monolith, but produced out of and with respect to a complex, translocal social field. For instance, in preparation for this stage of spooning, Cornelio had sent an assistant into the chapel to request of the catechist some fronds and a bowl. He accepted the fronds but rejected the bowl from the chapel as "too dirty" and dispatched his assistant to his own house for a clean bowl and a "silver spoon." In this ironic inversion of the stereotypical missionary obsession with hygiene and cleanliness (which also echoed other experiences the community had had with development agencies), we see the contestation and negotiation of multiple sites and modes of ritual authority entangling the chapel and catechist-led faith group with the dispersed households represented by the ayuno participants.

Against the backdrop of the ayuno—producing ayllu locality from a diversity of households—the ambiguous position of the catechists and the ritual knowledge and authority they control is stark. On the one hand is the structural ambiguity of the faith group. Distinct from the community—like evangelical churches—it is also a part of the community on the order of a household. As I demonstrate elsewhere (Orta 2004), these worship groups are quasi-households; relations among group members and catechists are explicitly analogous to the relations that constitute extended patrilocal households. Inculturation challenges catechists to negotiate a new footing for themselves, transcending their positions as fathers of their own household and (classificatory) fathers of their faith group. In the catechist course presenting the ayuno, Father Hernando exhorted the catechists to position themselves at the "center" of the ayllu. This is where mallkus and yatiris are said to practice, and the resonance with these markedly indigenous forms of social and ritual authority is not, I suspect, unintended. However it leaves the catechists in relatively uncharted (Catholic) territory.

At the same time, the catechists must wrestle with the ambiguity of the ritual knowledge they control (cf. Coleman; Engelke, this volume). Though inculturationist missionaries seek to downplay the importance of colonial Catholic knowledge, many catechists are valued in their communities as specialists adept in precisely this sort of religious knowledge. This knowledge, ironically, is held by many Aymara to be ancestral knowledge—once widely controlled by the achachilas. Moreover, this traditional Aymara (Catholic) knowledge is held to have once been routinely passed on from father to sons; this transmission is remembered as an index of traditional social integrity in Aymara communities. In this regard, the catechists and their faith groups are prototypical instantiations of Aymara household locality—though for reasons quite different from those imagined by inculturationists—and their participation in the enactment of the interpenetration of households within the ayllu becomes fraught with complexity.

As the offering bundling the community into a single body was completed, Bonifacio (who had entered the ritual space when his turn came to spoon co-pal) intervened, in effect taking control of the ritual. Using the oratorical style typical of a community meeting, he greeted all those present and declared his desire to speak. Noting that it was getting late, he said it was time for people to decide how they wanted to do the ayuno. Appealing especially to elders in the crowd, he offered to explain the ayuno "according to the word of God." Essentially he presented a cultural menu of three variants of the ayuno (thus softening the single prototype generated by Hernando). One began at 10 a.m. with the community reciting the Rosary until 11 a.m. or noon. This would be followed by a Via Crucis and a *letanía* (litany). "Then we will do . . . [long pause] . . . then that with the flowers probably gets done," he said, alluding uncomfortably to the offering prepared by the yatiris. After that comes "the rite of pardon, and when that is finished we are going to enter here and cel-ebrate the Mass of the ayuno. On top of that there is a communal meal," he concluded. The two other types are abbreviated versions of the first: one with-out the initial praying of the Rosary, the other without the Via Crucis and the burnt offering of the yatiris.

There was a period of debate as various ayllu members voiced opinions about the ayuno and about the catechists. The matter was decided by the mallku, who effectively ceded control of the event to the catechists, stating,

> Now elders and by the same token mother elders, all brothers and sisters, just as in the previous community meeting, we said that today is Santa Barbara and so per-haps we could fast, the entire community in the zone. And in that all of you have come, it is truly good. We the authorities [say] to you "very good." . . . We know in this community that since long ago we have been Catholic in our customs. But it appears that the entire community is not of the true Catholic religion. It is not that way with each sect today. Yes it's like that these days. Yes above all, all of this is clear, and so this morning we spoke with Alejandro, "each year you direct the ayuno. We count on you to say a few words. You have all the right [to speak and guide the ayuno]. This must be why we set you up on this path. Because in the community [we have] a voluntary ayuno, and sacred ayuno. This is what we have remembered. Above all, you cannot tell the community beforehand how it should be . . . we trust in you." This is how we spoke, we can clarify that. So above all, we authorities, all of the bases we can trust them, perhaps they can direct, and in that way we can complete/fulfill [the ayuno].

His speech does a number of things. First note that the mallku stressed the long-standing character of local custom as Catholic. Where missionaries see the performance of the ayuno as the reembrace of local non-Catholic tradi-tion, the mallku framed this popular practice as a re-embrace of Catholicism. Just as the mallku assimilates Catholicism as a presupposable local tradition, the recuperation of which is being performed in the ayuno, he also frames the catechists not as agents of foreign religious ideals, but as locally delegated rit-ual specialists, noting that the community set them on this path as catechists.

Finally, the mallku makes no distinction between Bonifacio's intervention in the event and his consultations with Alejandro earlier that morning. From his point of view they are interchangeable. From a faith group internal view, however, this is far from the case. Even as the mallku is assimilating the catechists as a component part of the local community, Bonifacio and Alejandro are performing a bitter and ongoing rivalry, with Bonifacio upstaging and humiliating Alejandro as he takes control of the ayuno.

With this, all entered the chapel under the direction of Bonifacio (to perform option two—the variant without the Rosary). The offering prepared by the yatiris was set on the altar in front of a saint's image. The faith group sang a hymn. The first station was performed inside the chapel. Exiting, some suggested that a Via Crucis ought to be performed barefoot ("the way the ancestors did it"), so we proceeded barefoot through the remaining stations, climbing a small hill behind the chapel to a calvario at the top. The yatiri bore the flower/copal offering and the mallkus a small cross from the chapel.

This hilltop shrine warrants further comment. Machaqueños often referred to such sites to illustrate their claims of cultural decline: the calvarios were no longer visited on fiestas, or they were in ruin—something consistently blamed on acts of vandalism by children who destroyed the structures and knocked down the stone cairns that often mapped Via Crucis stations up the side of the hill. (I suspect these were also targeted by catechists at some point). In this, and in the enthusiasm for performing the Via Crucis barefoot, and even in the exhortation that all offerings and participation in the ayuno must be "voluntary," there is a poignant self-consciousness of such cultural decline. Aymara are not as hardy as their ancestors, have not maintained local ritual sites, and cannot perform a sort of communal consensus of *voluntad* (will) believed to have once been part of the ayllu's ritual repertoire. Here the locality being produced through the ayuno is explicitly marked as a flawed, entangled, and challenged one.

The degradation of the hillside cairns turned out to be an issue: Bonifacio miscalculated and we arrived at the calvario at station seven. To my painful dismay, the remaining stations were completed on our knees, circling the calvario three times for each station. In the meantime, the yatiris prepared a fire of dung and straw. Cornelio called the mallkus out of the procession to make the burnt offering. This was the scene I described earlier, which, as is now apparent, was an improvisation building upon multiple contingencies. Moreover, Bonifacio used his improvisation of the Via Crucis portion of the ayuno to deftly braid together and acknowledge the complexity of the ayllu, inviting various authorities as well as a local Protestant pastor to perform the Bible readings at certain stations. This ritual ecumenism, it should be noted, is not the province of inculturationist-steeped catechists alone. Once the focal offering had been made by the mallkus, the yatiris then called each member of the ayllu (first other authorities, then men, then women) to hold a brazier of embers onto which they spooned the remainder of the copal. The effect was that each participant transited the apparently composite space of the calvario.

After the offering of flowers and incense, the community engaged in an act of pardon: each participant embraced every other participant and asked forgiveness for any insults or injuries committed during the previous year. The pardoning completed, the faith group gathered off to one side, where they sang a few hymns. Cornelio completed his sacrifice with an offering of wine arced high in the air toward the mountain peaks and sky.

The group then returned to the chapel, where the catechists performed a liturgical celebration, including the distribution of preconsecrated hosts. After the service, all retired to the churchyard, where we were fed at the misaqala by the mallkus, who had brought bread and wine—a traditional obligation of authorities at such events, I was told. The spatial segregation evident at other points in the ayuno was now largely overcome: Bonifacio and Alejandro, along with Cornelio, sat next to the mallkus. Bonifacio took over the distribution of the bread and wine; imitating the act of communion, he dunked each piece in the wine before handing it to the recipient, intoning *Kristun aychipaw* (flesh of Christ). This was followed by a communal meal, provided by the mallkus, to which Bonifacio invited everyone, saying, "now we have forgiven one another, we are a single family."

Cascades of Meaning

The ayuno bears discussion along a number of dimensions. It links the renewal of the growing season with the rotation of cargo posts. It is effectively the last act of the current mallkus, preparing the way for the next cohort of ayllu authorities, who for the first months of their tenure will be regarded as newly sown and sprouting seeds. This is significant, for the next year Bonifacio was obligated to represent his section by serving as p'iqi. One informant suggested that the rite of pardon was a way for incoming ayllu authorities to prepare themselves—i.e., by feeling humility and remorse for their past conduct—for the task of service ahead. Leaving aside the focus on humility, Bonifacio's intervention may have stemmed in part from his anticipation of a more public persona in the community.

The event might also be read as reinforcing many of the values and intentions of inculturationist pastoral workers. The ayuno is patently about performing community solidarity, so it was well chosen by the missionaries in this respect. The configuration on top of the hill might be read as valorizing the putative indigenous core of Andean Christianity. More significant, I believe, is the way the catechists moved from their respective peripheral positions in the event to positions of centrality. The scene of mallkus, yatiris, and catechists all serving their community is an inculturationist's fantasy, fleetingly embodied in the course of the ayuno. Bonifacio's improvised transubstantiation of the bread and wine would probably make many priests uneasy, and certainly exceeds his authority, but inasmuch as it entailed an insertion of his ritual authority within the context of a community-wide and community-producing practice, it conformed completely with messages conveyed by missionaries.

And yet this integration was not solely the objective of—nor solely controlled by—the catechists; nor did it imply the same things for all participants. The mallkus were also involved in situating the catechists as their delegates. Similarly, the yatiris recruited the catechists and the ritual paraphernalia they controlled as part of their offering. Who is centering whom? Whose locality is being produced?

In any event, this integration was fleeting, and highlighting it may lead us to overlook significant fissures in the event. There was a deep dispute within the faith group. Bonifacio had publicly upstaged Alejandro. Alejandro's wife and his other followers in the faith group were left seething, and in the following weeks Alejandro repeatedly attempted to criticize Bonifacio for screwing up the spatial arrangement of the Via Crucis (a position for which I, with my still sore knees, had much sympathy). There also remains Bonifacio's problematic history in the community. The mallku's diplomatic, cautious, and repeated stressing of the voluntary nature of the ayuno underscored the contentious ambiance of such practices, and despite the heroic integration of the catechists, the faith group repeatedly disengaged to huddle off to the side clutching their dog-eared Bibles and songbooks. Finally, there is Bonifacio's relation to his father, a yatiri-catechist pattern that is not unique.

But that this integration should be only fleetingly achieved underscores the insight that the production of locality is a constant, open-ended, and manifold concern. The point here is not to argue for or against an "optimistic" (inculturationist) reading of the ayuno. The intent of the missionary ayuno is premised upon a particular construction of indigenous locality as the site of an authorizing popular religiosity with specific social and political implications. However, the performance of the ayuno both underscores the complexities of this missionary construction and suggests a very different vision of locality—not as an embattled site of primordial cultural authenticity, but as an evanescent project continually produced by a range of situated actors.

Though by one line of analysis the ayuno and the catechists' participation in it are concordant with sensibilities of cultural production evident in such classical loci of Aymara authenticity as the household, the locality that is produced does not transcend the shifting contexts of its production. Missionization, and the frame of inculturation in particular, is just one example of a translocal cultural feature that entails the revalorization of dimensions of inside and outside and past and present, and asserts a specific sense of locality and of the articulation of past, present, and future. While the achievements of the ayuno certainly reflect the porous resilience of Andean locality, the ramifications of inculturation at the level of this ayuno performance involve other kinds of interpenetrations as well. As understood through references to cultural decline, through objectified menus of traditional cultural practice, through repeated invocations of the voluntary nature of ayuno participation, through the stubborn endurance of cross-cutting identities—faith group, Protestant sect—poised uneasily between the levels of household and ayllu in defiance of the homogenizing grinding of the yatiri's misaqala, the porously produced locality is not what it used it be.

Nor, then, is the meaning of the ayuno what it used it be—neither what it once was in an imagined machaqueño past, nor what it used to be in its contemporary codification in missionary courses, nor apparently what it was in the initial intents of Alejandro, the community authorities, Bonifacio, or his father Cornelio on that particular December morning. In this regard, Father William was right: "We don't yet know what people really understand by the customs that they do. *They* don't know." But he was wrong to take such understandings, clarified and aligned, as a plausible goal. This reading of Aymara "customs" such as the ayuno reflects an exegetical aesthetic of legibility, one that takes on particular force in settings of Christian missionization. The case of Andean Catholicism illustrates the ways that this aesthetic pathologizes local practices as the failed outcomes of an always unattainable ideal. The "second evangelization" represents a set of institutional efforts to correct this perceived flaw—efforts that inevitably became part of the complex social setting they hoped to transcend. That such efforts to determine always indeterminate cultural practices end inevitably in failure is not a surprising observation, though it does bear repeating. My aim here has been to highlight the limits of Christian meaning, and to examine the ways the institutions of Christian mission shape and participate in a veritable cascade of meaning, in the flux of which locally constitutive meaningful events such as the ayuno unfold.

Acknowledgements

This chapter is based upon field research conducted since 1989 among Catholic missionaries, Aymara catechists and Aymara communities in Bolivia, with a focus upon the ayllus of Jesús de Machaqa (Ingavi Province, Department of La Paz). This work has been supported by a Fulbright-Hays Doctoral Dissertation Abroad Fellowship as well as by travel and research grants from the Research Board and the Center for Latin American and Caribbean Studies of the University of Illinois at Urbana-Champaign. I am indebted to the many pastoral workers, catechists and faith group members who have assisted me in my research as well as to the ayllus and cabildo of Jesús de Machaqa who have allowed my ongoing research in the area. My thanks also to Matthew Engelke and Matt Tomlinson for inviting my participation in this volume and for their helpful feedback along the way.

References

Abercrombie, Thomas A. 1998. *Pathways of Memory and Power: Ethnography and History among an Andean People*. Madison: University of Wisconsin Press.

Asad, Talal. 1993. *Genealogies of Religion: Discipline and Reasons of Power in Christianity and Islam*. Baltimore: Johns Hopkins University Press.

Buechler, Hans C., and Judith Maria Buechler. 1978. "Combatting Feathered Serpents: The Rise of Protestantism and Reformed Catholicism in a Bolivian Highland

Community." In *Amerikanistische Studien*, ed. R. Hartmann and U. Oberem. St. Augustin: Haus Volker und Kulturen, Anthropos-Institut.

Keane, Webb. 1996. "Materialism, Missionaries, and Modern Subjects in Colonial Indonesia." In *Conversion to Modernities*, ed. P. van der Veer. London: Routledge.

Molinie Fioravanti, Antoinette. 1986. "The Andean Community Today." In *Anthropological Histories of Andean Polities*, ed. J. Murra, N. Wachtel, and J. Revel. Cambridge: Cambridge University Press.

Monast, Jacques. 1972. *Los Indios Aimaraes: ¿Evangelizados o Solamente Bautizados?* Buenos Aires: Cuadernos Latinoamericanos, Ediciones Carlos Lehle.

Nelson, Diane. 1999. *A Finger in the Wound*. Berkeley: University of California Press.

Orta, Andrew. 1995. "From Theologies of Liberation to Theologies of Inculturation: Aymara Catechists and Contemporary Catholic Evangelization in Highlands Bolivia." In *Organized Religion in the Political Transformation of Latin America*, ed. S.R. Pattnayak. Lanham, MD: University Press of America.

———. 1998. "Converting Difference: Metaculture, Missionaries and the Politics of Locality." *Ethnology* 37, no. 2: 165–85.

———. "Syncretic Subjects and Body Politics: Doubleness, Personhood, and Aymara Catechists. *American Ethnologist* 26, no. 4: 864–89.

———. 2002a. "Living the Past Another Way: Reinstrumentalized Missionary Selves in Aymara Mission Fields." *Anthropological Quarterly* 75, no. 4: 707–43.

———. 2002b. "Burying the Past: Locality, Lived History and Death in an Aymara Ritual of Remembrance." *Cultural Anthropology* 17, no. 4: 471–511.

———. 2004. *Catechizing Culture: Missionaries, Aymara and the "New Evangelization."* New York: Columbia University Press.

Platt, Tristan. 1987. "The Andean Soldiers of Christ: Confraternity Organization, the Mass of the Sun and Regenerative Warfare in Rural Potosi (18th-20th Centuries)." *Journal des Société des Américanistes* 73: 139–92.

Rafael, Vincente L. 1988. *Contracting Colonialism: Translation and Christian Conversion in Tagalog Society under Early Spanish Rule*. Ithaca: Cornell University Press.

Ramos Gavilán, Alonso. 1988 [1621]. *Historia del Celebre Santuario de Nuestra Señora de Copacabana y sus Milagros e Invención de la Cruz de Carabuco*, ed. I. Prado Pastor. Lima: Edición Ignacio Prado P.

Rappaport, Joanne. 2005. *Intercultural Utopias: Public Intellectuals, Cultural Experimentation, and Ethnic Pluralism in Colombia*. Durham: Duke University Press.

Scott, James. 1998. *Seeing Like a State: How Certain Schemes to Improve the Human Condition Have Failed*. New Haven: Yale University Press.

9

PARANOMICS:
ON THE SEMIOTICS OF SACRAL ACTION

James D. Faubion

Since 1985, Amo Paul Bishop Roden has declared herself a Branch Davidian Seventh-day Adventist. She has always rejected the teachings of the man who, even after his death in 1993, remains her more famous and (even after his death) more successful rival in prophetic authority, the man known as David Koresh. Like Mr. Koresh, however, she accepts the authority of five precursors whose messages jointly constitute the distinctive doctrinal heritage of her church, even if she must regard their messages jointly and severally as incomplete. Hence, she recognizes her distant debt to William Miller, a millenarian and evangelist of the Second Great Awakening who inspired the Adventist movement (cf. Barkun 1974, 1986; Faubion 2001: 43–45). She recognizes more proximate debts to Ellen White, the founding prophet of the Seventh-day Adventist Church; to Victor T. Houteff, the founding prophet of the Davidian Seventh-day Adventist Church; and to Ben and Lois Roden, the founding prophets of the Branch Davidian Seventh-day Adventist Church.

Sometime in the late winter or early spring of 1999, Ms. Roden received from her God what she would describe as "light." It was by no means the first time that she had understood herself to have been given such a gift, such a blessing, such an inflowing of the Holy Spirit. She had received many, and had already identified herself as the messenger appointed to announce and elucidate the sixth of the seven "messages" secreted in the "seals" or "vials" of the Book of Revelation.[1] But this light was one of particular intensity and particular moment. It permitted her to see her way toward the resolution of the enigma of the Second Coming. After years of interpretive labor, it permitted her to determine the identity of the returned Christ:

> [Whether] V. T. Houteff [was] the second coming of Christ is not a question many have asked. Christians should. Houteff was the founder and prophet of the Shepherd Rod church, the Davidian Seventh-day Adventists, a small man with no beauty that made

him desirable, a Bible interpreter who created a solid foundation for Bible students, an immigrant to America from Bulgaria.

Did he come as a thief as Christ said he would? (Rev. 3:3) Yes, indeed, Houteff came in the footsteps of Christ. Christ stole the righteous of the flock from the duly-appointed but corrupt priesthood (Num. 18:1–7) and justified himself because he was the true shepherd (John 10:1–11). So Houteff stole the righteous flock from the duly-appointed but corrupt priesthood of the Seventh-day Adventist Church.

. . . prophecy says: "And he (Christ) shall be for a sanctuary; but for a stone of stumbling and for a rock of offense to both the houses of Israel, for a gin and for a snare to the inhabitants of Jerusalem" (Isa. 8:14). Both the houses of Israel refers to the whole twelve tribes, the two tribes known as Judah and the scattered ten tribes known as Ephraim. . . . Did Houteff come to finally fulfill the downfall of the hypocrites among the ten tribes?

The answer is in Revelation, where Houteff clearly fulfilled two prophecies of the Lamb. The seven seals (Rev. 6–8:1) are on the seven thunders. "And when the seven thunders had uttered their voices, I was about to write: and I heard a voice from heaven saying unto me, Seal up those things which the seven thunders uttered and write them not" (Rev. 10:4). Those seven thunders are the revelation of the complete mystery of the Bible. "But in the days of the seventh angel (after the seven thunders), when he shall begin to sound, the mystery of God should be finished, as he hath declared to his servants and prophets" (Rev. 10:7). The first seal is opened by the Lamb, and this is the seal that reveals the prophecies of the Kingdom of God (Rev. 6:1–2). Houteff's writing specifically reveals these prophecies, explained and illuminated. Building on the work of Miller and White, he also explained all of the prophecies of the Book of Daniel. And that is important, because it proves that what I said about the seals being on the thunders is true. . . .

Not only was Houteff the Lamb that opened the seals, he was also the Lamb in the third angel's message of Rev. 14 [a forewarning of the punishment of the unrighteous, the "smoke" of whose torment will ascend "up for ever and ever"]. Houteff announced the beginning of Ezekiel 9 [a forewarning of the slaughter of the unrighteous among the residents of Jerusalem] in 1930: . . . ."The prophecy of Ezekiel gives the information in detail from the beginning of Luther's reformation to Ezekiel 9."

That the Holocaust fulfilled this prophecy went unnoticed in Houteff's time. God closed Houteff's eyes to it just as he hid the seven thunders from him so that Houteff might fulfill the suffering servant of Judah, Christ come as a thief, rather than Christ come in glory. . . .

The application of Ezekiel 9 foretold by Houteff actually took place [in accord with the prophetic chronology of Ezekiel] four hundred and thirty years after Luther's personal reformation. Luther was ordained a priest in 1507 and posted the Ninety-five Theses on the church door in 1517. That corresponds to the ten-year period from 1937 to 1947, the years of Holocaust that preceded the formation of Israel in 1948. . . .

. . . Houteff's sealed flock, which included Ben and Lois Roden of the Branch, stood as the holy angels that they will rise up to be, and Houteff stood as the Lamb he was during the Holocaust, and the smoke of the crematoriums arose in a sorrow and a horror that will never be forgotten. And because Houteff was the Lamb that took the Bible from God's hands, and also the Lamb on the earth during the Holocaust, he can be none other than Christ come as a thief, the second coming of Christ. (Roden 5: 1–8, abridged)

The prophet Malachi (4:5–6) foretold that Elijah, his distant predecessor, would return to proclaim the coming of the Messiah and the gathering of the Kingdom. The authors of the gospels of the New Testament understood him to have been fulfilled in the person of John the Baptist (Hayes 1971: 342). Before 1999, Ms. Roden had never ventured to cast herself as John's own proper successor and consummation. With the light of that spring, she could no longer resist the casting. Nor in retrospect did it surprise her that the final Elijah, the final John should not precede but instead follow the Christ. *Let's consider a good thief. A good thief comes unheralded and leaves unnoticed. It is obvious that the Elijah for a Messiah who comes as a thief must herald him after he is gone* (Roden 5: 1).

Ritual, Method, and Sacral Action

The psychoanalytic commonplace that ritual relieves anxiety is, as Georges Devereux (1968) reminded us, true of method as well. Both ritual and method establish discrete boundaries around objects or conditions that would otherwise remain amorphous. Both establish directions for the carrying out of processes and the enactment of transformations that would otherwise fail to occur, or whose occurrence can be recognized and consecrated only after the fact, only in hindsight. Ritual and method are selective. They relieve anxiety because they reduce complexity. They owe their productivity no less to the avenues they prescribe than to the myriad avenues they debar or displace. They are consequently capable of "working," even when they fail to produce a determinate result. A ritual well executed might appease our confusion even when its force or effect is insensible. A method well executed might be regarded as all the more unimpeachable precisely when it generates anomaly—indeterminate by definition—or worse. If nothing else, call it the semiotic attraction of good form.

Ms. Roden is a Biblicist, embracing the Bible as the Rosetta Stone of all human history, past and future. Her method of interpretation is typological, grounded in the postulate that the dramas and the dramatis personae of the Bible are "types" foreshadowing events that will come to full fruition and persons who will come to their full realization only in the final days of history itself (cf. Brumm 1970; Faubion 2001: 45–47)—that is, the days of the Second Coming, in which she understands herself to have been living at least since her conversion to Branch Davidianism and perhaps for several years before. By 1999, Ms. Roden was surely impatient to resolve the message that she believed herself called to deliver. The end of the century—which she was not alone in regarding as especially fateful—was looming. The vigil that she had been keeping for several years on the seventy-seven acres of Texas prairie known as Mount Carmel was no longer solitary; representatives of two rival factions of the Branch Davidian Church had joined her there and were busy staking claims of their own. She had friends, but few of her doctrinal supporters were nearby. Perhaps her revelation was thus overdetermined. Perhaps the pleasure she took in her own good methodological form merely galvanized a resolve at which she had already arrived. Whatever might have precipitated it and whether or not she knew it, Ms. Roden had in any case undergone a decisive change of mind. Few readers of what she had written to that point would have been taken aback at her recognizing herself as the fulfillment of Elijah. Quite a few—this one included—could not have helped but be startled at her identification of Victor

Houteff as the returned Christ. In what she had written to that point, almost everything had suggested or implied the contrary.

But then again, the sacral actor, the actor anointed or blessed, is himself a being of changes, of surprise and the thwarting of expectations, of the play of contraries. He (or she, or it) is a Janus, a double of himself, a cardinal embodiment of the Freudian uncanny. Positively hyperbolic, rhetorically exaggerated, aesthetically sublime, he is the Christ who comes in all his glory. Negatively hyperbolic, rhetorically understated, aesthetically grotesque, he is the Christ who comes like a thief but also the Christ of the Passion, the Christ humiliated and scorned. The former Christ is the standard-bearer of every pious monarch and the champion of the righteous oppressed. The latter is beloved of the humanist, the existentialist, the sinner. The synthesis of the two is not precisely a paradox, but it is an ambivalent and ambiguous figure of no obvious logical coherence. What is true of the Christ is, moreover, all the more true of those lesser immortals who are his counterparts, the saints. Method can once again only follow suit, ecclesiastical method included. Since the twelfth century, the Catholic Church has made a formal and appropriately elaborate affair of determining of who among its flock might be genuinely worthy of canonization. It has made several technical adjustments along the way but has kept its regulative criteria intact. On the one hand, the genuine saint must perform miracles—extraordinary and beneficent events in our world unaccountable in scientific terms—on at least two separate occasions as well as from beyond the grave. On the other hand, the saint must have lived a life of what the *Catholic Encyclopedia* (2003 [1908]) calls "heroic virtue," in fact a negative hyperbolization of ascetic self-denial and self-sacrifice that has its historical hypostasis in the early martyrs' often agonizing deaths. On the one hand, "consecrated"; on the other, "accursed," even "ruinous": thus, the decidedly dualistic definition of the Latin *sacer* itself.[2]

As we know. . . . Indeed, many anthropologists and numerous other scholars of religion have at least noted the contraries so often at play in sacral action, and many have noted the duality of the sacred itself. Few if any, however, have succeeded in sustaining the play of those contraries or the irreducibility of that duality as the basic premise of their analyses. The intellectual, rhetorical, and aesthetic legacy they have left is a legacy of diverse motivations, but for all of that it is largely a legacy of reductions. Our analytical comprehension of sacral action that is also ritual action can only be compromised as a result. Analytical adequacy is elusive in part because, as Ms. Roden is herself well aware, the sacral quality of an action, like the anointment or blessedness or election of the actor who performs it, is generally indeterminate and so in need of hermeneutical assessment, of an interpretation of one sort or another. Hence, it would be misguided (and surely frustrating) to attempt to specify any finite set of general conditions necessary and sufficient to qualify an action (or an actor) as sacral. For the same reason, it would be misguided to attempt to reduce the meaning of sacral action to its extension, to reduce its sense to its reference. A diverse range of very proper semanticists from Immanuel Kant (1987 [1790]) to Jean-François Lyotard (1994) would assert that the sublime does not allow of representation, that it does not refer, that it is a pure idea without any empirical content, a register of subjective rather than objective experience. Perhaps the semiotics of sacral action is quite as elusive as it still proves to be because it is distinguished with too little rigor, or too rarely, from the aesthetics of the sacred (not to mention the politics of the sacred). Whatever its sublimity, in any event, sacral action defies neither representation nor objective reference. In this respect (if only in this respect), Ms. Roden could agree with the Catholic postulators of the saints: if perhaps not precisely in the Catholic then at least in the Wittgensteinian sense, the criteria of sacral action are sufficiently stable and sufficiently widely shared to facilitate at the very least our discriminating between what is beside the point (say, walking on a footpath) from what is exemplary (say, walking on water). If assiduously applied, they might even facilitate our discriminating between mere pretense and the genuine article.

Whether the genuine article is a really genuine article is, of course, irrelevant from a semiological (as from an anthropological) perspective. From the anthropological perspective, sacral action is what I will venture to call "paranomic." I will return to a discussion of this neologism later; setting the parsing of that coinage aside for the moment, its motivation comes from two eminently well corroborated historical and ethnographic observations. The first of them approaches being an anthropological old saw: sacral action often encourages the reinforcement of the status quo ante. The second likelihood is equally familiar, if not as familiarly phrased: sacral action also very often encourages or effects the suspension—in part or in whole—of the normative force of the cognitive and evaluative codes that are operative within the status quo ante.

Similar observations may have motivated Weber's classic treatment of charismatic authority—but a pragmatics far more reductive than Wittgenstein's can have its way with semiotics even in analytical territories where it would seem least likely to be welcome. The exemplars with whom Weber opens his analysis of charismatic authority already clear its way: Cuchulain, Achilles, and the Arabian "berserk" (1946b: 245). All the members of this illustrious trio are men of violence; all are legendary warlords. None is distinctively a religious figure (though Achilles is reputed to have been born of divine Thetis and may have been an object of cultic devotion in archaic and classical Greece). If, moreover, Weber asserts that charismatic authority "is often most clearly developed" (1946b: 246) in the religious arena, he offers his own analysis as a more value-neutral and more empirically encompassing revision of Rudolf Sohm's (1967 [1912]), the latter having confined his conclusions exclusively to the religious arena. Thus expanded, the practice of the charismatic leader has the following hallmarks. It is unroutinized: "it knows no regulated 'career,' 'advancement,' 'salary,' or . . . expert training" (1946b: 246). It is unthrifty: "in general, charisma rejects all rational economic conduct" (1946b: 247); "it is the very force that disregards economy" (1946b: 248). It is at an inevitable remove from everyday life: "the holders of charisma, the master as well as his disciples, must stand outside the ties of this world, outside of routine occupations, as well as outside the routine obligations of family life" (1946b: 248).

It is absolutist: the charismatic leader does not derive his authority from the will of his followers but instead demands it without qualification as their duty (1946b: 246–47). It is indifferent to precedent: "charismatic justice . . . is the polar opposite of formal and traditional bonds, and it is just as free in the face of the sanctity of tradition as it is in the face of any rationalist deductions from abstract concepts" (1946b: 250). It is the sociological topos of the Nietzschean superman: "its attitude is revolutionary and transvalues everything; it makes a sovereign break with all traditional or rational norms: 'It is written, but I say unto you'" (1946b: 250).

The inference is inescapable: charismatic authority is antithetical in principle to any and every modality of social reproduction. The inference is, moreover, Weber's own, and famously so. Charismatic authority is "specifically unstable" (1946b: 248). It is inherently at odds with custom, with convention, with institutional order, and if it does not wane of its own accord it must either triumph in all its unbridled "enthusiasm" (1946b: 249) or be tamed through the application of one or another technology of "routinization" (1946b: 250). Weber identifies three such technologies: a "mechanism of rules" (as in those that govern the proceedings of moral-juridical ordeals designed to generate evidence of innocence or guilt); the mechanism of a kinship or ascriptive status system; and the mechanism of credentialization and the assignation of office (1946b: 251–52). In none of these cases does the domestication of charisma amount to its erasure. It might amount instead to its compartmentalization, its storage as a resource to be deployed only when exceptional occasions require it. It may thus be restricted to the "tactical" in Michel de Certeau's sense of that term (1984: xviii-xx). Or its legitimate exercise might be relegated strictly to the private sphere, as Weber seems to have thought it already was in the Bismarckian Germany of his own day (1946a: 155).

Weber's account of what might be thought of as the sociological calling of charismatic authority is nevertheless quite distinct from his account of its routinization:

> The provisioning of all demands that go beyond those of everyday routine has had . . . a *charismatic* foundation; the further back we look in history, the more we find this to be the case. This means that the "natural" leaders—in times of psychic, physical, economic, ethical, religious, political distress—have been neither office-holders nor incumbents of an "occupation" in the present sense of the word, that is, men who have acquired expert knowledge and who serve for remuneration. The natural leaders in distress have been holders of specific gifts of the body and spirit; and these gifts have been believed to be supernatural, not accessible to everybody. (1946b: 245)

More qualified versions of this thesis enter anthropology through Anthony Wallace's essay on "revitalization" (1956) and Clifford Geertz's treatment of "ideology" (1973: 193–233). In Weber's own more expansive version, the thesis has two fairly obvious entailments—at least once they come into view. The first—of functionalist tenor—might be put in the idiom of systems theory: like its biological counterpart, social autopoiesis is very likely to be in regular need of internal technologies—and perhaps the more the better—of emergency response and repair. The less routine that response and repair, the more likely it will fall into charismatic hands. The second entailment runs somewhat contrary to the first and is actually a non sequitur: it does not in fact follow from Weber's thesis that charismatic action is destined to lead to social reproduction or restoration, even when it is explicitly and intentionally carried out on behalf of society at large. In its ideal-typically most pure manifestations, it is far more likely to lead, by intent and by design, to the opposite end. It is sociologically radical in just this sense (cf. Bellah 1970).

Charismatic action, however, is usually more than merely that. As Weber's own inaugural examples suggest, it is often behaviorally radical as well, often expressed and exercised at the very edge of madness—or over it, as the unconvinced are ready to assert. Weber himself is fully aware of the precipice at issue, only to dismiss it with a toss of the relativist's head:

> For a long time it has been maintained that the seizure of the berserk is artificially produced through acute poisoning. . . . Shamanist ecstasy is linked to constitutional epilepsy, the possession and the testing of which represents a charismatic qualification. Hence neither is "edifying" to our minds. They are just as little edifying to us as is the kind of "revelation," for instance, of the Sacred Book of the Mormons, which, at least from an evaluative standpoint, perhaps would have to be called a "hoax." But sociology is not concerned with such questions. In the faith of their followers, the chief of the Mormons has proved himself to be charismatically qualified, as have "heroes" and "sorcerers." (1946b: 245–46)

As abstract as it is magisterial, this lesson in value-free science is clear enough in shifting the locus of charisma from the charismatic to the eye of the beholder. At the same time, it seems question-begging, even intentionally evasive. As the author of *Ancient Judaism* (1952), Weber is well aware that the adjacency, the intimacy of the charismatic and the lunatic is the transhistorical and transcultural standard, however variable the line drawn between the two might be. He is well aware that *ekstasis* is a criterion of charismatic qualification not as the transhistorical and transcultural exception but instead as the rule. Here, instead of solidifying the connection, he dilutes it twice—first in juxtaposing a case of intoxicated delirium with the symptom of a congenital disease, and then in juxtaposing both with what the untutored skeptic would suspect to be calculated subterfuge. He thus leaves us with little more than the impression that the criteria of charisma are heterogeneous, arbitrary, whatever the eye of the beholder might bear to believe.

Weber has as much (or as little) right as the rest of us to resort to a theoretical washing of hands—but this seems not, for better or actually for worse, to be an instance of it. In any event, ekstasis has an awkward place in the ideal-typification of an authority that Weber is deeply invested in locating in the political as well as the religious arena. It is only partially compatible with the one general—and positive—criterion of charismatic election that Weber is willing to posit. Peculiarly appropriate to the political arena, perhaps all too appropriate to that arena, the criterion is one of performance, of pragmatic success: "The charismatic leader gains and maintains authority solely by proving his strength in life. If he wants to be a prophet, he must perform miracles; if he wants to be a war lord, he must perform heroic deeds. Above all, however, his divine mission must "prove" itself in that those who faithfully surrender to him must fare well. If they do not fare well, he is obviously not the master sent by the gods" (1946b: 249). Ekstasis is often enough an instrument of just such proof, if less in the political than the religious arena. It does not, however, function merely as an instrument to ends of such semiological flat-footedness. Most broadly, it serves as a sign of divine contact or possession. Granted, it can do so only because it conforms at the very least to some array of standing expectations, of those commonplaces and implicit meanings on which, as Johannes Fabian and Thomas Csordas have appropriately emphasized, underlie the persuasiveness of any would-be proof of charisma depends (Fabian 1979; Csordas 1997). Perhaps it thus always bears the marks of the routinizing jaws of tradition. Yet, ekstasis in its revelatory service is not itself traditional. It, too, is transhistorical and transcultural; it is, in a word, transtraditional. It is in common company with a wide array of other conditions of the mindful body and the embodied mind, other suspensions and metamorphoses that bring the charismatic to the verge of madness and endow him with a double face. Weber's positivism (if you will) countenances only *Christos Pantokrator*, Christ the World-Ruler. It can countenance the figure dying on the cross only as the forsaken son, the champion whose "'virtue is gone out of him,'" whose "mission is extinguished" (1946b: 248). Such words are indeed the Bible's own, but Weber's citation of them is bluntly incognizant of the considerable number of Christians who saw and have continued to see in the crucifixion not the waning but the very consummation of the Nazarene's virtue and mission (cf. Bourdieu 1991). It is insensitive to what Leon Festinger and his colleagues have explored in territories well beyond those of Calvary: the semiotic attraction of good form, perhaps; the charismatic allure of failure most definitely (Festinger, Riecken, and Schachter 1964). It excludes from the charisma of the Passion the debasement of the self and diminution of its agency that link the Nazarene to the ubiquitous mythology of the Dying God but also to Job, to the ancient esotericist who must "suffer into truth," and to all their modern heirs.[3]

Prophets and Saints

An inspired Jeremiah serves as the angry vessel of these of his God's words:

> How canst thou say, I am not polluted, I have not gone after Baalim? See thy way in the valley, know what thou has done: *thou art* a swift dromedary traversing her ways; A wild ass used to the wilderness, *that* snuffeth up the wind at her pleasure; in her occasion who can turn her away? All they that seek her will not weary themselves; in her month they shall find her. (Jer. 2:23–25)

Ms. Roden receives them in the course of her exegeses as if they had always been addressed directly to her: *This is a harsh rebuke to me for sexual promiscuity and lack of faith in God* (Roden 6: 19). In an idiomatically more secular and less formal confessional, she doesn't hesitate to be blunt: *I always knew that I was too horny to be a saint; I really should have asked God about [my fourth husband]* (Roden 2: 32); . . . *trying to stay righteous while living in a ditch [was] like standing on a banana peel in an ice rink* (Roden 2: 35). She alludes to an especially difficult time in her life, a period following her decision to devote herself to what she understood as a divine call to elucidate and to promulgate the last of the mysteries of the Book of Revelation. By 1981, she had divorced her first husband and moved with her son from Canada to rent a small farm situated in the central Texas prairie only a few miles from Mount Carmel, at which a community of some forty or fifty Branch Davidians were making their home at the time, Ben and Lois Roden among them. Already in 1981 Ms. Roden had had the first inkling that she was being summoned to accomplish a sacral task, but what followed was not beatitude but torment. She suffered visions, *heartwrenching knowledge of the time of trouble* (Roden 2: 17). She was convinced that she was under attack: *My food was poisoned, my house was sprayed* (Roden 2: 17). In 1982 and again in 1984, she found herself—if briefly—a patient in the psychiatric ward of a local hospital.

Not until 1985 did she meet Ben and Lois's son, George, who converted her to Branch Davidianism *in an hour* (Roden 4). In the autumn of 1987, she married George, whose place as heir apparent to the leadership of the Branch Davidians was soon to be lost—not without violence—to David Koresh. She was forced to leave Mount Carmel with her husband once he was deposed, and not long after the two of them took refuge at her farm, she realized that she was pregnant. She would also witness the first of George's many entanglements with the courts and the first of his many incarcerations. Certain of the legitimacy of polygamy and just as certain of the illegitimacy of fornication, she contracted marriage with a man whom George, from his prison cell, had sent to protect her from her persecutors. It would be brief; her protector proved to have an insuperable addiction to alcohol. Subsequently, accused of neglect, she lost custody of the daughter whom she and George had parented. Alone, having consumed the last of her savings, unemployed, she would spend more than a year without a home, doing battle with the courts and the Koreshite community at Mount Carmel on George's behalf, occasionally *living in a ditch.* She is convinced that the Koreshites were partly to blame for her misfortunes and convinced that God's retributive hand ruled over the events that transpired at Mount Carmel between 28 February and 19 April 1993: a gun battle between the Koreshites and a team of agents from the Bureau of Alcohol, Tobacco and Firearms, who had come to serve them a search warrant, that left four agents dead; a standoff, soon under the supervision of the F. B. I; a fire that erupted on a windy spring morning on the second story of the Mount Carmel dormitories and led as cause or provocation to as many as eighty deaths, if one includes two unborn children among those counted.

Ms. Roden returned to the Mount Carmel properties some six months after the conflagration and set up her encampment there while the ruins of the dormitories were still under guard and enclosed within metal fencing. On a knoll near the entrance to the properties, presiding over a makeshift office and tables piled with pamphlets and typescripts and a small forest of posters and signs, she was quite durably encamped at Mount Carmel when I first met her in the summer of 1994. *Too horny to be a saint?* Perhaps, but the very judgment belies the nagging of what Ms. Roden took to be an unconditional obligation to strive toward embodying a sanctity that alone would spell liberation from her sins and full readiness for the task to which she had been appointed. She would have to cultivate the *patience* of those who *keep the commandments of God, and the faith of Jesus.*[4] She would have to cultivate the discipline of a daily routine of physical labors as well as the labors of exegesis and writing. She would have to follow a diet derived almost entirely from *the herb of the ground.* She would drink from the waters that pooled at that place where *by the grace of God, and for His glory, on April, 19, 1993 twenty-five children bought Mount Carmel for the world.*[5]

At the height of the summer of 1999, I traveled again to Mount Carmel to pay yet another visit to Ms. Roden, though without any special purpose. I was merely intending to update our conversations and my files. When I had last visited her, I found her residing in a small trailer—somewhat dilapidated, but a definite improvement over the cramped and exposed quarters of her tiny office. By the summer of 1999, the trailer had vanished along with the office and museum over which she had presided. A rival faction of the church was in the process of completing a Visitor's Center on the plot of ground where they had formerly stood. Ms. Roden had set up camp by the side of the road near the entry to the properties. Her home was a nylon pup tent. She had erected a plywood display board on which some of her voluminous writings were posted (including an account of how she had come to be by the side of the road; there had, it seemed, recently been another fire at Mount Carmel). When I arrived, Ms. Roden had just finished bathing in the pond that sat at one edge of the properties. Though the temperature, as usual, was well over ninety, though her skin was sere and her lips chapped by the wind and the sun, she was ready to talk. She simply needed a few moments to *tank up.* She proceeded to the pond with a plastic pitcher, filled the pitcher, returned to her tent and drank a considerable quantity of murky, yellow liquid that must have rivaled the temperature of the air and been saturated with aquatic bacteria. I recalled her having said during the course of a previous interview that even before they had married, George Roden had invited her to Mount Carmel to draw water from his well because he had learned that she required *a particularly pure drinking water* (Roden 4). I managed to suppress my surprise and revulsion, but did return the next day with six gallons of distilled water that I had bought at a Waco supermarket. *I cannot accept it,* she told me, as I should have known she would. She had been drinking only from those very waters, only from that very pond, *for five years*—her penance and her elixir, her holy portion, her blood of Christ.

Ms. Roden's self-disparagement, her visions and persecutions, her ascetic rigors and deprivations, her singular ablutions and infusions pale in comparison to those of St. Catherine of Siena, who began flagellating herself as a child, sat aghast night after night at the orgiastic hallucinations that unfolded before her as a novitiate, drank the pus from the cancerous lesion of one of the invalids to whom she was attending in order to obliterate her own sense of disgust, and survived on nothing more than the Eucharistic host for nine years until dying finally in 1380 at or near the portentous age of thirty-three (Bell 1985; Bynum 1987). The diverse methodical rituals or ritual methods of both women belong to a vast array deployed to effect what José Gil (1998) has called "metamorphoses" of the body, whether invited or suffered, which the numerous authors of the lives of the saints have taken particular care to record as evidence of sanctity itself. They should not, however, press us too rapidly toward the sheerly negative hyperbole, the darkness of the unqualified grotesque. Ms. Roden also shares her brighter and bolder side with an illustrious legion—even the very earliest of them. What Rudolph Bell has diagnosed as "holy anorexia" had its heyday between the fourteenth and the sixteenth centuries. Inarguably grotesque in its way, it was also the pious woman's adamantly sublime "no" to the compromises of earthly marriage and to a pervasive iconography of the female as fleshly path of temptation and repository of sin (Bell 1985; Bynum 1987; cf. Flinders 1993). St. Catherine of Siena's fortitude extended, moreover, well beyond her fasting and even beyond her ministrations to the poor and dying. She remains famous for the vigor and the scope of the reforms and projects that she urged on no less eminent a man than Pope Gregory XI—among other things, that he return to Rome from the more congenial Avignon and organize a crusade to boot (Flinders 1993: 121). Not merely in her ministrations but also in her insistent "no," St. Catherine seems thus to have established herself as the subject of a remarkably persistent mimesis.[6]

Methodologically, the saint may thus be of greater heuristic value than the prophet as an exemplar of the charismatic and the sacral actor alike, for at least three reasons. First, the roles most intimately associated with her rituals and methods in this as in the other world are homologous with, and so "objectively adjusted" to, roles that are integral to the political arena—but equally integral to other arenas as well. The saint thus accommodates the Weberian politicization of charisma without imposing upon charismatic authority the specifically political test of the achievement of particular and propitious ends. Second, she might be found almost anywhere. Finally—and to reiterate—she is a practiced dualist. Of her first characteristic, Peter Brown (1981: 31–35) offers a plausible if partial genealogy, arguing that the Christian imagination of the saintly role can be traced to the merely human figure of the patron, whose political, economic, and spiritual services became increasingly indispensable to the mobile and heterogeneous subjects of a Roman empire of ever vaster politico-economic and civilizational scale from the second century C.E. forward. The argument has a certain philological elegance and broad ethnographic resonance as well (cf. Kenny 1960; Christian 1972). One of the problems with it, however, is that the homology it implies is imperfect. Technically speaking, patrons have clients; the relation between patron and client is, in other words, a two-place relation. It is in fact isomorphic with relations between divine (or

quasi-divine) and human being more typical of pagan antiquity than of Christ-
ianized Rome, resembling those between Athena and the Athenians, say, or
between any of the Heroes and their classical or hellenistic devotees. Perhaps
it remains homologous with the relations that at least some of today's faithful
if heterodox laity understand themselves still to have with their municipal or
eponymous saints. From a strictly orthodox perspective, however, the only
true patron within the Christian pantheon is Jesus, which is to say God.

Saints, in contrast, are brokers. Like patrons, brokers have clients, but they
are further the agents or representatives of institutions or powers of restricted
access (such as God). Brokerage is thus a three-place relation. In its mundane
as in its saintly realization, its ethic is fiduciary and its specialties those of mediation and intercession. In the latter realization, it is structurally (and often
functionally) homologous with the principal stages of the *rite de passage*: it is a
personification of the ritual process. If what follows is that the saint is a "liminal" figure, so be it. What does not follow is that he or she is either a commu-
nalist or a communitarian or an egalitarian or has any of the other penchants
that Victor Turner much too blithely attributes to actors passing through or
dwelling within liminality (see Turner 1969). The saintly broker is also a uni-
tary personification of what Jacob Pandian (1991), echoing Bourdieu's (1991)
opposition between church and prophet, divides into the priestly and the sha-
manistic selves. The saint might be favored over that division not merely because she captures what priest and shaman have in common but also (and the
same must be said of church and prophet) because priest and shaman are not
themselves quite on a logical par. After Weber, the priest could as readily be
treated as a routinized derivative of the self that Pandian takes the shaman to
be—as Pandian himself admits (1991: 91).

Of course, the canonized legion are not exclusively female. Nor are they
only Christian. Though considered heterodox, North African (and many
other) Muslims recognize saints living and dead as well (cf. Gellner 1969; Wolf
1969; Gilsenan 1973; Rabinow 1975). Characterized as (and, yes, reduced to)
sacral broker, the saint is surely no less "universal" than Pandian (1991: 94,
106) asserts his shaman and his priest alike to be. It might even amount to
what the cognitivists call a template, a generative "recipe" for sacral action as
such (cf. Boyer 2001: 50). If not that, it is still in close step with a veritably
global cavalcade of professions and exercises, the diverse subspecializations
and multifarious local colors of which are so many variations on one and the
same functional and teleological theme. Brokerage between the domains of
the merely human and the more or other than merely human is the common
craft of the shaman. At least in settings not yet so liberalized as to understand
the goings on as all a matter of the manipulation of symbols, such brokerage
is the sacramental appointment of the priest. It is also the appointment of the
oracle, the channel, and the (appropriately named) medium. Whether among
the ancient Israelites, the nineteenth- and twentieth-century Nuer (Evans-
Pritchard 1940), or the current Branch Davidians, brokerage is also the stuff of
the prophet. It is plainly the virtue and the duty of the executor of a sacrifice,
and it is often the virtue and the duty of the sacrificial victim, especially when

he or she happens to be human. This last point merits emphasis—not because it illuminates the theoretical privilege of sacrifice, however, but instead because it does precisely the reverse. In spite of the pride of place it has found in the work of William Robertson Smith (1901) and Sigmund Freud (1950 [1913]), of Bataille (1989) and René Girard (1977), sacrifice stands apart from other types of sacral action neither because of its ends nor even because of its violent devices. The annals of sainthood are themselves replete with violence, and the saints are by no means always only passive victims of it. King Louis IX led two crusades. Joan of Arc led the charge on Orleans. Saint George is said to have slain dragons. Moreover, should we follow Bourdieu (as, in this instance, I think we should) in admitting that violence can be wrought just as effectively by symbolic as by literal devices, we would be hard-pressed to declare even many of the most intentionally pacifistic of sacral exercises entirely lacking in any display of weaponry (cf. Bourdieu 1977).

Paranomics

If at his most exemplary the sacral actor is sovereign, he is also the most obedient subject, a veritable slave. If she is a warrior, she is also the prisoner of her calling. If he is a contrarian, he is also the most unabashed conformist. If she is as brave as a lion of Judah, she is also as tired as an old woman. If she is harsh, a vengeful mother, she is also Mercy herself:

> "I will send them seven blessings," said the Shekinah. "The sign is my first blessing. I will send her to lead them into the Kingdom of the Saints of Yahweh. I will put a rod in her hand for the chastisement of the errant, and an olive Branch held out to the righteous. I will take her as the second lamb of the peace offering (Lev. 23:19). She shall be holy unto me. I will not set her over the meek or the poor; she is too harsh for the meek and the poor. I will set her over their exactors and she will make them to serve my people with tears and pity; not with persecutions and oppressions. My vengeance is a mother. She will make their exactors howl."
> "Yahweh, my Elohim," said Mercy, "I am as brave as a lion of Judah, and as tired as an old woman. I will do your will." (Roden 8: 17)

The Shekinah is the Holy Spirit. Ms. Roden follows George's mother, Lois, in using its Hebrew name and in inferring from the grammatical gender of that name the femininity of the Holy Spirit itself—or thus, herself. She follows Lois in understanding the godhead not as triune but as quaternary: Yahweh, the Shekinah, the Son, and a Holy Spirit Daughter who like her brother will also be incarnate in her proper day.[7] Ms. Roden is at home with such dualisms and at home with their multiplication.

But then again, there are dualisms and there are dualisms. Ms. Roden is not a Cartesian; for her, the difference of body and mind is superficial. She is not a Manichaean. She does not hesitate to point out that evil belongs to this world. Citing a passage in the Book of Isaiah (45:7) that has troubled churchmen for centuries, she even insists that it is God's creation. But she knows that it will not be triumphant. It is not eternal. Those dualisms that endure are matrices of unity. Their design evokes symmetry and balance. They are constitutive of destructive but always disciplined creation, of creative but always disciplined destruction. For the Taoist and the Confucianist, such dualisms are the parameters of the vital cosmos (cf. Faubion 2003). For the Hindu, they are the substance of Shiva. For the pagan Romans, they were the paradox of the *sacer* itself. Ms. Roden is sufficiently cosmopolitan to acknowledge that spiritual wisdom—a portion at least—might be found in other faiths besides her own. The dualisms that inform the wisdom that she has sought and suffered are the parameters of the cosmos, the substance of God, and the paradoxical unity of the sacred actor and her methods and rituals all at once. We who are infidels, we who are skeptics, might encounter their realization in the vengeful mother and her caring chastisements, even if we cannot recognize it in a thirsty woman sitting vigil among her books and typewriter and pens and papers at the edge of a dusty rural road in the middle of the Texas prairie only a stone's throw from a pond whose waters yellow and darken under the withering glare of the summer sun.

For Bataille, the *enfant terrible* of the Durkheimian tradition, the exemplary sacral actor—if actor he or she or it can be called—is the sacrificial victim, and the divine to which that actor is delivered and to which he or she or it gives access is in the region of immanent animality, of undifferentiated intimacy and presence, a region incompatible "with the positing of the separate individual" (1989: 51). For Gil, the shaman is the more instructive exemplar; the stuff that he retrieves, wielding his particular array of methods and rituals, from the regions of the presumptively uncoded is the "excess" or "surplus" power of "the body," but the body as undifferentiated fundament, as what Deleuze and Guattari construe as the body unproductive, sterile, unengendered, unconsumable but also the source of all energy, all power—the body without organs (1983: 8). Gil suggests that "primitives" have a variety of names for the surplus into which the shaman ritually taps in his capacity as a ritual conduit: *mana* and *wakau* and *hau* and *orenda* among others (1998: 94). Arabic names what is more or less the same surplus *baraka*. Its English name is "grace," from the Latin *gratis*, a cognate of the Greek *kharis*, whence "charisma." Following Claude Lévi-Strauss's analysis (1987: 61–63), Gil regards such names as "floating signifiers," but they are more precisely Peircean indices, pointing to an ontologically primary material and primary resource that "signifies nothing, says nothing" but on which all signification and all significance depends (1998: 99; cf. Faubion 2003: 78–82).

As a doctrine of that primary material, Gil's corporalism can only be as metaphorical as any other idiom one might choose. As a metaphor, it nevertheless has the benefit of suggesting what might almost pass as the template of sacral metamorphosis itself: the transformation of the organized body into the body as organ and more precisely into an intercessive and mediatory body capable of translating the raw stuff of power into a semiotic resource, a semiotic tool. Bataille insists that the service of the sacral body is entirely antithetical to the service of a merely profane and mundane tool, that sacral metamorphosis divests the body of its merely profane and mundane utility and renders it literally use-less (1989: 30–35). Perhaps. More immediately instructive is Gil's fascination with that "tribal" repertoire of techniques of metamorphosis that a somber, seri-ous, establishmentarian Christianity could only regard as "sacrilegious" (1998: 164–65). Such techniques provoke laughter. They "guard against seriousness and the possible heaviness of signs." They might be and sometimes are "genu-ine antipower devices." They direct us not to Turner's but rather to Mikhail Bakhtin's interpretation of Carnival and the carnivalesque. Through Bakhtin, they direct us—should we not already have arrived—once again to the aesthet-ics of the grotesque (Gil 1998: 170; cf. Bakhtin 1968). Bakhtin's grotesque body is opposed above all to the exquisitely contained, exquisitely self-contained classical body. The grotesque body is "open to the outside world." With it, em-phasis is placed on "apertures and convexities." This body has as its essence "the principle of growth" (Bakhtin 1968: 26; cf. Gil 1998: 171). It copulates. It defecates. It eats. It drinks. It gives birth. It dies.

Needless to say, such a body is ethnographically more familiar than the eth-nographer might sometimes care for it to be. As Bakhtin knew well but con-trary to what Gil seems to believe, it is by no means diacritically "primitive." Nor is it merely grotesque. Gil intends no insult in so designating it, of course, for he regards the effervescent primitive working his way through his grotesque metamorphoses as nobler, or if not quite that then at least more authentically human, than "we" who are Christian or post-Christian infidels could possibly be, whether because we (as Christian) can tolerate nothing short of the most tremendous and mysterious and unamusing ceremonialism as properly reli-gious or because we (as infidels) can comprehend the anointed brokerage of divine power only in economistic or sociologistic terms. The consequence of Gil's misplaced charity is, however, the reinforcement (perhaps unknowing) of that functionalist or pious bias that has impelled so many theologians and philosophers and rhetoricians to struggle so valiantly over the past two and a half centuries to absorb sacral experience and sacral action alike within the similarly restrictive and largely uncooperative aesthetics of the sublime. Better to admit that there is always something grotesque in the sublime and always something sublime in the grotesque. Better to recognize that if the antiheroic metamorphoses of the brokers of fecundity and the heroic metamorphoses of the brokers of husbandry and reaping and harvest are often very difficult to distinguish from one another, this is because their metamorphoses are of the same tropological type. To reiterate, both are hyperbolic. Both transpire as ex-aggerations—earthy and immanently animalistic in the one case, ascetic and ethereal in the other. Because they are hyperbolic, they are also reductive—but for once, appropriately so. Dualistic exaggeration distills the full dimensions of the profane and mundane self and its corresponding embodiment to the more austere dimensions of the sacral itself. What is left is the self as the body as organ, the body as the organ of a promise of which it is also the pledge and the testament: *I will do your will.*

The body of that organ who is the vengeful mother is excessive, then, but its excesses are not madness. Nor is its purpose annihilation, the production of chaos, the overthrow of all order, the crushing of all distinctions into indifference. It insists upon rectitude, the purgation of errancy, in the name of florescence, of the achievement of corporal and spiritual plenitude. The vengeful mother wages her war to establish peace, but not the peace of a world restored to what it once had been, a world in which she might reoccupy her former place. She is not a more humane but still jealous Medea (*pace* Girard 1977: 9–10), nor is she powered by that "prodigious effervescence of life that, for the sake of duration, the order of things holds in check." She is not "exactly comparable to the flame that destroys the wood by consuming it"; she does not call "for the general negation of individuals as such" (*pace* Bataille 1989: 52–53). She is neither conservative nor antisocial. She is not solely a therapist, but in her therapeutic intercessions she comes close to performing those dualistic operations that Gil discerns in a shaman's ritual surgeries:

> one . . . the decodification of the body that is "worn" or "sick," and the other . . . the revival of this same body as healthy and cured. The first corresponds to the setting loose of signification, necessary for the recodification that is underway. This setting loose is obtained through the pushing of codes and languages, for which the body is the emblem, to the point of extreme confusion—music, incantation, hallucinogens and drugs, dance, and the whole atmosphere pervading the event join forces in obtaining this result. It is a process that favors the progressive irruption of the uncoded body, which, significantly, can only exist in a state of trance or possession. It is only on this surface of inscription, rendered virgin, that new meaning can burst forth. (1998: 98–99)

She comes close—but only close. Gil has his shaman reestablishing "the order of symbolic codes" at the price of a "perilous journey to the regions of the uncodable" (1998: 99), a "voyage outside of all codes" (1998: 99). Even the shaman might object, and not only because he suddenly finds himself playing the part of the primitive ancestor of someone very like Deleuze and Guattari's capitalist—deterritorializing schizophrenic and reterritorializing fascist as the "process" requires (cf. Gil 1998: 84). Sacral actors are indeed manipulators of codes. They are not, however, universally obliged or universally compelled to act to reestablish semiotic systems that have fallen or have been brought into disrepair. They often might, but they are not universally obliged to enter into trance or surrender themselves to possession in order to achieve their ends. Above all, their success cannot be measured against the standard of clearing a surface of inscription of all its marks or of arriving at regions uncodable, outside of all code. What true gods might achieve is another matter. Sacral actors are only human. They have no power to return the inscribed body to a virginity that it will always already have lost. They have no power, either, to stand outside or beyond all code, not even in madness, not even in death. For mere humans, code has no outside. It allows of no exit.

As a fallback, one might, with the Gnostic eroticists and sinful messiahs through the ages, resort to the characterization of sacral actors as transgressors. Its titillations and provocations notwithstanding, such a characterization has at least two shortcomings of its own. One is that it is usually appropriate only if the body in question is lifted out of its performative context. It needs a more sober Durkheimian tempering, a revision that reflects a more rigorous acknowledgement of the intrasocial and intersocial relativity of transgression and conformity alike. Another is that it is excessively official; it suggests that a much more precise, much less vague boundary separates transgression from conformity than does so in fact, even in most official contexts. Norms permit of play. Their violation is rarely an all-or-nothing affair. It is not merely Bourdieu's strategic virtuosi who (unknowingly) know how to bend rules without breaking them. Religious virtuosi are equally adept, and like their economistic counterparts, they thus remain oriented toward rules, and so toward codes, instead of being either "outside of" or "beyond" them. Their methods and rituals thus are not deviant, much less beyond all determinacy.

Before or beyond being "high" and "low," "light" and "dark," their actions are—to spell out what I have so far noted only in passing—instead paranomic. The term is not merely a coinage but a coinage that I would be happy to discard if I could find a synonym formerly or presently in circulation, but my search has so far produced no plausible candidates. "Paranomic" is a hybrid composed of the Greek *para-*, a prefix indicating being beside or parallel to, and the Greek *nomos*, designating law or convention or rule or principle or standard. The paranomic does not (as I intend it to be understood) qualify sacral action alone. It is a property of any action that bends a given set of rules without breaking them and, at a more systematic level, a property of any practice similarly inclined. At the latter level, it is the property of virtuosity as such, in whatever practical arena or field it might be displayed. It is susceptible to considerable conventionalization, especially under the critical eye of administrative functionaries charged with keeping its excesses within proper administrative bounds and under proper administrative control. Nor is this surprising. Virtuosi are not transgressive, but as practitioners who do not always play in strict conformity to the rules, they can be dangerous. Their paranomics constitute a relativization in practice of the very rules from which they distance themselves, a questioning in practice of principles and standards that "go without saying." In their paranomics precisely, they are thus the potential agents or agencies of what Michel Foucault calls "problematization": the process of becoming intellectually detached from who one is or what one does, of constituting one's being or one's actions as an object of thought, of putting the one or the other or both into question (Foucault 1997: 117–18).

Virtuosi are thus events. At their most paranomically exemplary and most exemplarily paranomic, sacral virtuosi are transcendent events. They may be quite powerful agents or agencies of the renewal and inauguration of sacred symbols and sacred truths, but they are no doubt all the more dangerous as a consequence. If not method, ritual may for its part have its fundamental rationale precisely as a consequence. If ritual permits the suspension of the normative, it is also the mechanism of its assertion and reassertion. Or conversely: if it is tantamount to the imposition of order on what might otherwise threaten to devolve into chaos, ritual is also the very process that licenses such a threat becoming manifest. It is thus not merely conservative, not merely expressive, not the merely practical coding of an indexical icon of a given cosmos or cosmology. It is alive with possibilities. It is alive with the very possibilities whose volatility it releases but also functions to contain. Ritual is a technology. It is the technological sine qua non of the slow burn, of the controlled fission and fusion that are sacral virtuosity. It is the reactor of the sacral paranomic.

One might accordingly wonder less why a church so deeply established as the Catholic Church would have taken such pains to define and to hold fast to the criteria of sainthood than why it should not have seen as fit as many of its Protestant counterparts to declare sainthood itself an ecclesiological mistake, or if not that then at least a thing of the past. The obvious answer is again available in Peter Brown's study of the cult of saints at its Christian origins: these intercessors and mediators were and remain remarkably effective at galvanizing commitment to the institutional church itself (Brown 1980: 38 and passim). They are, after all, charismatic. The less obvious answer—until one recalls the history of Christianity from at least 1517, when Luther posted his ninety-five theses in Wittenburg, forward to the still schismatic present—is available from Ms. Roden. Pointing out to the Koreshites the consequences of what she could only see as their transgressions, their waywardness, our righteous and vengeful mother puts it this way:

> Jer. 8:17: "For behold, I will send serpents, cockatrices, among you, which will not be charmed,"
> Lois Roden was the serpent's root; Amo Paul Bishop Roden is the serpent's branch; [her daughter], the fruit of the cockatrice George Roden, is also the serpent's fruit.
> "and they shall bite you, saith the Lord."
> And we did.[8]

Notes

1. Here and throughout, Ms. Roden is cited in italics. Here and throughout, her words are taken from those of her unpublished writings and texts of interviews that I hold in a personal archive. The first of the two numbers that may document the citations indicates the corresponding text in the Bibliography; the second (if available) indicates pagination in the original text. By the time Ms. Roden wrote the text noted immediately below, she had come to understand herself as called to deliver not only the sixth but also the seventh of the messages of the angels of Revelation.

2. Matt Tomlinson (personal communication) suggests that the same semiotic doubling is hypostasized in the saintly relic, at once a repository of grace and a reminder of mortality.

3. The quoted phrase is more usually and more tepidly translated as "in wisdom there is suffering." The gloss I cite is that of Robert Fagles, from Aeschylus' Agamemnon (Aeschylus 1977: 179).

4. Roden 1: 12. The characterization is a quotation of Revelation 14:12.

5. Twenty-five children were among those who died at the culmination of the Mount Carmel standoff. The pronouncement quoted here is the text of a postcard that Ms. Roden printed and asked visitors to mail to then governor Ann Richards at the State Capitol in Austin, Texas.

6. Lena Gemzoe is currently conducting research among several provincial Portuguese families whose daughters have retired to their beds, there to dispense advice and take requests for

prayer while subsisting on nothing but their daily portion of the host (Gemzoe, personal communication).

7. To be precise, the "message" of the Holy Spirit Daughter originally came not from Lois Roden but from another member of the Branch Davidian Church, Charles Pace. Lois came to accept it only after considerable initial doubt (see Faubion 2001: 56). Amo argues that the Holy Daughter has in fact already been born—to her and to George Roden.

8. Roden 6: 119. On the daughter of Ms. Roden and George, see n. 6, above.

References

Aeschylus. 1977. *The Oresteia: Agamemnon, The Libation Bearers, The Eumenides*. Trans. R. Fagles. Harmondsworth, UK: Penguin.

Bakhtin, Mikhail. 1968. *Rabelais and His World*. Trans. H. Iswolsky. Cambridge, MA: MIT Press.

Barkun, Michael. 1974. *Disaster and the Millennium*. New Haven: Yale University Press.

———. 1986. *The Crucible of the Millennium*. Syracuse: Syracuse University Press.

Bataille, Georges. 1989. *Theory of Religion*. Trans. R. Hurley. New York: Zone Books.

Bell, Rudolph M. 1985. *Holy Anorexia*. Chicago: University of Chicago Press.

Bellah, Robert. 1970. *Beyond Belief*. New York: Harper and Row.

Bourdieu, Pierre. 1977. *Outline of a Theory of Practice*. Trans. R. Nice. Cambridge: Cambridge University Press.

———. 1990. *The Logic of Practice*. Trans. R. Nice. Stanford: Stanford University Press.

———. 1991. "Genesis and Structure of the Religious Field." *Comparative Social Research* 13: 1–44.

Boyer, Pascal. 2001. *Religion Explained: The Human Instincts that Fashion Gods, Spirits and Ancestors*. London: Heinemann.

Brown, Peter. 1981. *The Cult of the Saints: Its Rise and Function in Latin Christianity*. Chicago: University of Chicago Press.

Brumm, Ursula. 1970. *American Thought and Religious Typology*. New Brunswick: Rutgers University Press.

Burkert, Walter. 1996. *Creation of the Sacred: Tracks of Biology in Early Religions*. Cambridge, MA: Harvard University Press.

Bynum, Carolyn Walker. 1987. *Holy Feast and Holy Fast: The Religious Significance of Food to Medieval Women*. Berkeley: University of California Press.

Christian, William. 1972. *Person and God in a Spanish Valley*. New York: Seminar Press.

Catholic Encyclopedia. 2003 [1908]. At *New Advent*, ed. K. Knight. Http://www.newadvent.org/cathen/02364b.htm.

Csordas, Thomas J. 1997. *Language, Charisma, and Creativity: The Ritual Life of a Religious Movement*. Berkeley: University of California Press.

de Certeau, Michel. 1984. *The Practice of Everyday Life*. Trans. S. Rendall. Berkeley: University of California Press.

Deleuze, Gilles, and Félix Guattari. 1983. *Anti-Oedipus*. Trans. R. Hurley, M. Seem, and H.R. Lane. Minneapolis: University of Minnesota Press.

Devereux, George. 1968. *From Anxiety to Method in the Behavioral Sciences*. The Hague: Mouton.

Evans-Pritchard, E. E. 1940. *The Nuer*. New York: Oxford University Press.

Fabian, Johannes. 1979. "The Anthropology of Religious Movements: From Explanation to Interpretation." *Social Research* 46, no. 1: 4–35.

Faubion, James D. 2001. *The Shadows and Lights of Waco: Millennialism Today.* Princeton: Princeton University Press.

———. 2003. "Religion, Violence and the Vitalistic Economy." *Anthropological Quarterly* 76, no. 1: 71–85.

Festinger, Leon, Henry W. Riecken, and Stanley Schachter. 1964. *When Prophecy Fails.* New York: Harper Torchbooks.

Flinders, Carol. 1993. *Enduring Grace: Living Portraits of Seven Women Mystics.* San Francisco: Harper.

Foucault, Michel. 1997. "Polemics, Politics, Problematizations: An Interview with Michel Foucault." In *Essential Works of Michel Foucault, vol. 1: Ethics: Subjectivity and Truth,* ed. P. Rabinow, trans. R. Hurley et al. New York: New Press.

Freud, Sigmund. 1950 [1913]. *Totem and Taboo.* Trans. J. Strachey. New York: W.W. Norton & Company.

Geertz, Clifford. 1973. *The Interpretation of Cultures: Selected Essays.* New York: BasicBooks.

Gellner, Ernest. 1969. *Saints of the Atlas.* Chicago: University of Chicago Press.

Gil, José. 1998. *Metamorphoses of the Body.* Trans. S. Muecke. Minneapolis: University of Minnesota Press.

Gilsenan, Michael. 1973. *Saint and Sufi in Modern Egypt.* Oxford: Clarendon Press.

Girard, René. 1977. *Violence and the Sacred.* Trans. P. Gregory. Baltimore: The Johns Hopkins University Press.

Hayes, John H. 1971. *Introduction to the Bible.* Philadelphia: Westminster Press.

Kant, Immanuel. 1987 [1790]. *Critique of Judgment.* Trans. W. S. Pluhar. Indianapolis: Hackett.

Kenny, Michael. 1960. Patterns of Patronage in Spain. *Anthropological Quarterly* 33, no. 1: 14–23.

Lévi-Strauss, Claude. 1987. *Introduction to the Work of Marcel Mauss.* Trans. F. Baker. London: Routledge and Kegan Paul.

Lyotard, Jean-François. 1994. *Lessons on the Analytic of the Sublime: Kant's Critique of Judgment,* §§ 23–29. Trans. E. Rottenberg. Stanford: Stanford University Press.

Pandian, Jacob. 1991. *Culture, Religion, and the Sacred Self: A Critical Introduction to the Anthropological Study of Religion.* Englewood Cliffs, NJ: Prentice Hall.

Rabinow, Paul. 1975. *Symbolic Domination: Cultural Form and Historical Change in Morocco.* Chicago: University of Chicago Press.

Roden, Amo Paul Bishop.
  1. *Babylon is Fallen.*
  2. *Cracking the Cover-up.*
  3. Houteff and the Holocaust.
  4. Interview with William Dull, October 1995.
  5. Messiah and Elijah, The Second Coming.
  6. The Judgment of the Church.
  7. The Seven Seals.
  8. Yahweh's Song.

Smith, William Robertson. 1901. *Lectures on the Religion of the Semites.* London: Adam and Charles Black.

Sohm, Rodolf. 1967 [1912]. *Wesen und Ursprung des Katholizismus.* Darmstadt: Wissenschaftliche Buchgesellschaft.

Turner, Victor. 1969. *The Ritual Process: Structure and Anti-Structure.* Ithaca: Cornell University Press.

Wallace, Anthony. 1956. "Revitalization Movements." *American Anthropologist* 58, no. 2: 264–81.

Weber, Max. 1946a. "Science as a Vocation." In *From Max Weber: Essays in Sociology*, ed. H. Gerth and C. W. Mills. New York: Oxford University Press.

———. 1946b. "The Sociology of Charismatic Authority." In *From Max Weber: Essays in Sociology*, ed. H. Gerth and C. W. Mills. New York: Oxford University Press.

———. 1952. *Ancient Judaism*, trans. H. Gerth and D. Martindale. Glencoe, IL.: The Free Press.

Wolf, Eric R. 1969. "Society and Symbols in Latin Europe and the Islamic Near East: Some Comparisons." *Anthropological Quarterly* 42, no. 3: 287–301.

Afterword:
On Limits, Ruptures,
Meaning, and Meaninglessness

Joel Robbins

Throughout his book *Empire of Signs*, first published in French in 1970, Roland Barthes sustains a comparison between a place he calls "Japan" and one he calls "the West." The comparison turns on "the possibility of a difference . . . in the propriety of symbolic systems" between the two places (Barthes 1982: 3–4). His point is not to show that symbolic systems in the two places are different in the sense that they are possessed of different meanings—in a scholarly world punch-drunk on Saussurean insights and Levi-Straus's anthropological appropriation of them, that would not have been news. Rather, what Barthes wants to demonstrate is that the two systems actually work differently and that in particular they orient differently to meaning. Indeed, meaning is only the proper object of one of them. This becomes clear in the key chapter of the book—the chapter entitled "The Breach of Meaning"—in which we finally discover that Japan is understood as an "empire of signs" by virtue of its difference from the West, which is an empire "of meaning" (Barthes 1982: 70).

The burden of Barthes' argument is to demonstrate that the Japan of haiku and Zen koans, of elaborate politeness routines and presents in which the wrapping very much outdoes the gift, does not insist on signs bearing meaning in the way the West does. We should not be concerned here with whether he succeeds in making that argument convincingly, and even less so with whether he got Japan right. Although he visited Japan three times before writing the book, he was only there for a "few weeks" all told (Calvet 1995: 153). Moreover, he establishes from the outset that the Japan he talks about is his creation, a foil he constructs to point to our need someday to "write the history of our own obscurity" (Barthes 1982: 4). More interesting for present purposes than whether his argument about Japan is correct, then, is the way he uses his foil to draw out what lies behind the attachment to meaning in the West.

In the same key chapter of the book in which we learn that the West is an empire of meaning, Barthes turns to slightly more evocative phrasing to tell us that the "West moistens everything with meaning, like an authoritarian religion which imposes baptism on entire peoples" (Barthes 1982: 70). Readers of the book up to the point at which this statement appears will recognize that Barthes' simile is a motivated one, for he thinks that the Western problem of meaning is a specifically Christian inheritance, one that depends on the Christian "metaphysics of the person" in which the soul is interior and authentic and is the seat of meaning on earth, as God is in Heaven, and in which both people and God invest signs with meaning in order to express themselves (Barthes 1982: 65). And furthermore, through Christianity, the problem of meaning, of making it and finding it, confronts Westerners as an imposition, is experienced with a compulsive force; finding and making all of life meaningful is not an option, it is a duty. It is the compulsiveness of Christian meaning making in the West that renders meaning an unmarked term and meaninglessness a matter of special comment and harsh evaluation. It is, for Barthes, the Christian compulsion to moisten the world with meaning that raises the anxiety in people that they may have missed a spot, left a dry patch of senselessness that puts their whole project of salvation at risk. At the most general level, that possibility is what makes the papers collected here, so many of them taken up with moments of bone dry significative failure, ethnographically compelling and at times individually and certainly in the aggregate theoretically challenging as well.

I turn to Barthes at the beginning here for three reasons. First, he reminds us of the importance of comparative considerations in framing the topic of meaninglessness and religion. Comparison remains largely implicit throughout this book. No one, for example, takes the bait of examining some other religious tradition or traditions in detail to see if the vantages they could provide would frame the volume's core concerns differently (cf. Staal 1993). This is precisely what Barthes quite explicitly does do, and in so doing, even if he won't vouch for the truth of his account of Japan, he gives some force to the notion that meaning as it is taken up in these accounts is very much a Christian concern.

The second reason for starting with Barthes the semiologist is to emphasize the way in which meaning and meaninglessness really do succeed in staying in focus as the central topics of this volume. A majority of the contributors recognize the relevance to their concerns of Asad's (1993) critique of Geertz's definition of religion as too much built around Christian notions of belief to be universally applicable. And they are right to do so. In fact, at a crucial point in his set of reflections on Geertz's piece, Asad very much echoes Barthes' allusion to Christianity as an "authoritarian religion which imposes baptism on entire peoples" when he asserts that what Geertz misses when he notes that religions have to be meaningful, have to "affirm something," is that by virtue of the "requirement of affirmation . . . the entire field of evangelism was historically opened up, in particular the work of European missionaries in Asia, Africa, and Latin America" (Asad 1993: 43). But even as they follow Asad and

Barthes before him in locating the problematic of meaning within Christianity, they do not follow Asad in subordinating issues of meaning to those of discipline and power. Many situations that look ripe for analyses framed in the familiar language of discipline, power, domination, and resistance—Masowe prophets chastising their flocks, American NGO workers telling their sleeping African colleagues how to live, West Papuans turning Christianity to the cause of independence, a Fijian refusing to offer a sermon, even a Swedish preacher trying to force his audience to see the value of a moment of silence—go unanalyzed in such terms.[1] In this respect, even if the structuralist/semiotic framework that Barthes was steeped in and working his way out of when he wrote *Empire of Signs* is not much in evidence in these papers, still their authors develop their arguments within the universe of discourse that the structuralist/semiotic framework and others focused on meaning (ably reviewed in the introduction) did so much to establish.

There is, finally, a third reason to start with this little book of Barthes'. The fact that Barthes was working his way out of structuralism when he wrote *Empire of Signs* (*The Pleasure of the Text* would follow just a few years later) suggests that we might take as a truly radical observation his claim that Japanese systems of symbols functioned differently from Western ones—that is, that they did not function to produce meaning, at least not primarily or comprehensively. The idea that semiotic systems might work differently in different cultures is not one that anthropologists have taken up in a sustained way (Robbins 2001a, cf. Wagner 1981 and Parmentier 1994). It still represents a limit of our thinking about meaning. While the papers here do not provide a basis for carrying such an idea forward in a comparative way, they do direct us to continue with the initial, critical part of such a project by looking at the Christian background to what Barthes suggests may be the rather peculiar ways Westerners set their semiotic equations explicitly to solve problems of meaning.

Christianity and the Will to Meaning[2]

The Christian compulsion to create meaning is attested to throughout this volume. It is apparent, to mention just a few examples, in the "self-consciously voluble habitus" of the Swedish Word of Life members, the metasemantic insistences of the Fijian Methodist preachers, the slow, steady efforts Masowe Christians make to incorporate *mutemo*, and the Catholic missionaries' attempts to find a form of Christianity that might make sense (at least to them) in highland Bolivia. Given that the Christian insistence on meaning is patent, we can ask how Christianity makes the meaning of things appear to be such an important issue and whence the Christian drive for meaning derives it compulsive force. Assuming that we want ethnographic rather than theological answers to these questions, and relying primarily on the ethnographic evidence presented in this volume (though not ignoring that presented elsewhere), it is evident that Christianity motivates the problem of meaning by constructing the possibility of meaninglessness. Christians are driven to make meaning because of their sense that if they do not do so, they will be faced with a meaninglessness world.

Obviously too simple as it stands, this answer to the question of how Christianity motivates its problematic of meaning quickly becomes more interesting if we go on to ask how the possibility of meaninglessness is itself constructed. In addressing this question, we can take a cue from Gershon's observation that Samoans in New Zealand who convert from one form of Christianity to another come to see the kind of Christianity they formerly practiced as meaningless. I would suggest that the process Gershon documents, a process in which Christianity fosters a break in a person's life and then defines what is broken from as meaningless, can be taken as something of a paradigm for how Christianity more generally stages the meaningfulness of things as the outcome of dramas in which meaninglessness also has an important role to play. The key to discovering how widely important this paradigm is in Christianity is to recognize that it applies not just to individual conversions, but to a whole series of ruptures Christianity enjoins on those who embrace it. Thus, along with the rupture of one's own life narrative effected by one's conversion, we should also consider the rupture that many kinds of Christianity require believers to make with the "world" around them, as well as the rupture in the course of historical time that the apocalyptic event promises to bring about upon its arrival. All of these ruptures, I would argue, define what they break from as kinds of meaninglessness that believers are directed to strive against.[3]

Since Gershon does such a good job of showing how this paradigm works in the case of conversion (see also Engelke 2004; Meyer 1998), I will discuss only the other two kinds of rupture here. Evangelical Christians of various stripes, and all sectarians by definition, tend to emphasize the break with the social world.[4] Once their lives are governed by an ascetic moral code and a set of predictable routines, the worlds these Christians disavow generally appear to them to be relatively chaotic and devoid of meaning. Ammerman's (1987) study of North American fundamentalists documents this well, as does work on Pentecostal and charismatic Christianity from around the world (Robbins 2004). In these traditions, meaninglessness is often glossed as evil, or as the work of evil in the world—which suggests that there might be some value in scrutinizing the symbolism that surrounds meaninglessness more fully than the papers in this volume tend to do. In terms of the argument I am developing here, however, the important thing to note is simply that in breaking from the surrounding world, Christians construct that world as a realm of meaninglessness; henceforth, they need to work to avoid falling into it.

The way constructions of disjunction with the world foster images of meaninglessness also helps to explain the aptness of this volume's focus on ritual. Rituals always make and, at least for their duration, sustain such disjunctions inasmuch as those who practice them present them as movements away from routine, worldly activity (Bell 1992). In doing so, rituals both call into question the meaningfulness of those routines and raise the specter of their own failure to appropriately transcend them. Faubion puts the issue quite precisely when he writes of ritual that "if it is tantamount to the imposition of order on what might otherwise threaten to devolve into chaos, ritual is also the very process that licenses such a threat becoming manifest." Tomlinson sets it out neatly as well when he notes that "rituals of meaning-making necessarily create the possibility of a vague and chaotic realm in which meanings might be present but cannot be made, or might be absent and have attention called to such absence." As a paradigm for breaking from the world, then, ritual action quite clearly maps out the threat of meaninglessness.

Struggles over how exactly to construct meaning and meaninglessness around a break with the world, whether explicitly ritualized or not, figure prominently in several of the papers in this volume.[5] The employees of World Vision Zimbabwe negotiate the question of how to engage with the profane world in terms of their developmentalist goals while at the same time refusing to embrace the values of that world. The Californian World Vision board member who comes to run a prayer meeting with them further complicates the matter by suggesting that the goal of encouraging economic success, even if carefully delimited, is too worldly; from her comfortable position, she advocates a single-minded focus on the spiritual. Both among those who work in the Zimbabwe office and between them and the visiting board member, there are difficulties in knowing where to draw the line between the meaningful and Christian and the meaningless and worldly. As a result, the process of making Christian meaning stalls, producing the absurdity of ritual forms that do not construct orderly worlds. As Bornstein demonstrates very effectively, the failure of meaning in this case is related to the collapse of Zimbabwean society, a society that can no longer serve as "a ground of expectation" for anyone planning social action. But it is also important to note that Christians usually experience such failures as crises in their ability to make life meaningful, and in discussing resolutions for them, seek to discover ways to cordon off a meaningful church space from the meaningless space that surrounds it—something those who work for World Vision Zimbabwe are finding hard to accomplish.

Orta's discussion shares with Bornstein's a focus on missionaries, or at least in the World Vision case on those who work for an evangelistic group. It also documents in satisfying detail an ongoing struggle over how to define the relation of church and world among Catholic missionaries in the Bolivian highlands. The shifts Orta documents are striking. Charting the missionaries' course from a liberation theology deeply engaged with the world of contemporary capitalism by way of critique, to a theology of inculturation that insists on the primacy of the engagement with indigenous tradition—all of this foregrounded against a long history of efforts to define the point at which syncretism reaches the limits of Christian meaning—Orta's account indicates again how crucial the drawing—or erasure—of the lines between the church and the world is for Christians. The final discussion of the revived *ayuno* rite that he builds toward throughout the paper shows how the instability in missionary thinking on these issues over time eventuates in a struggle to control ritual meaning between Aymara who have connected with the missionaries in different times and in different ways. The result is a ritual cascade of meaning—even if not a failure, hardly the consensual, neatly bounded community of meaning the missionaries hoped to create.

In contrast to these two cases, in which the problem of drawing lines between the church and the world is fraught with difficulty, matters seem to be more settled for the overseas Samoan converts to evangelical, Mormon, and Seventh-day Adventist churches that Gershon writes about. Their new churches make meaning by defining as meaningless the rituals of social exchange—rituals at the center of overseas Samoan social life—that play a major role in the church practice of the mainline congregations to which their converts previously belonged. Hence the conversion of these Samoans illustrates the importance to Christian meaning production of not only the rupture of personal life narratives, but also the break with the world. Filled with the assurance of new converts, they have found the places where they want to draw the lines; meaninglessness is now behind them (as established by the break of conversion) and outside of their church (as put in place by their new understanding of where the world ends and the church begins).

To some extent, Ms. Roden presents another case of someone who, like the Samoans Gershon discusses, is confident that she knows where the line between her Christianity and the world should be drawn. She is, in a way that Faubion powerfully conveys, comfortable with the strict ascetic code she has adopted, and confident in her strictness. Yet as a sect of a sect—in effect a sect of one—her situation cannot help but raise the question of whether she has drawn the circle of meaning too tightly around herself, defined too much of the world as meaningless as the price of creating her meaningful world. This is why the specter of madness haunts Faubion's analysis. He fights it off gallantly—rescuing Ms. Roden's example for the light it can shed on common dynamics of religious action and creativity more generally. And to a large extent he succeeds—Jefferson, after all, also called himself a sect of one. But it remains true that cases like Ms. Roden's do represent the limit of breaking with the world as a meaning-creating strategy.

The Christian problematic of meaning—a problematic that, as we have just seen, shows its various guises in the way churches define themselves over against the world, and in the way converts define their present lives over against those they formerly lived—is posed in the most widely relevant terms in the apocalyptic narrative, which promises an absolute break in the flow of the ordinary, historical time in which all or almost all Christians must dwell to some extent (Robbins 2001b). The apocalyptic narrative forces the issue of the meaninglessness of ordinary time, not only by promising that at some point the future will come unstuck from the causal grip of the present, but also by asserting that history—both personal and impersonal—has a telos: the meanings of individual acts and the lives they amount to, and the meaning of the world itself, will find their ultimate specification at the end of time.

It is, for many Christians, the omnipresence and constant relevance of this plotting of time as a march toward a sudden final reckoning that most obviously compels them to make every moment meaningful and that most forcefully raises the specter of meaninglessness. As Löwith (1949: 4) puts it in his seminal account of the influence of Judeo-Christian eschatology on Western philosophies of history: "it is only within a pre-established horizon of ultimate meaning . . . that actual history seems to be meaningless." Here again—as with conversion and social withdrawal—we see how a posited rupture defines that which it breaks from as meaningless. To fail to respond to the meaninglessness of "actual history" by making every moment spent living within it a meaningful part of one's own salvational project—to let any moment rest in its meaninglessness—is in this scheme of things to fall into sin. And this meaning-compelling effect makes its demands not only at the level of individual lives. Anyone familiar with the hermeneutic practices by which dispensational premillennialists read current events into the scheme of salvation history knows that for many Christians, the potential coming of the millennium can be used to make everything that happens signify in meaningful ways (see, e.g., Boyer 1992).

The chapters here are largely silent on millennial themes, though they may be present for the people discussed in everyday, mundane forms and are probably pressing in their individualized version, where they appear as people's worries over the uncontrollable timing of their own deaths. It is noteworthy that the two chapters that do address millennialism to any extent, those by Faubion and Rutherford, are the same ones in which the possibility of meaninglessness appears to be least worrisome to people.[6] This is unsurprising, for millennialism, when adopted wholesale so that one attempts always to live for the world that will come after the break, is perhaps the most effective of Christian strategies for keeping meaninglessness at bay. As Faubion notes, it often retains its meaning-generating abilities even in the face of predictive failure. In the case of the West Papuans Rutherford discusses, the meaning-giving powers of the millennial break serve to secure a sense of the plausibility of other kinds of breaks, for instance with the colonial order and its churches or with the postcolonial state. The sense of steady purposefulness one gathers from her account is likely rooted in such millennial confidence.

Despite its meaning-giving powers, however, for many Christians, and certainly for most of those who figure in these chapters, the millennial rupturing of time merely represents the ultimate horizon of meaning; other breaks meanwhile do more to define the parameters by which they attempt to order their lives. Depending on these more modest strategies leaves one more open to failure—a topic so prevalent in these chapters that it demands discussion on its own terms.

On the Meaning of Failure

As many of the authors here recognize, the first thing to say about the failure of meaning is that it registers only where the compulsion to find meaning is strong. You go to an academic conference, sit in a hot room under buzzing fluorescent lights and listen to someone deliver a fifteen-minute paper. You don't follow it, nothing in your intellectual life changes—all told, it's a meaningless experience.

No one remarks on it, though, including you, and surely no one makes it the centerpiece of an analysis of the nature of meaning and meaninglessness. The chapters in this volume demonstrate that the same is not true in many contexts of Christian life, for by positing meaning making as a paramount goal, Christianity demands that failures to reach it be marked and attended to.

Slightly less obviously, from within Christian frameworks that take for granted the drive for meaning, meaninglessness tends to appear as an event. Meaninglessness is always something untoward, lobbed in unexpectedly from the rejected side of one or an other of the constitutive Christian breaks discussed above, rather than a stable, structured part of the Christian life and its routine reproduction. Or at least, so it appears in these chapters, where enduring representations of the meaningless or chaotic receive little play (see my point about the symbolism of meaninglessness above). Yet even as I agree that such representations exist, I also think the way the authors downplay them here is appropriate, for in the experience of most Christians, the worlds of meaninglessness depicted by such representations register on believer's lives only in eventful, untoward ways. Unlike representations of meaning and of the way meanings are made, which are always relevant to Christian people living their lives, representations of meaninglessness are only sporadically useful as equipment for living (to borrow Burke's phrase), and even then generally only when dwelling on the rejected side of a constitutive break (for example, in the context of evangelization). When living the Christian life with other Christians, failures of meaning are always surprises.

Because they deal with what the people they study regard as *events* of failure, the accounts of failure in this book take a particular shape that is somewhat novel in anthropological writing. In one sense they look very much like other anthropological reports in that their authors marshal fine-grained discussions of the nature of specific aspects of people's thinking (Masowe ideas about the importance of live and direct experience and slow, patient learning, for example, or Fijian Methodist ideas about the job of the preacher) and then bring them to bear on specific occurrences. But in another sense, they are odd by virtue of the fact that these occurrences, as true events, are really one-offs, nonce formations never to be repeated. Once, when an interviewer asked for an example of a rhetorical technique upon which anthropologists rely, Geertz responded by admitting that anthropologists often introduce a specific instance from their fieldwork, perhaps a quotation or something that happened during the course of their research, and analyze it in detail, all the while implying if not stating that they have hundreds of other examples just like it in their notes. The typical anthropological instance is not, that is, presented as an event, as a happening that is important because of its unique characteristics. It is presented as common, or at least as exemplary of issues raised by more common instances. Clearly the events of failure presented here are not meant to be understood in either of these ways. They are not Balinese cockfights or Japanese tea ceremonies, but are rather something akin to moments from a "blooper" reel of scenes rescued from the floor of the ethnographic cutting room. As such, they present a challenge to what Tomlinson, in a point I will return to, calls the anthropological will to meaning. How, then, do the authors here deal with them?

Engelke embeds his discussion of failure in a broader discussion of charisma and clarity. Much of the literature on charisma represents it as answering to failures of meaning: people seek out and accord authority to charismatic leaders when they need help making sense of their worlds or of their places in them. Masowe Christianity fosters the perpetuation of this dynamic by demanding at once "live and direct," unmediated, presumably firm and certain experience of the divine, and a recognition that religious knowledge/law (*mutemo*) is hard to master and that few can be confident in their grasp of it. By encouraging powerful experiences, Masowe charismatic leaders prove the efficacy of the world they hold out to followers; meanwhile, by refusing to let those experiences, or the reading of the Bible, authorize lay believers in their knowledge claims, those prophets also sustain their followers' need for them. Hence it is not surprising that when confronted with moments of failure in the responses of followers who cannot show knowledge or demonstrate faith, Masowe prophets and others can explain their failures away as proof of the hubris of claiming mastery, the continued need for patient learning, and the childlike nature of those in the church. Clarity is not the point for Masowe because among them, the meaning-making drive of Christianity more generally has been, as it were, sociologized, folded into the dynamics of charismatic leadership. What is meaningful is to find prophets to whom one can relate "live and direct," and it is out of relationships with prophets that a sense of the meaningfulness of the world comes.

"Virtuosi," Faubion tells us, "are . . . events." They also, as the virtuoso Masowe prophets demonstrate, thrive on events—even those of failure. In Christian congregations organized along other lines, such as the Swedish one Coleman discusses (which appears to be well along the path of routinizing the charisma upon which it was founded) or the Fijian one Tomlinson describes (which is not organized along charismatic lines at all), failure is less easily managed. In both cases, failure comes as a moment of silence. In the case of Pastor Rumar at the Word of Life service in Sweden, the silence may well, as Coleman notes, have been deliberate—meant to illustrate a point about the "right kind of stillness" (emphasis removed). In the case of the Fijian man, Jona, who read a Bible passage aloud as if he were going to preach but then offered no sermon, it is harder to tell—his may have been a "refusal" to make meaning, but it may have instead been nothing more than an upwelling of inadequacy. In both cases, however, the congregational response is the same: they sit bewildered for a while and then leave. The authors conclude that in neither case was any meaning made.

The anthropologists in both of these cases contextualize the events they discuss—a failed moment of silence and a moment of silent failure—by developing sophisticated accounts of the language ideologies and practices of speaking that give speech its force in the communities they discuss. For the Word of Life followers who keep up a constant stream of speech in order, one imagines, to talk the world into sense (the American English pun is intended here), elaborate chains of speech mimesis (see Harding 2000) between pastors and lay members hold the church together even as it expands around the globe. In a world in which chatter is circulated, recirculated, and above all simply kept up, a high-profile moment of silence might work to shatter the crust of routine that threatens to harden into spiritless practice. By positing this, Coleman is quite nicely able to redeem Rumar's failed act for his own analysis—though in its original context it remains meaningless for all that. Tomlinson shows us the work that goes into learning to sermonize in Fiji, and delineates the structures of authority that enforce proper study and practice. He gives us another vivid image of a religious life with talk at its center. But in the end he is no more able to make sense of Jona's silence than its original audience was. He shows how such moments of failure function in the Christian economy of meaning-making by motivating further efforts toward meaningfulness in terms I have echoed throughout this comment. But he cannot enlighten us as to what Jona thought he was doing or what it meant to others beyond the fact of its quality as a moment of failure. It comes and goes in his paper in sense as it must have come and gone for those who witnessed it—nothing more than a fleeting reminder of why it is better always to try to make meaning. This lesson pushes Tomlinson to end on a rather radical note by putting up for discussion the anthropological will to meaning—a will that makes Jona's failure a failure for us, unless we can make it meaningful. In the following concluding section, I want to take his lead and point out some questions about anthropology itself that are raised by this collection on meaning and meaninglessness in Christianity.

Christian Meaning and the Limits of Anthropology

The appearance of this book is something of a signal moment for a developing anthropology of Christianity. While there have been anthropological collections focused on Christianity in particular regions of the world such as Latin America, or on topics the discipline treats as of primarily Christian import (e.g., conversion; see Hefner 1993), this is one of the first such collections to my knowledge built around the assertion that anthropological studies of Christianity can contribute to questions of general theoretical import, such as the place of meaning and meaninglessness in human cultures.[7] Why, one wonders, should it be so late in coming?

The general anthropological aversion to Christianity is by now coming to be well known, and some general reasons for it have been canvassed (Harding 1991 is seminal in this regard; see also Robbins 2003). Here I want to pull out only one strand of what is surely an overdetermined history of neglect: the strand having to do with meaning. Coleman makes a telling point when he notes that anthropologists have tended to endorse quite literalist understandings of literalism. They have not thought it possible to produce the kind of nuanced account of Christian literalist practice they would want to have of most other kinds of practice in the world (the kind of account Coleman in fact gives here), or at least they have not been interested in providing one. In fact, they have tended to find Christian cultural elements rather meaningless—bits of syncretic foam floating on oceans of meaningful traditional culture (as Orta notes), or tired routines followed by alienated masses whose real culture, or real hope of finding a meaningful culture, must lie elsewhere. More times than I can count, anthropologists have told me that when they heard Christians talk in the field or at home, all they could hear was the robotic recitation of meaningless clichés. Often enough for anthropologists, then, Christianity has itself represented the limit of meaning.

We can return to Asad, by way of Tomlinson's portrayal of the anthropological will to meaning, to consider why this should be so. The heart of Asad's critique of Geertz's definition of religion, as I noted earlier, is the suggestion that anthropologists, by promoting belief as the defining quality of religion, have been guilty of promoting a Western folk model to the position of universally applicable scientific construct. The chapters here suggest an extension of this argument. The idea that the cultures of others should be meaningful, and should be so in some comprehensive way, also appears to be something of a Christian inheritance. Christianity does in fact say all semiotic equations should be set to solve the problem of meaning; anthropologists then assume this is true all over. To really ground this argument would take more space than is available here. But if it is a plausible one, then one possibility that follows is that anthropologists recoil from the Christian drive for meaning—its compulsiveness, its unwillingness to leave anything unaccounted for, its unrelenting wordiness—because it looks too much like their own. To define Christian culture as a failure—as the one culture with no meaning—then, like the Christian failures documented here, helps motivate the anthropological drive to find meaning everywhere else so as to avoid slipping back into the past from which it has broken.

Notes

1. Engelke's and Rutherford's chapters are partial exceptions. Engelke makes consistent and productive use of the notion of discipline, seeing it as something Masowe Christians use to generate meaningful attitudes in a way Asad would expect from his reading of the Christian tradition—though Engelke is careful to forestall any reading that attributes the charisma of prophets solely to their skills at mystification. Rutherford's chapter might be best seen as the exception that proves the rule on this point. She also, more than others, adopts some of Asad's language—that of "authorizing discourses." But she is clearly more alive to the meaning-bearing aspects of such discourses than Asad tends to be, and more to the point, her whole framework is build around a notion of "ideologies of institutionality" that insists that the entanglements of discipline with meaning must not get carelessly underplayed or left out of account in analyses of social life.
2. I borrow the phrase "The Will to Meaning" from Argyrou 2002.
3. It is of course true that different kinds of Christianity define these breaks differently, and that some do not make much of some of them—thus churches that allow infant baptism do not always stress the rupture of conversion, those that accommodate the world do not stress the break with the social surround, and those that downplay the second coming do not elaborate on the apocalyptic fracturing of historical time. In this comment I am not going to worry over these differences very much. My remarks are keyed to the kinds of Christianity taken

up in these chapters, which in all cases hinge on at least one of these dimensions of rupture. It is arguably true that the only form of Christianity in which none of them figures much is mainstream liberal Protestantism in the West—a form of Christianity that makes scant appearance here (except as the kind of Christianity Samoans in New Zealand often break from in Gershon's paper).

4. Niebuhr (2001[1951]) provides the classic typology of relations Christianity can contract with the culture around it, a theme that is also central to the voluminous church/sect literature.

5. The work of Hughes (2003, particularly chapters 7 and 8) provides an example of how a sophisticated contemporary theologian wrestles with this issue.

6. The millennial character of the situations Faubion and Rutherford discuss is obvious but not always analytically focal in their papers in this volume. They both offer more sustained discussions of this topic in their monographs (Faubion 2001, Rutherford 2003).

7. Saunders (1988) and James and Johnson's (1988) festschrift for Lienhardt are other volumes that do not fit under the "area studies" and specialized "Christian topics" rubrics. They are not, however, theoretically focused to the same extent as this volume.

References

Ammerman, Nancy Tatom. 1987. *Bible Believers: Fundamentalists in the Modern World*. New Brunswick: Rutgers University Press.

Argyrou, Vassos. 2002. *Anthropology and the Will to Meaning*. London: Pluto Press.

Asad, Talal. 1993. *Genealogies of Religion: Discipline and Reasons of Power in Christianity and Islam*. Baltimore: Johns Hopkins University Press.

Barthes, Roland. 1982. *Empire of Signs*. Trans. R. Howard. New York: Hill and Wang.

Bell, Catherine. 1992. *Ritual Theory, Ritual Practice*. New York: Oxford University Press.

Boyer, Paul. 1992. *When Time Shall Be No More: Prophecy Belief in Modern American Culture*. Cambridge: Harvard University Press.

Calvet, Louis-Jean. 1995. *Roland Barthes: A Biography*. Bloomington: Indiana University Press.

Engelke, Matthew. 2004. "Discontinuity and the Discourse of Conversion." *Journal of Religion in Africa* 34, nos. 1–2: 82–109.

Faubion, James D. 2001. *The Shadows and Lights of Waco: Millennialism Today*. Princeton: Princeton University Press.

Harding, Susan Friend. 1991. "Representing Fundamentalism: The Problem of the Repugnant Cultural Other." *Social Research* 58, no. 2: 373–93.

————. 2000. *The Book of Jerry Falwell: Fundamentalist Language and Politics*. Princeton: Princeton University Press.

Hefner, Robert, ed. 1993. *Conversion to Christianity: Historical and Anthropological Perspectives on a Great Transformation*. Berkeley: University of California Press.

Hughes, Graham. 2003. *Worship as Meaning: A Liturgical Theology for Late Modernity*. Cambridge: Cambridge University Press.

James, Wendy, and Douglas Johnson, eds. 1988. *Vernacular Christianity: Essays in the Social Anthropology of Religion Presented to Godfrey Lienhardt*. Oxford: Journal of the Anthropological Society of Oxford.

Löwith, Karl. 1949. *Meaning in History*. Chicago: University of Chicago Press.

Meyer, Birgit. 1998. "'Make a Complete Break with the Past': Memory and Postcolonial Modernity in Ghanaian Pentecostal Discourse." In *Memory and the Postcolony: African Anthropology and the Critique of Power*, ed. R. Werbner. London: Zed Books.

Niebuhr, H. Richard. 2001 [1951]. *Christ and Culture*. San Francisco: HarperSanFrancisco.

Parmentier, Richard J. 1994. *Signs in Society: Studies in Semiotic Anthropology*. Bloomington: Indiana University Press.

Robbins, Joel. 2001a. "Ritual Communication and Linguistic Ideology: A Reading and Partial Reformulation of Rappaport's Theory of Ritual." *Current Anthropology* 42, no. 5: 591–614.

———. 2001b. "Secrecy and the Sense of an Ending: Narrative, Time and Everyday Millenarianism in Papua New Guinea and in Christian Fundamentalism." *Comparative Studies in Society and History* 43, no. 3: 525–51.

———. 2003. "What is a Christian? Notes Toward an Anthropology of Christianity." *Religion* 33, no. 3: 191–99.

———. 2004. "The Globalization of Pentecostal and Charismatic Christianity." *Annual Review of Anthropology* 33: 117–43.

Rutherford, Danilyn. 2003. *Raiding the Land of the Foreigners: The Limits of the Nation on an Indonesian Frontier*. Princeton: Princeton University Press.

Saunders, George R., ed. 1988. *Culture and Christianity: The Dialectics of Transformation*. New York: Greenwood Press.

Staal, Frits. 1993. *Rules Without Meaning: Ritual, Mantras and the Human Sciences*. New York: Peter Lang.

Wagner, Roy. 1981 [1975]. *The Invention of Culture*. Chicago: University of Chicago Press.

CONTRIBUTORS

Erica Bornstein is an assistant professor in the Department of Anthropology at the University of Wisconsin-Milwaukee. Her book, *The Spirit of Development: Protestant NGOs, Morality, and Economics in Zimbabwe*, was published by Stanford University Press in 2005. In addition to her work in Zimbabwe, she has more recently begun research on humanitarianism in India.

Simon Coleman is a professor in the Department of Anthropology at the University of Sussex. His interests include conservative Protestantism, pilgrimage, and aesthetics in healing and religion. His books include *The Globalisation of Charismatic Christianity* (Cambridge) and two co-edited collections, *Pilgrim Voices: Narrative and Authorship in Christian Pilgrimage* (Berghahn) and *Reframing Pilgrimage* (Routledge).

Matthew Engelke is a lecturer in the Department of Anthropology at the London School of Economics. He is the author of a forthcoming book, *A Problem of Presence: Beyond Scripture in an African Church* (California), and has written articles on conversion, religious history, and spiritual healing. He is also the editor, with Marshall Sahlins, of Prickly Paradigm Press.

James Faubion is professor and chair of the Department of Anthropology at Rice University. His latest book is *The Shadows and Lights of Waco: Millennialism Today* (Princeton). He has also worked in Greece and has published several essays on social theory.

Ilana Gershon is an assistant professor in the Department of Communication and Culture at Indiana University. Gershon's research is on Samoan migrants, with a particular focus on questions of empathy, strategic ignorance, and rudeness. She has edited two special journal issues, "The Symbolic Capital of Ignorance" in *Social Analysis* and "Reflexivity in Others' Contexts" in *Ethnos*.

Andrew Orta is associate professor in the Department of Anthropology at the University of Illinois at Urbana-Champaign. The author of *Catechizing Culture: Missionaries, Aymara, and the "New Evangelization"* (Columbia), he has also published articles in such journals as *American Ethnologist* and *Cultural Anthropology*.

Joel Robbins is an associate professor of anthropology at the University of California, San Diego. His work has focused on issues of Christianity and cultural change. He is the author of *Becoming Sinners: Christianity and Moral Torment in a Papua New Guinea Society* (California) and is the editor of a special issue of the journal *Religion* focused on the Anthropology of Christianity.

Danilyn Rutherford is an associate professor in the Department of Anthropology at the University of Chicago. Her research interests include nationalism, Christianity, and money. She is the author of *Raiding the Land of the Foreigners: The Limits of the Nation on an Indonesian Frontier* (Princeton) and numerous articles.

Matt Tomlinson is an assistant lecturer of anthropology at Monash University in Melbourne. He has published articles on ritual, language, and Christianity in Fiji in *American Anthropologist*, *Oceania*, and the *Journal of the Royal Anthropological Institute*.

INDEX

Related Titles of Interest

New in Paperback
PATHWAYS TO HEAVEN
Contesting Mainline and Fundamentalist Christianity in Papua New Guinea
Holger Jebens

This study examines the tensions, antagonisms and outright confrontations that can occur within local Christian communities upon the arrival of global versions of fundamentalism through a rich and in-depth ethnographic study of a single case: that of Pairundu, a small and remote Papua New Guinean village whose population accepted Catholicism, after first being contacted in the late 1950s. Subsequently the villagers participated in a charismatic movement, before more and more members of the younger generation started to separate themselves from their respective catholic families and to convert to one of the most radical and fastest growing religious groups not only in contemporary Papua New Guinea but world-wide: the Seventh-Day Adventist Church. This case study of local Christianity as a lived religion contributes to an understanding of the social and cultural dynamics that increasingly incite and shape religious conflicts on a global scale.

Holger Jebens is Research Fellow at the Frobenius Institute and Managing Editor of *Paideuma*, and, from 2001–2002, was Theodor-Heuss Lecturer at the New School of Social Research.

August 2006. 256 pages, 1 map, bibliog., index
ISBN 1-84545-334-4, Paperback $27.50/£16.50
ISBN 1-84545-005-1 Hardback $85.00/£50.00 (2005)

RITUAL IN ITS OWN RIGHT
Exploring the Dynamics of Transformation
Edited by Don Handelman and Galina Lindquist

Historically, canonic studies of ritual have discussed and explained ritual organization, action, and transformation primarily as representations of broader cultural and social orders. In the present, as in the past, less attention is given to the power of ritual to organize and effect transformation through its own dynamics. Breaking with convention, the contributors to this volume were asked to discuss ritual first and foremost in relation to itself, in its own right, and only then in relation to its socio-cultural context. The results attest to the variable capacities of rites to effect transformation through themselves, and to the study of phenomena in their own right as a fertile approach to comprehending ritual dynamics.

Don Handelman is Sarah Allen Shaine Professor of Anthropology & Sociology at the Hebrew University of Jerusalem. **Galina Lindquist** was born in Russia, and trained as anthropologist in Sweden. She received her degree at the Department of Social Anthropology, University of Stockholm, for the study of urban shamans in Scandinavia.

2005. 240 pages, ills, bibliog., index
ISBN 1-84545-051-5 Pb $25.00/£15.00

Berghahn Books, Inc. 150 Broadway, Suite 812, New York, NY 10038, USA

Berghahn Books, Ltd. 3 Newtec Place, Magdalen Rd. Oxford OX4 1RE, UK

orders@berghahnbooks.com   www.berghahnbooks.com

Printed in the United Kingdom
by Lightning Source UK Ltd.
132497UK00001B/164/A